CASE STUDIES IN HYPNOTHERAPY

CASE STUDIES IN HYPNOTHERAPY

EDITED BY

E. THOMAS DOWD
University of Nebraska, Lincoln

AND

JAMES M. HEALY
Private Practice, Tallahassee, Florida

THE GUILFORD PRESS
New York London

A Division of Guilford Publications, Inc.
200 Park Avenue South, New York, N.Y. 10003

Printed in the United States of America

Library of Congress Cataloging-in-Publication Data
Main entry under title:

Case studies in hypnotherapy.

Includes bibliographies and indexes.
1. Hypnotism—Therapeutic use—Case studies.
I. Dowd, E. Thomas. II. Healy, James H. [DNLM:
1. Hypnosis. WM 415 C337]
RC495.C37 1986 616.89′162 85-27190
ISBN 0-89862-652-8

To Terri, Michael, and Kathy—E.T.D.

To Sara, Kembra, and Carrie—J.M.H.

And to the memory of Dr. David S. Kuypers, our hypnotic teacher.

CONTRIBUTORS

Marcia A. Angle, MD, Department of Social and Administrative Medicine, University of North Carolina, Chapel Hill, North Carolina

Daniel L. Araoz, EdD, ABPH, ABPP, Counseling Department, Long Island University, New York, New York

Elgan L. Baker, PhD, Department of Psychiatry, Indiana University School of Medicine, Indianapolis, Indiana

Joseph Barber, PhD, Department of Psychiatry, UCLA, Los Angeles, California

David L. Calof, Family Psychotherapy Practice of Seattle, Seattle, Washington

Bennett G. Braun, MD, Dissociative Disorders Program, Rush–Presbyterian–St. Luke's Medical Center, Rush University, Chicago, Illinois

John F. Chaves, PhD, Pain Management Program, Division of Behavioral Medicine, St. Louis University Medical Center, St. Louis, Missouri

Donna R. Copeland, PhD, Department of Pediatrics, University of Texas M.D. Anderson Hospital and Tumor Institute, Houston, Texas

Michael Jay Diamond, PhD, Department of Psychiatry and Biobehavioral Sciences, UCLA, Los Angeles, California, and Private Practice, Los Angeles, California

E. Thomas Dowd, PhD, ABPP, Diplomate in Counseling Psychology, Department of Educational Psychology, University of Nebraska, Lincoln, Nebraska

Albert Ellis, PhD, ABPH, Institute for Rational–Emotive Therapy, New York, New York

William L. Golden, PhD, Private Practice, New York, New York, and Institute for Rational–Emotive Therapy, New York, New York

Melvin A. Gravitz, PhD, Department of Psychiatry and Behavioral Sciences, George Washington University Medical Center, Washington, D.C.

James M. Healy, PhD, Private Practice, Tallahassee, Florida

Charles H. Madsen, Jr., PhD, Department of Psychology, Florida State University, Tallahassee, Florida

Clorinda G. Margolis, PhD, Private Practice, Philadelphia, Pennsylvania

John A. Moser, MA, Private Practice, Pensacola, Florida

Joan Murray-Jobsis, PhD, Private Practice, Chapel Hill, North Carolina

Charles B. Mutter, MD, Private Practice, Miami, Florida, and Departments of Psychiatry and Family Medicine, University of Miami School of Medicine, Miami, Florida

Belinda R. Novik, PhD, Private Practice, Chapel Hill, North Carolina

Dan C. Overlade, PhD, Private Practice, Pensacola, Florida
George A. Sargent, PhD, The Family Center, Vista, California
Judith B. Strauss, PhD, Private Practice, Philadelphia, Pennsylvania
Mathias Stricherz, PhD, University Counseling Center, Texas Tech University, Lubbock, Texas

PREFACE

This book is an outgrowth of a collaborative teaching effort at the University of Nebraska in the spring of 1982. The second editor (Healy) came to Lincoln to assist the first editor (Dowd) in teaching an introductory course in hypnosis and hypnotherapy. The collaboration extended to mutual consultation on the case of adolescent enuresis by Dowd that is contained in this volume. Discussions after teaching and practice centered increasingly on the lack of a book devoted to case studies in hypnotherapy of a wide variety of psychological problems. The present volume is the result of our effort to remedy this deficit and is particularly noteworthy in that it represents a collaboration between an academician (Dowd) and a practitioner (Healy). Each of us, however, operates partly in the domain of the other.

We attempted to enlist the services of active practitioners with a wide variety of theoretical orientations. We asked each participant to focus the discussion around a specific case, or cases, using actual transcripts, in order to provide as much detailed information as possible. Too often, case presentations are described in general terms only, leaving the reader to work out the details and specific applications alone. Each chapter author was free to develop his or her chapter around a case of particular interest. We were interested only in obtaining as wide a range of client problems as possible, rather than attempting to predetermine types of problems addressed.

We view this book as a reference manual to be spot used as needed, rather than read straight through. As a learning manual, the book can be approached in a variety of ways. The reader may focus on one particular problem or class of problems, using his or her own creativity to modify the procedures and hypnotic interventions presented. The reader may also wish to practice a specific hypnotic procedure across a range of concerns. The contributing authors hope that the material presented is utilized as a springboard for the creativity of each reader, rather than being approached as a complete "cookbook" with very rigid "recipes."

The practice of hypnotherapy currently enjoys an explosion of use. Each chapter represents one point of view regarding the solution of the client's (or clients') particular concern(s). A variety of procedures, however, are possible for each case. We hope that readers will modify and/or expand the methods outlined herein and will maximally utilize their own creativity. Only in that fashion will the field of hypnotherapy advance.

Hypnosis is a powerful technique for human change. The relationship bond established between client and therapist as a result of hypnotic interventions is extremely strong. Therefore, we urge that all mental health professionals obtain additional training in hypnosis before attempting the procedures outlined in this book.

E. Thomas Dowd
James M. Healy

CONTENTS

CASE STUDIES IN HYPNOTHERAPY

I
EMOTIONAL PROBLEMS

Emotional problems represent the largest class of mental health concerns for which individuals seek treatment. Indeed, depression has been called "the common cold of mental health," and in frequency of complaints anxiety is a close second. It is therefore appropriate that this section includes a wide variety and diversity of chapters.

In Chapter 1 Albert Ellis makes several interesting points. First, he discusses similarities between hypnosis and rational–emotive therapy (RET). Second, he has created a hypnotic variant in which he combines hypnosis and RET. Third, he describes his use of this technique in the solution of a frustratingly common problem in anxiety management: anxiety about anxiety itself, which can lead to a maladaptive spiral as the individual becomes more and more anxious.

William L. Golden takes a rather interesting tack in his chapter, in which he considers the phenomenon of resistance to the treatment of anxiety and the use of Ericksonian techniques for bypassing this resistance. Since resistance is a very common problem in all types of therapy, this chapter should be of interest. Golden also describes an integration between Ericksonian and cognitive–behavioral methods.

Dan C. Overlade describes a case of depression with a strong interpersonal component. Especially noteworthy is his combination of hypnosis and postural reorientation, as well as an immunization procedure against further depression.

Charles B. Mutter describes the treatment of a specific type of emotional problem, posttraumatic stress syndrome. With the recognition that Vietnam veterans have often suffered from this disorder, its treatment has become more important. Mutter describes four cases that testify to the multifaceted manner in which hypnosis can be used in the treatment of this problem.

At first glance, Joseph Barber's description of the treatment of dyssomnia, or sleep disorders, by hypnosis may not seem to fit this section. However, it is apparent that there was a strong anxiety component to the client's problem that was connected to the sleep disturbance. Hypnosis was used in a very creative manner to enable the client to recall the source of a deep conflict.

1
ANXIETY ABOUT ANXIETY
The Use of Hypnosis with Rational–Emotive Therapy

Albert Ellis

Rational–emotive therapy (RET) is often used in conjunction with hypnosis and has been shown to work effectively in several controlled outcome studies (Reardon & Tosi, 1977; Reardon, Tosi, & Gwynne, 1978; Stanton, 1977; Tosi & Marzella, 1977; Tosi & Reardon, 1976). There are several reasons why RET and hypnosis can be effectively combined:

1. Many authorities, such as Barber (1961, 1966), Bernheim (1886/1947), and Coué (1921), believe that therapeutic hypnosis itself largely works through suggestion and mainly consists of giving clients strong positive statements and inducing them to internalize and act on these self-statements. RET, particularly, teaches people how to dispute and challenge their negative self-statements (Ellis, 1962, 1971, 1973; Ellis & Whiteley, 1979). It also stresses (as do other forms of cognitive-behavior therapy) the use of repeated and powerful positive or rational coping statements (Ellis & Abrahms, 1978; Ellis & Becker, 1982; Ellis & Grieger, 1977; Ellis & Harper, 1975; Grieger & Boyd, 1980; Walen, DiGiuseppe, & Wessler, 1980; Wessler & Wessler, 1980).

2. Autohypnosis and regular hypnosis assume that humans upset themselves with ideas, images, and other cognitions and that they can be taught and trained to change these cognitions and thereby significantly change their feelings and actions (Araoz, 1983). RET strongly posits and implements this same assumption.

3. Hypnosis and RET are both highly active–directive methods and differ significantly from many other passive and nondirective therapies, such as psychoanalytic and client-centered therapies.

4. RET and hypnosis both emphasize homework assignments and *in vivo* desensitization and frequently urge clients to do the things of which they are afraid and to work against their feelings of low frustration tolerance and their self-defeating addictions.

Albert Ellis. Institute for Rational–Emotive Therapy, New York, New York.

Because some of the basic theories and practices of hypnotherapy and RET significantly overlap, I have combined RET with hypnosis since the early 1950s; one of my first published papers on RET was "Hypnotherapy with Borderline Psychotics" (Ellis, 1958; expanded version, Ellis, 1962). At first, I had several sessions with clients with whom I used hypnosis, so that they could be trained to go into a moderate or fairly light trance. I noticed, however, that a number of clients who only achieved light trance states—or states of deep relaxation but hardly hypnosis—did just as well or better with the RET I taught them as did clients who achieved deep or "true" hypnotic trances.

I therefore created a new hypnotic method that saved me and my clients hours of therapy time. Using this method, I put the clients in what is usually a light hypnotic (or deeply relaxed) state, employing a modified version of Jacobson's (1938) progressive relaxation technique, which takes only about 10 minutes to effect. I follow this with 10 minutes of RET instruction, designed to show the clients that they have a few specific irrational beliefs (iBs) with which they are creating some major problem (e.g., anxiety, depression, rage, or self-downing) and that if they keep actively and strongly disputing these iBs (as I have previously taught them to do in several nonhypnotic sessions), they will change their beliefs—and thereby also appreciably change their self-defeating feelings and behaviors that stem from and help reinforce these iBs.

The unique feature of this RET hypnotic procedure is that I often use it only once, for a single session, to work on a client's main presenting problem. I record both the 10 minutes of hypnotic relaxation induction plus the following 10 minutes of RET instruction on a 60-minute audio cassette. I give the cassette to the clients to keep listening to everyday, at least once a day, for the next 30–60 days. Using this method, I only see the clients for a single 30-minute hypnotic session; but they get 15, 30, or more hours of recorded RET hypnotic therapy at their own home or office for the next month or two; and if they actually use this time as I direct them to do, they often develop deeper and deeper trance states, even though during the original live session they develop only a very light trance—or, as many of them report, no real trance state at all.

CASE DESCRIPTION

To illustrate the use of this method, I report here the case of a 33-year-old unmarried borderline female who had a 20-year history of being severely anxious about her school, work, love, and sex performances and who became classically anxious about her anxiety, had a severe case of phrenophobia, and was sure that she would end up as a bag lady, without any friends, lovers, or money. Actually, she was quite attractive, could have 10–15 orgasms a week when she felt secure with a love partner (which was rare), and made a large salary as a sales manager.

I had 13 sessions with this severely anxious woman, and at times she used the main message of RET—that you largely feel the way you think—and notably decreased her feelings of terror about failing in love, sex, and business. But a few weeks later she would fall back again almost to zero and make herself exceptionally upset—especially about her anxiety itself. After hearing that one of her friends was helped to stop smoking by hypnotherapy, she asked me if I used it along with RET. I said that I sometimes did but that I often did not encourage clients to resort to it because they thought of it as a form of magic and used it instead of working at the RET.

I agreed, however, to try it with her and used it once. The following is a transcript of my first and only hypnotic session with her.

HYPNOTIC SESSION

First loosen your toes and then tense them up. Just tense your toes. Now relax them. Relax. Relax. Now I'm going to put you through a series of relaxation exercises like the one you just did with your toes, but emphasizing the second part—focusing on physical relaxation. I want you to relax your toes and only focus on relaxing them. Think about your toes and focus on relaxing them. Relax them, relax them, relax them. Then relax the rest of the muscles of your feet—all your sole, instep, heel, and ankle muscles. Let all your feet muscles sink into a nice, easy, free, relaxed state. Relax the soles of your feet, your ankles, your heels, your whole feet. Just relax, relax, relax, relax.

Then relax the calves of your legs, let both calves relax—easy, free, warm, nice and relaxed. Then relax your knees, let your knee muscles go—nice, free, flexible, warm, relaxed. Then your thighs; relax your thigh muscles, focus on those thigh muscles, and relax, relax, relax them. Relax them, relax them, relax them. Now your hips; let your middle region, your hips, relax, relax, relax. And now go back to your toes again and let your toes, your feet, lower legs, your calves, your knees, your thighs, and your hips relax, relax, all of them relax. Let the whole lower part of your body relax, relax, relax, relax, relax. Now your stomach muscles. Think of your stomach muscles, focus on your stomach muscles, relax all those stomach muscles, relax them, let them go easy, nice, warm, flexible, and free.

And now your chest muscles. Breathe easily—in and out, in and out, let go, relax your chest muscles, let your whole chest, as well as your stomach, your legs, and your feet, relax, relax, relax, relax.

Now your shoulder muscles. Let go your shoulder muscles and relax them. Let them sink, sink, sink into themselves. Let them sink, sink, sink into any sofa, bed, or chair that you are resting on. Just let them go. Let them relax. And now your upper arm muscles, let them go—easy, warm, free, relaxed. And your elbows—let your elbow muscles relax, relax, relax. And your forearm muscles—let them go, let them go. Warm, free, easy, relaxed. And let your wrist muscles relax. Easy, free, relaxed, flexible, warm. And the muscles of your fingers and your hand. Let them go—flexible, free, nice, warm, easy, relaxed.

Now your whole body's sinking into a totally, nice relaxed state from the tip of your toes to your neck. Your shoulders and arms are getting more and more and more relaxed. Now focus on your neck muscles. Let them go. Let those neck muscles, which are sometimes tense, relax, relax, relax. And now your jaw muscles. Let your mouth hang slightly open. Let your jaw muscles relax, relax, relax. And you can even relax your cheek muscles. You can let them go a little, let them get flabby and relaxed, more than they normally are. And the muscles of your mouth, your lips—relax, relax them, relax them, relax them.

And now the top of your head, your scalp muscles—wrinkle your scalp a little and let the muscles relax, relax, relax. And especially your eye muscles, which are now tense. Let those eyes relax, relax. Easy, free, and flexible. You now *want* to let your eyes close into a nice relaxed, easy state. And you focus on letting those eyes relax, relax. And they're closing. Easy and free, warm and relaxed. They're getting tired. They *want* to relax and you *want* them to relax. Along with your whole body, you especially want to let your eyes relax, let go. They're closing, getting tired, tired and more and more relaxed. And now your eyes are closing and becoming more and more relaxed. You really *feel* the relaxation in your eye muscles. They're closing, closing—becoming more and more relaxed. You *want* to go, you *want* to let yourself go and feel fully calm and relaxed. You *want* to sink into a totally, totally relaxed state.

Your eyes are getting heavier and heavier and you want to let yourself sink, you're trying to let yourself sink, into a deeper, deeper, relaxed state. You want to let your whole body, especially your eyes, go *deeper*, and *deeper* and *deeper into a totally free, warm, nice, flexible, relaxed state. And now you're letting yourself go deeper, deeper, deeper, deeper*. You want to fully relax and get your body out of your way and go *deep, deep, down deeper, down deeper*, into a fully, fully, fully free and easy relaxed state. You're only listening to the sound of my voice, that's all you're focusing on, that's all you want to hear—the sound of my voice, that's all you're focusing on, that's all you want to hear—the sound of my voice. And you're going to do what I tell you to do, because you *want* to, you *want* to do it. You *want* to stay in this relaxed state and be fully aware of my voice and do what I tell you to do because you *want* to do it, you *want* to be relaxed. You *want* to rid yourself of your anxiety and you *know* that this will help you relax and listen, relax and listen, go into a fully free and relaxed state.

You're only focusing on my voice and you're going to listen carefully to what I'm telling you. You're going to remember everything I tell you. And after you awake from this relaxed, hypnotic state, you're going to feel very good. Because you're going to remember everything and use what you hear—use it for *you*. Use it to put away all your anxiety and all your anxiety *about* your anxiety. You're going to remember what I tell you and use it everyday. Whenever you feel anxious about anything, you're going to remember what I'm telling you now, in this relaxed state, and you're going to fully focus on it, concentrate on it very well, and do exactly what we're talking about—relax and get rid of your anxiety, relax and get rid of your anxiety.

Whenever you get anxious about anything, you're going to realize that the reason you're anxious is because you are saying to yourself, telling yourself "I *must* succeed! I *must* succeed! I *must* do this, or I *must* not do that!" You will clearly see and fully accept that your anxiety comes from your self-statement. It doesn't come from without. It doesn't come from other people. *You* make yourself anxious, by demanding that something *must* go well or *must* not exist. It's *your* demand that makes you anxious. It's always you and your self-talk; and therefore *you* control it and *you* can change it.

You're going to realize, "*I* make myself anxious. I don't *have* to keep making myself anxious, if I give up my demands, my musts, my shoulds, my oughts. If I really accept what is, accept things the way they are, then I won't be anxious. I can always make myself unanxious and tense by giving up my musts, by relaxing—by wanting and wishing for things, but not *needing*, not *insisting*, not *demanding*, not *must*urbating about them."

You're going to keep telling yourself, "I can *ask* for things, I can *wish*. But I do not *need* what I want, I never *need* what I want! There is nothing I *must* have; and there is nothing I *must* avoid, including my anxiety. I'd *like* to get rid of this anxiety. I *can* get rid of it. I'm *going* to get rid of it. But if I tell myself, 'I *must* not be anxious! I *must* not be anxious! I *must* be unanxious!' then I'll be anxious.

"Nothing will kill me. Anxiety won't kill me. Lack of sex won't kill me. There are lots of unpleasant things in the world that I don't like, but I can *stand* them, I don't *have* to get rid of them. If I'm anxious, I'm anxious—too damn bad! Because *I* control my emotional destiny—as long as I don't feel that I *have* to do anything, that I have to succeed at anything. That's what destroys me—the idea that I *have* to be sexy or I have to succeed at sex. Or that I *have* to get rid of my anxiety." In your regular life, after listening to this tape regularly, you're going to think and to keep thinking these things. Whenever you're anxious, you'll look at what you're doing to *make* yourself anxious, and you'll give up your demands and your musts. You'll dispute your ideas that "I *must* do well! I *must* get people to like me! They *must* not criticize me! It's terrible, when they criticize me!" You'll keep asking yourself, "Why *must* I do well? Why do I *have* to be a great sex partner? It would be *nice* if people liked me, but they don't *have* to. I do not *need* their approval. If they criticize me, if they blame me, or they think I'm too sexy or too little sexy, too damn bad! I do not *need* their approval. I'd *like* it, but I don't *need* it. I'd also *like* to be unanxious but there's no reason why I *must* be. Yes, there's no reason why I *must* be. It's just *preferable*. None of these things I fail at are going to kill me.

"And when I die, as I eventually will, so I die! Death is not horrible. It's a state of *no* feeling. It's exactly the same state as I was in before I was born. I won't feel *anything*. So I certainly need not be afraid of that!

"And even if I get very anxious and go crazy, that too isn't terrible. If I tell myself, 'I *must* not go crazy! I *must* not go crazy!' then I'll make myself crazy! But even if I'm crazy, so I'm crazy! I can *live* with it even if I'm in a mental hospital. I can *live* and not depress myself about it. *Nothing* is terrible—even when people don't like me, even when I'm acting stupidly, even when I'm very anxious! *Nothing* is terrible! I *can* stand it! It's only a pain in the ass!"

Now this is what you're going to think in your everyday life. Whenever you get anxious about anything, you're going to see what you're anxious about, you're going to realize that you are demanding something, saying "It *must* be so! I *must* get well! I *must* not do the wrong thing! I *must* not be anxious!" And you're going to stop and say, "You know—I don't need that nonsense. If these things happen, they happen. It's not the end of the world! I'd *like* to be unanxious, I'd *like* to get along with people, I'd *like* to have good sex. But if I don't, I *don't*! Tough! It's not the end of everything. I can always be a happy human *in spite of* failures and hassles. If I don't *demand*, if I don't insist, if I don't say, 'I must, I must!' Musts are crazy. My *desires* are all right. But, again, I don't *need* what I *want*!" Now this is what you're going to keep working at in your everyday life.

You're going to keep using your head, your thinking ability, to focus, to concentrate on ridding yourself of your anxiety—just as you're listening and concentrating right now. Your concentration will get better and better. You're going to be more and more in control of your thoughts and your feelings. You will keep realizing that *you* create your anxiety, *you* make yourself upset, and *you* don't have to, you never have to keep doing so. You can always give up your anxiety. You can always change. You can always relax, and relax, and relax, and not take *anyone*, not take *anything* too seriously.

This is what you're going to remember and work at when you get out of this relaxed state. This idea is what you're going to take with you all day, everyday: "*I* control me. I don't *have* to upset myself about anything. If I do upset myself, too bad. I may feel upset for a while but it won't ruin my life or kill me. And I can be anxious without putting myself down, without saying 'I must not be anxious!' At times I will make myself anxious, but I can give up my anxiety if I don't *demand* that I be unanxious."

And you're going to get better and better about thinking in this rational way. You'll become more in control of you. Never *totally* in control, because nobody ever is totally unanxious. But you'll make yourself much less anxious and able to live with it when you are anxious. And if you live with it, it will go away. If you live with it, it will go away. Nothing is terrible, not even anxiety. That's what you're going to realize and to keep thinking about until you really, really believe it.

Now you feel nice and free and warm and fully relaxed. In a few minutes I'm going to tell you to come out of this relaxed, hypnotic state. You will then have a good day. You will feel fine when you come out of this state. You will experience no ill effects of the hypnosis. You will remember everything I just said to you and will keep working at using it. And you will play this tape every day for the next 30 days. You will listen to it every day until you really believe it and follow it. Eventually you will be able to follow its directions and to think your way out of anxiety and out of anxiety *about* being anxious without the tape.

You will then be able to release yourself from anxiety by yourself. You can always relax and use the antianxiety technique you will learn by listening to the tape. You can always accept yourself *with* your anxiety and can stop telling yourself, "I must not be anxious! I must not be anxious!" Just tell yourself, "I don't *like* anxiety, I'll work to give it up. I'll conquer it. I'll control myself, control my own emotional destiny. I can always relax, make myself feel easy and free and nice, just as I feel now, get away from cares for awhile and then feel unanxious. But I can more elegantly accept myself first with my anxiety, stop fighting it desperately, and stop telling myself it's awful to be anxious. Then I can go back to the original anxiety and get rid of it by refusing to awfulize about failing and vigorously disputing my irrational beliefs, 'I must do well! I must not be disapproved!'".

Now you feel good, you feel relaxed, and in a couple of minutes, I'm going to count to three and when I count to three you will awake and feel quite alive, have a good day, and experience no bad effects, no headaches, no physical discomfort! Everything is going to be fine and you'll have a good day. You will remember all this and, as I said, you will listen to this tape whenever you possibly can, at least once a day. And you will think and act more and more on its message. You'll be able to control yourself and reduce your anxiety appreciably. And when you do feel anxious you'll live with the anxiety, accept it, and refuse to panic yourself about it. All right, I'm going to count till three and when I say *three* you'll wake and be fully alive and alert and feel great for the rest of the day. One, two, three!

THERAPEUTIC OUTCOME

My client used the recording of her hypnotic RET session once or twice a day for the next 45 days and reported a significant decrease in her anxiety level, and especially in her anxiety about her anxiety. She stopped being phrenophobic, convinced herself that if she had a breakdown and went to the mental hospital it would be highly inconvenient but not horrible or shameful, and then hardly thought at all about going crazy. When she did, she was able to feel comfortable within a few minutes by strongly telling herself, "So I'll be crazy! Tough! I'm sure I won't stay that way very long—and if I do, that will just be tougher. But not shameful! No matter how crazy I am, I'll never be a turd for being that way!"

As she began to get over her anxiety about her anxiety, this woman's enormous fears of failure, particularly of sex failure, for awhile almost completely disappeared. When, weeks later, they reappeared, they were relatively light, and she was almost invariably able to cope successfully with them. She continued in RET nonhypnotic treatment for 14 months more, but only had 18 half-hour sessions during that time. For the last 11 years she has maintained her gains, with occasional moderate setbacks when a love affair ended, and is now happily married and unanxiously highly productive. Once in a while she still listens to the original hypnotic tape and believes that it was quite instrumental in helping her make much greater progress than she had previously made in RET.

I tend to agree with her, partly because I have used similar taped sessions to good avail with about 80 other clients (although with little or no success with 18 others). One important question I have not yet resolved is: Does the benefit presumably derived from this tape of recorded hypnotic sessions stem from the use of the entire 20-minute tape, including the hypnotic relaxation instructions, or would equal benefit stem from the client's listening a number of times to the 10 minutes of RET instruction on the tape even if this were heard apart from the hypnotic section? I have tried to induce several researchers to do a controlled study of this question but so far no one, to my knowledge, has done so. I still hope that this experiment will be done one day. Until then, I shall continue to use this recorded hypnosis–RET procedure with some amount of faith in the clinical results I have thus far achieved with it.

REFERENCES

Araoz, D. L. *Hypnosis and sex therapy*. New York: Brunner/Mazel, 1983.

Barber, T. X. Physiological effect of "hypnosis." *Psychological Bulletin*, 1961, *58*, 390–419.

Barber, T. X. The effects of "hypnosis" and motivational suggestions on strength and endurance. *British Journal of Social and Clinical Psychology*, 1966, *5*, 42–50.

Bernheim, H. *Suggestive therapeutics*. New York: London Book Company, 1947. (Originally published 1886.)

Coué, E. *My method*. New York: Doubleday, Page, 1921.

Ellis, A. Hypnotherapy with borderline psychotics. *Journal of General Psychology*, 1958, *59*, 245-253.

Ellis, A. *Reason and emotion in psychotherapy*. Secaucus, NJ: Citadel Press, 1962.

Ellis, A. *Growth through reason*. North Hollywood, CA: Wilshire Books, 1971.

Ellis, A. *Humanistic psychotherapy: The rational emotive approach*. New York: McGraw-Hill, 1973.

Ellis, A., & Abrahms, E. *Brief psychotherapy in medical and health practice*. New York: Springer, 1978.

Ellis, A., & Becker, I. *A guide to personal happiness*. North Hollywood, CA: Wilshire Books, 1982.

Ellis, A., & Grieger, R. (Eds.). *Handbook of rational-emotive therapy*. New York: Springer, 1977.

Ellis, A., & Harper, R. A. *A new guide to rational living*. North Hollywood, CA: Wilshire Books, 1975.

Ellis, A., & Whiteley, J. M. (Eds.). *Theoretical and empirical foundations of rational-emotive therapy*. Monterey, CA: Brooks/Cole, 1979.

Grieger, R., & Boyd, J. *Rational-emotive therapy: A skills based approach*. New York: Von Nostrand Reinhold, 1980.

Jacobson, E. *You must relax*. New York: McGraw-Hill, 1938.

Reardon, J., & Tosi, D. The effects of rational stage directed imagery on self concept and reduction of stress in adolescent delinquent females. *Journal of Clinical Psychology*, 1977, *33*, 1084–1092.

Reardon, J., Tosi, D., & Gwynne, P. The treatment of depression through rational stage directed hypnotherapy (RDH): A case study. *Psychotherapy: Theory, Research and Practice*, 1977, *14*, 95–103.

Stanton, H. E. The utilization of suggestions derived from rational emotive therapy. *International Journal of Clinical and Experimental Hypnosis*, 1977, *25*, 18–26.

Tosi, D., & Marzella, J. N. In J. L. Wolfe & E. Brand (Eds.), *Twenty years of rational therapy*. New York: Institute for Rational Emotive Therapy, 1977.

Tosi, D., & Reardon, J. P. The treatment of guilt through rational stage directed therapy. *Rational Living*, 1976, *11*(1), 8–11.

Walen, S., DiGiuseppe, R., & Wessler, R. *A practitioner's guide to rational-emotive therapy*. New York: Oxford, 1980.

Wessler, R. A., & Wessler, R. L. *The theory and practice of rational emotive therapy*. San Francisco: Jossey-Bass, 1980.

2
AN INTEGRATION OF ERICKSONIAN AND COGNITIVE–BEHAVIORAL HYPNOTHERAPY IN THE TREATMENT OF ANXIETY DISORDERS

William L. Golden

Cognitive–behavioral methods for treating anxiety and phobic disorders have been developed by Ellis (1962) and Meichenbaum (1972a, 1972b, 1977). These techniques include rational–emotive methods, relaxation procedures, exposure to anxiety-provoking situations via imagery, the use of coping imagery, coping self-statements, and other cognitive restructuring procedures. Several writers (Araoz, 1981, 1982; Golden, 1983a; Spanos & Barber, 1976) have pointed out the similarity between these cognitive–behavioral methods and hypnotic procedures. Spanos and Barber (1976) have proposed a cognitive-behavioral model of hypnosis. They claim that "hypnotic" behavior is the result of the same factors that are involved in cognitive-behavior therapy:

1. The motivation and cooperation of the individual receiving the treatment or the suggestions.
2. The attitudes and expectations of the individual toward the treatment or the suggestions.
3. The wording of the instructions or the suggestions.
4. The individual's involvement or "absorption" in "suggestion-related" thoughts and imagery.

Several hypnotherapists (Araoz, 1981, 1982; Boutin, 1978; Ellis, 1962; Golden, 1983a; Gwynne, Tosi, & Howard, 1978) have integrated hypnotic procedures with rational–emotive therapy (RET) and other cognitive–be-

William L. Golden. Private Practice, New York, New York, and Institute for Rational-Emotive Therapy, New York, New York.

havioral approaches. Hypnotic induction procedures are employed along with a combination of hypnotic, cognitive, and behavioral treatment strategies (see Golden, 1983a, for a description of various cognitive–behavioral hypnotherapy methods).

The treatment methods in cognitive-behavior hypnotherapy are direct and didactic. Clients are taught self-hypnotic and other self-control procedures as coping skills and are instructed to practice and employ them. Success in cognitive–behavioral hypnotherapy depends on the cooperation of the client, the willingness of the client to collaborate with the therapist, and the client's conscious and persistent application of the treatment procedures.

On the other hand, in Ericksonian hypnosis, indirect suggestion is employed, either with or without formal hypnotic induction procedure. Usually these suggestions and instructions are given without the client's full awareness of their purpose. Erickson (Erickson & Rossi, 1979; Erickson, Rossi, & Rossi, 1976) and strategic therapists, such as Haley (1976), believe that resistance is inevitable and that efforts to directly influence a client will often increase resistance. Therefore, although they do talk about unconscious learning, they do not directly teach coping skills to their clients. Instead, Ericksonian hypnotherapy includes methods such as confusion techniques, paradoxical interventions, indirect suggestions, and other techniques that involve joining or utilizing resistance, as well as utilizing clients' frames of reference, associations, strengths, and even their symptoms.

Elsewhere (Golden, 1983b) I have argued that Ericksonian and strategic therapy procedures are appropriate in treating very resistant clients who will not cooperate with a cognitive–behavioral approach. However, many of these techniques are unnecessary with cooperative clients who do very well with the cognitive–behavioral problem-solving approach. Even when resistance is encountered, a cognitive–behavioral approach often can be used to overcome it (see Golden, 1983b, for a cognitive–behavioral problem-solving approach to treating resistance). In cognitive-behavior therapy, the factors contributing to the resistance are examined and appropriate interventions are planned, usually with the cooperation of the client. The therapist and the client work together on the impasse as a problem to be solved. The client is taught to use the same methods that are used in cognitive-behavior therapy to deal with any problem: self-monitoring, cognitive restructuring, training in the development of new skills needed to overcome the problem, desensitization to higher order anxieties, and so on.

Nevertheless, there are a number of clients who will (at least initially) resist any and all direct efforts to help them. For these individuals Ericksonian techniques seem to be an important, if not indispensable part of their treatment. The purpose of this chapter is to describe an integration of Ericksonian and cognitive–behavioral methods in the treatment of anxiety disorder. Two cases are described where Ericksonian principles and techniques were used to bypass or overcome the client's resistance, thereby increasing the client's receptivity to cognitive-behavior therapy.

CASE 1

John C, a single, black, 30-year-old community college student, came to therapy for treatment of test anxiety, poor concentration, and difficulty studying. His grades were poor and he was on probation at school. Not having very much money, he worked at night and went to school, taking 12 credits a term, during the daytime. Although his eye contact was adequate, John appeared extremely shy and withdrawn. He spoke very little, did not display any affect, and only gave information when it was asked of him. He would probably be diagnosed as a borderline personality. He lived alone and spent most of his spare time alone. His functioning was minimal. He did not have any friends, worked as an unskilled laborer, and had a long history of being a marginal student.

At his initial session, John requested hypnosis for his academic problems. He reported that he had been to five different hypnotherapists, and all had failed to hypnotize him. Various methods and approaches had been attempted by some very competent hypnotists. However, all of them had employed traditional hypnotic methods that involved direct attempts to hypnotize John.

I asked John if he would consider some treatment method other than hypnosis. He knew that I had been doing research on the treatment of test anxiety and had sought my help because of my expertise in that area. Nevertheless, he insisted that I treat him for his test anxiety, and only his test anxiety, through hypnosis.

I felt that I was being set up to fail, just as those therapists before me who attempted to treat John through hypnosis as he requested. On the one hand, John was demanding that I hypnotize him. On the other hand, he was saying he could not be hypnotized. In fact, he actually said, "I want you to hypnotize me, but I don't think you can. So far, no one has been able to hypnotize me."

My answer was immediate and directly in response to John's challenge. "You know you're right John, I can't hypnotize you, but I'll tell you what, I'll show you how I hypnotize myself."

Without further ado, I proceeded to demonstrate and teach John how I hypnotize myself:

"First I find a comfortable position in a chair like this one or like the one you're sitting on. I let myself sink into the chair into a comfortable position." (I paused and looked in John's direction. Apparently in response to my implicit suggestion, he repositioned himself in the chair. I waited for him to get comfortable, before I went on.)

"Usually I close my eyes, but I don't have to. But it often helps to close your eyes when *you* are first learning to relax." (I was giving John indirect suggestions to relax. However, I was being very careful to give John choices, such as the choice to close his eyes or to keep them open and the choice to either experience relaxation or to simply listen and learn how he might go about hypnotizing himself.)

I closed my eyes and continued to talk about how I hypnotize myself. I peeked to see if John had followed suit. His eyes were closed and he was proceeding with the next step, which was my indirect suggestion to take long, slow, deep breaths.

"Next, I take several long, slow, deep breaths . . . and each time I exhale, I start to let go of a little tension . . . letting my arms . . . and my legs go loose and limp . . . letting my body sink into the chair . . . letting my back go loose and limp . . . letting my shoulders hang comfortably . . . letting my jaws hang slack." (I continued to model the breathing and progressive relaxation, occasionally opening my eyes, observing John, and pacing my comments to match changes in his breathing and other cues, such as his posture, that indicated he was becoming more relaxed.)

As he exhaled, I would give indirect suggestions such as, "And as you exhale you can sink further into the chair and experience a more relaxed feeling." (At this point I switched from speaking about my experiences and stopped using the word "I" and began talking more directly to him using the word "You.")

After John exhibited signs of deep relaxation, I gave him suggestions that now that he was relaxed, he could enter a deep hypnotic trance. I used relaxation imagery, counting, and the image of walking down a long stairway as deepening techniques. Then, before terminating the trance, I gave John suggestions that he was a good hypnotic subject and that he could recreate the trance by repeating the procedure using the same techniques of deep breathing, progressive relaxation, imagining pleasant scenes, counting, and the stairway image. I also gave him suggestions that during trance he would be receptive to constructive suggestions that would aid him in achieving his goals.[1] I then suggested that after he opened his eyes he could reinduce the trance because he now knew how to hypnotize himself. John responded to these suggestions and demonstrated that he could induce self-hypnosis. At his next session John reported that he practiced his self-hypnosis exercises several times a day.

1. The rationale for these suggestions was not that the client would be more suggestible to them because he was in a deep trance. Rather, the successful trance induction allowed him to accept other suggestions (i.e., the relaxation that he experienced increased his belief in hypnosis as being capable of producing change in him).

In subsequent sessions, John was cooperative and receptive to rational-emotive hypnotherapy (REH; Golden, 1983a). First, imagery was used to uncover the negative thoughts, attitudes, and fantasies that aroused anxiety in John and impaired his concentration. By imagining himself in test-taking situations (called activating events in RET) while in a trance, John was able to get in touch with his anxiety-producing cognitions.[2] Through this evocative technique, John was able to pinpoint his beliefs that he was stupid and worthless and that he would fail no matter how hard he studied. The test-taking imagery also evoked a series of images, or fantasies, in which John pictured himself going blank on tests and failing. John reported these internal events while in the trance state.

Next, cognitive restructuring procedures were utilized during the trance state. Rational-emotive imagery (REI) was the main technique used to help reduce John's test anxiety. Often, in REH with the help of the therapist, clients will dispute (i.e., question and reevaluate) their self-defeating thoughts and attitudes while they are in the trance state. However, in John's case Ellis's (1962) technique of disputing irrational beliefs was not employed, because of John's expectation and request that I give him the suggestions while he was in the trance state passively listening. His preference was respected, and during the REI, I gave John rational-emotive suggestions[3] (such as, "You can do well on your exams as long as you study, but no matter how you do, you are still worthwhile, and can treat yourself well"). As part of the REI, John was instructed to imagine himself taking exams. He was asked to imagine himself coping with the examination situation and responding appropriately (calming down and doing well on the exam).

A similar hypnotic procedure was used for studying. After undergoing a similar induction procedure, John was asked to imagine himself employing various study skills (e.g., mentally rehearsing important facts). He was given rational suggestions about studying (such as, "No one can remember everything they read; you can do well even if you forget some important information") and was given suggestions for improved concentration. John practiced these exercises at home as part of his self-hypnosis.

John received a total of five hypnosis sessions spread out over the course of one school term. He reported feeling less anxious while studying and during examinations. He passed all of his exams and attained a 2.2 grade point average as compared to his past average of 1.7. Follow-up during the next term indicated that John maintained his gains.

2. Cognitive-behavior therapists often use this and other imagery techniques without first inducing trance. Trance was incorporated into the procedure in this case because it was what the client expected.

3. Rational-emotive suggestions are self-statements that are formulated on the basis of RET principles and are employed as hypnotic suggestions.

CASE 2

Paul D was a 33-year-old white male, who sought treatment for anxiety attacks, or what he called "adrenalin rushes." Paul had been referred to me by a former client who was successfully treated for agoraphobia and anxiety attacks. At first, Paul requested the same treatment, which was cognitive-behavior therapy, that his friend received.

Paul was unable to pinpoint the onset of his anxiety disorder. He was also unable to say what triggered these anxiety attacks. He was taught Jacobsonian relaxation and was instructed to monitor the situations and his thoughts when he felt anxiety or any "adrenalin rushes." The self-monitoring revealed that Paul's anxiety attacks occurred in response to internal cues; feelings and sensations such as headaches, stomach pains, and the manifestations of anxiety (rapid heartbeat, sweating, the warm sensation of adrenalin, etc.). His negative self-statements were that he "could not handle these feelings" and that if they did not go away, eventually he would become "helpless and out of control." A search for external cues proved to be futile.

Because Paul requested the same type of therapy that his friend who referred him had received, "coping" desensitization (see Meichenbaum, 1972a, 1972b) was presented as the treatment of choice. As part of the desensitization procedure, Paul was relaxed and was asked to imagine experiencing each of the sensations that he feared. He was instructed to calm himself down and use relaxation techniques and coping self-statements (such as, "I can cope with anxiety. These sensations are uncomfortable but not dangerous. I don't have to totally eliminate the anxiety. Just reduce it to a manageable level. It will pass," etc.) whenever he experienced anxiety during the procedure. Furthermore, he was given the assignment of employing these coping techniques whenever he felt anxious between sessions.

Paul reported some success and decrease in his anxiety. Despite this success he said that he felt that there was something else that was needed. Attempts to explore what this something else might be were unsuccessful. Then, after Paul's 10th session, he came to therapy very enthusiastic about what he considered to be a great revelation. He had been watching a movie on television about a married couple who both had the same symptoms as he was experiencing. They ended up consulting a psychiatrist who employed a hypnotic regression procedure to uncover the source of their anxiety. According to the story, hypnotic regression revealed that they had been captured by aliens from outer space who had hypnotized them and gave them suggestions that they would have amnesia for their experience. As the story goes, once the repressed memories were lifted, the couple's symptoms were alleviated.

Paul did not believe that he was captured by aliens from outer space. But he *strongly* believed that he had some deeply repressed memories that could only be retrieved through hypnotic regression, and once the memories were brought to his awareness he would be cured.

Coming from a cognitive–behavioral orientation, I at first resisted Paul's request and encouraged him to continue with the cognitive-behavior therapy, since he was getting better. At Paul's next session, he insisted he was getting worse and that he was not getting the right treatment. He needed hypnotic regression. At this point I realized I had better join the resistance.

A total of two hypnotic sessions were employed, after which, the client reported a complete alleviation of his symptoms. The first session was devoted to hypnotic induction via hand levitation. He was shown how to create sensations of lightness by becoming absorbed in thoughts and images consistent with the goals of the suggestion, that is, hand levitation (see Katz, 1979, and Spanos & Barber, 1976, from descriptions of this cognitive skills approach to hypnosis). Paul proved to be an excellent hypnotic subject and reported experiencing a high degree of dissociation. During the hand levitation, he experienced a spontaneous dissociation from his hands which became anesthetized without his being given suggestions for numbness. During his first hypnotic session Paul was trained in self-hypnosis. He was given suggestions while he was in the trance state that he would be able to induce a hypnotic state in himself through the same hand levitation technique. Then, as in the first case (John), it was suggested that, after I terminated his trance, he could reinduce the trance state on his own, which he did.

During the second hypnotic session, Paul was trained in regression and was gradually brought back in time to the onset of his anxiety disorder. Hypnosis was induced by my asking Paul about what he experienced during his first hypnotic session. I have found that good hypnotic subjects, like Paul, often reexperience hypnotic phenomena when they are asked to recall what they felt during previous experiences with hypnosis. This type of recall induction technique is very well suited for clients who show an interest in hypnotic regression. The recall induction procedure utilizes their curiosity for regression and, at the same time, is itself an exercise in reexperiencing the past, thus paving the way for further work with regression.

I asked Paul, "Do you remember what you felt when you were experiencing hypnosis last week?"

"Yeah," he responded. "My arms started to feel light after I imagined a helium balloon under each of my hands."

At that point, Paul held out his arms in exactly the same position as he did the previous week when he experienced hand levitation. His arms were outstretched and he held his hands just slightly above his thighs. I continued the questioning,

"And what else did you experience?"

"My hands started to go numb," he replied.

Paul was already exhibiting a great deal of responsiveness to the procedure. His arms remained outstretched while we continued to talk. Paul appeared to be experiencing hand levitation as a result of recalling his previous experience with it. I took his high degree of responsiveness to my questioning as an indication that Paul was ready for more direct suggestions to reexperience the past.

"And just as you experienced those sensations then, you can feel them again, now . . . just by recalling them. All you have to do is close your eyes, and go back in your mind to when you imagined those helium balloons . . . making your hands feel light and buoyant. . . . And what are you feeling now?"

"I, I feel it again. My hands feel light, and they're going numb. They feel like they're not attached to my body."

"Very good," I said. I wanted to reinforce his responsiveness. "Now you can just let yourself go loose and limp. Letting yourself sink into the chair into a deep, deep hypnotic trance. . . . And whenever you want to go into a trance, all you have to do is just recall what it feels like to go into a trance, and you'll begin to reexperience those same feelings, the same sensations that you feel when you go into a deep trance. . . .

"And in this trance your mind is very clear, and you can remember things very clearly, like this morning, when you were home, before you left your house. . . . Where are you?"

"I'm in the kitchen," he slowly uttered. "I'm at the table eating breakfast."

"What are you eating?"

"I'm having toast and some orange juice."

Once I established a pattern of having Paul describe the past as if he were actually there experiencing it, I asked him to go back further and further in time, 1 week ago, 1 month ago, 1 year ago, closer and closer to the time when his symptoms began. When I thought we were close to that point in his life I suggested, "And, as you already know, you are able to remember things when you are in a trance that you have repressed . . . memories, events, feelings that are related to your problem . . . And you can tell me about them now . . . as you remember them."

Paul reported his symptoms began after a bad LSD trip where he felt out of control and in a state of panic. I then suggested the following:

"And now, Paul, that you are in a hypnotic state, you can reexperience those same sensations and perceptions that you did then when you were on that LSD trip. And you can feel confident that now you can master those feelings and overcome your fear of them. . . . You're going back, going back to that LSD trip . . . recalling what you felt on that trip . . .

and as you recall those sensations and perceptions you will begin to reexperience them."

Paul was very responsive to these suggestions and experienced hallucinations such as his hands disappearing and his body distorting in size and shape. At first, Paul felt intense anxiety. However, with prolonged exposure (approximately 25 minutes) his anxiety subsided, and he was able to experience the sensory and perceptual distortions while feeling relaxed.

The next step was to provide Paul with hypnotic control over the sensory and perceptual distortions. I suggested that his hallucinatory experiences would end. Then they were recreated once again through the same suggestion that they would reoccur by his remembering what they felt like. This symptom-utilization procedure (symptom induction and reduction) was repeated until the sensory and perceptual distortions could be reliably induced and removed.

Finally, Paul was taught to induce and remove the sensory and perceptual distortions on his own, through his self-hypnotic skills. Once he demonstrated that he could exercise control over these hallucinatory experiences and his anxiety symptoms, trance was terminated. Follow-up contacts throughout the next year indicated that the regression and symptom-utilization procedure dramatically brought an end to Paul's symptoms.

DISCUSSION

Both of these cases demonstrate how cognitive–behavioral methods can be integrated with Ericksonian techniques. A similar approach was taken in both cases. However, in the first case, the resistance was anticipated and aborted before it developed. In the second case, the resistance was joined after it developed.

These cases are typical of my approach when treating anxious resistant clients. My goal with all anxious and phobic clients is to get them to confront and cope with their anxiety through whatever means possible. The cognitive–behavioral treatment of anxiety and phobic disorders involves some sort of exposure to anxiety-provoking stimuli (activating events), whether they are external cues (such as test-taking situations in the first case) or internal cues (such as those in the second case). Often the exposure is first done in imagination and then *in vivo*. In addition, clients are taught how to control their anxiety and overcome their phobias by using coping skills such as relaxation techniques and coping self-statements.

On the other hand, there are many clients (such as the two described above) who cannot or will not cooperate with, or who simply do not respond to, the usual cognitive-behavior therapy approach, which is based on a didactic self-control model. For these clients, modifying the self-control model by employing Ericksonian techniques and concepts appears to be helpful.

However, one does not have to abandon the cognitive–behavioral model as a result of employing Ericksonian techniques (or for that matter, any techniques from a different theoretical orientation). Although Ericksonian techniques were employed, I maintained a cognitive–behavioral perspective in both of the cases previously described.

In the first case, a cognitive–behavioral modeling procedure was employed that provided the client with indirect suggestions for relaxation and trance induction. John was not given direct suggestions for trance because other hypnotists had attempted to hypnotize him that way and failed. Rather than provide the client with more of the same, I anticipated and preempted the resistance by agreeing that I could not hypnotize the client. Then I paced my discussion about my own self-hypnosis to the client's behavior (i.e., his breathing, body movements, etc.).

After the client responded to indirect suggestions for relaxation and trance via the modeling techniques, I took the lead and switched to more direct self-control methods, such as self-hypnotic training and REH (see Golden, 1983a).

In the second case, the Ericksonian methods that were employed included joining the client's resistance, utilizing his expectations for cure through hypnotic regression and symptom utilization techniques (the symptom induction and reduction procedure described on p. 20). As the client requested, hypnotic regression was employed. However, the hypnotic regression provided me with an opportunity to "flood" the client through exposure to anxiety-provoking stimuli, thus allowing extinction to take place. Behavior therapists and cognitive-behavior therapists often use flooding, a technique that involves confronting one's fear or phobia. In this case, the client attributed his cure to his gaining insight through the regression procedure. I, on the other hand, consider his use of the regression procedure as an example of flooding. It is my belief that the client's symptom relief was due to extinction from the flooding and the development of self-efficacy from the self-hypnosis training and the symptom utilization procedure. Self-control was taught to the client by teaching him how to induce and remove the sensations he feared. From a cognitive–behavioral viewpoint, the regression procedure not only provided the client with prolonged exposure (flooding) to the sensations that first elicited his anxiety attacks and the sensations of anxiety themselves (i.e., his adrenalin rushes, rapid heartbeat, sweating, etc.) but also provided him with an opportunity to practice and develop skill in applying self-control procedures.

Of course, there are limitations to *post hoc* analyses of individual cases. One can never be certain about which interventions were responsible for change and which were superfluous. Even more difficult to evaluate are the principles used by clinicians to account for therapeutic success. However, as pointed out by Marks (1976), most behavioral approaches to the treatment of phobic disorders and compulsive rituals involve some sort of exposure to the cues that trigger anxiety and avoidance. Certainly this principle was made use of in the two cases reported here.

There also appears to be enough evidence, provided by these two cases, taken in conjunction with those reported by Erickson and his students, that demonstrates the usefulness of recognizing and utilizing whatever the client brings to treatment (i.e., the client's expectations, requests, experiences, and even resistances). As demonstrated in the two cases described here, this utilization concept can be integrated within cognitive-behavior therapy and hypnotherapy, thus expanding the range of clients treatable by cognitive and behaviorally oriented therapists.

REFERENCES

Araoz, D. L. Negative self-hypnosis. *Journal of Contemporary Psychotherapy*, 1981, *12*, 45–52.

Araoz, D. L. *Hypnosis and sex therapy*. New York: Brunner/Mazel, 1982.

Boutin, G. E. Treatment of test anxiety by rational stage directed hypnotherapy: A case study. *American Journal of Clinical Hypnosis*, 1978, *21*, 52–57.

Ellis, A. *Reason and emotion in psychotherapy*. New York: Lyle Stuart, 1962.

Erickson, M. H., & Rossi, E. L. *Hypnotherapy: An exploratory casebook*. New York: Irvington, 1979.

Erickson, M. H., Rossi, E. L., & Rossi, S. L. *Hypnotic realities*. New York: Irvington, 1976.

Golden, W. L. Rational-emotive hypnotherapy: Principles and techniques. *British Journal of Cognitive Psychotherapy*, 1983, *1*(1), 47–56. (a)

Golden, W. L. Resistance in cognitive-behavior therapy. *British Journal of Cognitive Psychotherapy*, 1983, *1*(2), 33–42. (b)

Gwynne, P. H., Tosi, D. J., & Howard, L. Treatment of nonassertion through rational stage directed hypnotherapy (RSDH) and behavioral rehearsal. *American Journal of Clinical Hypnosis*, 1978, *4*, 263–271.

Haley, J. *Problem solving therapy*. San Francisco: Jossey-Bass, 1976.

Katz, N. W. Comparative efficacy of behavioral training, training plus relaxation, and sleep/trance hypnotic induction in increasing hypnotic susceptibility. *Journal of Consulting and Clinical Psychology*, 1979, *47*, 119–127.

Marks, I. M. The current status of behavioral psychotherapy: Theory and practice. *American Journal of Psychiatry*, 1976, *133*(133), 253–262.

Meichenbaum, D. Cognitive modification of test anxious college students. *Journal of Consulting and Clinical Psychology*, 1972, *39*, 370–380. (a)

Meichenbaum, D. *Therapist manual for cognitive-behavior modification*. Unpublished manuscript, University of Waterloo, Waterloo, Ontario, Canada, 1972. (b)

Meichenbaum, D. *Cognitive-behavior modification*. New York: Plenum Press, 1977.

Spanos, N. P., & Barber, T. X. Behavior modification and hypnosis. In M. Hersen, R. M. Eisler, & P. M. Miller (Eds.), *Progress in behavior modification*. New York: Academic Press, 1976.

3
FIRST AID FOR DEPRESSION

Dan C. Overlade

Of all the emotional disorders, depression is unquestionably the most common. It is estimated (Gallant & Simpson, 1976) that depression is the presenting symptom in half of the admissions to psychiatric institutions and that the disorder afflicts half the population at one time or another. It is easy to imagine that outpatient psychotherapists encounter at least that fraction of clients in whom depression is either the primary presenting problem or a significant component of the decision to seek therapy; people do not go for help because they are happy.

Hill (1970) recalls that in the fourth century B.C., Hippocrates viewed melancholia to be caused by the black bile and Aristotle believed that the ideal therapies for melancholia were catharsis, wine, music, and aphrodisiacs. Hill also points out that both Asclepiades and Celsus introduced the concept of psychotherapy to the Romans. Asclepiades recommended pleasant music, intellectual stimulation and, for the treatment of melancholia, forming of good emotional relationships. Celsus emphasized the importance of the individual patient–doctor relationship along with group recreational activities. With Kraepelin the view developed that depressive illnesses were a manifestation of manic–depressive psychosis.

A more current view holds that the "depressed mood may be characterized by the individual as feeling sad, blue, down in the dumps, or low" (American Psychiatric Association, 1980, p. 301).

Klein (1976) suggests that depression is a " . . . pervasive impairment of the capacity to experience pleasure or to respond affectively to the anticipation of pleasure." That writer points out that such an inhibition of the mechanism of pleasure can result in a significantly diminished interest and investment in the environment: The depressed individual may often be incapable of enjoying hobbies, food, or even sex.

Lewinsohn, Biglan, and Zeiss (1976), after questioning the meaningfulness of a distinction between "abnormal" and "normal" mood states, point out that feelings of hopelessness, helplessness, and sadness—along with frequently accompanying symptoms such as sleeplessness and loss of

Dan C. Overlade. Private Practice, Pensacola, Florida.

appetite—are within the repertoires of all people under certain circumstances. The same writers point out that such factors as genetic or biochemical predispositions and previous life experiences may, in combination, influence the duration, intensity, and frequency of dysphoric feelings.

An individual might be trained, for example, by childhood models to be more disposed to responding depressively. It is also possible (Becker, 1974) that an individual might be genetically predisposed to respond depressively to certain types of psychological events in a manner that imbalances neurotransmitter, hormone, and electrolyte balances.

In the past 25 years, advances in biochemical research have fomented the debate about a dichotomy of depressive disorders: endogenous depression, thought due to biochemical abnormality, and exogenous (or reactive) depression, thought to represent an exaggerated response to the vicissitudes of life. Simplistically, one might suppose that the two types would be amenable to distinction on the basis of whether or not the client knew what was depressing him or her. However, the immediacy of the cathexis of the depressive affect to a plausible explanation means that even the person depressed as a response secondary to a psychotropic drug administered for the alleviation of anxiety or mania will almost always be capable of identifying a circumstance that can be utilized, cognitively, to account for the lowered mood. In those cases in which there is a clear history of recurring episodes of depressed affect without a rational precipitant identified, or the onset of the depression was longer ago than 2 months and has continued without respite, or there is indication of suicide risk, then medical treatment should be the immediate consideration. But when the depression is of quite recent onset, has an identified precipitant of significance sufficient to account for the intensity of the depression presented, and is not possibly a response secondary to medication, then there are hypnotic techniques that can be applied immediately toward the objective of fostering the early amelioration of the depression.

CASE STUDY

The subject of this case study is Michele R, a 41-year-old white woman who presented an acute situational depression. She had no prior treatment for any kind of emotional disturbance, but she had consulted me 2 years earlier in order to learn self-hypnosis; at that time her identified objectives were to be better able to express herself, to understand herself better, to make decisions more readily, to have better relationships with people (although she had no real difficulty with that), and to find solutions to her then 18-year-old son's problems, which chiefly involved irresponsibility, acting out, and mild drug abuse. She proved an apt student of self-hypnosis and was seen a total of seven times in the course of her training.

Michele's first marriage, which endured for 14 years, produced a daughter, now 14 years old, and the son, now 20 years old. After her divorce and a cross-continent geographical move, Michele met and married her second husband, Frank, 7 years before the onset of her depression. Her daughter lived with her and Frank; her son sometimes did and sometimes did not. The son sometimes was and sometimes was not applying himself to acquiring a college education with Frank's support. The son had not lived with Michele and Frank throughout their marriage; sometimes he had lived with his father in a distant state, and sometimes he had been in a boarding school.

Frank had been married to his first wife for 6 years; that union produced no children. He was divorced from her before meeting Michele. He had been referred to me 2 years before my first meeting with his wife for treatment of a very specific phobia. That treatment had been effective, and Frank had shown a most remarkable aptitude for self-hypnosis (perhaps he was the "star pupil" within my experience); his effectiveness in dissolving his phobia had been directly responsible for Michele's initial motivation in coming to me for treatment.

Frank, 6 years Michele's junior, was a highly successful fashion photographer in a southeastern city. The nature of his business was such that he frequently traveled to New York and to many other locations in order to complete a particular fashion photographing contract. Frank and Michele had traveled together extensively, but it was not always practical for her to go on all of the business trips. When other stressors accumulated, Michele's response to Frank's frequent traveling had at times included some apprehension, jealousy, and suspiciousness. Both she and Frank were quite attractive and easily could have been fashion models, but at certain times Michele was sensitive about Frank being off on location with several pretty models, even though there were staff assistants and often male models involved in the on-location shootings.

Not long after Frank and Michele completed a ski trip to the Rocky Mountains and a vacation in Switzerland, it became necessary for Frank to fly to New York for 2 days of business negotiations. From his point of view it did not seem sensible for her to make the trip with him—both because of the expense and because there would be no real time for them to seek entertainment—and he announced that he would go alone. Although he frequently made such business trips (both with and without her), her response to his announcement was highly emotional, suspicious, and accusatory. When he reversed himself and said that she might go with him if she felt that strongly about it, she declined to accompany him.

Although there were many stressors present (not the least of which was exasperation and frustration with her acting-out son), she cathected the depression she was experiencing to behavior of Frank, which she could view as justifying feelings of insecurity, jealousy, anger, and resentment.

Her suspicions and jealousy were unfounded, and it was at Frank's insistence that she reluctantly returned to see me while he was in New York.

Michele was, then, already acquainted with me. We had enjoyed a good rapport, and this had been sustained by Frank's periodic returns for what he termed "maintenance checks" in his continuing control of his phobic tendencies and by the fact that they would occasionally consult me via long distance telephone regarding her son, whom I had also briefly treated. She knew something of my style and of my appreciation of humor.

I share the view of Fay (1978) that "the use of contrast and exaggeration—and in general, the promotion of levity in our lives—tend to be beneficial." Fay points out that a sense of humor and the capacity to laugh at oneself are important ingredients in psychological well-being. Some might suppose that depressed persons *lose* their humor; it would be more accurate to say the sense of humor is "put on hold." This occurs because the physiologic postures and facial expressions associated with the humor experience are incompatible with the physiologic postures and facial expressions of depression. It is precisely this incompatibility that is ultimately capitalized on when the suggestions for ameliorization of depression are given. Without this explanation, readers unfamiliar with my work might think that some of my responses to Michele were flippant or perhaps insensitive. The responses were neither; a depressed person is helped not at all by serious commiseration. If Michele had not been acquainted with me, I might have responded to her differently, but the difference would have been slight.

VENTILATION

The treatment approach utilized has four parts: ventilation, education, amelioration, and immunization. At the beginning of the session Michele was allowed to enumerate those episodes with Frank and his behaviors that she felt were responsible for her feelings of hurt, resentment, and depression. This ventilation was accepted uncritically, except that questions were from time to time interjected so as to keep clear in my mind—and hers—what was fact and what was suspicious conjecture.

EDUCATION

The second, educational, phase began by presenting to Michele (in the waking state) an understanding that emotions are primitive and mammalian responses that then receive substantiation and often perpetuation by the human intellect. Monkeys and humans present the same posture in deep depression—shoulders rolled forward, chin and gaze downward, and arms drooping. It was pointed out to her (and this lays the groundwork in understanding for the third phase) that one is not likely to succeed in relinquishing a depression at an intellectual level: The intellect, in its impelling drive to substantiate the felt emotion, will only persevere at arguing for the right to feel depressed. But, posturally, depression is heavy head on spine and shoulders and impotent arms. Making the conscious decision to change the posture can result in an improved feeling; then the intellect can begin searching for reasons for feeling better or good.

I would interject here that with regard to the correctness or scientific validity of the concepts offered to the client about emotional response mechanisms generally or depression particularly, I am in agreement with the view expressed by Meichenbaum and Turk (1976) that the important aspect of the educational phase is that the conceptual framework be plausible to the subject and that its acceptance would permit the practice of specific coping techniques that could then be recommended. The plausibility or face validity of the conceptualization is more essential for the client than is the scientific validity.

Further concepts about emotions and depression were developed. It was noted that mammals typically have a "tucking" reflex—a closing posture that serves to protect the vital organs and communicates to other animals a willingness to capitulate. This is as true of people as it is of puppies or turtles or armadillos. The infant, chided for the first time by an adult, instinctively drops the chin and extends the lower lip in a pout, and the adult eases up the intensity of the criticism. With this experience, the child reinforces the reflex and begins to learn the lesson that one can sometimes protect himself or herself from the bigger animals by looking penitent.

But notice something: If we were to extend that round-shouldered, slight chin-dropping posture of capitulation, we would very soon be into the posture of depression. Now we have a way to understand why we sometimes might seek depression. Whereas anxiety could be caricatured as a feeling that, "I have messed up and now I am going to suffer, and I don't know how dire the consequences will be or whether I will even survive them," depression would be represented by, "Well, I may have messed up, but God knows I'm suffering—and I am surviving." At some level of my mammalian mind I surmise that God, gods, fates, or the powers that be are obliged to ease up on me when it is clear that I am whipped.

When I escape anxiety through the depressive route, I must believe my depression is genuine; just as I must believe my rationalization for it to be effective in rescuing me from anxiety. But some part of me believes that if I were not depressed I would be shunted back into anxiety, and thus I hang onto the depression as respite. This expectation, developed through repetitions of the anxiety-to-depression escape, is invalid if one deals with depression at a somatic rather than an intellectual level. Depression can often be resolved without any increase in anxiety.

Michele had listened attentively throughout the education phase and had become increasingly hypnoidal. Taking note of that, I then began to shift the giving of generalizations to bring the focus back to Michele. By a gradual pacing of her breathing and giving emphasis to certain words, she was easily led into trance and into the third phase of the treatment procedure.

AMELIORATION

"It's easy to let go of depression. It is only difficult to decide that we're ready. If *you're really feeling* in the pits and your best friend tries to cheer you up, you may feel like punching her out, because she just doesn't understand how seriously down you are feeling. But now that you understand that emotion is in the body and that the intellect only justifies or substantiates it—and that you *have the ability* to *change the way things feel* in your body—perhaps you would be willing to *learn some things* that you can do when *you are ready* to relinquish depression. Would you like to do that? (*Michele: "Yes."*)

"I call them first aid for depression." Here is the first. If you will—just now—close your eyes. Take a deep breath. Hold it. Now, let go. . . . Do that again. . . . Now let go. . . . And a third time. . . . Now, if you will, imagine that at the top of your skull at the vortex there is a hook. And from that hook a string goes straight up to the ceiling . . . through a pulley and across the ceiling a short distance to another pulley . . . and down out here in front of you. . . . And at the other end of that string is a contrivance that permits the adding or removing of various sized weights. . . . And you have two benevolent helpers whom you now direct to place weights on the other end of that string . . . with the objective of counterbalancing the weight of your head on your spine and shoulders. And if they get too much weight, so that your neck feels stretched, signal them and they change the combination so as to only counterbalance the weight of your head. And if you are still able to feel some weight of your head on your spine and shoulders, you let them know that, so they can change the combination to increase the counterbalancing weight. And as soon as your head is essentially counterbalanced, imagine that your two benevolent helpers place a small sandbag on each of your shoulders. They balance it there, position it there, drape it there. And now each places on top of that sandbag a second and, ultimately, a third. And all six of these sandbags are filled with very fine, very white, very dry sand. And now your benevolent helpers are introducing into the sacks a great many pencil-sized holes. In your imagination, step aside and watch as sand begins to trickle from the sandbag, falling to the ground around you. Watch as the bags get thinner and emptier and flatter . . . until all that is left on your shoulders are the limp empty sacks. These your helpers soon remove. And, when that is accomplished, you can open your eyes. (*She does.*) I think it might be a good idea for you to practice that one daily for the next few days; it only takes a few minutes.

"For this next one, I should like to come stand behind your chair and actually lift your head. Would that be all right? (*Michele: "Yes."*)

(*Now standing behind her chair.*) "I'm trying to find a notch here in your skull that I can get a hold of (*seeking the mastoid prominence just behind the ear at the level of the lobe*). There. Now, what I'm going to do is simply take some of the weight off of your spine and shoulders so that you can experience exactly what that would feel like. You know, for a long time we have acknowledged that we humans frequently replay old neurotic tapes—acting in the present as if we were in a prior scene or situation. But it has been only in recent years that we have come to capitalize on the fact that we can also replay old constructive tapes. And, having once experienced the sensation, you will forever be able to elevate your mood by thinking that you would like to feel as if I or someone else who cared about how you felt were actually carrying part of the load. Now in a minute I am going to give you back your head . . . but not all of the weight.

(*Returning to my own chair.*) "Now, here is a third first aid for depression. See if you can identify in your mind some friend or acquaintance who seems very often to be smiling or laughing. Discover that as you search your memory bank for a smiler, the corners of your own mouth turn up, and as you identify and more clearly see such a person in your imagination, the smile broadens further still. Imaging is a powerful means for influencing the physiology directly. Almost certainly in your lifetime you have seen at least pictures of a guard at Buckingham Palace standing at stiff attention outside his sentry box, with his tall, bearskin, Beefeater hat and its chinstrap. And as you try to picture such a person in your mind, just now your own shoulders went back. Both a shoulders-back posture and a smile are incompatible with depression. And the imaging of both the posture and the facial expression will initiate a dissolving of the depression.

"Here is another technique. With your eyes closed just now, attempt to place a soft warm smile[1] on your lips. This will be very difficult to do and will feel very awkward because the smile is not physiologically compatible with depression, in which the corners of the mouth tend to turn downward. Attempting to turn the corners upward when your mood is low may result in some facial clonus or involuntary muscle movements as the physiology seeks to reconcile the incompatible expression with the mood.

1. An unpublished construction gleaned from a workshop on depression with Maxie C. Maultsby, Jr., on April 29, 1983, at Gulf Breeze, Florida.

But if you keep trying to introduce a smile for perhaps as much as 30 seconds, you will initiate a reduction in depression. Typically, these techniques are going to begin working at once, but you may not become aware of the change until some minutes have passed. (*Michele opens her eyes and begins to come out of her trance.*)

"You may find it difficult to believe, but there is a magic word [Mangan, 1963] that will dispel depression very quickly. I might hesitate to tell you what the word is if you were really getting any mileage out of your depression. I mean, if your depression were a tool in your manipulation of Frank by letting him see how miserable he has made you, then it might be a mistake for you to know the word, because if you were accidentally to think the word it could ruin your presentation. Well, maybe that's not a real consideration. I used to think so. Now I find that when people want to stay depressed they curiously repress the word. You don't even have to believe it for it to work. Even thinking the word can start change, but saying the word can be devastating to a depression. I'm not sure you're ready for it. (*Michele, recognizing she's being toyed with: "Come on!"*)

"OK, but you have to agree not to use the word when you want to be depressed. The word is: BUBBLES. Say it. (*Michele: "Bubbles"—she is smiling.*) Say it again. (*Michele: "Bubbles"—she is grinning broadly.*)

"So (*recapping*), you now have five techniques that you could employ if you were to decide that you wanted to relinquish depression. You could imagine the string attached to the skull and counterbalancing weights and the draining sandbags on the shoulders. You could close your eyes and think to yourself that you would like to feel as if I or someone were standing behind you and actually lifting some weight from your spine and shoulders. You could picture a smiler and a person standing with shoulders back. You could, with eyes closed, spend part of a minute trying to put a soft, warm smile on your lips. Or you could think the magic word. What was it?"

(*Michele says, "Bubbles," and she is smiling broadly as both stand. "I'm feeling better already."*)

DAN: (*walking toward the door with her*) That's what is supposed to happen. But I want you to agree to something if you will.

MICHELE: What's that?

DAN: That if you start to feel even still better—

MICHELE: Yes?

DAN: —don't fight it. (*Michele exits to speak to the receptionist about her next appointment.*)

IMMUNIZATION

After his return from New York, Frank was seen for one session before Michele's first follow-up appointment. He related that she seemed to be feeling much better and that communications between the two had been meaningful and cordial since his return. She presented a similar report when she was next seen, but she admitted to some apprehension about how she might feel the next time Frank was on location, taking photographs of attractive models—an event that she knew would be frequently repeated for many years to come. Because of this (and with her mood now substantially lifted), it was appropriate to begin a series of procedures having the purpose of "immunizing" her against a recurrence of depression as the result of cues similar to those that had been associated with her depression. She was assisted in rehearsing the self-hypnotic procedure she had learned 2 years earlier, and she was able to identify the changes she wanted in her emotional response sets. After she concluded her procedure and while she still appeared to be in a light trance, I related the following anecdote:

"Some years ago my own attorney referred to me a young woman who, 2 years earlier, had been involved in a minor automobile accident. Although there would later be medical testimony stating that she had incurred no physical injury or trauma in the incident, it was nevertheless true that within an hour after the accident she began spotting and soon miscarried her first pregnancy. In the 2 years intervening she had been unable to reconceive (even though she and her equally young husband were eager to start building a family), and her attorney, reasonably suspecting a psychological infertility, referred her to me for treatment.

"Ultimately, the case reached litigation, and I was subpoenaed to testify. I experienced some apprehension about appearing. For one thing, I knew who the defense attorney would be and I knew how he cross-examined a psychologist: straight out of the old manual! It would be, *Mister* Overlade this and *Mister* Overlade that, interspersed with questions like, You're not a *real* doctor, are you? or astonished observations such as, You mean, you never went to medical school?! For another thing, I knew that I might easily be led into answering questions pertaining to the apparent triggering of a miscarriage by psychological trauma and that my competency to respond to such questions would receive immediate challenge. I had prepared myself for that by placing in the hands of the woman's attorney a copy of William Kroger's book, *Clinical and Experimental Hypnosis* [Kroger, 1963], and knew that in his direct examination of me the woman's attorney could ask me if I recognized Dr. William

Kroger to be an expert in his field of obstetrics and gynecology as well as a past president of the American Society of Psychosomatic Medicine and the American Society of Clinical Hypnosis and I could respond that I did. Then he could ask me whether I knew that on page 202 of Dr. Kroger's book he stated that there is anatomical evidence that strong emotions can contract the uterine musculature and thus cause placental separation. I could say that I knew that, and then he would ask me whether I agreed with Dr. Kroger, and I would respond that I had no reason not to—and that would be the end of that.

"But the morning of the trial had been busy and somewhat rushed; I completed two hospital consultations before driving to the county seat of the neighboring county, arriving at the courthouse only 1 minute before the 10:00 a.m. subpoena time. I was about to bolt and run for the third-floor witness room when I decided that I would take time for a trance. Behind the wheel of my van, I went into a trance that lasted no more than a minute, and among other suggestions I gave myself, I programmed myself not to be *startled* by anything that happened in the courtroom that morning. Within minutes I was on the stand and under direct examination by my friend, the woman's attorney. Perhaps he was in a dramatic mood that morning. He interrupted his questioning of me, turned his back and took two or three steps away from me, then abruptly spun around and, throwing both hands up into the air, shouted, Boo! The jury jumped, the spectators jumped, and the judge sitting beside and behind me, uttered under his breath an oath not ordinarily sworn in a courtroom. I didn't bat an eye. During a recess, the attorney said to me, Some kind of cool character you are! I'm trying to demonstrate that everyone is subject to a startle response—and you didn't give me one. The attorney (who has learned some things about self-hypnosis) understood when I told him what my self-suggestion had been; the literalness of the unconscious mind resulted in my startle response being on hold while I was in the courtroom."

The barely perceptible affirmative nod of Michele's head made it clear to me that her unconscious mind had already grasped the implication of the anecdote for her own immunization, and to avoid sabotaging the effect, I said nothing about it.

At her second follow-up visit, a week later, she still had had no further difficulty with depression, and immunization efforts continued. I induced a trance that was patterned very closely to that which Barber (1977) has presented for rapid analgesia. I have found that Barber's well-thought-out procedure, which was so remarkably effective in producing analgesia for experimentally induced dental nerve pain, with its emphasis on the suggestion, "nothing to bother, nothing to disturb," is equally effective with emotional pain.

At the end of that session, Michele announced the obvious: that she was back in control and didn't require any further visits. She agreed to return if she encountered any recurrence.

Contacted 6 months later, Michele reported that she had continued to feel well and had no recurrence of depression.

REFERENCES

American Psychiatric Association. *Diagnostic and statistical manual of mental disorders* (3rd ed.) (DSM-III). Washington, DC: APA, 1980.

Barber, J. Rapid induction analgesia: A clinical report. *American Journal of Clinical Hypnosis*, 1977, *19*, 138–149.

Becker, J. *Depression: Theory and research*. Washington, DC: V. H. Winston, 1974.

Fay, A. *Making things better by making them worse*. New York: Hawthorn Books, 1978.

Gallant, D. M., & Simpson, G. M. (Eds.). *Depression: Behavioral, biochemical, diagnostic and treatment concepts*. New York: Spectrum, 1976.

Hill, D. Perspective on depression. In D. Hill & L. E. Hollister (Eds.), *Depression*. New York: Medcom, 1970.

Klein, D. F. Differential diagnosis and treatment of the dysphorias. In D. M. Gallant & G. M. Simpson (Eds.), *Depression: Behavioral, biochemical, diagnostic and treatment concepts*. New York: Spectrum, 1976.

Kroger, W. S. *Clinical and experimental hypnosis in medicine, dentistry and psychology*. Philadelphia: Lippincott, 1963.

Lewinsohn, P. M., Biglan, A., & Zeiss, A. M. Behavioral treatment of depression. In P. A. Davidson (Ed.), *The behavioral management of depression and pain*. New York: Brunner/Mazel, 1976.

Mangan, J. T. *The secret of perfect living*. Englewood Cliffs, NJ: Prentice-Hall, 1963.

Meichenbaum, D., & Turk, D. The cognitive-behavioral management of anxiety, anger and pain. In P. A. Davidson (Ed.), *The behavioral management of anxiety, depression and pain*. New York: Brunner/Mazel, 1976.

4
POSTTRAUMATIC STRESS DISORDER

Charles B. Mutter

Posttraumatic stress disorder (PTSD), is a commonly known syndrome characterized by a series of debilitating symptoms following a psychologically traumatic event that overwhelms the ego-adaptive mechanisms. The victim interprets the event as one that threatens his or her survival, that is, one that is outside the range of usual human experience (American Psychiatric Association, 1980). Prior to 1980, this condition has had different labels; yet, the definitions have included a continuity of characteristics. In this chapter a brief historical background of PTSD, its characteristics, and treatment will be discussed, followed by a series of case histories in which varied hypnotic techniques have been used in conjunction with treatment.

HISTORY

The term "traumatic neurosis" was first used by Oppenheim (1889). He believed that symptoms were due to molecular disturbances of neurones, which were produced by concussion. Freud (1958) studied stress reactions associated with combat during World War I; however, he did not sustain an interest, because Oppenheim's theory challenged his belief that all neuroses have their origin in childhood (Parker, 1977). The term was later expanded to "traumatic neurosis syndrome" (Modlin, 1960); and, for the first time, recurrent dreams were seen as pathognomonic of this condition. Little attention was given to PTSD until the post-Vietnam war era when the incidence became more prevalent.

Charles B. Mutter. Private Practice, Miami, Florida, and Departments of Psychiatry and Family Medicine, University of Miami School of Medicine, Miami, Florida.

ETIOLOGY

There are various types of trauma that may precipitate a PTSD. They can generally be characterized as: (1) reactions to war or combat; (2) civilian disasters (e.g., earthquakes, fires, terrorism); (3) reactions of holocaust survivors; and (4) peacetime trauma (e.g., automobile or work-related injuries, sexual battery) (Moses, 1978). In each of the above traumas, physical injury may or may not be present.

There is a differing belief among clinicians about the role of the premorbid personality in the formation of PTSD. The psychoanalytic literature attributes earlier personality structure to symptom formation. Moses (1978) believes a traumatic reaction is seen in an individual who has had prior vulnerability and susceptibility dating back to childhood. In a colloquium on trauma (Geerts & Rechardt, 1978), Ginat presented his opinion that victims of war neuroses have problems dealing with earlier aggressive feelings. In contrast, some investigators do not feel that there is any pretrauma personality pattern associated with PTSD. To illustrate this point, Titchener and Kapp (1979) reported a study of the victims of a 1972 Buffalo Creek disaster in which 90% of the victims who had symptoms of more than 2 years' duration were of varying personality types. An earlier long-term study of a marine disaster (Leopold & Dillon, 1963) illustrates the same point, that is, it was the trauma and not the premorbid personality that explained the observed reactions. Braverman (1977) found no specificity with respect to age, sex, site of injury, or premorbid personality formation. I believe that both viewpoints have merit. Examples of each viewpoint will be illustrated in the case histories.

ONSET AND SYMPTOMS

PTSD is usually subdivided into acute and chronic, or delayed, forms. The acute form occurs within 6 months posttrauma and lasts no longer than 6 months (American Psychiatric Association, 1980). The cause of the latent interval is not always clear. Moses (1978) believes that the onset takes place when a stimulus threatens the adaptive capacity of the ego and brings about physical symptoms related to autonomic nervous dysfunction. Parker (1977) described two patients in an auto accident whose symptoms occurred immediately after they realized they could have been killed. In the author's experience, it is not the trauma but the victim's interpretation of that trauma in terms of his or her survival and/or adaptive control. An auto crash case illustrates this point. I treated a patient involved in an automobile accident who suffered a crush injury just above her knees. The onset of PTSD did not occur until 2 months after physiotherapy and complications, at which time she realized that she might be physically incapacitated for the remainder of her life.

The diagnostic criteria of PTSD have been established by the American Psychiatric Association (1980) (see Table 1).

Symptoms vary, depending on the nature of the stress. Braverman (1980) studied 110 PTSD victims and found that 92 showed irritability as the initial symptom. Anxiety, depression, nightmares, and phobic avoidance of anything related to the stressor event are other common characteristics. The symptoms often are aggravated when a victim repeatedly reviews the traumatic event, especially during frequent medical consultations and interrogations for purposes of litigation. Anxiety is intensified with (1) the patient's recall and, often, the reliving of the traumatic experience and (2) the patient's belief that his or her condition must be quite serious because so many specialists are involved.

TREATMENT

Many methods have been used for the treatment of PTSD, including chemotherapy, psychotherapy, psychoanalysis, systematic desensitization, and behavior modification. Because the scope of this chapter is limited,

TABLE 1. *Diagnostic Criteria for Posttraumatic Stress Disorder*

A. Existence of a recognizable stressor that would evoke significant symptoms of distress in almost everyone.

B. Reexperiencing of the trauma as evidenced by at least one of the following:
   1. recurrent and intrusive recollections of the event
   2. recurrent dreams of the event
   3. sudden acting or feeling as if the traumatic event were reoccurring, because of an association with an environmental or ideational stimulus.

C. Numbing of responsiveness to or reduced involvement with the external world, beginning some time after the trauma, as shown by at least one of the following:
   1. markedly diminished interest in one or more significant activities
   2. feeling of detachment or estrangement from others
   3. constricted affect.

D. At least two of the following symptoms that were not present before the trauma:
   1. hyperalertness or exaggerated startle response
   2. sleep disturbance
   3. guilt about surviving when others have not, or about behavior required for survival
   4. memory impairment or trouble concentrating
   5. avoidance of activities that arouse recollection of the traumatic event
   6. intensification of symptoms by exposure to events that symbolize or resemble the traumatic event.

Note. From American Psychiatric Association, *Diagnostic and Statistical Manual of Mental Disorders* (3rd ed.), Washington, DC: APA, 1980, p. 238. Reprinted by permission.

I will confine my discussion to the use of hypnosis and psychotherapy. It is important to clarify that hypnosis is not a treatment in itself, but a technique that facilitates treatment.

In general, psychotherapy emphasizes the importance of recalling, abreacting, and assimilating the traumatic event to decathect the psychic charge associated with the experience. Psychotherapy should help the patient deal with the subjective feelings surrounding the trauma (Walker, 1981). Medication may also be an important adjunct, especially when pain and depression persist (Ross, 1966). Thompson (1977) found that the response to medication alone was greater than the effects of conventional psychotherapy; yet, his study revealed the presence of symptoms after 1 year regardless of the method of treatment. Onset of treatment is an important factor. Van Putten and Emory (1973) believe that early intervention will usually produce a more favorable prognosis. Moses (1978) contends that war neuroses tend to be chronic and may be refractory to treatment. He attributes this to masochistic personality trends and resistances of the negative therapeutic relationship. Hellekson-Emery (1981) points out the need for long-term treatment, especially with hostages.

RATIONALE FOR HYPNOSIS

Patients with PTSD usually suffer from physical symptoms. Pain is often present, and physical deformity may exist. In acute trauma wherein resolution occurs rapidly, the pain will usually be of short duration; the patient does not develop psychic sequelae. In trauma where duration of healing is more protracted and debility or deformity is existent, greater anxiety and depression occur, because these symptoms tend to serve as day-to-day "reminders" of the traumatic event and interfere with resolution. A feeling of loss of control occurs. As the patient becomes more anxious and/or depressed, he or she becomes more self-preoccupied and focuses greater attention on his or her pain. The pain increases, resulting in heightened anxiety and depression. The patient has "reminders" of past pain and now anticipates future pain. A vicious cycle is established, and the patient feels helpless and, sometimes, hopeless. The patient feels entrapped in a body that he or she cannot control and fears that this will become his or her ultimate fate.

When a patient experiences a traumatic event, an imprint is formed. At the time of the trauma he or she becomes disoriented, develops a fear of death, either on a conscious or unconscious level, and may experience pain (Ewin, 1980). Dreams subsequent to the trauma serve as a means to work through and resolve the threat to the ego; however, nightmares reinforce the feelings of loss of control. The ego attempts to resolve the problem and remove the life-threatening imprint by developing a more effective defense system to seal off or repress the event, but the conscious "reminders" of pain, debility, and nightmares deter resolution.

Hypnosis is a useful tool in the treatment of PTSD because of its multifaceted effects. Not only can it be used to produce hypermnesia when needed to uncover repressed traumatic events, but it may be instrumental in producing amnesia of the traumatic event—thus enhancing the ego's capacity to resolve the conflict. Suggestions can be used to help control pain and alter dreams. Of greatest importance is the ego-strengthening effect, enabling the patient to believe that he or she has greater mastery of his or her body and mind—a belief most desperately needed by victims of this condition. It is because of these many values that hypnosis should be considered an important adjunct to treatment.

USES OF HYPNOSIS

There is a paucity of literature describing the use of hypnosis in the treatment of PTSD. Ewin (1980) described hypnoanalytic treatment for patients with chronic pain following a traumatic event. Dempsey and Granich (1977) described a hypnotherapeutic treatment of a stutterer who retained his affliction for 19 years following a traumatic war event. Hypnotic intervention has been used more recently with Vietnam veterans (Brende & Benedict, 1980; Spiegel, 1981).

One may use hypnoanalysis as a hypnotherapeutic technique. The patient is regressed to the traumatic event to allow him or her to remember, abreact, and decathect the charged material. The therapist serves as a guide who helps the patient work through and resolve the conflict. Often, hypnotherapy uncovers pertinent data that explain the dynamics of symptom formation. Case 1 illustrates this point.

Hypnosis may also be used to alter symptoms. Intensity of debilitating symptoms can be diminished and healing can be effected as illustrated in Case 2. Restructuring the traumatic event is another hypnotic strategy. One can change the sequence of events, or even distort the event, through imagery. The restructured event is coupled with some aspect of reality to facilitate ego reintegration. An example is described in Case 3.

Hypnosis has been found useful in the desensitization of a traumatic event through the use of coupling techniques that decrease the emotional charge of the event. A positive aspect of the traumatic event is suggested each time the patient thinks of the event in order to diminish anxiety and facilitate resolution. Case 4 illustrates this strategy. In each technique described, emphasis on survival plays an important role in resolving the conflict. Often techniques can be mixed. Choice of techniques employed should depend on the patient's dynamics.

Other hypnotic techniques are useful in the treatment of PTSD. Erickson (personal communication, 1978) believed that an individual did not need to consciously know the source of his or her problem because the unconscious mind knows. He employed the direct suggestion that the unconscious mind would find the source of the problem and solve it. He also used metaphors as a form of indirect suggestion.

CASE HISTORIES

CASE 1

A 26-year-old, divorced female was seen for psychiatric evaluation following an automobile accident, which occurred approximately 14 months earlier. When asked to describe the accident, she stated, "I was out to dinner with a friend. I was on my way home; I was driving slowly. I remember a car passing me. I don't remember what happened after that, but I remember being taken to the hospital." Additional records revealed that the patient struck her head on the windshield, shattering it. She suffered severe lacerations of her forehead and face; she experienced head and neck pain and multiple contusions of her body. She had plastic surgery on her face with good results. The contusions healed, but her head and neck pain persisted despite negative neurologic findings. Brain scan and EEG were normal. Before the accident she had worked as a professional model and partner in a successful business venture. Subsequent to her injury she had a 20-pound weight loss; she lost all interest in her appearance and became disheveled, apathetic, and withdrawn. She experienced recurrent nightmares and headaches. Psychological testing revealed depression and diminished self-esteem but no signs of organic damage. Her description of the details of the incident was very vague; however, she expressed the desire to remember because she was suffering and could not alleviate her symptoms.

The patient was found to be a good hypnotic subject. She was placed in a trance and regressed to the time of the incident. She remembered driving and swerving to avoid contact with another car. She struck a concrete column under an overpass, rendering her unconscious. Her next memory was a feeling of head and neck pain with a sensation of blood trickling down her face. She felt confused and disoriented. She visualized a crowd gathering and someone exclaiming, "My God, she's dead!" In this disoriented state she was able to describe two conflicting emotions, the first, that she may have died and secondly, that she wanted to remain alive.

The above memory explained the basis of her symptom formation. One part of her mind accepted the concept of death, thus explaining her apathy; she actually walked around like a "zombie," as one who was dead.

Yet, another part of her mind struggled for survival through the persistence of pain, "If I feel something, then I know I am alive."

The hypnotherapeutic approach was designed to enable the patient to realize that she did survive. It was suggested that she had means other than pain to prove that she was alive; for example, she could feel, touch, hear, and see; she could use these other senses for validation. A suggestion was then given that in her own way she would eliminate her discomfort because she no longer needed to prove to herself that she was alive. She was told, "You have survived, and all the forces that helped you survive this experience are still with you, and they will last the rest of your life."

During trance she granted me permission to suggest that she would remember the experience. She was crying profusely when trance was terminated. She then expressed a feeling of relief that a tremendous weight had been lifted from her. She was seen for three additional sessions over a 5-week period. Her headaches and nightmares gradually subsided and ceased after 1 month, and her depression lifted. Her self-image was restored; she improved her appearance, and she eventually resumed her former life pattern.

In this particular case, hypnoanalysis was utilized to retrieve repressed material in a brief, direct manner within a protective environment. The data were essential to understanding the dynamics of her symptom formation. The hypnotic regression enabled her to abreact, work through and restructure her thinking about the trauma, and resolve the conflict.

CASE 2

A 29-year-old police officer was injured in a motorcycle accident. He was leading a funeral procession when he was struck by a car and thrown from his motorcycle. He was not rendered unconscious. There was a gasoline explosion; he caught fire, and suffered second- and third-degree burns on 45% of his body. He received intensive treatment in the burn care unit, followed by corrective surgery and multiple skin grafts. During his hospital stay he developed hyperirritability and insomnia with nightmares of the accident. In these dreams he reexperienced the traumatic event, seeing himself and others burning and running. He had no prior history of psychiatric illness. There had been no other major stressors in his environment; he had a stable marriage and was a model officer. Despite medications to control pain, anxiety, and depression, his symptoms failed to abate. He was referred to me approximately 18 months after the injury.

At the time of examination, the patient complained of pain in his hands and elbows, where healed scars were noted. The major physical residual from this incident was tightening of the skin over both dorsal surfaces of his hands due to scarring. Plastic surgery had been effective for the most part; yet, his skin cracked and bled even with regular applications of cocoa butter and continuous physiotherapy. He had not returned to work. His major concerns were the persistence of pain, nightmares, and feelings that he would suffer debility the rest of his life. The 1st year of treatment consisted of supportive psychotherapy and pharmacotherapy to assist him in restructuring his thinking so that he could overcome his problems. His nightmares diminished, but his anxiety, hyperirritability, and pain still persisted, impairing his everyday functioning. It was felt that hypnosis would be effective for symptom alteration.

Hypnosis was used primarily for pain control and healing. The suggestion was given that his body would break down just enough scar formation to produce greater elasticity. A second suggestion was given that the raw materials of healing would flow to those parts of his body to heal the tissues more effectively and prevent further breakdowns. Suggestions for pain control were also given. The patient responded quite well; he discovered that he had greater mastery over his body than ever before. This produced a ripple effect (Spiegel & Linn, 1969), and within 2 months his nightmares stopped completely. His mental attitude changed, and he was able to function more effectively in his daily environment. He eventually returned to work in an allied profession. Treatment sessions were tapered to biweekly, then monthly, and he was discharged after 1 year of hypnotherapy.

Restructuring the events of a traumatic incident is a useful technique accomplished through the use of hypnosis. Case 3 describes an example of how debilitating symptoms can be alleviated via suggestion to help the ego gain greater mastery.

CASE 3

A 28-year-old painter was working on a scaffold on the 13th floor of a building. The scaffold broke, and as he was falling, he grabbed a balcony railing two floors below. He struck the right side of his head and suffered facial and oral injuries. He was not hospitalized but required oral surgery. Shortly thereafter, he developed hyperirritability, anxiety attacks without any apparent provocation, and avoidance of heights. He described flashbacks of his fall and facial pain. He would awaken in the mornings feeling tired but did not recall any dreams. His wife later stated that he would thrash about kicking and screaming during the night, but he had no conscious awareness of this upon awakening. He was referred to me 1 year after his injury because of his persistent symptoms. He had no history of psychiatric illness. He had a good marriage and functioned well until the accident. He was treated with antianxiety medication and supportive psychotherapy for approximately 2 months. His anxiety diminished, but his sleep pattern was still disturbed, and his flashbacks failed to subside. He complained of feeling nervous, irritable, and short-tempered, whereas he had been a tranquil and easy-going individual prior to his injury.

The patient was hypnotized, and survival suggestions were given similar to those in Case 1. It was then suggested that his unconscious mind would find a way to help him solve his problem. Although these suggestions gave him some relief, he still had recurrent flashbacks. He was subsequently rehypnotized and regressed to the incident. He revivified the experience of falling and the thoughts of death. A suggestion was then given that he would not see a balcony as he fell, and at the same time, a very strong wind would develop beneath him and diminish the speed of his fall so that he would land safely on his feet. A posthypnotic suggestion was given that, anytime a flashback recurred, this new imagery would immediately be coupled with the flashback, resulting in the realization that he had survived. It was further suggested that he set aside some time each day for the purpose of consciously producing the flashback with the new imagery. The restructing of the traumatic event as experienced in the flashback diminished his anxiety and enabled his ego to resolve the traumatic event. His sleeping pattern improved, and he was able to resume his previous work. His avoidance of scaffolds persisted at the time of discharge 18 months later.

CASE 4

This case is unique in that it describes an individual with PTSD without any physical trauma. A 52-year-old air traffic controller was seen for evaluation as a result of a work-related incident that occurred 11 months earlier. He stated that, as he was tracking planes on radar and giving instructions, there was a near collision of two aircrafts in the same pattern. Although he was instrumental in averting the disaster, he developed diaphoresis, acute anxiety, and irritability. He felt an aversion toward his job and frequently called in sick. The Federal Aviation Administration examined him and found him to be totally disabled because of severe anxiety and depression. Prior to this incident he was an outgoing individual who had many friends and a very close family relationship. He had no history of psychiatric illness. He had an excellent work record of 30 years and was known to be a very conscientious employee. He had been a pilot during World War II and had flown privately on frequent occasions; however, he avoided any type of aircraft, private or commercial, subsequent to this incident. He had difficulty functioning in his everyday life; he experienced weight loss and was most troubled by the increasing frequency of nightmares of planes colliding. The nightmares began approximately 2 months after the incident. At times he was afraid to fall asleep for fear that he would have recurrent dreams. During the evaluation he stated, "I keep thinking of what almost happened and feel responsible that I could have caused those people to die."

Hypnoanalysis was initially used to explore his feelings of guilt since, in reality, there had been no disaster. During trance he identified with the passengers and in some way saw himself as one of the victims. Despite repeated hypnotic efforts to fragment the traumatic imprint, his symptoms persisted. A coupling technique was then suggested as follows: "Whenever a thought about this incident recurs, whether in a waking state or dream, you will add to this thought the reality that you averted the collision by giving appropriate instructions to both pilots. You will immediately visualize the planes separating on the radar screen and experience relief."

During the initial use of these suggestions the patient was diaphoretic and tremulous; however, with additional reinforcement, his symptoms subsided. The nightmares abated within 4 months, he was able to function more effectively in his daily life, and he made an adequate adjustment to retirement. He is now able to travel on commercial airlines with minimal discomfort. Course of treatment was twice weekly for 1 month, weekly for 1 month, and gradually tapered to his being seen on an as needed basis after 14 months. As an interesting footnote, he returns for hypnotic reinforcement whenever there is a reported plane crash.

There may be circumstances in which the premorbid personality plays a major role in the resolution of trauma. The following case demonstrates the value of hypnotic search.

CASE 5

A 59-year-old hotel desk clerk was seen for psychiatric evaluation regarding an injury that had occurred 6 months earlier. He was robbed and shot in the hand and abdomen. He was hospitalized for 17 days and underwent exploratory surgery. His condition upon admission was critical; however, he had full physical recovery. Following his discharge from the hospital he became fearful of crowds, hyperirritable, and sensitive to noise. He avoided his place of employment because he feared another assault by the same assailant. He became more withdrawn and remained at home, refusing friendly visitors or phone calls. He developed insomnia and nightmares after discharge from the hospital. He had no history of trauma or psychiatric treatment. His premorbid personality was one of a shy but easy-going individual with a passive–dependent personality pattern. Clinically, he appeared anxious and depressed.

The patient was treated with antidepressant and antianxiety medications and supportive psychotherapy; however, he failed to respond. Hypnotherapy was then utilized to desensitize him to the trauma. Suggestions were given that he had survived and that the probability of further confrontation with the assailant was minimal. The patient reported that he felt less anxious after the sessions; yet, his nightmares continued with the same frequency, and he remained withdrawn.

Another hypnotherapeutic technique was utilized. The patient was placed in trance and was asked to imagine that he saw the assailant being bound and rendered helpless and under his control. It was then suggested that he see himself punishing his assailant for causing this problem. This technique is important because it allows the victim to discharge repressed rage and hostility. The patient expressed a great deal of hesitation in complying with this suggestion. He was unable to fantasize being overtly aggressive to the assailant, even though he had the assailant in his control. It was then decided that further exploration was indicated. The patient was regressed to earlier periods in his life. It was discovered that, in childhood, he had a punitive father who would beat him whenever he showed any attempt to assert himself. It was discovered that the patient interpreted his assault as punishment for his earlier, repressed aggressive feelings. Once this repressed material was worked through psychotherapeutically, his symptoms subsided.

SUMMARY

PTSD is a condition that is becoming more recognized by clinicians in all disciplines, but treatment should be confined to therapists well versed in psychodynamics and psychotherapy. The key to the appropriate type of hypnotic intervention is the understanding of the dynamics of symptom formation. Hypnosis is an important adjunct to treatment, because it can shorten the length of treatment and render a more favorable prognosis. In my experience, most of the PTSD patients have been effectively treated within 6 months to 1 year when hypnotherapy has been employed; however, contributory stressors such as marital conflicts, death of family members, job stress, and any other factors that increase integrative task may complicate and prolong treatment. The presence of guilt, especially in holocaust and disaster victims, must be recognized and treated. One must also consider the effect of secondary gain and litigation. Patients who receive compensation following trauma and are involved in litigation often hold on to symptoms that produce suffering so as to justify recompense. The clinician must be cognizant of all the above factors and must carefully evaluate the patient before beginning hypnotherapeutic intervention.

REFERENCES

American Psychiatric Association. *Diagnostic and statistical manual of mental disorders* (3rd ed.) (DSM-III). Washington, DC: APA, 1980.

Braverman, M. Validity of psychotraumatic reactions. *Journal of Forensic Sciences*, 1977, *22*, 654–662.

Braverman, M. Onset of psychotraumatic reactions. *Journal of Forensic Sciences*, 1980, *25*, 821–825.

Brende, J., & Benedict, B. The Vietnam combat delayed stress syndrome: Hypnotherapy of "dissociative symptoms." *American Journal of Clinical Hypnosis*, 1980, *23*, 34–40.

Dempsey, G. L., & Granich, M. Hypnobehavioral therapy in the case of a traumatic stutterer: A case study. *International Journal of Clinical and Experimental Hypnosis*, 1978, *26*, 125–133.

Erickson, M. H. Personal communication, Phoenix, Arizona, January 4, 1978.

Ewin, D. M. Constant pain syndrome: Its psychological meaning and cure using hypnoanalysis. In H. Wain (Ed.), *Clinical hypnosis in medicine*. Chicago: Year Book Medical Publishers, 1980.

Freud, S. Remembering, repeating and working through. In *The complete psychological works of Sigmund Freud*. London: Hogarth Press, 1958.

Geerts, A. E., & Rechardt, E. Colloquium on trauma. *International Journal of Psychoanalysis*, 1978, *59*, 365–375.

Hellekson-Emery, C. Post-traumatic stress disorder of a former hostage. *American Journal of Psychiatry*, 1981, *138*, 991.

Leopold, R. L., & Dillon, H. Psychoanatomy of a disaster: A long term study of posttraumatic neurosis in survivors of a marine explosion. *American Journal of Psychiatry*, 1963, *119*, 913–921.

Modlin, H. G. The trauma in traumatic neurosis. *Bulletin of the Menninger Clinic*, 1960, *24*, 49–56.

Moses, R. Adult psychic trauma: the question of early predisposition and some detailed mechanisms. *International Journal of Psychoanalysis*, 1978, *59*, 353–363.

Oppenheim, H. *Die traumatischen Neurosen*. Berlin: Hirschwald, 1889.

Parker, N. Accident litigants with neurotic symptoms. *Medical Journal of Australia*, 1977, *2*, 318–322.

Ross, D. W. Neuroses following trauma and their relationship to compensation. In S. Arieti (Ed.), *American handbook of psychiatry*. New York: Basic Books, 1966.

Spiegel, D. Vietnam grief work using hypnosis. *American Journal of Clinical Hypnosis*, 1981, *24*, 33–40.

Spiegel, H., & Linn, L. The "ripple effect" following adjunct hypnosis in analytic psychotherapy. *American Journal of Psychiatry*, 1969, *126*, 53–58.

Thompson, G. N. Post-traumatic psychoneurosis: Evaluation of drug therapy. *Diseases of the Nervous System*, 1977, *38*, 617–619.

Titchener, J. L., & Kapp, F. P. Family and character change at Buffalo Creek. *American Journal of Psychiatry*, 1976, *113*, 295–299.

Van Putten, T., & Emory, W. H. Traumatic neurosis in Vietnam returnees: A forgotten diagnosis? *Archives of General Psychiatry*, 1973, *29*, 695–698.

Walker, J. I. Post-traumatic stress disorder after a car accident. *Postgraduate Medicine*, 1981, *69*, 82–86.

ADDITIONAL READING

Keiser, L. *The traumatic neurosis*. Philadelphia: Lippincott, 1968.

Krystal, H. (Ed.). *Massive psychic trauma*. New York: International Universities Press, 1968.

5
THE CASE OF SUPERMAN
Integrating Hypnosis and Gestalt Therapy in the Treatment of Dyssomnia

Joseph Barber

The grass was cool and damp beneath his bare feet, but it was the sound of breaking glass that caught his attention. Or a sound *like* breaking glass – he wasn't sure. "They're after me!" he thought. Feeling more frightened than he'd ever been in his 24 years of life, feeling sure the police were chasing him, he began running across the lawn. As he scaled the 8′ fence, he felt sure he would get a police bullet in his back. But he didn't. Jumping off the fence into the alley, he began running, running as if he were a college quarterback again. It was while he was running down the moonlit alley that he began to "wake up," to remember that he'd been sleeping at Ann's house, in her bed. And he suddenly realized that he was naked, running down an alley of an unfamiliar neighborhood in the early hours of the morning.

Gradually orienting himself, he found a plastic bag in a garbage can with which to clothe himself. Since he was unfamiliar with the neighborhood, he was unable to find his way back to her house by way of the alley. Frightened and utterly bewildered, he walked round the block, and finally made his way to her front door. He rang the bell, repeatedly, with no response. And then as he knocked frantically, the police car arrived.

The police had been summoned by neighbors who had been awakened by a woman's screams. One officer seated John in the patrol car and provided first-aid treatment for the severe laceration of his right arm and chest. The other officer went into the house to take care of Ann. He emerged a half hour later with the following story: Ann had been sleeping with John and was awakened with him astride her, beating her in the face with his fists. She had screamed, he had jumped off the bed, and then he had leaped through closed drapes and a closed window.

Joseph Barber. Department of Psychiatry, UCLA, Los Angeles, California.

The police took John to the emergency room for treatment of his wounds; Ann did not press criminal charges. (John paid her substantial surgical bills.) John had no memory of the events related by Ann. He was as incredulous about them as you would be if you were accused of beating someone in your sleep last night. It was as if he were in a nightmare.

The next morning, feeling that "something must be very wrong with me," John telephoned a psychology clinic. He was seen by a young clinical trainee, who took on his case. John presented his problem as concern and confusion over the events of the previous night. He wanted to know why it had happened and wanted to prevent such a terrible thing from happening again. He reported being unaware of having any other problems in his life.

John was diagnosed as a "hysterical dissociative," and psychodynamic therapy was initiated. Sixty-five therapy sessions later, John had little more understanding of his condition than at the outset, and had experienced increasingly frequent episodes of somnambulistic behavior. He had frequently awakened in the night, out of bed, always utterly bewildered, disoriented, slowly coming out of a nightmare, sometimes having done some violence to his bed or his furniture. Once he awakened after shoving both his arms through a bedroom window (resulting in wounds that required extensive suturing). After 9 months (65 sessions of psychotherapy) the incidence of these somnambulistic episodes had increased to as many as four nights a week, never fewer than twice a week.

It was at this point that I was asked to take over the case.

At our first meeting John presented as a well-dressed, unusually handsome man, smilingly charming, somewhat apprehensive about seeing me. During the interview he was articulate, expressive, obviously very bright, enjoying a successful career, and remarkably unaware of his own psychology. His behavior during that night 9 months previous was totally outside his ability to grasp as coming from him. He was a gentle man, with no awareness of any violent thoughts or feelings. He was absolutely mortified and stunned that he had apparently hit a woman—that he had in fact beaten a woman. He was athletic, very physically active, muscular, and what might be described by his friends as a "gentle giant." He was a model of the good-looking, friendly, all-American young man. He did not swear, he drank only at parties "to have a good time with the guys," had many friends, was close to his parents and siblings, worked hard—there was absolutely nothing in his appearance or behavior to provide a clue to the understanding of the bizarre and terrible violence unleashed during his sleep.

There also seemed to be an underlying sadness about him and a remarkable lack of awareness of it on his part. In our initial conversation, I asked him what he was feeling (at a moment when I thought he looked momentarily sad). His reply, "Nothing." "Might you be feeling a little sad?" "No." "What were you thinking about, just a moment ago?" "I was remembering an old lady I saw on my way here. She was crossing the street, and was having a lot of trouble, a lot of trouble walking. I guess she has arthritis or something. I thought it was sad that she was having trouble walking."

Thus it was that I began to be aware partially of the extent of John's lack of awareness of his affective experience. I also had the benefit of the results of his psychological testing. Testing had revealed that John feared he was crazy, felt he had had strange experiences (appropriately enough, I thought, considering what had happened), and felt someone might have control over his mind (again, I thought, understandable, given the circumstances). His MMPI and TAT results both indicated the presence of a homosexual panic. The therapist he had been seeing had written, "Specifically, the patient appears to be struggling with some sexual identity confusion, fearing possible homosexual impulses which have a paranoid flavor to them." It was apparent, then, from the extreme nature of John's symptoms, that there was tremendous conflict at an unconscious level—conflict that centered around control over impulses that were terrifying to him.

A striking feature of this man was his attitude toward women as expressed in his language. He consistently referred to women as "broads" and "chicks." He had had one significant relationship with a woman while in high school. It had ended with a feeling of tremendous pain and loss for him. He felt he had never gotten over that loss. Subsequently, he had had no significant romantic relationships. On the contrary, he had had sexual experiences with many, many dozens of women, and almost never more than once with the same woman. Asked to describe the kind of woman he would like to have a relationship with, he replied, "a tall blonde."

Another striking feature of this patient was his total disinterest in and understanding of the meaning of his dreams. Further, his dreams were not characteristic of adult dreams. John's nightmares were consistently the type that terrify small children. For instance, he might dream of being chased by "bad guys," or "Martians," or of being harassed by gigantic bumblebees. All his nightmares contained childhood creations of terror and helplessness: monsters or malicious men of one sort or another. John could not remember having nightmares about his present reality. He could not remember having nightmares that contained members of his family, his work colleagues, and the like.

John's only understanding of his problem was that the stress of his job must somehow contribute to it. What he didn't understand was why he couldn't handle the stress, since he always had in the past.

Careful review of his childhood history was made. Of significance is the fact that at age 2 John had had an episode of meningitis with associated high fever and subsequent history of night terrors. In college he'd had a few minor and inconsequential somnambulisitic experiences. There was no evident precipitating variable that could predict or explain his earlier somnambulism or his current episodes.

To rule out the possibility of organic etiology (e.g., temporal lobe epilepsy), neurologic workup was done, including routine EEG studies. All results were within normal limits. It was of concern to me, however, that the EEG studies were made without associated episodes of somnambulism (so the brain activity associated with that behavior had not been observed). What, I wondered, characterized John's EEG prior to and during such an episode? Preparations were made for hospital admission to accomplish sleep monitoring. Sleep monitoring of EEG revealed normal sleep patterns, with no evidence of epileptic activity. However, just prior to three somnambulistic episodes, the EEG showed a transitional period subsequent to slow-wave sleep (Stage 4) but prior to what could definitely be considered to be an REM period. It was as if the normal motor inhibition that characterizes REM onset did not occur at these times, and the REM period took place with active motor behavior.[1] (Lesioning of the locus ceruleus nucleus produces similar results. One could speculate that the childhood episode of meningitis with its high fever might have altered the functioning of part of the motor inhibitory system). So it appeared that there was no evidence of epileptic etiology of this syndrome. Further, there was no clearly indicated medical treatment for this syndrome. This is a rare entity (Pedley & Guilleminault, 1977), and the only reported treatment involves chronic use of tranquilizers before sleep to prevent the possibility of somnambulism.

Because hypnosis is effective in the modification of physiologic processes, including sleep, and because hypnosis can alter dreaming, in particular, hypnosis seemed to be the treatment of choice for John. Initially, hypnosis was used to modify the somnambulistic behavior, which by this time had become frequent and potentially very dangerous. Subsequently, hypnosis was used in the context of psychotherapy to effect curative changes in the syndrome as a whole.

Therapy was initiated as a problem-oriented process. Our stated and agreed goal was to end his somnambulistic episodes and to prevent their recurrence. I explained that, by way of reaching this goal, it was likely that John would also learn a good deal about himself. This was satisfactory to him.

1. Preparation for hospital admission (for EEG monitoring) took several weeks. During this time, hypnosis was successful in stopping the somnambulistic behavior entirely. In order to obtain somnambulistic behavior for purposes of the EEG monitoring, hypnosis was successfully used to suggest temporary onset of the symptoms again.

The therapeutic agenda, then, was to work toward greater awareness of John's person and his conflicts and to help him to integrate a new understanding of himself. However, my initial and primary concern was for his physical safety (as well as that of others with whom he might come in contact during his somnambulistic activity). He had had at least two experiences of somnambulistically jumping out of windows. When I learned that he often traveled to other cities and often stayed in highrise hotels, I asked what precautions he took to prevent his jumping from those windows (with more potentially serious consequences than he'd previously experienced). With an amused smile he replied, "Nothing."

At the first session, as a consequence of my concern for his physical safety, two interventions were made: (1) John was instructed to make his bedroom relatively safe for his somnambulistic behavior (removal of dangerous objects, moving a bureau in front of the window, etc.). (2) He was hypnotized and told that, whatever the necessity of these "terrible and frightening occurrences," from now on "it is not necessary for you to get out of bed while you are sleeping, and you will not do so." Such suggestions were given repeatedly and quite emphatically. Suggestions were offered in an indirect manner (e.g., "You can really be proud when you awaken in the morning, and feel rested, and pleased that you spent the whole night in bed"), as well as in the clear and direct manner described above. My own attitude was absolutely clear and firm and confident with respect to these suggestions. There was no doubt in my mind that it was dangerous for John to get out of bed in his sleep, and I communicated that to him.

Further, as a result of concern for the safety of others, John's own precaution of not sleeping with someone else now was very strongly encouraged. There was no suggestion that he ought not have sexual experiences with others, only that he not actually go to sleep with someone.

At the second session, 2 days later, John reported that he had not found himself out of bed during the nights following our meeting, but that he had awakened from a nightmare the previous night, still in his bed, having thoroughly messed up the bedding (indicating that the hypnotic suggestions may have had a salutary effect).

Because of John's understanding that his problem was associated with his sleeping and dreaming and because the somnambulism apparently was associated with nightmares, dreams and their meaning became the focus of treatment at this second treatment session. Although I remained curious about the events that surrounded John's assault of Ann and believed they must be important to an understanding of John and his problems, I also felt that there was little likelihood of successfully investigating the events of that evening, at least for now. (I had the benefit of John's previous therapist's experience. That therapist's focus in therapy had often turned toward the assault itself and the events in John's life at that time; this attempt had met with failure and, in the therapist's view, resistance and hostility from John). I would not learn what happened that evening until much later.

Since John's dreams were consistently a puzzlement to him and since he never had any conscious idea of their meaning, at the second session I hypnotized John and suggested, "Some night this week, and I don't know which night will really be best . . . but some night this week, you will have a dream. This dream will be interesting to you, and will tell you something you need to know about your life right now. As soon as the dream ends you will awaken, and you will remember the dream vividly as you write it down so you don't have to memorize it. And you can bring in your notes about the dream next time." I gave suggestions for amnesia about the dream instructions, John awakened, and without further discussion he left.

It was my judgment that John was not prepared for rapidly uncovering unconscious material. He needed to discover for himself that there was more to his mind than he was consciously aware of, and at least initially, the hypnotic experience would best be kept separate and out of his conscious awareness.

At the third session, 1 week later, John was hypnotized and asked if he had dreamed. He said he had had an interesting dream the night before and had written it down. I asked him if the dream meant anything to him.

"Well, is it possible to have, like, two parts of yourself? Like a private self and a public self? Could you have two parts of your self that were, like, in conflict?"

The astuteness of this question surprised me and was the first evidence of any awareness on John's part of an existence of his inner mental life. I responded by asking John to tell me more about what he might know, or even suppose, about those aspects of himself. The discussion that followed involved his new-found understanding about himself, based on his recall of a dream he'd had the previous night. He recounted the dream, in which he found himself standing, suddenly, and without explanation, atop a water tower in an unfamiliar town. He was frightened of being up there and wanted to get down and did not know how. He felt that one part of himself didn't want to admit how frightened he was, seeing himself, literally, as Superman (who could fly up to and down from the tower, effortlessly and fearlessly). The other part of himself, he was aware, was privately frightened and unwilling for anyone else to know that he was frightened. Discussion was focused, very gently, on things John was afraid of, and of the fact that he really could not admit this fear to anyone. This discussion took place entirely within the context of a hypnotic state. Toward the end of the session, suggestions were made again that John would have a dream in the next week, that the dream would be interesting and meaningful to him, that he would remember it when awakening and write it down. I also suggested that he would continue to remain in his bed at night (as he'd successfully done now for the past week), he wouldn't mind not remembering our session when he left the office, but he would probably leave with a sense of accomplishment and well-being.

Each subsequent session, usually one per week, for 9 months, focused almost exclusively on the use of hypnosis to suggest a night dream during the week, and then working with that dream, using Gestalt techniques, to bring gradually to awareness unconscious material to be dealt with in therapy.

While the out-of-bed somnambulistic behavior essentially stopped subsequent to the 1st week's hypnotic suggestion that he not get out of bed, there was continuing, though progressively less frequent, episodic messing up of the bed during nightmares. These episodes, too, diminished, and, within 2 months had ceased entirely. There was always the threat, though, of future episodes, since this was at least partly an organic problem, and his susceptibility to its exacerbation probably still existed. (It is likely, for instance, that emotional upset was, for John, a precipitant to the neural dysfunction underlying his somnambulistic episodes. So long as he had no better way of coping with fear and anger than through denial and repression, and so long as a significant amount of John's stress was caused by intrapsychic conflict, the possibility of future somnambulism was quite real. Given the potential for harm as demonstrated by his assault on Ann, this possibility was taken very seriously. I wanted to avoid future somnambulistic episodes.)

Subsequent to the third treatment session, we began an almost unvarying pattern of treatment. John would arrive in the office, seat himself in his chair, and, in response to posthypnotic suggestion, quickly and "spontaneously" develop a deep hypnotic state. While in this state, he would recount a recent dream that was of interest to him. I would then ask him to retell the dream, allowing its vivid recreation in his imagination, in the present tense, from his point of view. Many of the dreams were of nightmare or near-nightmare quality and evoked significant anxiety, which was managed by supportive suggestions. Following the narration of the dream from his point of view, he would be asked to reexperience and narrate the dream again, this time from the point of view of a different character in the dream. When appropriate, he would be asked to have a conversation with one or more of these characters. This process would be repeated so long as there seemed fruitful material to be obtained by going through the experience of still other characters in the dream (Polster & Polster, 1973). I almost never made interpretations. Rather, I would encourage John to come to his own meaning, or would ask him what the dream (or part of a dream) meant to him. John was almost always able to come to significant meaningful awareness of some part of his character or life conflict through the dream.

The speed with which he developed new awareness about himself was quite remarkable. Within the first 4 months of psychotherapy, John became consciously aware of the following powerful conflicts: He had a peculiarly strong identification with the character of Superman. He felt inadequate as a man and feared that he was a homosexual. He felt enormously guilty about masturbating (which he did ritualistically and after much planning). He felt that he would be enormously successful in his career, yet paradoxically felt himself a total failure. He became consciously aware of the extent of his excessive alcohol intake and of his use of marijuana and became afraid of his dependence upon these substances. He became aware of a strong ambivalence toward his mother, now realizing that he hated her as well as loved her (though he did not yet know the reasons why he felt the hatred). All these conflicts are evident of deep-seated confusion and conflict over his view of himself and, particularly, of his quest for and fear of personal power. Again and again in working with his dreams, he would refer to himself as Superman and comment that he both liked being Superman and loathed the artifice. This theme of ambivalence toward power was consistent throughout John's therapeutic experience.

A persistent nightmare developed, in which John found himself (in the dream) in his bedroom, on his bed, frightened that there were bombs ("booby traps") hidden around his room, and unable to leave his bed without possibly exploding one. John interpreted these dreams to be his way of keeping himself in bed during his sleep.

Otherwise, the incidence of nightmares began to quickly diminish, and the character of the nightmares changed from the childish fears of monsters and giant insects to more adult themes (as illustrated, for instance, by a dream in which he confronted a man in the park who was intending to seduce him into sexual behavior). John quickly became fascinated with the process of psychotherapy, and his motivation to "be better" was now combined with the birth of an interest in discovering more about himself in the process of "getting better." His characterization of "getting better" became more and more oriented toward becoming freer to express himself and toward being able to have more intimate contact with others.

John began the seventh treatment session with a wish to talk about what he was discovering. Up to this point, therapy had consisted almost entirely of work within the hypnotic state, nearly always focused on a recent dream. At this session, however, John discussed the fact that he realized his life was changing, he was sleeping better, he no longer got out of bed at night, he was having fewer and fewer nightmares, and he was feeling less afraid in his waking life. After this point, then, the dreamwork more often began after a discussion in the normal waking state of a new awareness that interested John, or sometimes of a discussion of a life problem that was troubling him. (At the 10th session, for instance, John talked for the first time about disappointments and difficulties in his professional career. Up to this time, John denied any but the most blissful characterizations of his career.)

It is unlikely that any of these issues were unknown to John's previous therapist. He had, in fact, made interpretations about many of them to John. Although John had "resisted" those interpretations then, he now was developing them himself.

An example of the dreams that John worked with in these early months is the following:

> I'm asleep in my bed, then I dream that I wake up. I realize that my room has been booby-trapped, and that I have to find and disarm the bomb before it goes off. I very carefully crawl around the room, scared that I'll set off the bomb, trying to find it. I wake up, thinking my bedside lamp is going to fall on the floor. But it doesn't.

> My girlfriend lives in a bad part of town—the gay part of town. I feel scared visiting her. I'm with her in the swimming pool of her apartment building, and the gay men share this same pool. I'm scared, but I don't know why. I go to her apartment to find her, and she isn't there. The place is dark except for gays. I'm scared.

> I'm in an airplane—a biplane—my dad is the pilot. We're doing an airshow down by the park for a huge crowd of people. I'm standing on the wing. I'm supposed to perform some kind of stunt, while my dad flies the plane. He doesn't seem to be watching where we're going. We're heading straight for the cliff. I'm out on the wing and can't control the plane from there. I shout to my dad to turn, but he doesn't seem to hear me. I see the faces of the crowd as we flash by. They're smiling, enjoying the show. But I know we're going to be killed.

In working with the dream of the airshow, John retold the dream from the point of view of his father. In doing so, he became aware of his father's pride in him, his love for him, his confidence in his son's abilities. John retold the dream from the point of view of an anonymous woman in the crowd, during which he became aware of the expectations others have for his abilities, and for his belief that women see him as incredibly sexy and have tremendous sexual needs for him. It was during the working through of this dream that John became aware of his ambivalence toward his father, of his wish to wrest control from his father (whom he sees as incompetent and weak), and of his terrible sadness at that impulse. He said he hated the idea of taking away control from his father. It made him feel embarrassed for his father, he said. (This issue of taking over from the father was a theme that became significant later in his therapy, as we will see.)

About 4 months into therapy, John became gradually interested in a woman to a far greater degree than he'd been familiar with previously. Up to this time, his experience with women (except for his high school sweetheart) had been to see them once or twice only, purely for the purpose of sex. This woman, Christine, had become a steady interest of his, and he began seeing her exclusively. He still maintained the prohibition of actually *sleeping* with someone else, however. (This was no difficulty for him, since he did not want emotional closeness with anyone, anyway.) His interest in Christine prompted conscious anxiety for him about being trapped by a woman. His dreams began to be more and more clearly dreams about sexuality and power. His homosexual fears seemed to diminish (particularly as he experienced Christine's absolute fondness and attraction to him). At about the 7th month of therapy, John had the following dream:

> I'm Superman. I get my kicks by helping people, fighting bad guys, saving women and children, you know. And I'm in bed now with Christine, and we're making love, and she asks me to take off my Superman outfit. I tell her I can't, that it doesn't come off, that I've never taken it off. But she insists that it is only clothing, that it will come off, and she insists that I do take it off. We have a fight, and she won't make love with me if I'm wearing my suit. And I'm so horny that I agree, so I take it off. Only now I can't. I can't make love with her. I'm impotent. Christine is disgusted with me. I feel helpless now. It's like my genitals shrunk, got tiny, and I feel like a little boy, and I'm scared.

In working with this dream, John became aware consciously of his desperate need for power over women, fearing that they would otherwise have a fatal power over him. It was a frightening session for John, and a significant amount of time was taken with helping him to integrate this issue consciously.

In the week following, John had the following dream:

> I'm locked in a dark place. I can't see anything. It's hard to breathe. I'm being punished. My mother's mad at me. I don't know why. I did something bad. I don't know what. It's all dark, and I'm getting really scared. I bang on the door, but she won't let me out. No matter what I do or say, she won't let me out.

In working with this dream, I asked John to take the role of his mother and reexperience the dream. He felt totally incapable of even pretending to know what his mother felt or thought, or to even guess why she was punishing him (although he had not previously experienced difficulty in dreamwork).

After 9 months of psychotherapy, John rarely had nightmares, was seeing Christine on a steady and exclusive basis, was contemplating asking her to move in with him, was succeeding very remarkably in his career, and had developed a very vivid interest in his inner life and in his personal growth. He became interested in philosophy and psychology, particularly the psychology of consciousness. He read books on the subject and more and more wanted to talk with me about these subjects. He was freer in his social behavior and was more readily willing to let others see his human, non-Superman self. He was developing a quite psychologically intimate relationship with Christine, and in fact told her about his experience with Ann. (He'd previously told no one but his therapists and his attorney.) In short, he was becoming a psychologically well-developed man.

Although the nature of his sleep disorder warranted continued monitoring, his need for therapy was rapidly becoming satisfied. At about this time, he asked me if I thought he was ready to find out what happened the night he assaulted Ann in his sleep. (He had previously mentioned his curiosity about this only in our initial interview. He almost never mentioned the event, and had not expressed curiosity about it.) I asked him to develop a hypnotic state, and after he had done so, I used ideomotor signaling to inquire about his unconscious readiness to learn this information at a conscious level. He indicated that he was ready to let his conscious mind learn what had happened that night. I then suggested, as I had so often suggested before, that one night in the following week he would have a dream and the dream would be interesting and meaningful to him. This time, however, I suggested that the dream would reveal to him what actually happened the night he assaulted Ann. I suggested that this dream would reveal to him what had precipitated the event and what he was doing in his sleep as it occurred. I also suggested to him that he would be free to not consciously remember this dream until he worked with it in my office.

The next week he arrived feeling, he said, very excited. He said he'd had a dream the night before that he knew must be very important because he couldn't remember any of it. (By now he had a great appreciation of and interest in defense mechanisms such as repression.) I asked him if he was ready to work with the dream with me. He indicated that he was, and promptly developed a hypnotic state within which to work with the dream.

> I'm in bed with Ann. We're making love. She teases me, and I get my feelings hurt. I don't know why, but I hate her for teasing me. So we stop making love, and we each turn away from the other and go to sleep. Now I'm sleeping. I begin to dream. In the dream I'm in bed with Ann, just like I really am, and we're making love, and she begins to laugh at me, to make fun

> of me. And suddenly I realize she isn't really Ann, she is my mother, in disguise somehow. And I'm in bed fucking my mother! And she's laughing, saying, "I finally got you. I finally got you!" And I'm so ashamed, so embarrassed, I just start hitting her to make her stop. Then she starts to scream, and I jump off the bed and jump out the window.

As John was describing the events of the dream, he was becoming progressively more agitated and upset, and, by the end of the account, was alternately panicky and crying. I offered the support of his knowing that I now knew what had happened and was not offended or horrified by what I knew; but rather, that I understood the terrible dilemma he had experienced as a child. I further offered an opportunity simply for time and quiet in which to absorb and integrate this experience. After a few minutes of more quiet sobbing, John began to awaken from the hypnotic state. The remainder of the appointment was taken with consciously integrating this experience.

During the treatment sessions that followed, John and I worked toward a conscious understanding of that dream, and of the childhood memories it had released. In the days following that dreamwork, John began to remember bizarre and painfully confusing incidences of sexual seducton by his mother. These incestuous incidences, it became evident, led him to his confusion over his feelings for his mother—his very deep love and affection, and his equally deep hatred and fear. His view of his own sexuality, and of his terrible need for both control over and distance from women, was also undoubtedly rooted in these early experiences. Finally, it became clear why the strength and unemotionality of Superman had seemed necessary to protect him from his sexual and emotional vulnerabilities. Memories of the actual torture of being locked in the dark closet (one of his punishments for not satisfying his mother), made clear how John had developed his dissociative capacities. Reviewing his early childhood fears of taking his father's place as his mother's sexual partner helped him to understand his contemporary view of his father as weak and incompetent (and of his current ambivalence about trying to take his father's place in the business world).

John experienced enormous relief from discussing these memories' meaning to him. He rapidly became more relaxed and at ease with himself and less fearful still about his own nature. After eight treatment sessions, John terminated therapy with the understanding that he could call and/or resume treatment again if he wished. From time to time since then, John has briefly reentered therapy for the purpose of sorting out current life problems.

It has now been over 7 years since the night John assaulted Ann. In the past 2 years he has had no somnambulistic episodes. (In the previous 2 years he had one episode, of a very minor character.) John and Christine have been living together for over 3 years and are contemplating marriage. John's professional career has become very successful, and his life is that of a lively, increasingly self-aware man struggling with the same dilemmas life presents us all.

The successful resolution of John's problem might have been achieved through therapeutic means other than hypnosis. Hypnosis was used as the major therapeutic technique for two primary reasons:

1. The primary syndrome involved behavior during sleep. Hypnosis has a rich history of use for treatment of sleep disorders and offers the potential for rapidly altering their symptoms. In this case the symptom necessitated rapid alteration, since there was the potential for serious harm to the patient and others.
2. The patient's symptom involved troubling dreams, so dreams offered the obvious focus for working through issues that were outside the patient's conscious awareness. Since Gestalt therapy includes techniques for dreamwork that are easily combined with hypnotic techniques, it was natural to combine these therapeutic techniques (Barber, 1983).

Surely, hypnotic suggestion to alter the symptom of somnambulism would not in and of itself have been sufficient for treating the problem. John's deeply felt confusion over power issues, combined with the extremely ambivalent incestuous relationship with his unusually seductive mother, required a working through of these themes to remove the need for the nightmares. The goal in therapy (once the immediate danger of the out-of-bed experiences was past) was to enable John to become aware of himself (particularly his confusion over issues of power) and to integrate this awareness with a growing sense of his own inner wholeness and strength.

John is now able to use his lessened need for power and control within the healthy context of his work and no longer needs to hide what he regarded as his base and evil self. Superman had been needed to save a little boy from pain and terror from which he could not save himself. Superman is no longer called upon to polarize John's impulses. John is now a man and is learning to master the power and strength he now knows is his own.

REFERENCES

Barber, J. Hypnosis and awareness. In J. Zeig (Ed.), *Ericksonian psychotherapy* (Vol. 1). New York: Brunner/Mazel, 1985.

Pedley, T. A., & Guilleminault, C. Episodic nocturnal wanderings responsive to anticonvulsant drug therapy. *Annals of Neurology*, 1977, *2*, 30–38.

Polster, E., & Polster, M. *Gestalt therapy integrated*. New York: Brunner/Mazel, 1973.

II
FAMILY AND RELATIONSHIP PROBLEMS

Hypnotherapy traditionally has been practiced using the individual psychotherapy model, one client at a time. Students learning hypnosis at first might not consider using this powerful tool in the practice of conjoint family, marital, or relationship therapy. The authors contributing to this section illustrate efficacious methods in the treatment of these concerns.

The editors would like to underscore a common thread that many of the authors develop and explicitly discuss in the following chapters. In hypnotic image development, these authors evoke the hypnotic subject's images rather than directly control the internal images. Daniel L. Araoz specifically speaks to allowing the client to "fill in the blanks" with the client's own set of images. If the therapist attempts to direct all the imagery without giving the client the freedom to choose and create, the therapist not only would miss the possibly rich material that may be brought forth, but also may trigger resistances within the client.

Each author in this section also uses the client's own frame of reference. Michael Jay Diamond underlines this metaphoric problem description for the benefit of the client. This almost too obvious fact can, unfortunately, be easily forgotten in the search for the perfect hypnotherapeutic intervention. Besides beautifully showing the process of using the client's "world view," these authors also display the elicitation and use of the client's own resources to resolve their problems.

George A. Sargent shows how hypnosis can be efficiently used in family treatment. Of interest is the use of hypnosis with the spouse present and its effectiveness as a learning tool. He illustrates a "ritual of purification," a ritualized reintegration process that can be used in various ways. Sargent explicitly suggests that the client may well have been in a trance during the ritual itself and therefore may have profited more profoundly from the experience. He gave her the ritual as an assignment to be done while she was in a light trance, thereby eliciting a subconscious commitment.

Araoz presents his well-conceived method of using hypnotherapy with sexual dysfunctions. He outlines a seven-point model for sex hypnotherapy, distinguishing between the circumstances, operations, and consequences of the therapy. This model could easily guide therapists in all their work, not just in sexual dysfunction therapy.

Diamond eloquently states that to accurately treat the whole person the therapist must "go beyond" the DSM-III classifications. He asserts that the treatment of choice is a function of many other factors as well. His chapter teaches the importance of honoring and respecting the whole person as well as the implicit and explicit contract with the person. Readers can learn much from a careful and repeated reading of the written analysis of his fourth session. It is suggested that the reader can review and work into their own practice a few of his suggestions. Diamond's summary and concluding remarks speak for most authors when he says, " . . . the reader should not regard this as a simple and rather packageable hypnotherapy procedure."

6
SEX HYPNOTHERAPY IN A CASE OF ORAL SEX INHIBITION

Daniel L. Araoz

Traditional hypnosis, especially in the last 50 years or so, has dealt with sexual dysfunctions in all their varieties (Araoz, 1982a; Beigel & Johnson, 1980). The hypnotic approach used was often direct suggestions combined with imagery. Some specialists used indirect imagination methods or subconscious exploration of the origins of the dysfunction. The new hypnosis, on the other hand, prefers indirect methods and is very concerned with *the hidden symptom* in sexual dysfunctions, namely, the person's reaction to and cognitive operations resulting from the problem. Because of this awareness, modern sex hypnotherapy starts with the thoughts, images, self-talk, and so on that the person is using, often without realizing it. The general outline in the mind of the sex hypnotherapist would run something like this:

1. Be sure that medical aspects of the problem have been resolved or ruled out and the sexual *relationship*—if any—is constructive.
2. How is the person reacting to the problem? Check negative, defeatist *statements* made to self.
3. How is the person reacting to the problem? Check negative, defeatist *images* entertained/fostered.
4. Check at which times these statements and images are more prevalent.
5. Propose statements and images slightly more positive, hopeful, and joyful, using hypnosis.
6. Recommend daily practice of number 5, together with proven techniques of nonhypnotic sex therapy such as sensate focus, and the like.
7. Check progress weekly until dysfunction is overcome.

Daniel L. Araoz. Counseling Department, Long Island University, New York, New York.

Ascertaining that there is no medical cause for the sexual dysfunction is necessary in order to avoid mistakes in treatment due to misdiagnosis. Once the problem is identified and the relationship checked to be sure it is ego-enhancing, it is necessary to examine how the person is reacting to the sexual difficulty: What is the person saying to himself or herself regarding it; what mental images are occurring in relation to the sexual problem? Many people fall into this trap unawares: They castigate themselves because of the problem, and they mentally rehearse the next failure with increased anxiety. The time at which these negative cognitions take place is important in order to advise the person to practice self-hypnosis during those times more intensely than at other times. Number 5 is the point at which treatment specifically takes place. If the person is saying: "It will happen again, I know it," a new statement could be "Next time we are together, I'll pay special attention to my sensations and feelings in other parts of my body." This cognitive switch always is made experientially, rather than intellectually, rehearsing in one's mind the next sexual encounter, the client's being relaxed and paying attention to other parts of his or her body. Clients are taught how to do this by themselves, and frequently the use of an audiotape proves helpful for the clients to practice with the tape—at least initially—until they have acquired the habit of "thinking" differently about their problem.

Sex hypnotherapy is not a substitute for traditional sex therapy techniques, and this is the reason for prescribing traditional sex therapy techniques for the couple to do alone in private. That sex hypnotherapy should follow a weekly schedule that is ideal and reflects the need for continuity and for overseeing the progress made. I prefer to see the person weekly for half an hour rather than every 2 weeks for a whole hour.

The following clinical illustration is an example of the application of sex hypnotherapy. Both the medical and relational aspects were found to be positive, namely, there was no reason to deal with these two aspects as part of the therapy. The client's reaction to her problem, however, was of paramount importance. Both her self-talk (defeatist statements) and imagery needed special attention. As long as she continued to give herself negative suggestions about her problem and as long as she continued to process defeatist mental images about her difficulty, there would be no hope of resolution. Therefore an important part of the treatment centered on these two points—her negative self-statements and her negative imagery about the problem—in order to transform them into constructive, ego-enhancing and positive mental activity. The process of hypnosuggestion is the same in both self-defeating and ego-enhancing cases. The content, however, is radically different. When the content is changed, as in the following case, progress starts to occur.

PROBLEM DEFINITION AND GENERAL BACKGROUND

A 32-year-old nurse, Reena, had not been married before. She presented with what she described as "a phobia of fellatio." Just placing her lover's penis in her mouth made her gag and become dizzy and changed her mood from sexual to angry. She was in a good relationship with a man who did not insist she do this; but she wanted to do it, because in some part of her mind she knew that she would enjoy fellatio, and also because she felt that it was a tender sign of love for her lover. She knew exactly why she had this problem, but no matter how much she had tried, she had been unable to overcome it. When she was only 5 or 6—and she had a clear memory of this—a male cousin 9 years her senior had forced her to engage in this activity, although she had no recollection of his ejaculating in her mouth. The cousin would reach orgasm by masturbating vigorously in front of her after she had excited him through fellatio. She had never told anybody about this, because the cousin was someone who, otherwise, was very good to her and he made her swear that she would not tell, since this was a sign of the great and special liking that he had for her. This lasted during a whole summer and it had happened at least 10 or 12 times.

Now, as an adult woman, she realized that there was no reason for hate toward this cousin, since this had happened when he was a "stupid 14- or 15-year-old." As a matter of fact, she was still quite fond of her cousin, seeing him at least once a month, and on occasion, several years earlier, he had apologized for that behavior. Other than that time, they had not talked about it ever again.

As mentioned, the relationship she was having with her lover was very positive. As is usually the case in sexual dysfunction, I had requested that her lover accompany her to the first interview. He was sensitive, caring, and articulate, expressing that he did not see this as a problem in their relationship but that he was willing to cooperate in any way he could because she was upset about her reaction. He added that he had suggested that she stop trying fellatio since this was not important to him, but that she insisted on "solving this problem." They both had separate places to live, although they spent at least one night a week together and had sexual intimacy two to four times a week.

Reena had read one of my books and looked me up for a consultation. She was well motivated, explaining the dynamics of her relationship in terms of having to solve this for herself. She knew that hypnosis could help although she did not expect miracles. As a matter of fact, she was prepared for brief therapy, thinking in terms of 10–15 sessions. As it turned out, I saw her only four times and she was surprised at the prompt resolution of her problem.

TREATMENT

Hypnosis was used from the very first session, which lasted a whole hour. The next three sessions lasted from 30 minutes to an hour. Reena's problem was centered on her past experience with her cousin. She said: "I know it's crazy, but I still feel—at least a part of me does—that that was horrible and that that made me somehow bad. I know this is stupid but I can't help it." I asked her whether this feeling had come up before, in other relationships, especially when she had started to date. Reena didn't know for sure but believed that, yes, when she was a teenager and very much in love with a boy about 5 years older than she, she had thought of that "horrible incident" and because of the fear of fellatio had lost her interest in that older boy.

My thinking at that point went along two separate lines. First, the trauma suffered as a 5- or 6-year-old little girl had to be resolved. Connected with this was the reaction suffered as a teenager. Both issues required resolution. Second, Reena had mentioned "a part of me that knows this is ridiculous." How could I combine these two elements therapeutically? My treatment plan was formulated in terms of four steps: First, to focus on the trauma itself and to use Reena's current resources and strength in order to resolve it. Second, to address myself to the beginnings of her conscious sexuality as a teenager. Third, to help her rehearse a new enjoyment of her sexuality without the remnants of her past trauma. Finally, to work toward an integration and harmonization of the different parts of her personality.

The rationale for this therapeutic plan was based on her current inner strength and mental health. My therapeutic alliance with her strong "parts" would weaken the traumatic memory of past events. In other words, by emphasizing her inner resources and strengths, less and less mental energy would be spent both in negative mental review, as she had been doing habitually (going over in her mind the traumatic experiences of the past), and in negative mental rehearsal (going over in her mind the next "failures" she would experience in attempting to perform fellatio with her man).

To this effect, I taught her to use hypnosis, regressing to the time when she was a 5- or 6-year-old, and her cousin was initiating her into fellatio. Reena was quick to regress and reexperience the unhappiness with her situation. At this point, however, I suggested that she introduce another figure into the scene, namely, herself as a grown-up. The adult in Reena had much understanding, wisdom, and sensitivity that little Reena did not possess. I asked her to see in her mind's eye the two Reenas with as much detail as possible, compare their sizes, observe their way of dressing, their hairdos, their shoes, and so on. I suggested she hear the voice of little Reena—

anxious, frightened, upset—and that of the adult Reena, angry perhaps but reassuring, helpful, soothing. I invited her to listen carefully to what the adult was saying to the child. The adult would know what to say and how to say it, in order to give little Reena all the support and consolation she needed at the time. An excerpt of our verbal exchange follows:

THERAPIST: The adult Reena is consoling the little Reena. Hear carefully what she says. Notice little Reena's reaction, her progressive feeling better, her smile perhaps.

REENA: (*obviously relaxed and breathing slowly*) Yeah, I'm there. It feels good to console the little me. She feels better now.

THERAPIST: Continue the conversation. . . . What else can the adult Reena do to help little Reena?

REENA: I see myself hugging the little me, sitting her on my lap and wiping her tears. She feels so good now.

THERAPIST: You know what to do, what to say, to make little Reena feel good about herself. Tell her that you will meet her again several times in the next few days. On your own, you may want to do this at home, meet little Reena again, have a conversation as you just did—until the whole thing is resolved.

Notice that even though I was talking about little Reena, she referred to her as her own self. The grammar and the logic were faulty, but the experience was real and meaningful for her. She also came up with the right thing to do without any direct suggestion from me, hugging little Reena, wiping her tears and sitting her on her lap. Finally, my last suggestion to meet again with little Reena was a way of introducing self-hypnosis and of recommending daily practice of this exercise.

However, the first session was not over with this encounter. After having discussed this experience briefly, I suggested that she relax again and then that she meet the young adolescent who had been uncomfortable with her sexuality. Reena went back into hypnosis and used her mental and personality resources as an adult to help the teenage Reena. Once more, she was told to feel free to renew this meeting between these two inner realities, that is, her current, adult self, and her past, adolescent self, if she felt the need to do so.

The last part of the session was a *mental rehearsal* of a caring sexual encounter with her lover. My instructions, while she was in hypnosis, were rather general: "You feel absolutely free and happy to be with him. You enjoy everything about him. Every part of him gives you joy. Every part of him is beautiful. You feel free and happy, relaxed and without a care in the world. You are with your lover 100%, all there. Your whole body makes love to him. Every part of your body makes love to him. And you love every minute of it," and so on.

Reena discussed this last exercise as being very positive in that she found herself enjoying *the thought* of fellatio, though she did not see herself doing it yet. I stressed the need to repeat this exercise many times, even in a less formalized manner than that used at the office, such as in lost moments during the day, and to monitor how her whole being reacted to this imagery. With this the first session was finished.

The second session found Reena very surprised. She reported that she had practiced faithfully every day during the 10 days that had elapsed since the first session. During that time, her lover had to be out of town for business the first 3 days but when they were together on the 5th day, she had felt very different—more relaxed, less concerned about fellatio and feeling freer in the sexual encounter. She had not performed fellatio. But then on the 6th day when they had spent the night together, she woke up in the middle of the night, and following the norm they had established of waking each other when one could not sleep, she awakened him and started to make love. She claimed that she had been very sleepy but feeling "very mellow." Somehow, without thinking, she found herself very centered on her lover's penis, "as if I were worshiping it." Then, spontaneously, she had started to kiss his penis, to lick it, and to introduce it into her mouth—without any gagging, discomfort, or displeasure. Nothing else happened but this was a major step for Reena. She was delighted with the results of "my self-psyching," as she called it.

Then, the next day they had spent a couple of hours together at his place. They had made love without any problems, and Reena felt that she could have initiated fellatio with her lover without any problem. Fellatio did not take place, but she felt sure that it could have happened. She was very happy with this. Her words were revealing: "I knew, and I still know, that something inside of me was really changing. Now I'm looking forward to fellatio. I want to do it, to enjoy it. And I know I will!"

During the rest of the session, I suggested that she start with mental rehearsal—going over a very pleasant sexual experience, including fellatio, in her mind's eye. As implied earlier, I find it helpful *not* to direct clients with many details but to guide them in general terms such as those used with Reena this time: "You become more aware of your total enjoyment, *being* with him. Your whole body responds completely, in a natural, healthy way to your lover. You enjoy everything about your lovemaking. You enjoy every part of your lover's body," and so on. Her reaction to this mental exercise became very enjoyable and included fellatio without any direct suggestion on my part. I asked her to become especially conscious of her body. Was her body in any way showing some disagreement with her mental imagery? This "disagreement" would be manifested in any form of tension, physical discomfort, or pain. Nothing of the sort was experienced. On the contrary she felt "very relaxed, with great peace inside me," as she said.

After the above practice I suggested that she go back to meeting the little Reena. She responded that it was really not necessary for "that problem" any more, but that she wanted to spend some time with the little self anyway. I guided her into this experience, and she found herself playing hide-and-seek with her little self. After coming back to her ordinary way of thinking, she expressed curiosity about this new development, namely, the hide-and-seek play she had not encountered before in practicing this exercise at home. Whenever patients become interested in interpretations I suggest that they go back to the mental experience itself and that, frequently, in it they'll find what they are looking for. Therefore, she went back to the play of hide-and-seek—her adult playing it with her little self—and after a few minutes smiled and said in a sleepy voice, "Now I know what it means." After hypnosis, she explained: "I know there is no little girl any more. I am the adult and I like it this way. I like myself! But I know that at times many of the feelings that belonged to the little girl will be there. It'll be like hide-and-seek. Once in a while the little girl's feelings will come out of hiding. But that's OK now. I know what to do with those feelings." The interpretation of her spontaneous imagery came through experiencing it fully, not through thinking about it.

When I asked her to renew the contact with the young teenager, afraid of sex, as she had done in the first session, her response was that it was not necessary to do that. By having resolved the problem of the little Reena, she had also taken care of the problems experienced as a teenager.

She was reminded of practicing these mental exercises every day, even if she thought the problem was completely solved, and with that she was dismissed until the following week. For reasons beyond Reena's control, she was unable to keep her third appointment. She was therefore seen 2 weeks after the second session.

Reena was subdued but very pleased with the results. She had enjoyed fellatio three times. She reported that all the negative self-talk had stopped and that everytime she found herself starting to be negative, she "turned on her beautiful scene" (meaning the sexual scene with her lover), which absorbed her more every time she focused on it. At this session, we worked on checking whether every part in her personality was happy with what had changed in her sexuality. To do this, I used the hypnotic state to ask if there was any part in her who objected to the changes she had experienced. Following Watkins's (1978) and Edelstien's (1981) technique, three "parts" appeared. One of these parts called herself "Nostalgia." In essence what she said was that she did not know whether she would like giving up what had been part of her life for so long. At one point she said, "I don't care whether she likes it or not. I feel funny doing it." I encouraged Reena to respond as the grown-up self to Nostalgia. First, she did it by herself. Then she reported to me what had transpired. The adult had told Nostalgia that she did not have to be part of fellatio, she could stay out of it altogether and it would be all right not to have to worry about it. She added that she would give Nostalgia other things to worry about. Again, here we see an interesting but frequent phenomenon: The client herself handled the situation creatively, firmly, and definitely without the therapist's direct intervention.

Another "part" that came up was a mischievous one, though she did not reveal her name. She simply said that she was delighted with the changes because she always had wanted to enjoy "the big lollipop." She had to remain hidden because of that "silly, prudish Reena" who was still holding on to something that happened 25 years ago. At this point I suggested "Perhaps you and Reena can become real good friends now," to which this "part" responded, "We've always been friends, but you are right, now we can become real good friends."

Finally, Reena experienced a part called "the real me." This part expressed pride in Reena: She was now a whole woman, able to do what she wanted, when she wanted. Now she was acting as a free agent, not inhibited by her past but freed from it once and for all. This part gave her deep feelings of satisfaction and inner peace. No other "parts" came up, and so I suggested that she could have a meeting with all these parts to be sure they were all together integrating her total personality. This she did in silence for a few minutes, after which period of time she said: "Everything is OK now. I am happy." She was still told to practice any of the mental exercises we had done in the three sessions, and a last appointment was made for 2 weeks later.

Reena was, again, pleased with the progress made. She mentioned, however, that on a couple of occasions she had reverted to the old negative attitude, but that she had been able to "take care of the situation both times." She had used self-hypnosis to call a meeting of her three parts and in a few minutes was able to recover the good feelings she had experienced before. She was now sure she had learned the right way to handle her difficulty. She felt she could go on without my help. I invited her to use the rest of the session to review hypnotically the whole process of change since she had started working on it with me. She did this in a very relaxed state and came out of it more confident than ever before. I asked her to call me over the telephone in about 3 weeks to let me know how things were going. This she did exactly as requested. Reena commented over the phone that her problem seemed so far away, that it was difficult for her to believe that she had been so miserable for so long, but that "the whole thing" seemed very removed from her now. She was satisfied with the results and grateful for having experienced "such a transformation."

Three months later Reena called again, just to say hello and to let me know that everything was still going on as well as before. She also added that she was seriously considering living together with her lover since things between them were so good now "that my mind is clear."

COMMENTS AND CRITIQUE

In any therapeutic intervention we need to keep in mind the three elements that validate each other; namely, what is the condition we are concerned with (diagnosis is the most commonly used term, with medical flavor), the outcome or change we expect to attain (a model of health, normalcy, or happiness), and the operations or interventions or techniques we have to elicit or start in order to obtain the desired result? Obvious as this may sound, it is not always kept in mind by therapists of many persuasions, with the exception of the behavior therapists. In the case of sex therapy, this model of *circumstances–operations–consequences* (Mahrer, 1983) is especially important. I chose the case of Reena because it affords a clear, almost pure example of such a model. Of the seven points outlined in the beginning of this chapter, 1–4 belong to the *circumstances* or the behavior analysis, 5–6 belong to the *operations* or treatment, and 7 belongs to the *consequences* or outcomes.

The *circumstances* are of special interest because they are always a mixture of external events *and* cognitions (inner activity of the individual, most frequently nonconscious). This is what is referred to as the hidden symptom; that is, what the person is doing to himself or herself, as in the case of Reena, that reinforces the problem and makes useless any intervention not considering it. Because *circumstances* are of an inner nature, they can be labeled negative self-hypnosis (Araoz, 1981), and thus hypnotherapy is the treatment of choice to counteract it. As was mentioned earlier, however, other methods should be combined in order to establish an effective regimen. Together with hypnotherapy Reena was encouraged to engage in sexual activities with her lover as part of her therapy and as a means of monitoring the changes in her mental attitude.

It should also be noted that the hypnosis used with Reena was not the traditional type with emphasis on hypnotizability, ritualized inductions, and concern about hypnotic depth. The hypnotic approach described is that of the new hypnosis (Araoz, 1982b, 1983), which assumes that all normal individuals are able to use hypnosis and uses naturalistic methods of induction, disregarding depth of hypnosis.

I could strengthen this one case with many other examples of clients with sexual problems who have been greatly helped through hypnotherapy. In my teaching seminars to sex therapists, I request that they start using the hypnotherapeutic approach with at least one patient. I stress that they should always remember that sex hypnotherapy is a method to strengthen pure sex therapy, not one to do away with the proven techniques used to help people with sexual problems. Many of my students have told me that after seeing the therapeutic benefits in one client they became encouraged and started using this approach more often. Many would never do sex therapy without adding hypnosis to it, after having realized the advantages of this combination.

The addition of hypnosis to sex therapy addresses itself to the problem already mentioned by Masters and Johnson (1966) early in their research and, more recently, by Kaplan (1979)—namely, *spectatoring* and *the turn-off mechanism*, respectively. Though aware of the unproductive consequences of negative cognitions and imagery in their patients, neither Masters and Johnson nor Kaplan had developed any meaningful techniques to deal with the problem. The "hypno" in sex hypnotherapy goes directly to the very core of this clinical difficulty.

As in Reena's case, past traumatic sexual experiences seem to have programmed the nervous system adversely, and only a very vivid and experiential "reprogramming"—not convincing reasoning and logical understanding—is capable of freeing the person to enjoy sex fully. This "reprogramming" of the nervous system can be accomplished effectively and expeditiously through hypnosis.

REFERENCES

Araoz, D. L. Negative self-hypnosis. *Journal of Contemporary Psychotherapy*, 1981, *12*, 45–51.

Araoz, D. L. *Hypnosis and sex therapy*. New York: Brunner/Mazel, 1982. (a)

Araoz, D. L. *The new hypnosis*. Paper presented at the annual meeting of the American Society of Clinical Hypnosis, Denver, 1982. (b)

Araoz, D. L. *The paradox of the new hypnosis*. Paper presented at the annual meeting of the American Society of Clinical Hypnosis, Dallas, 1983.

Beigel, H. G., & Johnson, W. R. (Eds.). *Application of hypnosis in sex therapy*. Springfield, IL: C. C. Thomas, 1980.

Edelstien, M. G. *Trauma, trance, and transformation*. New York: Brunner/Mazel, 1981.

Kaplan, H. S. *Disorders of sexual desire*. New York: Brunner/Mazel, 1979.

Mahrer, A. R. *Experiential psychotherapy*. New York: Brunner/Mazel, 1983.

Masters, W. H., & Johnson, V. E. *Human sexual response*. Boston: Little, Brown, 1966.

Watkins, J. *The therapeutic self*. New York: Human Sciences Press, 1978.

7

WHEN THE KNIGHT REGAINS HIS ARMOR

An Indirect, Psychodynamically Based Brief Hypnotherapy of an Ego-Dystonic Sexual Impulse Disorder

Michael Jay Diamond

Sexual disorders reflect various problems including biologic and maturational inadequacies, educational deficits, behavioral and learning disorders, problems in impulse control, affective and self-image dysfunctioning, as well as interpersonal and object relational impairments. Difficulties in several of the forementioned areas occur irrespective of the primary etiologic locus of overdetermined sexual problems (e.g., impulse disorders index self-esteem and interpersonal difficulties). The psychotherapist's diagnosis must go beyond a DSM-III classification to include accurate assessment of the most efficaciously treated component in the patient's personality (Kaplan, 1983). The treatment of choice is a function of this problem-oriented diagnosis along with careful assessment of the patient's ego strengths and capacity for psychological treatment, as well as consideration for the patient's economic and environmental realities. The following case illustrates an unusually successful brief hypnotherapeutic treatment of an ego-dystonic sexual disorder diagnosed in the realm of weak impulse control. The case exemplifies the importance of accurate problem diagnosis and assessment of healthy ego functioning. In addition to several theoretical and technical considerations to be delineated, the case underlines the essential importance of psychodynamic understanding within a brief hypnotherapy that might otherwise be classified as Ericksonian-oriented arising from the permissive, albeit primarily indirect and strategic, approach to the presenting problem.

Michael Jay Diamond. Department of Psychiatry and Biobehavioral Sciences, UCLA, Los Angeles, California, and Private Practice, Los Angeles, California.

CASE BACKGROUND

Mr. T, a middle-aged man residing a considerable distance from my urban private practice, telephoned after being referred by my teaching university. He requested hypnosis for something he "would rather not discuss with me on the telephone." Nonetheless, he responded to my mild intake-probing with an interesting and self-revealing statement concerning his motive for treatment. He said, "Let's just say I have a 'chink' in my armor." He elaborated briefly by stating that this "chink" was something he disliked in himself. An initial appointment was arranged.

The client's metaphorical problem description provided the first hint of his prevailing frame of reference, and ultimately, led to a series of client-based metaphorical hypnotic suggestions designed to enhance patient autonomy and self-control (Diamond, 1980). While the meaning of any symbolically based therapeutic communication must inevitably be obtained from the patient, the empathic therapist's associations provide useful leads to obtaining and working with patient material that might otherwise remain unconscious or preconscious. My visual and verbal associations to the telephone communication were knight in armor, Middle Ages, grandeur, gallantry, discipline, pride, passion, shame, and respect for privacy. As the reader can note, the treatment and most particularly the assessment began on the telephone. Prior to our meeting, I had the impression of a rather developed, yet deeply troubled man. Moreover, I felt optimistic about treatment although unsure why.

I wasn't surprised to find Mr. T a rather formidable and nice-looking gentleman who described himself as a successful executive, happily married father of two daughters and three grandchildren, and an important and respected church official in his community. He was physically active, and in good health aside from sleep disturbances produced by his "chink." He had never seen a psychotherapist and only reluctantly did so in this circumstance due to the nature of his problem and the likelihood of serious censure within his religious community were he to discuss the difficulty in the usual church setting. It was both a sign of his own psychological maturation as well as quite propitious in view of his treatment by a non-church-affiliated therapist that his distress did *not* extend to a moral sense of failing the Church or God.

Mr. T explained his problem as "recent homosexuality," and he was experiencing considerable guilt and distress. He was definitely "not interested in discovering the reasons why." He stressed not wanting his wife to know about his treatment (or problem) and wished help quickly with hypnosis. He willingly committed himself to five or six sessions, while emphasizing his strong motivation to alter the problem so as not to jeopardize his church and community standing nor his marriage and family. He reported considerable loss of self-esteem in not being able to overcome the problem on his own, as well as guilt, anxiety, disturbed sleep, and reduced job performance.

A general discussion of his problem and its background ensued and provided a better understanding of the most efficaciously treated problem component (i.e., controlling his homosexual impulses). In short, Mr. T had recently become involved in a homosexual relationship with an artist whom he met during a business transaction. They had been illicitly seeing each other twice weekly for several months. He enjoyed the sex, genuinely liked his lover, and concomitantly, would feel extremely depressed and guilty following each meeting. Moreover, he strongly disapproved of his infidelity and secrecy *vis à vis* his wife.

Mr. T had been aware of what he considered to be "insubstantial" homosexual impulses throughout his adulthood and recalled early adolescent homosexual peer experimentation. He had had a strong junior high school "crush" on a male teacher, who had unfortunately committed suicide during the school year by hanging after exposing his homosexuality. The recent involvement was Mr. T's only adult homosexual experience. He remained sexually active with his wife, albeit recently less so. He was satisfied with his marriage. It seemed however, that Mr. T had been rather isolated from close male relationships. These factors, along with the recency of his homosexual activity and ensuing emotional disturbance rendered the behavior ego-dystonic and apparently directly treatable. In addition, Mr. T evidenced considerable overall psychological health and ego strength manifested in creative sublimatory activity (i.e., church, physical activity, and art) and well-developed functioning in conflict-free ego spheres. There were no significant impairments in his ability to work, love, and enjoy life.

Mr. T was a good hypnotic subject, previously experiencing trance states during meditation, prayer, and outdoor adventure activities. He evidenced little resistance to hypnosis and agreed to the hypnotherapy treatment plan to help him to not act on his homosexual impulses, appropriately terminate his homosexual relationship, and strengthen his heterosexual feelings toward his wife. Toward this end, strengthening of nonsexualized male relationships was discussed as a therapeutic goal.

TREATMENT RATIONALE AND OVERVIEW

Treatment ran five sessions on a once-weekly basis. Follow-up data were available 2 months, 6 months, and 5 years later. Hypnosis was regularly used in a permissive and primarily indirect manner both to strengthen mature ego functions and adaptive defenses while minimizing resistance, which would have been more likely to occur with uncovering techniques and/or direct suggestion. As Erickson (1954a, 1964) suggested, it is therapeutically unwise to generate (and work through) resistance in brief treatment. The present treatment was thus designed to keep the patient's anxiety and intrapsychic conflict highly contained and therapeutically manageable while limiting defense and resistance. Elicitation of verbal expressions of guilt-charged material as well as verbalized "insight" were kept minimal within an implicit, unspoken patient–therapist understanding. Interventions were construed to be congruent with the patient's healthy self-image and prevailing world view, while maintaining a generally positive transference and strong therapeutic alliance. The specific procedures used maximized choice, autonomy, patient values, and self-control. The therapeutic framework was essentially ego-psychological and mastery-oriented (Diamond, 1980; Fromm & Gardner, 1979; Gardner, 1976). Self-hypnosis was taught to enhance these ego processes, while verbal (i.e., nonhypnotic) psychotherapy was limited to reality-oriented strengthening of relevant assertive communication skills (i.e., in sensitively terminating the homosexual relationship) and adaptive ego-syntonic behaviors (e.g., enjoyable activities with wife, exercise, male comraderie, and self-hypnosis).

Hypnotic procedures were used in order to establish rapidly a therapeutic context for the patient to attend to and use his internal change resources. The hypnotic interventions indicated considerable therapist activity, paradoxically in order to evoke client responsibility for change. Thus, the therapist's extensive hypnotic verbalization was employed to actively support client independence and self-control. Hypnotic suggestions were primarily designed to foster the patient's ability to listen to himself, a process contemporary hypnotherapists refer to as "trusting the unconscious" (Erickson, Rossi, & Rossi, 1976). Erich Fromm (1968) suggested that listening to ourselves is so difficult because it requires the rare ability of "being alone with oneself." This rather sophisticated intrapsychic capacity is related to being "alone in the presence of the other" (Winnicott, 1965) and has been considered essential in effective hypnotherapy (Diamond, 1984). Therapeutic utilization of this process was based on assessed patient ego strengths.

The first two sessions focused on obtaining relevant information, establishing rapport and a therapeutic alliance (with agreed-upon goals), and providing a rewarding hypnotic experience while assessing Mr. T's hypnotic talents (e.g., ability to dissociate, become absorbed in imagery, and respond to hypnotic suggestion). Hypnosis occurred in session 2, using a standard eye fixation, relaxation, and imagery-based (i.e., escalator-downward) deepening technique. Additional suggestions employed Mr. T's use of physical exercise (i.e., jogging) to increase absorption and rapport. Ideomotor finger signaling was established for communicative purposes, and an ideomotor suggestion (i.e., hands moving apart) was successfully employed to ratify the patient's trance (e.g., the patient spontaneously commented that "that convinced me I was hypnotized"). An ego-strengthening suggestion to experience himself "in a place and time feeling carefree and without guilt" resulted in a spontaneous regression to when he was 8 years old on a river raft with a friend. This was later employed for positive self-image work. Motivationally oriented posthypnotic suggestions were made concerning both improving hypnotic talent with subsequent trancework and obtaining the therapeutic benefits of trance.

Sessions 3 and 4 employed hypnosis for achieving specific therapeutic goals, and the fifth and final session reinforced prior hypnotic work while strengthening patient use of self-hypnosis and related autonomous processes in the context of terminating the therapeutic relationship. Indirect and permissive hypnotic suggestions were used for induction, deepening, and therapeutic purposes.

Session 3 involved telling the hypnotized patient a simple and patient-relevant metaphorically based story (Erickson *et al.*, 1976). The story involved a warrior climbing a mountain, encountering obstacles along the way, acquiring strength by authentically facing obstacles, and concomitantly, responding to obstacles by choosing paths consonant with his ultimate purposes. Additional hypnotically embedded material concerned the humanness of varied impulses, desires, thoughts, and feelings, along with the function of emotional pain as signaling a need to attend to inner conflict (i.e., obstacle). Indirect suggestion was used to strengthen the patient's healthy ego while minimizing maladaptive harsh superego functioning. He was told, for example, that "a warrior recognizes and accepts his own imperfections and limitations, while proceeding to act, when possible, to achieve goals, giving his life its meaning." Finally, direct suggestion involved the hypnotic visualization (i.e., behavioral rehearsal) of not acting on homosexual impulses as he found alternative gratification and self-confidently reexperienced himself with pride in his mastering ability. A posthypnotic suggestion established the cue words, "deep relaxation," for further self-hypnotic induction.

The patient reported sleeping much better with improved homosexual impulse control in the ensuing week. An annotated segment of the complete hypnotic procedure used in session 4 is presented to enable a detailed examination of the hypnotic style used. The final session emphasized strengthening Mr. T's self-hypnotic skills as well as his libidinal ties to his wife. A "pseudo-orientation in time" (Erickson, 1954b) was employed to enable Mr. T to experience his problem as solved. Follow-up contact was arranged.

HYPNOTHERAPEUTIC SESSION: A DETAILED ANALYSIS OF SESSION 4

The fourth session epitomized the general treatment framework. Progress was evident by the onset of the session. Initially, there was an empathic reflection of Mr. T's concerns in terminating his homosexual relationship (i.e., his wish to not harshly reject his lover as a "person"), while providing reality-based assertive role-playing experiences to facilitate this goal. The remainder of the session used hypnosis to enhance patient self-control and mastery abilities. A variant of Stein's (1963) "clenched fist" technique, related to the "anchoring" procedure of Dilts, Grinder, Bandler, Bandler, and DeLozier (1980) was employed to provide an autonomous and bodily based, symbolic, and conditioned self-control technique. This technique was embedded within the framework for "listening to oneself" and "trusting the unconscious." Consistent with an indirect Ericksonian *modus operandi*, the homosexual issue was never directly mentioned during trancework. The accompanying comments attempt to provide a more detailed understanding of the basis for specific interventions.

Therapist's verbatim hypnotic suggestion	*Clarifying comments*
"Starting with your being comfortable. . . .	Setting stage for hypnosis.
Let's begin with your just recalling the words that we used last time, *deep relaxation*. As you hear the words, you feel the words.	Hypnotic induction using cue words.
You can begin by letting your eyes close and going into a state of deep relaxation . . . , letting yourself move down into the state, . . . calming your mind . . . so that you're conscious and yet unconscious, . . . alert and yet relaxed (*pause*).	Deepening suggestions (involving previous induction techniques) employing eye closure, relaxation, imagery (downward), focused breathing, and indirect suggestion.
With each breath you may find that you become more and more relaxed. I wonder if you are going to go into a deep or very deep state of hypnosis today.	Indirect, permissive deepening suggestion.
You may wonder what you'll remember and what you'll forget.	Indirect, permissive amnesia suggestion.
It really doesn't matter what you remember or what you forget. For as you know, the most important thing is creative work that takes place on an unconscious level.	Relaxation-based trance state provides internal setting for using ego resources.
You may hear my words very consciously or [you] may not. But unconsciously, you are fully capable of responding, processing, and using the information that fits for you.	Permissive suggestion to "trust the unconscious" and "listen to oneself."
"As you relax more and more, with each breath . . . you may find that you feel as you felt . . . some time before in the past . . . a time when you were younger, . . . perhaps when you were that little boy, running . . . freely through the fields, feeling the wind and the sun,	Induced positive age regression, with ego-strengthening elements.
or walking on the sand at the beach, feeling the cool, wet sand underneath your feet, . . . feeling the spray from the waves hitting you, soothing (*pause*). Feeling the warm sun and the blue sky, hearing the crashing of waves, smelling the salt air, opening yourself, . . . wondering how far back you	Permissive provision of alternative, comforting sensory images (to increase response likelihood).

can go, . . . knowing that so much rests within you, so many experiences, memories, . . . thoughts, and beliefs. And within that there is an important place, a place where you have the choice, . . . the choice to choose . . . to choose to act . . . as you wish to act. To choose to live life the way you wish to live life (*pause*). Just as you know . . . your mind powers are immense, . . . if you wish, you can find yourself back in a very pleasant and positive memory situation. Where you felt strong and good and confident (*pause*). When you felt loving and compassionate (*pause*). You may wish to see how you look in the situation, . . . hearing the sound of your voice when you feel this positive way. Feeling the feelings that you feel when you are in this positive, confident, compassionate state of mind. And you know that you can go back and feel these kinds of feelings when you need to feel them. You know that these feelings are very much attached to you (*therapist touches patient's right knee*); when you need them (*pause*). And just as you can recover these feelings of strength, you know, too, there is a part of you that is very capable of experiencing very negative feelings . . . that you can go and recover and feel the feelings of guilt and insecurity, disappointment in yourself (*therapist touches patient's left knee*). But you know there are situations where you can feel these kinds of feelings, you can see what you look like when you feel this way, you can hear the sound of your voice when you are in this negative place, . . . you can feel the feelings from this negative place, . . . and that does not feel very good (*pause*). Just as you can in the other place, these feelings, too, are available to you. The feelings that you can activate and experience, and you know just as the positive is available (*therapist touches right knee*), the negative is available (*touches left knee*). . . . And just as the negative, so are the positive. You might find that both can be active, and at the same time, you can make a choice, . . . a choice to choose to feel good, to feel strong, . . . to feel the ability to choose to see yourself feeling strong, to hear your voice, the strength to feel feelings of compassion, security, and self-confidence. . . . And when you need these feelings, they are available to you. When you need them they are

Indirect suggestion for responsibility for change concomitant with "being alone with oneself."

Facilitating ego-syntonic choice by "listening to oneself."

Ego-strengthening suggestions (to minimize resistance surrounding ego-syntonic choice).

Augmenting suggestion effect by employing multiple sensory experiences.

Suggested linkage of positive "ego state" to autonomous, bodily based symbolic stimulus.

Suggested linkage of negative "ego state" to establish self-control cues (*vis à vis* unpleasant experience).

Use of multiple sensory modalities to intensify effect.

Helping patient acquire hypnotic self-control over both positive and negative "ego states" by alternating them.

Suggesting and reinforcing self-control technique by emphasizing positive ego-strengthening choice experience.

there (*pause*). You might find that when you choose . . . in a way that is congruent with you needs, . . . your values, . . . you have a great deal more energy, because we fight when we are in conflict and we lose energy (*pause*). When we are not in conflict, when we act in accordance with what we truly value, . . . we feel we have more energy (*pause*). Energy to go through the day (*pause*). Feeling good, . . .	Indirect suggestion providing experiential reinforcement for ego-syntonic choice (i.e., reduction of conflict; increase in energy).
energy to accomplish so many more of the things we wish to accomplish in life (*pause*). Energy to go through downtimes of the day not feeling so tired but rather feeling alert,	Reinforcement of effects (and affects) of ego-syntonic choosing.
with more energy, . . . energy that lets us sleep well and soundly (*pause*). Using all of our senses to experience life as fully as we can, . . . seeing those things, those people, the wonders of nature around, . . . hearing	Suggested sleep improvement.
the sounds of the symphony, . . . the sounds of other voices, . . . the sound of our own breathing, . . . of our loved ones (*pause*). The feeling is good, strong, warm, compassionate. Human feelings that are so much a part of all of us. Smelling the wonders, the tasting, the fruits of life (*pause*). As you con-	Suggested increased enjoyment of preferred activities.
tinue to breathe and relax, you know that the solution to your problem lies within you (*pause*). Your conscious mind, of course, is capable of being confused, being impatient, being dissatisfied. Your unconscious mind, the part of you that I am speaking directly to now, knows very well what the solution for your problem is. It also knows that it is capable of communicating that solution to the rest of you, to the conscious part of you, . . .	Reinforcement of healthy adaptive ego functions and concomitant capacity of "being alone with oneself" (while utilizing potential resistance to maintain therapeutic goals).
when the conscious part of you is ready to hear that message, to take it, and to act upon it fully. I don't know the solution to your	Permissive self-control suggestion.
problem. That is something that only you know (*pause*). We know that the solution is there, though. Don't know exactly when the problem will be fully resolved (*pause*). It might be a matter of hours, perhaps days, . . .	Suggested autonomous functioning (listening to self).
maybe it will be weeks or even months. We don't know that for sure. But we know that the solution is there (*pause*). As I speak here to your unconscious, if your unconscious can hear me, I would like it just to signal to me	Suggestion respecting patient's "readiness" and possible resistance to change (i.e., attending to patient defenses and self-protection needs).
by simply moving the index finger of your right hand. Fine (*pause*). Ready now to let go all of that tension. Breathing in all of that re-	Use of ideomotor signal to ensure rapport and alliance maintenance.

laxation, . . . climbing your mountain, moving on in your own very unique, very special way through life, calling upon your own resources, your own creativity, . . . your own sources of strength, . . . and you know what we don't know (*pause*). And as you find yourself in your own unique way, working your own unconscious mind in whatever way your mind works, you know that it is not important what you consciously remember, or what you forget (*pause*). For the answer and the solution lie within you, and they are moving at their own pace towards integration with your conscious mind. You know, too . . . that you have the choice, the choice to feel good or not good (*pause*). Whichever way feels better, the choice is available to you, and in making that choice, further choices . . . become easier (*pause*). Coming from a place of strength, compassion, and confidence enables us to choose many other things much more easily, much more clearly, much more comfortably. And you know, too, that you can continue in your work, practicing self-hypnosis, letting yourself go into this altered state of mind, deepening as you wish, and letting your own unconscious create solutions for you (*pause*). Develop the solution, and continue to contribute to your own sense of well-being, and now when you are ready, at your own pace, when you know . . . there are at least two ways for the solution to come about, I would like you then to begin to bring yourself back to the present state of reality, your present state of consciousness, bringing yourself back into the room, opening your eyes when you are ready, feeling fully back, alert, refreshed, and feeling good, but not until we know of at least two ways to solve your problem (*pause*). When you are ready you can then come back. . . . "

Indirect suggestion utilizing previously established images for autonomous functioning.

Permissive amnesia suggestion (to minimize resistance of an obsessive nature).

Suggested utilization of hypnotically activated capacities.

Reinforcement of self-control skills.

Posthypnotic suggestion of increased ease in ego-syntonic choosing (made contingent on experienced ego states).

Posthypnotic suggestions to use self-hypnosis and maintain self-control (in preparation for termination of treatment).

Reinforcement of self-control skills (pertaining to capacity to "listen to oneself").

Trance termination contingent upon accomplishment of ego-syntonic therapeutic goal.

Note on patient's response: Patient mentioned at least three ways, only one of which was acceptable to him as a solution.

TREATMENT OUTCOME AND FOLLOW-UP

Mr. T reported successfully terminating his homosexual relationship, increased self-esteem, and substantial reductions in depression, anxiety, and guilt. His sleep patterns and work output were again normal, and he regularly used self-hypnosis for stress reduction and ego support. A follow-up telephone conversation 2 months later indicated maintenance of gains along with increased and satisfying heterosexual relations with his wife "about once or twice weekly." Six-month follow-up data became available when a new patient referred by Mr. T spontaneously reported that Mr. T felt he "was greatly helped by hypnosis," a statement Mr. T corroborated 5 years later when referring a relative. This long-term telephone follow-up enabled Mr. T to speak of the success of his treatment while disclosing his continued use of self-hypnosis for mastery purposes.

SUMMARY AND CONCLUSION

The patient, who presented with the problem of "having a chink in [his] armor," responded to a fairly straightforward and uncomplicated nondirective treatment. In my experience, such rapid success is more the exception than the rule, and thus, the reader should not regard this as a simple and rather packageable hypnotherapy procedure. Rather, this case highlights the interplay of several important treatment processes. These include (1) an accurate assessment of both patient pathology and strength; (2) patient's motivation to change and "faith" in the treatment process; (3) patient–therapist match or "chemistry;" (4) the establishment of a strong working alliance with agreed-upon treatment goals (Bordin, 1979); (5) therapist ability to empathize with the patient's narcissistic vulnerabilities and thereby create the therapeutic and partially curative "conditions of safety" (Eagle & Wolitzky, 1982); (6) modulation of negative transference elements; (7) patient internalization of the therapist's more benign superego characteristics (via identification and introjection), lessening intrapsychic conflict; and (8) employment of therapeutic activities that are congruent with treatment goals (e.g., utilizing nondirective hypnosis as a self-control skill within the context of patient's learning a new adaptive–defensive style).

The case strongly underlines the importance of patient ego strength plus an ego-dystonic symptom along with therapist psychodynamic and developmental understanding for successful brief, symptomatically oriented treatment. The case prognosis was initially highly favorable due to the patient's healthy ego functioning, intact psychic structure, and paucity of serious psychopathology. The presented disorder was viewed as problematic from within the client's framework rather than from a prevailing nosological or therapist-based viewpoint. Therapeutic interventions attempted to exploit healthy, adaptive ego processes and were undoubtedly partially effective due to a positive therapeutic alliance resulting from both the patient's mature ego and the therapist's respect for the patient's need to work at an ego-supportive level. Moreover, both the transference and countertransference remained positive and were characterized by mutual respect and implicit understanding. Additionally, the therapist was both highly active and relatively nondirective, creating the appropriate working environment and "conditions of safety" for this patient's self-initiated change(s). No substantial psychic reorganization occurred, and the sexual problem may reemerge during times of stress, regression, and/or unconscious conflict. Nevertheless, Mr. T acquired an effective self-control tool and probably will not return to psychotherapy. The "tool" has helped him create a context for "listening to himself."

The key change ingredients, however, remain unclear, as multiple processes were involved in this successful treatment. It is naive and fallacious to attribute the positive findings to hypnosis, indirect suggestion, metaphor and storytelling, ego strengthening, or any other isolated technical intervention. Therapy occurred on multiple levels, always embedded in an ongoing relationship with the therapist-other. Treatment took place *in* hypnosis, not *by* hypnosis. Hypnosis was an effective tool, due to its congruence with Mr. T's expectations and wishes, as well as its capacity to produce therapeutically relevant alterations in consciousness and active cognitive processing (Sheehan & McConkey, 1982). Thus, hypnosis enhanced the therapeutic frame by augmenting such therapeutic elements as the working alliance, positive transference, therapist recognition of countertransference issues, therapist empathy, physical setting parameters, patient imagery and free association, patient autonomy, reconditioning experiences, insight, and faith. Hypnosis apparently augmented the patient's access to internal processes, sensory-based imagery (including visual, auditory, and kinesthetic sensations), and believed-in-efficacy (i.e., faith) in treatment. The approach thus used hypnosis to facilitate therapeutic goals rather than creating therapeutic goals in order to use hypnosis.

REFERENCES

Bordin, E. S. The generalizability of the psychoanalytic concept of the working alliance. *Psychotherapy: Theory, Research and Practice*, 1979, *16*, 252–260.

Diamond, M. J. The client-as-hypnotist: Furthering hypnotherapeutic change. *International Journal of Clinical and Experimental Hypnosis*, 1980, *28*, 197–207.

Diamond, M. J. It takes two to tango: Some thoughts on the neglected importance of the hypnotist in an interactive hypnotherapeutic relationship. *American Journal of Clinical Hypnosis*, 1984, *27*, 3–13.

Dilts, R., Grinder, J., Bandler, R., Bandler, L. C., & DeLozier, J. *Neuro-linguistic programming* (Vol. 1). Cupertino, CA: Meta Publications, 1980.

Eagle, M., & Wolitzky, D. L. Therapeutic influences in dynamic psychotherapy: A review and synthesis. In S. Slipp (Ed.), *Curative factors in dynamic psychotherapy*. New York: McGraw-Hill, 1982.

Erickson, M. H. Special techniques of brief hypnotherapy. *Journal of Clinical and Experimental Hypnosis*, 1954, *2*, 109–129. (a)

Erickson, M. H. Pseudo-orientation in time as a hypnotherapeutic procedure. *Journal of Clinical and Experimental Hypnosis*, 1954, *2*, 261–283. (b)

Erickson, M. H. The burden of responsibility in effective psychotherapy. *American Journal of Clinical Hypnosis*, 1964, *6*, 269–271.

Erickson, M. H., Rossi, E. L., & Rossi, I. *Hypnotic realities: The induction of clinical hypnosis and forms of indirect suggestion*. New York: Irvington, 1976.

Fromm, E., *The revolution of hope*. New York: Harper & Row, 1968.

Fromm, E. & Gardner, G. G. Ego psychology and hypnoanalysis: An integration of theory and technique. *Bulletin of the Menninger Clinic*, 1979, *43*, 413–423.

Gardner, G. G. Hypnosis and mastery: Clinical contributions and directions for research. *International Journal of Clinical and Experimental Hypnosis*, 1976, *24*, 202–214.

Kaplan, H. S. *Evaluation of sexual disorders: Psychological and medical aspects*. New York: Brunner/Mazel, 1983.

Sheehan, P. W., & McConkey, K. M. *Hypnosis and experience: The exploration of phenomena and process*. Hillsdale, NJ: Erlbaum, 1982.

Stein, C. The clenched fist technique as a hypnotic procedure in clinical psychotherapy. *American Journal of Clinical Hypnosis*, 1963, *6*, 113–119.

Winnicott, D. W. The theory of the parent–infant relationship. In *The maturational processes and the facilitating environment*. New York: International Universities Press, 1965.

8
FAMILY SYSTEMS AND FAMILY HYPNOTHERAPY

George A. Sargent

The Adrian family was referred to me by the probation officer for their son, Dan, aged 16, who had been arrested for possession of marijuana. Although Dan was not going to be prosecuted for his drug possession, his family agreed with the juvenile probation authorities that Dan would benefit from some family therapy. The family was quite willing to come in.

At the first session, attended by all four members of the Adrian family—which included the younger daughter, Julie, aged 12—it became apparent that the mother had assumed the role of primary disciplinarian. Father, Frank, was a Marine Corps Master Gunnery Sergeant but did not fit the stereotype. He was mild mannered at home, did not give orders, and spent a good deal of his time with the children encouraging them not to aggravate their mother, Lillian, who described herself as the "bad guy." "I'm the screamer and the hitter," she stated. "My husband is softer on the kids than I am." The husband explained, with tears in his eyes, his deep love for his wife and the fact that he could never be angry with anyone in his family. They all meant far too much to him. The dynamic was set for therapy. The father in this enmeshed family was laying all the problems for ineffective discipline at his wife's doorstep, indirectly communicating his criticism of her way of handling the children by encouraging the children not to get their mother upset. The indirect message was clear: "If you get your mother upset she will yell and make life miserable for all of us; she has to be treated gently. You know she is not too stable."

His description of his wife's emotional state was not totally inaccurate. She was deeply troubled by her son's drinking and ditching school classes, as well as by his marijuana use. "How could you do this to us?" both father and mother said to Dan in the first therapy session. "You are hurting the family and hurting yourself."

Dan Adrian was the most interesting personality of all. He made an ingenuous presentation and was handsome, intelligent, and soft-spoken.

George A. Sargent. The Family Center, Vista, California.

He had many friends at school and a string of ex-girlfriends. He cut classes and lied to his parents with great ease. When he was caught doing wrong, his eyes would cloud as he admitted his guilt and his sorrow at burdening his family. When his parents would lift their restrictions, however, Dan was quick to get himself into trouble again. For example, he misused the family car. Several days after Dan had been told he could not use the car for 2 weeks, his father let him use it to go see his girlfriend, because—as he explained to his irate wife—"the boy can't have *all* his freedoms taken away or he'll totally rebel." Instead of simply taking the car (on this reprieve), visiting his girlfriend, and returning home, however, Dan went out and got drunk. He arrived at his girlfriend's house so inebriated she refused to go out with him. He finally brought the car home 4 hours later than his father had demanded he return it. There was yelling by Mrs. Adrian, anger tempered by protectiveness from the father, apologies, and "I don't know why I keep hurting you" from Dan, and sad withdrawal by his sister. This pattern was well established by the time therapy began.

THE FAMILY THERAPY FRAMEWORK

One way of conceptualizing this family, from a family systems viewpoint, is that the family is caught in a nonproductive repetitive pattern or sequence of behaviors that maintain Dan, as the identified patient, in his role of acting-out teenager. The family's enmeshment and boundary problems (Minuchin & Fishman, 1981) are seen in the father's protectiveness of his wife, which is actually collusion with the children not to irritate an "irrational" mother. This enmeshment and protectiveness prevents individuals in the family from communicating more directly and coping with their problems in more healthy ways. Dan, for example, did not smoke marijuana to hurt his parents. He smoked and drank because it made him feel good. Father was neither so void of anger nor mother so empty of compassion as their established roles seemed to indicate. The therapeutic question, from a family therapy perspective, was how best to begin the family in a process of individuation; how to help break up the destructive father–son collusion (often father would not tell his wife if Dan got into some trouble), and how to get husband and wife to struggle directly with their differences in disciplining their children. Mother did not want to always be the "bad guy." She clearly loved her children, but her anger at her husband's passivity in dealing with her—under the guise of protectiveness and adoring compassion—was often misdirected at the children, and especially at Dan. Father would not deal directly with his criticism or anger with anyone in civilian or military life. His style of working with his Marine subordinates also seemed to be protective and paternalistic. Dan's best chance of learning to live with limits seemed to lie in the unification of mother and father's approach to him.

THE HISTORY OF THE FAMILY

Mr. Adrian had been married before, but his first wife had been unfaithful to him. When Sergeant Adrian had found out that his wife had had a series of lovers, he divorced her immediately. As a result of his distrust and deep hurt from this first marriage, he was quite watchful of his second wife, Lillian, and had developed a habit of calling her twice a day at exactly the same time. If she was not there at 10:30 a.m. and 2 p.m. to answer the telephone, he would become quite distraught, demanding to know where she had been and why she had not answered the telephone. He was within a 15 minutes' drive of his house and would go home when she did not answer. Sometimes he would drive home if she told him directly—or indirectly, by being silent when he asked how things were—that Dan had gotten into trouble again.

Frank Adrian had adopted Dan. Dan had been conceived in a union between Lillian, when she was 23 years old, and her one-time-only lover, a man named Rolland, who had wanted her to abort. He deserted her long before Dan was born. Mrs. Adrian was raised in a Filipino household of 10 children by a very abusive father. She recounted how when one of the children did something wrong, her father would whip them all and make his children kneel for hours on a rice-sprinkled floor. She still had the scars on her knees from these times. He especially picked on Lillian, hitting her, telling her she was stupid and no good. She attributed this particular abusiveness to her on his part to the fact that she had been born the first child of two twins, the second of whom was a boy. Her umbilical cord had been wrapped around her infant brother's neck and he was stillborn. Her father never forgave her. Mrs. Adrian even remembered how her father had beaten her once so severely during her pregnancy with Dan that she thought she would die; certainly she expected to abort but did not. After Dan was born, even though he had been conceived out of wedlock—a fact that had caused the family great shame—Lillian's father doted on him, giving him everything he had ever denied his own daughter. Her mother had been passive, nonprotective of her, and very much in the background, partially because of illness. Not surprisingly, Lillian Adrian grew up with an extremely poor self-image and modeled her father's verbally abusive and physically assaultive behaviors. She treated Frank Adrian with great deference, since he was "like a kind father to her, the one she always wanted but never had." She was a victim of his benevolent dictatorship. Small wonder husband and wife had difficulty fighting *directly* about their differences in discipline. She had never received any fair discipline, nor had she seen her parents struggle to forge a consistent and fair child-rearing policy. Her husband was afraid to fight for an evenhanded and mutual approach, fearing he would push her away into another relationship (the way he felt he lost his first wife).

THE FIRST USE OF HYPNOSIS

It became clear very early in the therapeutic work with the Adrians, which was organized along directive family therapy lines (Lange & Van der Hart, 1983), that Mrs. Adrian's overreactions to her children's behaviors were based in her earlier abusive family history. I concluded that age regression might be useful in helping her to relive some of the pain of her abuse by her father and, more importantly, to gain enough perspective on the abusiveness that she could direct her anger at him directly instead of misdirecting it to her own children. In front of her husband, explaining to him what I was going to do, I suggested she close her eyes and begin to breath fully and deeply. As I gradually regressed her back to her childhood in her Filipino family, the effect was profound and somewhat frightening. Mrs. Adrian proved to be an excellent hypnotic subject, and her husband watched, fascinated, looking ready to protect her but not knowing how to do so.

"Now, Lillian, I want you to close your eyes and take a deep breath. That's right, let it all out, and as you take the next breath I want you to feel your chest rising and notice the rush of air through your nostrils."

"Frank, I want you to watch her face closely. See how the muscles around her eyes relax even as they flutter? Her face will continue to soften each time she exhales." (*to Lillian again*) "Another breath in—hold it—relax and let it out."

"Now, Lillian, I want you to bring your father here. I want you to remember a time when you were little. Can you see his face?" She frowned, paused—eyes closed, then nodded slowly. "Keep breathing, Lillian, and notice where you and he are meeting. Feel your feet heavy on the floor. Are you inside?" Her brow wrinkled slightly, as if looking inward more intently. Slowly her hands rose to her chest as if holding a doll or a pet nestled there. "What do you have there, Lillian," I asked. "My cat," she said with a toss of her head like a 10-year-old. She stroked the cat contentedly then frowned.

"I just found him outside, Daddy, can't I keep him?" she said, clasping softly her imaginary cat tighter to her chest. Her face was soft, her voice pleading and youthful. She clearly was frightened of her father, however;

suddenly, she cringed as if she had been struck. "Ouch, Ouch! Oh, please, Daddy, don't hit me," she said, as the cat apparently was yanked from her arms. She writhed in her chair, her hands and arms above her head, warding off blows. She cried. "I'm sorry, Daddy. No, I'll never do it again. I know it was wrong. Ouch, Daddy, you're hurting me!" Her head yanked backward as if he were pulling her hair. She cried out again, "Daddy, you're hurting me." Then it seemed as if he were gone. She was left alone, her arms empty, sobbing softly.

"Lillian," I said, "just relax, he's gone now." The tightness began to leave her face. "Let it all go and breathe. That's right" (*reassuringly*), "that's right. You can leave that place and time and feelings and begin to come back here. Perhaps you can hear my voice more clearly, or Frank's breathing." (*long pause*) "When you're ready you can be back here fully with Frank and me, with a full recollection of all that you want to remember. Ten—nine—eight—seven—you might notice the feeling of your feet on the floor six—five—four—three—breathing easily again—two—one—zero." Her eyes slowly blinked open, her face immobile. She looked around the room, then quizzically at her husband and then at me. "I guess I was really gone, wasn't I?" she asked.

"It's OK honey," said her husband in a protective tone, looking worried.

"I feel better," she responded. "He was wrong to take that cat. The *cat* wasn't causing any trouble."

Lillian and her husband left soon thereafter. Mrs. Adrian was far more clear about how abused she had been as a child, and she seemed more aware of how unfair the abuse had been, how unjustified.

THE COURSE OF FAMILY THERAPY

Dan and his parents began talking more about his behavior as a result of my push in therapy in the first several sessions for clearer communications. The goal was to hammer out a mutual policy between husband and wife concerning disciplinary approaches. Dan's attendance at school improved, and his drinking and pot smoking were diminished. Then he was arrested for breaking and entering into a neighbor's house and stealing some camera equipment with several other neighborhood boys. His behavior had not changed. What had begun to change significantly was his mother's reaction to trouble. As Lillian realized how angry she was at her father, she was less angry with the children. She did not call her husband during the daytime to have him rush home when this problem was reported. She did not fly off the handle at Dan. Dan was amazed to see that she dealt with him as if he were a mature adult (he had celebrated his 17th birthday since the therapy had begun). Mother told son and husband that if Dan stole he should face the consequences. Instead of flying into a rage, yelling, or hitting, she told Dan how much she loved him and how worried she was about his breaking the law. Dan was sent to juvenile court where he was given a work program and extra probation. He was directed to make restitution for the stolen equipment.

In the course of working with the Adrian family, I had determined that Dan, although being bright, likeable, handsome, and apparently regretful for all the problems he had caused his family, was developing all the characteristics of a true sociopathic personality. His sorrow was usually about getting caught, and his promises only held up until the next time it was discovered that he had not kept them. The girls at school seemed to be "getting smart" about Dan's "love-'em and leave-'em" philosophy, and most of them dropped their contacts with him. Faced with his real fear of incarceration for any more infractions, Dan actually began to improve his behavior. He again stopped smoking marijuana and drinking, and he began attending classes regularly. Meanwhile, I continued working with Mrs. Adrian, because she was motivated to change herself and her relations with the family. As long as she allowed her husband to collude with Dan—protecting her from his actual misdeeds and giving in on rules the parents had made mutually—Dan would never receive consistent limits at home. Already society, as represented by the court, was imposing its limits on him because he had not learned to abide by limits within his family. As long as the split between mother and father existed, there could be no real consistency of consequences.

Mrs. Adrian continued to grow. Although her husband was invited to attend the sessions, he found excuses not to come. "You go," he would say, "you need it and deserve it. I'm just too busy." Secretly, his wife told me, he resented her reliance on therapy. "I can talk to my therapist," she told him, "you don't listen to me or take me seriously." His listening problem had been graphically demonstrated months before.

The Adrians had first come into therapy in January. In March, just after Dan had been charged with the felony burglary and released to his parents' custody, there was an incident. The first afternoon, as Mrs. Adrian picked Dan up from school, she had a sudden impulse to run over him with the automobile. Initially slowing, she had actually stepped on the gas pedal again, aiming the car at him. Her daughter, sitting beside her in the car, had yelled "Mother, don't! You'll hurt Dan!" The mother had braked the car hard and swerved, and no damage was done, but she was well aware she had wanted to kill her son and had almost succeeded, at least in hurting him.

"At that point," she told me, "I actually wanted to kill him. I thought of all the hurt and pain he was causing Frank, me, and his sister, and I just wanted to kill him. I would have if Julie hadn't yelled."

It was clear to me that the mother was terrified of her murderous impulse, and that it was very real. As I had her confront her husband about it later, however, he minimized it.

"Lillian, you would never hurt Dan," he said. "You're just not the type."

His manner was irritatingly condescending and paternalistic. I pushed him to understand that his wife was utterly serious about the accident that had almost happened that week. Finally he heard her words and saw, from her tears and intensity, that indeed she had wanted to kill Dan.

"You don't take me seriously," she said, "you never have." He left that session a very concerned, perplexed, and shaken man.

As Mrs. Adrian faced her anger, she became less angry and volatile. Her behavior with the children was much more mature and rational. She no longer hit or wanted to hit. She no longer yelled. For example, after another minor incident and her reaction to it, Dan said, "Mom, you've changed!" In private with me he repeated time and time again how much nicer it was to be around his mother and how different she was.

As she became more tolerant, her husband became more upset. He could see she was growing more independent, and he must have secretly worried that if she became too independent she might leave him. Mrs. Adrian began receiving comments from her friends and neighbors who were watching her mature, watching her feel better about herself.

"Frank always had you so much under his thumb," they said. "We always wondered how you could stand it."

Of course, compared to her father's way of treating her, her husband's benevolent control had been heaven, but as she became more aware of her own needs and feelings, she realized that she also resented his control.

"I don't feel I should have to be home every day at 10:30 a.m. and 2:00 p.m. just to answer his calls," she said. "And I certainly don't have to call him every time something goes wrong with Dan. I can at least handle that until Frank gets home."

Together we planned how to alter the telephone patterns. First she began by suggesting to her husband that she make the 10:30 a.m. call to him, instead of vice versa. He enjoyed this, but was suspicious. "I love you and want the enjoyment of calling you sometimes," she said, being quite honest. (She heard from her husband's secretary that he would tell her at 10:28 a.m., "Please hold all other calls, I'm expecting a call from my wife.") For 2 weeks she kept to the morning schedule religiously, then gradually began calling a bit earlier or later than 10:30 a.m. "Sorry, I was at the grocery," she would explain, or "I would have called later but I wanted to get my hair done." The husband could hardly object, particularly when her messages were so kind and essentially reaffirmations of her love for him. She truly loved him, by the way, just not his controlling paternalism. She began making the messages shorter.

"I love you, honey. Have a good morning. Bye."

Or, she would be silly. Occasionally she would miss a call (unforgivable in the past), and he would not even mention it.

It was now time to work on the afternoon calls. At my suggestion she set up a schedule of alternating responsibility for who was to make the afternoon call; that is, on the first 2 workdays of the week it was his responsibility, the next day hers, the following day his, then the next 2 workdays hers, and so on. Of course, with such a complicated schedule, sooner or later one of them forgot to make the call, or even whose call it was, so they had difficulty blaming the other or feeling guilty about it. Within 2 months Mr. and Mrs. Adrian were only talking to each other on the phone two or three times a week.

"Only when I really want to say hello or have a real problem do I call," she said.

Meanwhile, another pattern was being changed at home with far more dire circumstances. As Mrs. Adrian became more moderate and reasonable, her husband was expressing more irritation with Dan.

"I woke up the other night to hear Frank and Dan yelling at each other downstairs," she said. "I used to be the one who stayed up when Dan was out beyond his curfew, but Frank has taken over that job. I never saw Frank so angry, I thought he was going to hit Dan. Another incident occurred several nights later when Dan went out the window against our instructions. Frank was pounding Dan's head against the screened porch wall, yelling and waking up the entire neighborhood. He's really losing control."

Although she thought it would be a good idea for Mr. Adrian to come into therapy, he still resisted.

"I'm not going to mention it to him anymore," she said. "Perhaps he will decide to come in himself. I know he's worried that he's blowing it." But Dad stayed out despite increasing tensions at home.

The most drastic legal problem Dan got into involved a charge of rape of a 15-year-old girl, Lydia. One result of his arrest and conviction on the burglary charge was probation. Dan's parents were charged with enforcing a curfew for him and reporting to his probation officer any changes or deviations from agreed-upon rules of the house. He was not to smoke marijuana or drink, nor was he to spend any time with the boy with whom he had burglarized the house. One Friday evening he did not return home at the specified dinner hour. The parents were worried and called his girlfriend Lydia's house. She was also gone. Finally, at 11 p.m., Lydia's parents called. She had been found upstairs drunk in bed, having snuck by them an hour before. Lydia said that she and Dan and Tom, the boy from the burglary, had been drinking at the beach. She had left them and come home. Dan came home an hour later, also drunk. The next morning the parents called the probation officer, in accordance with the suggested court procedures, and reported Dan's violation of probation. The probation officer took no immediate action.

Two nights later a knock came on the door of the Adrian's house at 5 p.m. There stood Lydia. She proceeded to tell Mr. and Mrs. Adrian that Dan and Tom had raped her that night at the beach. Mrs. Adrian was horrified and concerned for Lydia.

"Have you told your parents?" she asked.

"No," said Lydia.

"You could have been hurt," said Mrs. Adrian.

Apparently Lydia showed no real affect about this comment, nor did she seem terribly upset.

"I could see that several young girlfriends of Lydia's were sitting outside in her car," said Mrs. Adrian, "but I was more concerned that her parents know what was going on. At that moment, with all the terrible history Dan had introduced into our household, I had no doubt that he had done it. If he did it he has to be punished by the law, I thought."

She and Mr. Adrian told Lydia to go home and tell her parents, and the Adrians would come over in 15 minutes. Actually they came over in 30 minutes and Lydia had still not told her parents of the accusation against Dan and Tom. The police were soon involved, as were lawyers. Lydia and her parents disappeared out of town for a week or two, apparently to escape from some of the publicity, although none of it appeared in the papers. Many of the children at school knew. Dan began to receive threatening phone calls, and the Adrians received harassing calls from young students calling their son a rapist. Mrs. Adrian began to get very upset and began to get accusatory with Dan again. He steadfastly maintained that he had not raped Lydia.

In fact, the accusation seemed arbitrary, somehow. It was not clear whether or not the case would go to trial. Lydia stated that she did not want to prosecute, but the district attorney's office had apparently decided to prosecute on the state's behalf. More striking from the clinical standpoint was Mrs. Adrian's reaction to the entire event. She was amazed to realize how totally she sided with Lydia, even though it was her son who stood accused, and even though the way in which Lydia presented the accusation was inconsistent and provocative. In fact, many other young men from Dan's school had told Mrs. Adrian that they believed Lydia simply was out to hurt Dan. Dan and she had made love many times before. She was also known around the high school for being promiscuous. Under these conditions even Mrs. Adrian wondered about her continued strong identification with Lydia. In order to understand more about this situation, I suggested using hypnosis with Mrs. Adrian, and she readily agreed. The results were startling.

THE SECOND USE OF AGE REGRESSION

"My parents didn't let me date," she said as we discussed her early relationships with men. "They only let me go out with one man, Rolland, their godson, because they trusted him. Eventually we wound up going to bed together, just once. But, that was enough. I got pregnant and had Dan. My parents thought they were protecting me, but ironically they set up the mess I got into. I shamed my family, and they practically disowned me."

"Are you willing to go back to that night you and Rolland decided to go to bed together," I asked, "because it must have been a terribly important time for you."

She nodded, already starting to lie sideways on the couch, pulling down a cushion from the back to put under her head. She closed her eyes.

"Lillian, I want you to breathe deeply. Just let yourself go. That's right. Feel the texture of the couch material on your arms and hands. Breathing out—relaxing." Her face quickly softened, then she pulled another soft cushion from the back—without opening her eyes—and held it lovingly embraced to her chest. "Rolland is there, Lillian. Just you and he. Remember and breathe and feel."

There followed a quiet period of her caressing the pillow lovingly, smiling softly, and breathing deeply. Then, without further prompting—she began to speak.

"No, please stop, Rol, it hurts," she said.

Her hands pushed at the cushion, his imaginary chest.

"No, I don't want to. Please, please don't."

She struggled for a while silently, one arm clutching the cushion toward her, the other hand pushing it away.

Her actions and her words became even more agitated, her voice filled with anger, fear, and pain. She cried and whimpered, in supplication. And then, he was through with her. She clutched herself, shivering.

"Take me home," she said in a low, emotionless voice. "I feel dirty, I'll never be clean." In a low tone of disgust, she said, "I'm dirty." Then angrily she said, "Don't touch me!" She half rose to a sitting position and the cushion slid off the couch. She fell back, looking exhausted.

"Lillian," I began softly, after a few seconds, "you can relax and breathe now. Let it all go and just breathe. He's gone. You can relax, and as soon as you want to you can come back here, remembering what you want to. Perhaps, as you breathe . . . " her eyes fluttered open. She looked at me wonderingly, the tears still fresh in her eyes. Her gaze went to the pillow on the floor she had nearly torn apart in her anger, then back to me.

"I do feel dirty," she said as if for the first time aware of it. "I guess that's why sometimes I still resent it when Frank makes love to me. I resent him." Thoughtfully, she said, "I was raped. I was raped, just like Lydia was raped."

We spoke about her feelings about her rape at length. She had never admitted, not even to herself, that Dan had been the product of a rape. She finally understood her strong identification with Lydia. Almost simultaneously, she expressed her need to separate herself from the experience of her son's girlfriend. Having had some experience in the use of prescribed rituals in therapy to help a client say goodbye to a lost someone or to an experience that would not die (Sargent, in press), I suggested to Lillian that a ritual leave-taking of Rolland and the rape experience might help her separate her experience from that of Lydia's. Knowing her excellent capacity as a hypnotic subject, I had little doubt that she could carry out the ritual with the correct level of deep involvement required to make it effective (Van der Hart, 1983). While the use of a prescribed ritual does not require the use of hypnosis, the ritual that speaks symbolically to the client's therapeutic issue often produces a trance-like state in the doing.

THE RITUAL OF PURIFICATION

I suggested to Mrs. Adrian that she close her eyes again, breathe regularly and deeply, and relax more and more fully. I then outlined the ritual task for her. What was needed was to say goodbye to Rolland once and forever, I explained. She was to find a photograph of him (she did not have any, but her sister did) and place it on a table between two burning candles. Using the ritual prescription described by Van der Hart (1983) she was to write a letter to Rolland in which she would express all the hate and venom that she had for him in her heart. She was to tell him how many problems Dan had had, and how confusing it was for her to deal with Lydia's rape. She was to say how he had broken her parent's trust in him and anything else that she had to express, good or bad, that came into her head. When this was over she could burn the letter, tear it up, bury it, or bring it into me to decide what to do with it. Since Rolland was still alive, the question of mailing it to him was not irrelevant, but she should discuss it with me first. After writing the letter she was to take a shower and use lots of soap, washing off all the "filth" from the experience. She would then finally feel clean again in a new way, I suggested.

It took 3 hours for Mrs. Adrian to write the letter to Rolland, and she made an audiocassette while she wrote, talking and writing simultaneously. She burned the letter after reading it over three times, and, after prying the cassette apart, she pulled the tape into long strands and burned them as well.

"At first, I felt silly," she said, "it was difficult to get started writing. But soon the words and the feelings began to flow, and before I knew it 3 hours were gone."

Once she burned the tape she took the picture and looking at it said, "Rolland, you bastard, you will never bother my life again. Never!" and she burned that picture as well.

"I don't know what to tell my sister about the picture," she laughed, "but I just had to burn it too."

Once the burning was done, she got into the bathtub and soaked in a bubblebath for over an hour.

"Then I went into the shower," she said, "and I scrubbed and scrubbed. In some places on my head and back I almost made myself raw, but it was a good kind of pain, if you know what I mean. When I got out and dried off I felt really clean, I can't describe it. I mean clean like I hadn't been in years. As I walked into my bedroom I passed my mirror and I looked at myself and said, 'You know, Lillian, you're not a bad-looking woman.'"

Later that afternoon she cooked a fancy meal for her family and used the best linen and silverware on the table.

"I wanted to share the goodness with them," she said, "but I didn't tell them what had happened. I don't know if I will ever tell Frank that I was raped; probably, but I don't know. Anyway, that night I called my mother and asked why she never gave me any sex education. She told me—I never knew this—that she had known that night I came home from Rolland that something had happened, but she didn't know how to talk about it. Sex wasn't discussed in our family. I was really angry when I heard that, I guess I read her the riot act. Anyway, we cleared the air. That was Thursday night, the same day I left your office."

"Oh, and guess what else," she said, although I could hardly absorb any other revelations from her ritual, "Frank and I made love on Saturday afternoon and he held me and cuddled me like he never did before. He usually is pretty much businesslike about sex, you know, but he was so sweet, and he caressed my face and held me afterwards. And guess what, I had my first orgasm ever!" (I had not known Mrs. Adrian had been nonorgasmic until this moment.)

TREATMENT OUTCOME

Dan was not convicted of rape because Lydia had trumped up the charges, but the experience shook him to the core. He was vulnerable because of his prior history of using others. His schoolwork improved enormously, and his drug use and alcohol use ceased altogether. He then knew that behaviors, not words, are what would convince his family of his love and concern for them. Still, we can hardly claim a successful treatment outcome in Dan's case. Only time will tell whether his late-developing conscience will prevail. His mother and father have a much different relationship, however. Their sex life is much more loving and egalitarian, as are the rest of their interactions. They are more individuals, less enmeshed and less driven together by their past deprivations. Mr. Adrian trusts that his wife loves him, because she is independent enough to leave him and chooses to stay and love him even more. Mrs. Adrian knows she can be loving, demanding, and rational. She knows she is an individual, separate from her husband, from her son (she is no longer jealous of her father's attention to him instead of to her) from Lydia, and from her own parents. Mr. and Mrs. Adrian are consistent in their discipline of Dan and his sister, Julie. They won't make the same mistakes with her. The use of the family approach affected the system beyond the presenting problem of the identified patient.

Hypnosis was used in the family treatment at points where important awarenesses could not be (or, at least, had not yet been) discovered because of unconscious resistances. It was performed formally with the husband present and was used with the wife alone. There is no question in my mind, because of Lillian's vivid description of the profound quality of her experience, that she was also in a trance state when she performed her ritual of purification and leave-taking. We might even speak here of self-hypnosis or of the ritual performance as a posthypnotic suggestion for induction. Of course she was an excellent hypnotic subject, who needed little training to go deeply into her past experiences.

The overall case is an apt example, I believe, of how hypnosis integrated with therapy and drawing upon already established, learned but unconscious family connections can be a powerful additional technique in the armamentarium of the family therapist.

REFERENCES

Lange, A., & Van der Hart, O. *Directive family therapy*. New York: Brunner/Mazel, 1983.

Minuchin, S., & Fishman, H. C. *Family therapy techniques*. Cambridge, MA: Harvard University Press, 1981.

Sargent, G. Burial at sea. In O. Van der Hart (Ed.), *Leave taking rituals in psychotherapy*. New York: Irvington, in press. (A translation from the Dutch of Sargent, G., Een begrafenis aan zee. In O. Van der Hart (Ed.), *Afscheidsrituelen in psychotherapie*. Baarn, The Netherlands: Ambo, 1981.)

Van der Hart, O. *Rituals in psychotherapy: Transition and continuity*. New York: Irvington, 1983.

III
HABIT CONTROL

The control and elimination of objectionable habits represents one of the more problematic aspects of hypnotherapy. All practitioners have experienced clients who wanted to "be hypnotized" in order to stop smoking or lose weight. Such habits have proved to be extremely resistant to change by psychological interventions, and hypnosis has often been disappointingly ineffective in modifying such entrenched habits. Experience has shown that level of motivation is a better indicator of an ultimately successful outcome than is the type of intervention used. It has been our experience that many, perhaps most, clients who want to "be hypnotized" to overcome such habits generally do not want to overcome the problem, they "want to want to" overcome it. In other words, they are hoping that the therapist will be able to provide an intervention that will eliminate the desire and increase the motivation with no effort on their part!

It should therefore be no surprise that this section does not include chapters on many of the more common habit problems. Instead, some less common habits such as enuresis are discussed. Smoking is covered, however, in the context of substance abuse.

In Chapter 9 Judith B. Strauss and Clorinda G. Margolis describe one successful case of smoking cessation and briefly discuss the utility of hypnosis in the treatment of drug and alcohol abuse. Significantly, their successful smoking case involves a multifaceted treatment plan, including interpersonal interaction, motivational enhancement, age regression, and follow-up contact. The latter intervention may be especially important, as it is increasingly recognized that ongoing support is of critical importance in enabling individuals to maintain their treatment gains in cases of long-term habits.

The two cases involving hypnotherapy in the treatment of adolescent enuresis are interesting in that they both involve a removed father in addition to disturbed mother–son relations, with family therapy used as an adjunct to hypnotherapy. However, each case approaches the treatment of enuretic behavior from a very different point of view.

Bennett G. Braun describes enuretic treatment from a psychodynamic perspective, in which understanding of the origin of the problem behavior is important to final resolution. Hypnotherapy involved inculcating in the client feelings of control and coping ability. There are strong indications of the transmission of learned maladaptive behavior patterns across generations. Therapy with an additional family member was done in order to make it easier for the child to give up his enuresis by removing the mother's overprotective control.

Many of the same themes appear in E. Thomas Dowd's chapter, in particular the overprotective mother, the removed father, a passive–aggressive behavior pattern in the client, and disturbed mother–male child relations. However, Dowd is much less concerned with understanding the etiology of the problem behavior and operates more in the present. In addition, his approach involves behavioral structuring and more indirect hypnotic induction (although a direct instruction was in one instance more useful than an indirect one). Both cases illustrate the likely family-oriented nature of enuretic behavior and the desirability of incorporating elements of family therapy into the treatment plan.

9
HYPNOSIS WITH SUBSTANCE ABUSERS

Judith B. Strauss
Clorinda G. Margolis

Hypnosis has been used to help patients reduce or eliminate drug abuse, including abuse of tobacco, alcohol, barbituates, opioids, amphetamines, and cannabis. Successful hypnotic treatment of smoking cases has been documented most carefully, and by and large, tobacco smoking represents the least difficult substance disorder problem to treat. The case we are presenting is a smoking case. Hypnotic intervention with alcohol and drug abusers will be discussed in the last section of the chapter, where treatment of nicotine addiction as a paradigm case of substance abuse must be questioned.

Although more attention has been paid to hypnotherapy for smoking, the overall results are equivocal.

HYPNOSIS AND TOBACCO DEPENDENCE

Much more attention has been paid to hypnotherapy for smoking than for other addictive substances. Holroyd (1980) reviewed 17 studies conducted from 1970–1979 and evaluated them in terms of long-term abstinence, a measure of the effectiveness of the treatment. It seems apparent from that review that hypnosis for smoking is most effective when there are several hours of treatment, interpersonal interaction, personalized suggestions that trade on patients' motivations, and where there is additional counseling or contact. She concludes that when these conditions are met, 55% to more than 66% of smokers remain abstinent for at least 6 months. Long-term abstinence results are impressive in a study that used a group treatment modality but emphasized individual patient involvement (Kline, 1970). Sixty patients were asked not to smoke for 24 hours prior to treatment and

Judith B. Strauss. Private Practice, Philadelphia, Pennsylvania.
Clorinda G. Margolis. Private Practice, Philadelphia, Pennsylvania.

then participated in a 12-hour marathon session in groups of 10 each. Every participant was individually hypnotized until eventually the entire group was in trance. They were made aware of feelings associated with smoking deprivation and alternately had periods of deep relaxation induced. At a 1-year follow-up, 88% of the patients had not resumed smoking.

Herbert and David Spiegel (1978) are well known for their short-term treatment strategies in using hypnosis for cigarette smoking. Initially, a brief clinical history is taken, which includes the number of years smoking, the average number of cigarettes smoked, who else in the household smokes, any successful cessation in the past, physical symptoms if any, and the events leading to the decision to look for help at this time. The patient is taught an exercise that must be repeated a minimum of 10 times a day. The exercise is composed of a self-hypnosis procedure and what the authors call the critical points.

1. For your body, not for you, for your body, smoking is a poison.
2. You need your body to live.
3. You owe your body this respect and protection.

The follow-up data revealed that only 20% of the sample of 615 were not smoking 6 months after the single session.

Wadden and Anderton (1982) in their review of a number of studies involving hypnotherapy and smoking conclude that hypnosis does not offer a more unique strategy for smoking cessation than other treatment efforts.

TREATMENT PLAN FOR SMOKING DEPENDENCE

This case is typical of the successful cases that we see for hypnosis. It is interesting to note that our treatment plan consists of measures that Holroyd (1980), in her analysis and evaluation, stated were most effective in producing abstinence. Several hours of treatment, interpersonal interaction, individualized suggestions, and additional counseling suggest positive therapeutic outcomes.

Our first session is a detailed initial interview rather than simply a brief smoking history. This is important in terms of maximizing the individual life experiences of the patient and determining whether this is the right time to stop smoking. For example, when someone is about to take comprehensive or professional examinations or is initiating divorce proceedings would probably not be the best time to begin treatment. We encourage the patient to prove to us that he or she is ready to stop. In fact, the patient must convince us that this is the right time. At this first session, behavioral techniques are suggested that will be used the 1st week. As many smoking rituals as possible should be changed—smoking with coffee, after meals, with alcohol, in the car, at the desk, and so on. The patient should immediately switch to a less favored brand of cigarette.

The second session is the key session—a double session in which the patient will be hypnotized several times and not smoke again.

The third session is basically a follow-up and reinforcement session. There is an additional session in 1 month and also 6 months later.

CASE STUDY

First Session: Initial Interview

The patient, Mr. B, a 50-year-old white male, was referred by his family physician, who had been encouraging him to stop smoking because of a chronic sinus condition. Mr. B had two grown children who lived away from home, and with whom he maintained a close relationship. Mr. B had been adopted 1 month after birth, and for the first 5 years of his life he had been frequently hospitalized because of allergy and sinus problems. Because of this condition, his family moved to Arizona. As a young man, Mr. B began his career with a major corporation that required him to move about the country. His father, who lived in Florida, had been a heavy smoker, but because of health reasons, had not smoked for the past 10 years. His mother had never smoked. Mr. B began smoking as a teenager behind his parents' back and was smoking two packs a day at the time of the initial interview.

He considered his job very demanding and stressful but identified no major or unusual problems. He stated that he drank a lot of coffee at work, about an average of 15 cups, always accompanied by cigarettes. As many of his colleagues had stopped smoking, Mr. B was embarrassed by his smoking behavior and uneasy about smoking in meetings. When he traveled, he no longer sat in the smoking section. He normally had a martini for lunch and drank a few beers at home in the evening. He had not had much exercise in the past 3 years, and though he used to jog, he stopped because he became short of breath so quickly.

He stopped smoking about 15 years ago for about 2 years, but started again at a cocktail party. His wife of 27 years was a moderate smoker who had no plans to stop.

There were marital problems several years ago based primarily around their frequent moves. The couple had brief marital counseling, which improved their relationship.

Mr. B was concerned about going to the best hypnosis practitioner—the best providing the most effective treatment. He was worried that he might not be hypnotizable. Additional historical material was gathered around his childhood, and some happy experiences were elicited.

Careful questioning revealed no overt psychopathology; he appeared to be a well-functioning man in control of and generally pleased with his life. At the end of the session, he agreed to change many smoking habits. For example, he was to switch to a mentholated brand, not smoke when he drank coffee or with his lunchtime martini or evening beers, not smoke when he spoke on the telephone, and give up the after-meal cigarette. The patient was not instructed to cut down on his smoking behavior, but to change it.

Second Session

When the patient arrived for this double session, he appeared tense, agitated, and distracted. Mr. B said, "I've been bad. I didn't try hard enough. I guess I should get a D, because I only tried the first day. I couldn't separate coffee and cigarettes. I really thought it would be easier than this to change my habits." Together we agreed not to hypnotize him that day and used only a single session to explore his resistance and to question whether this was the right time for him to stop smoking. The behavioral changes were again discussed, and specific suggestions were made. For example, if he drank coffee in his office he could not have a cigarette, but he could have tea with a cigarette.

Third Session: Double Session

Mr B arrived early for his appointment and appeared to be elated and in a buoyant mood. "I give myself an A+ this week," he said. He had been able to give up drinking coffee in his office, and he no longer carried cigarettes in his pocket. The patient claimed to be at a 90% motivation level. "I'm a good problem solver at work," he said. "I ought to be able to solve this easily."

Given his present motivation, hypnosis was induced four times. The first induction was an eye fixation technique. A purpose of the initial hypnotic induction was to help him learn to become a good hypnotic subject and to give us information about helping him become a good subject. We wanted to see how comfortable he could become, how he responded to hypnotic suggestions, and note his breathing, facial pallor, and peripheral changes in vision. The patient was told to stare at something on the wall, to notice his eyes becoming tired, and to let his eyes close when they became heavy. As his eyes closed, he might feel himself becoming very relaxed. The eye fixation induction took a very long time; he appeared tense, moved slightly in the chair several times, and showed uneven breathing. Eventually, Mr. B closed his eyes, his body quieted, his breathing slowed, and he seemed to be in a mild hypnotic trance. Ego-strengthening and motivational suggestions were given. One suggestion was that he was learning to become a good hypnotic subject in order to achieve his goals, that his problem-solving skills were evident, and that he was usually able to succeed at what he tried. We then alerted him by counting to 10. The patient volunteered that during trance his body first felt numb all over and then began to feel heavy. He felt very relaxed. His report of his first induction indicated to us that he had been able to experience a hypnotic trance. He was amazed at how relaxed he had become and was enthusiastic about trying this experience again.

The material to be used next was gathered from the initial interview and his early history. Mr. B had had fond memories of his childhood. His favorite pastime had been playing ball, and he had been outdoors at every opportunity. In the summer he and his friends would gather at a corner near a field. They would play ball and "kick the can" until their parents would drag them indoors for the night. "I wanted to rush out at every possible chance to be with my friends," he had said. Mr. B felt close to his family and had told how his mother had been famous in their neighborhood for her outstanding cooking. He himself couldn't wait to look in the various pots on the stove when he arrived home from school to see what was being prepared for dinner.

The second induction used a hand levitation technique. Mr. B closed his eyes and was told to feel sensations of lightness in his right hand. When it was obvious, because of slight movements in his fingers, that he was experiencing some lightness, he was told to imagine a balloon tied to his wrist gently moving and pulling upward. His hand raised about 3 inches and remained cataleptic. He appeared to be in a hypnotic trance, so age regression to his boyhood was suggested. This took him to a time before he was smoking and when cigarettes had no meaning to him. During the initial interview, Mr. B had told us that he used a cigarette to signal himself to stop eating at the end of his meal. When we suggested that he return to a happy time during his childhood, he chose age 9, when he was living in the southwest. Using his own descriptions and words, we suggested he was playing with his friends and then going home to dinner. Once inside, he smelled the aromas of various delicacies that his mother had prepared. However, after gobbling his food his memory of fidgeting in his chair, anxious to rejoin his playmates, was vivid. We suggested that he was hungry and that the food was delicious. He felt happy being with his family. Outside he heard the cries and shouts of other children who had luckily been released from their dinner tables. His concentration was focused on making a speedy getaway himself. He didn't need a cigarette then to signal the end of the meal. He reported how funny it sounded when the idea of ending the meal with a cigarette was mentioned. The patient was extremely impressed with both the hand levitation and the age regression. The hand levitation seemed to give him the proof and assurance that he had been really hypnotized, and the age regression allowed him to recapture pleasant memories, moods, and feelings.

The third hypnotic trance was to reinforce his reasons for wanting to stop smoking. The reasons were his embarrassment at business meetings, because most people in his company do not smoke; his fear of cigarettes ruling him; his desire to have a strong, healthy body and feel fit enough to resume an exercise program; and his admiration for his father who had given up cigarettes 10 years earlier. We used a coin technique as an induction. The patient extended his hand palm upward, and a coin was placed on the edge of his palm. He was told that with each count the hand would turn a little until the coin fell off, his eyes would close, and he would become completely relaxed, arms resting at his side. The coin fell off at the count of 90. We then reinforced and reflected Mr. B's resolve to stop smoking, reminding him of his discomfort at meetings, his fear that "a little white thing" was stronger than him, the wonderful way it feels to be able to run and not get out of breath, and how successful his father had been in conquering his lifelong cigarette dependence.

In the fourth and final hypnotic experience for this session, Mr. B was taught autohypnosis. He was asked to choose one of the inductions and hypnotize himself. He chose the hand levitation. When in trance, we did a life progression. This involved activities that he would participate in during the next week as a nonsmoker. Life progression is similar to behavioral rehearsal but includes suggestions for improved sense of smell, taste, and sensory awareness. Specifically, we traced life's events step by step.

"You waken a nonsmoker. You get up in the morning and brush your teeth. Your mouth feels scrubbed and fresh and clean. You get dressed and sit down to breakfast and enjoy the taste of food. As a nonsmoker, everything has a better taste. The orange juice is tart and delicious, the cereal crisp and crunchy. You get in your car and open the window. The fresh air feels good on your skin and smells good as you drive to work. You arrive at your office and you're a nonsmoker. You sit at your desk and begin to review some reports that you have written, the telephone rings, you answer it, and you do not smoke. When you go to your morning meeting, it feels good not to be smoking. The papers you are holding feel crisp in your hands. You smell your fingers and they have a pleasant smell. You meet some of your associates and go out to lunch as a nonsmoker."

The life progression was continued to complete the day-long activities and ended with:

"When you go to sleep tonight, all of these suggestions will be reinforced, and when you awaken tomorrow, you will be aware of being a nonsmoker."

Fourth Session

At the fourth session Mr B was jubilant, and he gleefully expressed these thoughts: "I feel as if a huge weight has been lifted off of my chest. One of the most dramatic changes for me is the sense of smell. I found that I didn't have to use my nose spray for my sinuses at all. I could actually feel my sinuses draining. When I got home last week, I saw my smoking gear and felt as if it belonged to someone else. I knew then that the smoking person was gone, and that there wouldn't be any conflict anymore. The sense of smell has been incredible. I could actually smell honeysuckle as I was running, and the way the city smells during a light rain is unbelievable." However, he was worried that he wouldn't be able to sustain this, and he recognized his need for a cigarette. There were times during the week that he felt incomplete, as though part of him were missing. He was ambivalent about cigarettes because they smelled good when they were lit and smelled bad when they were put out in the ashtray. In general, Mr. B felt very good. He hadn't smoked all week and was running a mile every evening. He'd had a dream the other night that he had a cigarette. He awoke scared to death that it wasn't a dream. In this session we did a relaxation induction and incorporated suggestions for self-hypnosis. The relaxation induction was fairly standard. However, this particular one had the patient experiencing a wave of relaxation moving slowly down his body and releasing tension. Interwoven were suggestions to the effect that just as Mr. B had learned to hit a ball, had learned to run, one foot in front of the other, he would learn to hypnotize himself. It was suggested that each time he attempted autohypnosis, he would become increasingly relaxed. The patient reported "I feel more confident and more relaxed than I have ever felt before in my life, the tension just melted away." Mr. B expressed the fact that he had experienced some uneasiness in his body that had felt like withdrawal, but he believed that he would not smoke again. He left feeling alert and in control.

The final session was a half-session follow-up and was held 1 month later. Mr. B had had his teeth cleaned. He was enjoying food because it tasted so much better. However, he had not gained weight. He was running a mile in less than 10 minutes. He admitted that there still were difficult times when he wanted a cigarette, but these were not severe and they were controllable.

At his 6-month half-session check-up, he was still astounded by his success. "I feel good about myself. This is getting easier all the time. My awareness has also improved. I actually can't believe that I've done it." We asked him to call in 6 months to let us know how he was doing.

HYPNOSIS AND DRUG ABUSE

It has been within the last few years that hypnosis was first applied as a therapy in the treatment of drug abuse. Bourne (1975) feels that hypnosis allows the patient to go back to the years before the use of drugs was acquired and to relearn behavioral patterns. Hypnosis may be used in aversive conditioning, as a way of substitute gratification, anxiety reduction, and for systematic desensitization. In an individual case study, Diment (1981) focused primarily on inducing relaxation in hypnosis with a 59-year-old widow dependent on barbituates. The approach taken, gradual reduction in medication paired with deep relaxation training, resulted in a reduction of her daily barbituate level from 600 mg to an average of 150 mg per night. Lamanno (1975) found that there were positive indicators as to the appropriateness of hypnoanalytic suggestion in the rehabilitation of the drug addict. In other studies (Greer, 1975) hypnoaversive techniques were effective in decreasing drug taking behavior of narcotics abusers, and Manganiello (1981) found that hypnotherapy was effective in the treatment of methadone addicts. The group that received hypnotherapy achieved a significantly reduced methadone dose level, had less incidence of illicit drug use as a group, and suffered less discomfort.

HYPNOSIS AND ALCOHOL ABUSE

Surprisingly, alcohol abuse has received the least attention in hypnotherapy studies. Wadden and Penrod (1981) summarized the research on the hypnotic treatment of alcoholism appearing since 1964 and concluded that the extent of hypnosis's effectiveness in treating alcoholism has not been determined. They feel that positive results must be viewed with caution because of methodological shortcomings. They suggest that future investigators systematically examine the relationship between hypnotic susceptibility and therapeutic outcome. They also propose several steps that could be undertaken in treatment. Relaxation training may alleviate the severe anxiety that accompanies alcohol withdrawal. Hypnosis may then be used to facilitate the understanding of the events that maintain the problem drinking. Lastly, coping imagery and modeling of adaptive behaviors may be instituted.

Katz (1980) agrees that hypnotic approaches can be used in a variety of ways to enhance treatment of alcohol abuse. He mentions the use of hypnotic suggestions for aversion to alcohol, confidence building, and amnesia for past pleasure with alcohol. The following are among the most successful of the results reported.

Miller (1976) used a modified hypnoaversive technique in which the suggestion was made that patients would reexperience the worst hangover of their lives if they resumed drinking. This program was instituted on a weekly basis lasting from 4 to 6 months and then whenever needed. More than 60% of the individuals treated were abstinent 1 year later. Gabrynowicz (1977) included hypnotherapy with transactional analysis, group support, cognitive restructuring, and problem solving. He found that 76% of the 25 patients were abstinent when contacted 9–32 months after treatment.

DISCUSSION

Since prehistoric time, people have used central nervous system intoxicants to alter states of consciousness, relieve physical or mental pain, and produce euphoria. Although the most popular drug has been nicotine (Davison & Neale, 1978), alcohol, opium, and cannabis have been universally used. In contemporary times, synthetic drugs like barbituates and amphetamines have become available. Only when drugs produce behavior unacceptable to the community or cause serious health problems to those who use them does the problem of substance abuse arise and the need for treatment is identified. Because the abuse of any of the drugs is assumed, at least initially, to be under the voluntary control of users, abuse is learned (Wadden & Anderton, 1982). Whether abuse or addiction is best understood as an impulse disorder (Spiegel & Spiegel, 1978) or as neurotic symptoms (LeCron & Bordeaux, 1949), we think about substance abuse as pathological dependence and a habit. Habits can be altered by hypnotic intervention depending upon the motivation of the patient and the appropriateness of the hypnotherapeutic work engaged in by both the hypnotherapist and patient. The extent of pathology present in any patient can easily influence outcome and may explain successful treatment of smoking cases and the paucity of reported successes in other substance abuse cases. We have found that hypnosis as medical treatment has the advantages of shortening the time needed to establish a therapeutic relationship, helping in ego building, benefiting the learning of relaxation techniques, increasing suggestibility, and promoting behavioral methods such as aversive conditioning.

We have been successful in achieving cessation of smoking behavior in our patients. One indicator of a positive outcome is patient motivation. We believe that hypnotherapy can enhance motivation but it cannot create it. We will not begin to hypnotize a patient unless we are convinced that he or she is motivated. Positive expectations are also extremely important. Mr. B, the patient in the case described, responded well to hypnosis although the initial induction required more time than usual. He believed it to be important "to be seeing one of the best" practitioners of hypnotherapy. His elation on his success at being able to be hypnotized certainly had a positive therapeutic effect.

The importance of individualizing or tailoring the hypnotherapy experience cannot be overemphasized. It is the knowledge of intimate details that often precedes a successful experience. For example, in Mr. B's case, we were able to utilize his childhood experiences creatively during the age regression. Happy childhood memories and vivid recollections of sensory experiences formed a positive anchor.

The life progression technique is most effective when it is done in depth and in as detailed a way as possible. For Mr. B, the sense of smell was keen and vivid. The olfactory senses had special meaning for him. In the life progression, smell was used as the other senses would be. This is bound to vary from patient to patient.

We saw Mr. B five times. There are patients who would benefit from lengthier treatments and should be seen more often if it is indicated by their excessive anxiety. We recommend some changes when the model is applied to alcohol and drug abuse. We feel that lengthier treatment is indicated and that these patients should initially be in an intensive treatment program while going through withdrawal and detoxification.

Tobacco dependence and hypnotherapy has received more attention in the literature than either drug or alcohol abuse in conjunction with hypnotherapy. Perhaps this is because it is easier to obtain a population to work with, and this population may tend to remain available for the duration of the study. It should be noted, however, that we do get conflicting results in the research that has been done, which makes it difficult to assess the efficacy of using hypnotherapy with the addictions. On the other hand, we have had successful results when certain guidelines have been followed. We concur with Wadden and Anderton (1982) that research in clinical hypnosis is in its infancy and should be pursued with increased vigor.

REFERENCES

Bourne, P. Non-pharmacological approaches to the treatment of drug abuse. *American Journal of Chinese Medicine*, 1975, *3*, 234–244.

Davison, G., & Neale, J. *Abnormal psychology: An experimental clinical approach*. New York: Wiley, 1978.

Diment, A. A use of hypnosis in a case of barbituate dependence. *Australian Journal of Clinical and Experimental Hypnosis*, 1981, *9*(2), 104–105.

Gabrynowicz, J. Hypnosis in a treatment programme for alcoholism. *Medical Journal of Australia*, 1977, *64*, 643–656.

Greer, E. *The use of a hypnoaversive technique with narcotics dependence*. Unpublished doctoral dissertation, University of Tennessee, 1975.

Holroyd, J. Hypnosis treatment for smoking: An evaluative review. *International Journal of Clinical and Experimental Hypnosis*, 1980, *28*, 341–357.

Katz, N. Hypnosis and the addictions: A critical review. *Addictive Behaviors*, 1980, *5*(1), 41–47.

Kline, M. The use of extended group hypnotherapy sessions in controlling cigarette habituation. *International Journal of Clinical and Experimental Hypnosis*, 1970, *18*, 270–282.

Lamanno, E. *Hypnosis in the psychodynamic appraisal and rehabilitation of the heroin addict: A case report*. Unpublished doctoral dissertation, United States International University, 1975.

LeCron, L., & Bordeaux, J. *Hypnotism today*. New York: Grune & Stratton, 1949.

Manganiello, A. *A comparative study of hypnotherapy and psychotherapy in the treatment of methadone addicts*. Unpublished doctoral dissertation, University of San Francisco, 1981.

Miller, M. Hypnoaversion treatment in alcoholism, nicotinism, and weight control. *Journal of the National Medical Association*. 1976, *68*, 129–130.

Spiegel, H., & Spiegel, D. *Trance and treatment: Clinical uses of hypnosis*. New York: Basic Books, 1978.

Wadden, T., & Anderton, C. The clinical use of hypnosis. *Psychological Bulletin*, 1982, *91*, 215–243.

Wadden, T., & Penrod, J. Hypnosis in the treatment of alcoholism: A review. *American Journal of Clinical Hypnosis*, 1981, *24*, 41–47.

10
CONJOINT HYPNOTHERAPY OF AN ENURETIC CHILD AND A POLYPHOBIC MOTHER

Bennett G. Braun

PRESENTATION OF CASES AND HYPNOTHERAPY

Michael K, an 11-year-old boy, presented with his mother, father, and 15-year-old brother. During the first interview the family presented as a "united front" (Kramer, 1980), with Michael being the designated patient because of his enuresis. During this session Michael was embarrassed, quiet, and retiring.

It was quite obvious that there was an extreme competitive relationship between the two brothers (sibling rivalry). For example, the older brother would intentionally use long words. Michael had to ask what they meant or would feel embarrassed and left out. The brother also teased Michael about the enuresis.

The father (Mr. K) was basically quiet and would only respond to questions asked. He was approximately 32 years old, a steelworker, and had dropped out of school at the end of the eighth grade.

The mother (Mrs. K) carried the conversation. She had finished eighth grade before terminating school in order to go to work. She ran her own business as a dog obedience trainer and poodle clipper and worked out of her home. Mrs. K had a lot of underlying anger, but it was not expressed except as concern for Michael and a desire to help him get well.

Both parents appeared much more intelligent than their formal education would indicate. Mother and father both enjoyed reading and had a very good vocabulary. There appeared to be an underlying problem between the parents that could not be dealt with during the course of therapy.

Michael's enuresis was discussed with the whole family during the first session, and it was thought that Michael had a secondary enuresis. However, the onset of the enuresis was unknown by any family member. All

Bennett G. Braun. Dissociative Disorders Program, Rush–Presbyterian–St. Luke's Medical Center, Rush University, Chicago, Illinois.

they could say was that it had started several years ago, and he had been wetting 7 nights a week since then. They had tried medication, including imipramine. He was made to take care of his own sheets, including washing them and remaking his bed. It was agreed that they would return the following week to begin weekly visits.

At the second session mother came in and reported that there had been no changes, that he was still wetting his bed 7 days a week. She reported that the whole family would come back if necessary, though they preferred not to since it was Michael's problem.

Attempts to communicate with Michael at the beginning of the session were basically unsuccessful as he was very anxious, somewhat agitated, and quiet. He would not converse; rather he would answer questions with a yes, no, or a shake of the head. I decided to use hypnosis as a means of helping him relax. I introduced the hypnosis by asking him if he would like to relax and be more comfortable, and if he would be willing to cooperate in a small experiment. After finding out that hypnosis had nothing to do with hypodermic needles, he agreed.

A trance was induced via progressive relaxation and counting backward from three to one. He was informed that he would be able to speak while relaxed in trance.

Since he was so frightened, a fractionation technique of helping him into and bringing him out of trance was used. Several different techniques were used for induction and deepening; they included eye closure, hand levitation, and reverse hand levitation (starting with hands up and having them get heavier). When he entered a light state of trance, he was brought out to see that "all was well." Each induction took him a bit deeper. In this way, he was introduced to the idea of hypnosis.

In the next session trance was easier to achieve. I asked him if he liked to watch television. He said yes, and I asked him what his favorite TV show was. He answered "Gilligan's Island." So as a deepening technique, I asked him to visualize a television set on which he would see "Gilligan's Island" and would be able to enjoy the program and relax even deeper. When questioned as to what was happening on "Gilligan's Island," he reported that Gilligan was being chased into the water by a monster. This experience was a major factor in building rapport with him and a turning point in therapy.

Michael turned out to be a good hypnotic subject. In the succeeding session, after helping him relax, I had him view the television set and watch another episode of "Gilligan's Island" to deepen the trance. I next suggested to him that we would have a channel on this television set that was hooked into our own private TV station. With this channel we would watch a boy Michael's age go through his day, because we had a special camera that could follow the boy around. Michael was instructed to tell me what he saw on the TV set. This was, in essence, the beginning of a technique of uncovering information about Michael, while allowing him temporarily to disown it.

We watched the boy go to school. It was noted that "the boy" read too fast and made mistakes; he was in the middle reading group. (Michael was also in this middle reading group.) This indicated Michael's perfectionism, and the concept was reinforced later in the session when he reported he won a spelling bee. Over the next few sessions, I gave Michael suggestions that he could like himself and would be more kind to himself. (This indirectly dealt with his perfectionism. His mother reported that he could take criticism better.)

The boy was observed to come home from school. He played outside and then had dinner. Michael made a special point of saying that the boy's parents argued a lot, especially at dinner time. He did some homework, had a coke, and went to bed.

I suggested that the camera would be set by the bed and could observe him through the night. I called off times from 9:30, when he went to bed, to 11:00 and we watched the boy fall asleep. As I counted off the hours, he would describe what the boy was doing: "He's sleeping, he's rolling over, he's dreaming," and so on. He would not tell me the dreams. He abruptly moved in his chair when I said "2 a.m." I asked him what happened, and he said that the boy wet his bed. "After that," he said, "he rolled over a bit and then fell comfortably asleep." He continued through the night with nothing else unusual happening except that the boy woke up, and his brother teased him about wetting his bed while he changed his sheets (a parallel to reality).

After a couple of weeks, more rapport building, and information gathering, we then allowed the boy to become Michael. We then had the special camera follow *him* through the day: going to school, doing well at school, returning home, having his parents argue and go out for the evening, being teased by his brother, his drinking a 16-ounce Coke and going to bed. Again at 2 a.m. he bolted in his chair and said that he had wet. I suggested to his parents that he not be allowed to have liquids after 6:30 p.m. This had only a minimal effect: a rare dry night.

Later I made the association between the nocturnal fluid intake and "Gilligan's Island." I asked him if Gilligan was safe when he ran into the water. He replied, "Yes." It appeared that the enuresis was related in some way to his safety. We began to investigate why he needed the "ammunition."

Next I started having his parents wake him at about midnight to take him to the bathroom to urinate. This resulted in an occasional dry night, which was appropriately praised, but the reinforcement appeared to have no particular effect in maintaining dry nights.

Increasing resistance to entering trance was encountered around times when he was ambivalent about therapy (including growing up, individuation, and aggression). Resistance also occurred prior to my going on vacation. Perhaps he saw my vacation as abandonment of him to his mother as his passive father had done. However, once trance was achieved, he could work well. Automatic writing was used to discover how he felt about being dry and to see if there was any unconscious resistance. He wrote, "I am thinking about a dry night. I wish I had all dry nights." This was appropriately reinforced both in and out of trance.

Approximately 3 months into the case, I decided to use a fantasy technique (Braun, 1984) to further investigate the psychodynamics of the enuresis. I hypnotized Michael and suggested that he would learn something about the enuresis. No attempt was made to program what he would learn, merely that he would learn something.

Trance was induced by a previously taught cue of counting backward from five to one and was deepened by color imagery. The patient was instructed to see a series of colors starting with a black area that contained a growing white spot. This grew until he had a white area surrounded by black in the center of which there was a red spot that was growing, and so on. This was done to help break the patient's grounding in reality, to decrease defensiveness, and to heighten the ability to respond to the fantasy.

Next I suggested that the colors would swirl together, mix, and fall away so as to leave him in front of a flight of 10 stairs. He would ascend into a room in which he would learn something about his enuresis. As he went up the stairs, I started to give mild strengthening suggestions; however, with each stair that he climbed, he became visibly more anxious. On the fifth stair, he started to exhibit some movement in the chair, which appeared to be pelvic thrusting. I stopped him and asked what was happening. He said that he was afraid to go into the room. When asked why he was afraid, he responded, "Because there's a monster in the room." I suggested that he continue, he would be able to handle whatever he found in the room, and I would be available to help him. He went up the sixth stair while I gave strengthening suggestions and on up to the seventh stair, the eighth stair; at the ninth stair he started shaking so much that we stopped. I gave him suggestions about his increasing his size and strength, and I reassured him that he could handle whatever he found behind the door. Finally, he decided to go up the 10 stairs and enter the room. He opened the door and entered the room. At this point his movements became quite noticeable, and his face blanched. He became more scared and started the equivalent of writhing in the chair. I asked him what was happening, and he said that he was backing up and the monster was coming after him. At this point he appeared even more shaken, and being afraid he might wet my chair, I just hollered out, "Stop!" He stopped moving and I asked him what was happening. He said, "I stopped and the monster stopped." I said,

"Good. That shows that you have more power than he does. Go toward him. Get him." He did. I asked him what was happening, and he reported that the monster was backing up. At this point he appeared calmer, so I asked him what the monster looked like. He reported that the monster was very tall, had four red eyes, eight legs, and was green.

I then reassured him of his strength and encouraged him to keep after the monster. (At this point the technique was aimed at assertiveness and mastery.) He reported that he was doing so and the monster was backing up. Suddenly he became quite noticeably relaxed, and the color returned to his face. I asked him what happened, and he replied that the monster had fallen out of the window. I suggested that he look out the window and tell me what he saw. He said that the monster was lying still and that his eyes were black. I interpreted this to him as "the monster has died."

Next I suggested that he go down the stairs, go to the monster, and see what would happen. He went down the 10 stairs and out a doorway, turned to his left, and walked over to the monster that was lying underneath the window. I asked him what was happening, and he said that the monster was not moving, but he again looked anxious. I gave calming and strengthening suggestions. I had him go over and touch the monster. He did and when asked what the monster felt like, he reported that the monster felt cold, wet, and rubbery (perhaps like the rubber sheet that covered his mattress).

I proposed to him that it would be a good idea to dig a hole and bury the monster. He agreed, so I told him to look to his right and against the wall he would find a shovel and a pickax with which he could dig this hole. After a bit of work he said that the hole was completed. He "pushed" the monster into the hole and covered it up. He appeared quite relaxed and pleased with himself when he left the office.

At the following session his mother reported that he had had 2 dry nights during the week. He indicated that he wanted to dig up the monster to make sure that the monster was still there. He was afraid that the monster had gotten out. After verbally reinforcing his successful dry nights, I hypnotized him and suggested that we go back to where the monster was buried. He dug down to find that the monster was still there and in a minor state of decay.

Hypnotically over the next several weeks, we had to continue to reinforce the fact that the monster was dead, that the monster was buried and decaying. We repeatedly examined the grave until we found nothing left of the monster but bones. By the 4th week even the bones were gone (a hypnotically sped putrefaction process and/or desensitization). During this period the patient was consistently dry about 2–3 nights a week.

At this point in the therapy, it was still unknown as to when the enuresis started. While investigating why the enuresis had not improved beyond 3 dry nights per week, I was told that another monster existed. There was an implication that the monster had some relationship to myself. I was unable to figure this out for another week at which time we did another hypnotic session in which I attempted to understand the meaning of the color green. Using green as the associative stimulus, I asked him (under hypnosis) to associate to green. The green was, of course, the green monster, green grass, green doctor. When asked what he meant by "green doctor," I found out from him that doctors "were green," that is, wore green surgical scrub suits. At this time we discovered that he had been very scared when he had undergone a tonsillectomy.

His mother was extremely overprotective. It turned out that both his brother and he had had tonsillectomies on the same day, by the same doctor, and had shared a hospital room. His mother was absolutely convinced that both children would be dead by the end of the day. Despite her attempts to conceal it, she had conveyed her anxiety to him.

The monster was the two orderlies in green that pushed him to the operating room. Two orderlies are large and have four eyes and eight limbs. With this understanding, he improved, being dry approximately 4 nights a week.

After the tonsillectomy, Mrs. K, being overprotective, and having fears of both children bleeding to death, would not let Michael or his brother go upstairs to sleep in their bedroom. She had them sleep in the living room, since her bedroom was downstairs next to it. Michael slept on the green couch where his first episode of enuresis occurred. After history gathering from Mrs. K and other family members, it was finally determined that the enuresis was intermittent for the first weeks and then settled into a stable pattern. This, along with minor speech problems—stuttering and hoarseness (which lasted approximately 2 months)—gained him quite a bit of attention from Mrs. K. This attention reinforced the enuresis, which remained.

It is interesting to note that none of the family members knew when the enuresis started until Michael discovered it through hypnosis. They were then able to confirm that this was indeed when the enuresis started.

Serendipitously, the next week when he came into the office with his mother, I discovered she was polyphobic. Michael teased his mother about the fact that she always took the stairs up to my fourth-floor office. His mother had an elevator phobia and an incredible fear of heights, which she stated were life-long. She had never taken an elevator. Michael would take the elevator, and she would walk up the stairs. It was at this time I suggested that perhaps Mrs. K might like to use hypnosis to help her with her phobias. Since Michael had been using hypnosis and she had witnessed it, she agreed. She was further motivated by the fact that her fear of heights had ruined the family's vacation to the Colorado Rocky Mountains the previous year, and in a few weeks they planned to return to Colorado. (The parallel between this passive–aggressive-control family dynamic and enuresis can be seen: Family going to Colorado and mother's fear of "ruining" the trip; mother's overprotective control and Michael's enuresis are only two of many examples.)

I did hypnosis with her while Michael waited in the waiting room. Before doing the actual hypnosis, I taught her a scaling technique using zero to ten. Zero was established as the deepest relaxed you could be, and ten was the most incredible tension/terror you could imagine just short of dying. This was done to enable her to later determine her level of relaxation prior to, during, and after hypnosis and while dealing with various stimuli. I induced hypnosis by a technique of progressive relaxation, then trained her to continue to deepen the trance by counting backward from five. She was also trained in self-hypnosis using counting backward from five to one as both a heterohypnotic and autophynotic signal to relax.

I used typical desensitization techniques. She was instructed to imagine herself in a chair looking out the window of the building toward the same floor of another building. This allowed her to be inside the room, away from the window, and not have to experience any particular fear about looking down. When she was able to do this. I then suggested imagery of her getting up and walking to the window, but not looking down or opening the window. Doing this caused her to become a bit more tense. After counting backward and relaxing her, I had her look down one story. She became quite anxious, yielding an increase of four points on the scale. I again helped her to relax by counting backward and had her look down another floor. After looking down 10 stories she had exactly the same amount of anxiety with each new story as when she was first asked to look. Since there was no desensitization effect, I recognized that the building must be infinitely tall. It was at this time that I found out that she had never looked out of even a second story window. I recognized that *in vitro* desensitization was valueless in her case.

We continued the session by moving from my office to a large office in which her son was waiting. The building that we were working in was a U-shaped building so that when one looked out of this particular office, one would see another part of the building across the way. I had her, *in vivo*, do exactly what we had just had her do *in vitro*. I had her walk to the window, relaxed her, and stood with her. I touched her shoulder to create both an anchoring point and to reassure her. Next, I had her open the window and relaxed her again in front of the opened window.

I then had her look out the window to the window of the same floor across the way, having her look down a floor, and so on, until she could see the grass. When she became tense to a scale level of four or five, I would help her relax until she reached two or three before continuing. At the point that she could see the grass on which there happened to be a pigeon, I suggested that she look at the pigeon, which was a bit closer to us than the first patch of grass she had viewed. Next I had her look at a squirrel. By good luck the squirrel happened to start running toward our building. This forced her to look even more vertically until she could see some gravel at the base of the building. At this point I indicated that she was leaning out the window, looking down, and had achieved a great success. She was absolutely surprised and for a second became anxious; however, she was able to control herself. The procedure was repeated out of trance.

After processing her success with Michael present, we decided to go to the stairwell on the fourth floor and have her look down to the basement, which was five stories below. We repeated the process by going up to each landing and looking down (relaxing her each time) until we reached the eighth floor. When we reached the eighth floor, Michael, who was accompanying us, said, "Wow, that's a bit scary." This was used to point out to her that Michael had his own control systems and that she could let go of some of her control of him.

During many therapy sessions prior to this one, I had worked with Mrs. K about allowing Michael to ride his bike, allowing him to go places without her, and his taking responsibility for himself—with only a modicum of success. However, after this session, her relationship with him changed. She started to let go of him. During the next week, Michael had only 1 wet night. This was a first for him, and his achievement was appropriately reinforced. He then was successful at remaining dry a full week.

Prior to the family leaving on their trip to Colorado, Mrs. K practiced self-hypnosis desensitization *in vitro*, and in many other *in vivo* circumstances. The trip was a major success. Mrs. K was able to share in the beautiful Rocky Mountain views. Michael had only one accident while traveling to the mountains, but after they arrived, he was dry for the rest of the trip; 13 consecutive days.

On returning home, his mother got into a fight with the neighbors. This was the precipitant that started Michael wetting again. He intermittently wet his bed once a week for the next few weeks.

At this point his mother, a religious Catholic, found out she had unexpectedly become pregnant. The dynamics of this appeared to relate to her letting go of Michael, his growing up, and her substituting the new baby.

The emphasis of the therapy shifted to working with Mrs. K about whether she wanted a therapeutic abortion or not. This was at a time (1970) when abortions were illegal in the state of Illinois, except to save the life of the mother. She stated that the pregnancy was an accident, and she did not want the baby. After working with her religious beliefs and guilt, arrangements were made so that she could have a therapeutic abortion in the hospital. With having the freedom to choose and not feeling forced to have the baby, she decided to have the baby and was able to cleanly let go of Michael. He became consistently dry.

Shortly after this, I entered the army. In mid-1972 I received a call from Mrs. K saying that she was having a problem. She recognized that she was being overprotective toward her new daughter. We discussed some things she could do, and I suggested a therapist in her area. I later found out she did not follow through.

In 1973 I returned to Chicago and set up practice. Two years later I received a call from Mrs. K stating she was having significant problems with her daughter. When interviewing Mrs. K, I learned that Michael was in high school and had had no problem with enuresis since I had last seen him.

However, her daughter's behavior was moderately disturbed. The daughter was belligerent, inappropriate, unmanageable, and was also enuretic. On taking a history, I found out that there was absolutely no structure to the child's life. The marriage between Mrs. K and her husband had deteriorated. She could not consider a divorce because of her religious beliefs and felt extremely trapped. We worked on the issue of control and her choice to remain married or not. She chose to stay married and saw that as a choice, no longer feeling trapped. This was very similar to the work that had been done around the issue of the abortion. She recognized that this baby was an unplanned baby and was indeed a substitute for the child she had let grow up. She realized that she had to work on this issue, let her daughter grow up, and put some organization into their daily life. Accomplishing this was a matter of having her substitute concepts and techniques that she already knew from her obedience training of dogs. She applied the concepts of consistency and contingency to the relationship with her daughter. Her daughter responded quite readily, and the total therapy lasted approximately 8 weeks. In this case the enuresis was handled with the aid of an alarm sheet.

DYNAMIC FORMULATIONS AND HYPNOTHERAPEUTIC INTERVENTIONS

Generally, it seems appropriate to think about symptoms as having three contributing phenomenon, which I call "three Ps": (1) predisposing factors, such as genetics, target organ, or systems (this can be a learned target); (2) precipitating event(s), such as tonsillectomy and accidental urination; and (3) perpetuating interactions, mother's attention.

In Michael's case one of the predisposing factors that determined target organ choice was the attention his mother paid to the enuretic symptom, rather than the expected one, the speech problems that occurred simultaneously with the enuresis, after the tonsillectomy. There were indications of problems in Michael's toilet-training process. At the age of 6, bladder control had not been perfected for a long enough time. Regression under stress affected this less solidified system first. Also, under stress and fear, there probably was a decrease in the output of antidiuretic hormone and a subsequent increase in urine production (see Williams, 1981).

The precipitating events were Mrs. K's conveying her fears to Michael, Michael's own fear, and his accidently urinating on the green couch.

The perpetuating interactions were overdetermined and occurred on many levels. Dynamically, for Michael, it allowed him an oedipal triumph of sorts, since he had more of his mother's attention than his father (or brother). It enabled him to assert himself and be in control of an area of his life, albeit negative. It also reinforced his existential belief in his devaluated position.

On a didactic level, it allowed him to passive–aggressively express his anger at his mother and brother while remaining regressed and a child. His symptom was reinforced by his mother's overprotectiveness and the attention she paid to it and to him, especially in the beginning. There was an interactive reinforcing system going on between his being a child and his mother's need to keep him regressed. It also served to punish his brother who degraded him, as the odor often drove his brother out of the bedroom they shared.

On a family systems level, his problem decreased the strife in the household by keeping energy and attention focused on him and away from the underlying problems between his parents. These problems could not be dealt with effectively in therapy. The parents united to help their child and did not have to deal with their own issues and conflict.

The family's main interactive way of expressing itself was reciprocally passive–aggressive, which could be seen between father and mother, Michael and brother, Michael and mother. This process could also be seen in the choice of vacation type (by camper trailer with an enuretic) and destination (the mountains with someone who has a fear of heights).

On a social level, the enuresis kept him isolated because he could not sleep over at friends' houses. His repeated refusal to accept and/or offer invitations led to a decrease of interaction with others his own age and kept him closer to home and mother. His being at home helped reduce his overprotective mother's anxiety. It also yielded an increase of interaction between mother and Michael that was mutually reinforcing on more levels than anxiety reducing.

The psychotherapy in this case was conducted in all possible combinations of the mother–son dyad. Most often I would see Michael first, then Michael with his mother, and finally the mother alone, though this order was varied as indicated by the therapy situation.

During sessions in which hypnotherapy was used, Michael or Mrs. K worked both in and out of trance. When emotionally laden material was exposed, permissive amnesia was suggested (i.e., "You will remember what you are able to deal with and the rest of the information will be temporarily forgotten. You will be able to recall it when you can handle it.").

Hypnosis was interwoven into the changing therapeutic approach (family, individual child, individual mother, and dyadic) in several different ways and toward different subgoals and goals. It was first used to help Michael relax so we could better relate. With the increased communication and relaxation, came an increase in rapport and trust. Next hypnosis was used as a projective technique via the television set imagery. (It's interesting that the favorite program of an enuretic boy was "Gilligan's Island.") Then the TV set was used to help him give me information while being "removed" from it indirectly, like play therapy. When he was ready, the association of the patient and events he had described was facilitated hypnotically by having the camera follow him and not "the boy."

The issues of assertiveness and mastery were partially addressed during the employment of the explorative technique, of going up 10 stairs to a room where he would learn something. They were further reinforced by the desensitization technique of repeatedly examining the monster and noting his degree of decay. The discovery of the onset of the enuresis was aided by the use of hypnotic, free association techniques to the color green.

Behavioral techniques such as decreasing fluid intake and deciding on the time to wake him to go to the bathroom were shaped by the information gathered hypnotically. Behavioral reinforcement was also given both in and out of trance. Positive suggestions about self were given in both states also.

Mrs. K, in order to let go of Michael and allow him to grow and individuate, had to deal with her phobias, which were learned from her overprotective, polyphobic mother. Autohypnosis was taught and used in conjunction with heterohypnosis to obtain a sense of mastery via *in vitro* and *in vivo* desensitization. The separation of mother and son was aided by the sense of mastery Mrs. K obtained over her phobias[1] and her life. As she felt more in control of herself *vis-à-vis* her phobias and fears, she could allow Michael to physically and emotionally move away. He, with his newfound mastery, could take the risk to individuate. During the *in vivo* desensitization, while Mrs. K was in a hypnoidal, if not a hypnotic, state, she received suggestions about Michael's ability to protect himself and her letting go of him.

It appeared that the final step in Mrs. K's letting go of Michael was via "symptom" substitution—getting pregnant with her daughter. When she had the freedom to choose between a therapeutic abortion and hav-

1. A successful treatment of phobia will often generalize to other areas, and in this case, it did.

ing her child, she indirectly dealt with her issue of control. None of her interrelated issues—overprotection, individuation, and control—were completely resolved, as can be seen from the phone call I received in 1972 and from her presentation with her daughter, who was enuretic and out of control. Further therapy appeared to have been successful in helping deal with these issues more rapidly.

This case represents the integration of hypnosis with both direct symptom relief and a psychodynamic approach with behavioral therapy and an early version of family therapy.

EPILOGUE

In a 13-year follow-up, the following was reported by Mrs. K:

1. Michael had no recurrence of his enuresis. He is married and the father of two children. He was hurt in an accident in a steelmill, but has recovered and will start college shortly.

2. Mrs. K and her husband are relating much better. "We've learned to live with each other and support each other."

3. Mrs. K has had no recurrence of her fear of heights and has even taken a hot air balloon ride.

4. The daughter has had no recurrence of her enuresis. She developed a snake phobia at the start of high school, but overcame it without therapy, has a pet snake, and became the leader of a local group that studies them.

5. The oldest son became a computer designer and overprotects his daughter.

REFERENCES

Braun, B. G. Hypnosis in family therapy. In A. H. Smith & W. C. Wester (Eds.), *Comprehensive clinical hypnosis*. New York: Lippincott, 1984.

Kramer, C. H. *Becoming a family therapist*. New York: Human Sciences Press, 1980.

Williams, R. T. *A textbook of endocrinology*. Philadelphia: Saunders, 1981.

11
HYPNOTHERAPY AND FAMILY THERAPY IN THE TREATMENT OF ADOLESCENT ENURESIS

E. Thomas Dowd

Enuresis, or bed-wetting, is a difficult problem to treat. At the same time, however, its treatment outcome, or lack of it, is clear and unambiguous, thus making it an excellent vehicle for the demonstration of the utility of hypnosis. In the following case description, the focus is on the combination of hypnosis and family therapy in the treatment of adolescent enuresis. This case is particularly interesting because of its demonstration of major etiologic themes explicated in the literature.

The causes of enuresis can be divided into two broad classes, those attributable to physical problems and those attributable to psychological problems (Kroger, 1977). Physical causes involve both maturational factors and congenital and mechanical factors. The majority of children are physiologically mature enough to control their nighttime urine by age 3, although there are large individual differences. Organically based problems, such as diabetes, hyperacidity of the urine, a kidney condition, or a tendency toward deep sleep, can significantly raise the age at which bed-wetting ceases or can prevent its elimination entirely (Gibbons, 1979). It is therefore important that physiologic or physical causes be ruled out before psychological interventions are begun.

There have been a number of psychological causes of enuresis noted in the literature. These include emotional immaturity (Kroger, 1977), a method of expressing resentment, hostility, or aggression toward parents (Kroger, 1977; Gibbons, 1979), sibling rivalry (Kroger, 1977), underlying insecurity (Gibbons, 1979), disturbed relations with the mother (Kroger, 1977; Braun, Chapter 10, this volume), or as a family symptom expressing poor parental relations (Gibbons, 1979; Calof, 1982; Ritterman, 1983;

E. Thomas Dowd. Department of Educational Psychology, University of Nebraska, Lincoln, Nebraska.

Braun, Chapter 10, this volume). It is significant that most identified psychological causes are family-related interpersonal in nature, thus suggesting that effective treatment should focus on interpersonal relations within the family. Calof (1982) has graphically illustrated how the therapist's assumptions regarding the nature and cause of the enuresis can affect the treatment interventions used and result in the ignoring of significant sources of data. The following case nicely illustrates not only many of the above etiologic agents but also how a shift in conceptual and treatment focus during treatment can result in greater therapeutic gains. For the purposes of this chapter, the "identified patient" is referred to as George Smith.

PATIENT'S HISTORY

George was a 14-year-old boy referred to me for treatment by a doctoral student in clinical psychology. The student had heard of my work in hypnosis and thought that it might help George. It should be noted that this is not an unusual type of referral to those who practice hypnosis, where the client or referral source prescribes the treatment in advance. Accordingly, I met with George and his parents to ascertain the nature of the problem and to decide if hypnosis might be warranted in this case.

George presented himself as a physically and socially immature 14-year-old, who spoke little and kept his eyes cast down much of the time. Although he appeared shy and somewhat withdrawn, he did not seem hostile or resistant. The father was a tall, athletic-looking man, with a forceful and articulate manner of speaking. Although he had definite opinions about the nature and cause of his son's problem, he did not seem hostile or resistant to hearing other opinions. The mother was considerably smaller than her husband and was not nearly as articulate as he. She appeared to defer to him on most things, yet I perceived that he would often look to (and at) her after some of his statements, as if seeking her acquiesence or approval. Both parents appeared genuinely concerned about their son and eager to help in any way they could.

Mr. and Mrs. Smith described George as a mentally mature, emotionally and physically immature, shy, and introverted pleaser, who did well in school and caused no trouble to parents or school. He was a physically active boy, who fished and played sports (primarily soccer), Atari, and chess. Although he was usually relaxed and affectionate toward the parents, he had difficulty expressing anger openly and would displace it by such activities as slamming doors. He had been adopted when a baby and had been told this fact early. Neither parents felt that his adoption was in any way related to the enuresis. He had been enuretic all his life. They had taken him to a urologist on several occasions, who had indicated that there were no medical problems, but that George had a small bladder. He urinated frequently during the day (five or six times), but no longer "dribbled." He had taken medication on several occasions (7.5 mg Tofranil), but the primary result had been to make him more introverted and had given him headaches. For this reason, the medication had been discontinued. They had not been to the urologist in several years, and were at their wits' end. They had never seen a psychologist regarding George's problem. They stated that George was a deep sleeper, but that he would not wet the bed if gotten up during the night to urinate. He had a bowel movement every 2 or 3 days.

George had a younger (by 4 years) brother, who was the parent's natural child. The brother (who for the purposes of this chapter will be called John) was described by Mr. and Mrs. Smith as extraverted, lazy, and loud. George did better in school than John, although John had more friends. There appeared to be a great deal of conflict between the boys, described as "teasing, competition, and fights." John was aware of George's problem and would often tease him about it. John was not, nor had he ever been, enuretic.

Until this point Mr. and Mrs. Smith had basically agreed with each other regarding George's situation and problem. There were now some significant areas of disagreement. Mr. Smith did not think the competition between the two boys was excessive or out-of-hand, while the mother felt that it was. The father thought that the enuresis was George's fault and that he could stop if he really wanted to. The mother thought that it was not his fault and that the father was excessively angry at George for something that he could not help. Mr. Smith admitted that he would become angry at George and that that probably did not help the situation. Two things were immediately apparent to me: First, these disagreements had been going on for some time, and second, that Mrs. Smith felt uncomfortable with conflict and protected both boys. She appeared to protect George from his father by disagreeing with her husband and undercutting his efforts to overcome George's enuresis and by siding with George against an angry and unreasonable father. There were indications that she protected John from George. It should be noted that the father did not display anger toward George either in the session with George or in the session with the parents alone.

In an individual session with Mr. and Mrs. Smith, I asked them to describe the sequence of events during a typical enuretic night. Assuming that they had not awakened George, he would generally wet the bed sometime between midnight and 3 a.m. He would then awaken and either sleep on the floor for the remainder of the night or go to his mother's room and get in bed with her, usually the latter. In the morning, the mother would change and wash George's sheets. When I asked Mr. Smith how he felt about George joining them, he stated that he did not sleep with his wife, but slept in a separate bedroom on the first floor (both George and his mother slept on the second floor). He stated that the reason was that he preferred the waterbed in the first-floor bedroom, but that Mrs. Smith did not like the waterbed.

The dynamics between Mr. and Mrs. Smith were not characterized by anger or hostility. Mr. Smith was articulate and forceful in his statements, while Mrs. Smith was more timid and passive. There seemed, however, subtle hints that she controlled the direction of family life more than was initially apparent. She seemed to do this by passive–aggressive behavior, such as "not doing." For example, Mr. Smith was adamant that George's problem was due to a small bladder and an excessive intake of sugar. Mrs. Smith did not feel this way and "contrived" to ensure that George had a supply of sugar via cookies, ice cream, and soda kept in the house. Since Mr. Smith was away on business several days each week or two, Mrs. Smith effectively controlled the home atmosphere.

A subsequent interview with George indicated that he typically watched TV in the room he shared with his brother until 10:30 p.m., drank a soda, and went to bed. He confirmed that he would urinate frequently during the day. He characterized relations with his brother as "OK," but said that they fought a lot. He loved both his mother and father, but felt a little closer to his mother.

It was apparent that there were incestuous overtones to the relationship between George and his mother and some relationship strains between Mr. and Mrs. Smith. This, together with the father's periodic absences from home and the mother's protection of George from his father and John from George, tended to point to a mother–child alliance with the weaker member. George's enuresis could be seen in part as an attempt to bond himself to his mother. It was hypothesized that the mother had some reasons for resisting the elimination of George's bed-wetting and might resist a solution to the problem. At the same time, George was obviously distressed by his enuresis, especially as it prevented him from spending the night at his friends' homes, a popular adolescent pastime. Accordingly, a hypnotic intervention was planned that would structure, via metaphors (Gordon, 1978), appropriate ways of growing, loving, and relating.

HYPNOTIC SESSIONS

Because I sensed that George was resistant to change at some level, I structured an indirect induction that he could control. I told George that in hypnosis he could close his eyes or not, talk or not, and relax or not, and I counted backward from 10 to one, asking him to concentrate on my voice.

Somewhat to my astonishment, the indirect suggestion that he could close his eyes if he wished failed to produce the effect; I finally was successful with a *direct* instruction that he close his eyes and relax progressively as he paid closer and closer attention to my voice as I continued talking. I then used the following hypnotic routine (summarized). Embedded suggestions are italicized and were vocally stressed.

"Just relax, George, and as you concentrate on the sound of my voice, you can, *George, allow yourself to become* as *relaxed* as you wish. You are here [i.e., hear] to learn what I have to say, but your conscious mind is not important, so you can go play soccer till later, and your unconscious will hear [i.e., here] as I speak. Growing up well is important for you; learning and unlearning; things, *George, change* as you, *George, change*. When K______ [my daughter] was an infant, she was often angry, but did not know how to express that anger. As she grew older, she learned its appropriate expression and these expressions changed. So too: in growing up relationships, *George, develop*:

- How you have heard your father talk about his family.
- How you share and don't share with John.
- How you, *George, love your mother* and father *differently*.
- As a child you hugged and loved one way, but now as you cross to being a man, George, your love will grow like you; how you love will, *George, change*.

"When you were a small child, walking seemed so difficult, but you learned; when you were a child, the alphabet seemed so difficult, but you learned; as you begin to drive a car, it seems so difficult, but you will learn. Now, as you are ready to, *George, be a man*, I know you really want to *hold* your head high, *George*, and you can as you, *George, change the ways of childhood*.

"Just as you learned to, *George, remain dry during the day*, so can you now, *George, use that knowledge* to continue to remain dry daily. Yes, *George, remain dry during the days*. You already know how to remain dry during the day, George, definitely. Remain dry between the days.

"But, we are not here [i.e., hear] to hear [i.e., here] me tell you what you already know, but how to learn and accomplish much more besides within yourself. So, I'll speak to both your conscious and unconscious at different states. And your conscious and unconscious minds will hear here what they want to hear, need to hear, and will be able to use all that they want to use in the way they want to use. And you will be able to use those things that are valuable for you in a very special way sometime soon. And you can allow yourself to be surprised at the changes you are able to make."

George was then brought out of the trance by counting backward from ten to one. He initially claimed that he had not been hypnotized because he "remembered everything," but when asked what he remembered, he actually was able to recall very little.

The next two sessions were with George privately. We spent about half the session working in hypnosis and the other half exploring his motivation and strategies for overcoming his enuresis and exploring his results achieved thus far. The hypnotic sessions basically followed the preceding format, with some additions. I suggested to George that he would of necessity stumble when learning new things, but that the more he practiced, the more he would succeed ("just like learning to ride a bicycle; at first you are conscious of every movement, but later you do it so well and so unconsciously that you wonder one day why you ever found it difficult"). Since he liked fishing with his father, I structured a fish metaphor for George, organized around the repetitive usage of the terms "catch and hold, catch and hold," a metaphor both for fishing and for urine retention. I continued to use the growing and developing metaphor ("And as you are learning new ways of growing, new ways of being close in different ways, different but deeper as you develop"). Discussions with George indicated that he had some ill feelings toward his father for the latter's anger at his constant bed-wetting. It also appeared that George continued to drink liquids just before bed, although he was aware that this made a wet bed much more likely. He did say that he had told himself not to pee one night, and he hadn't. These discussions indicated the likely presence of strong secondary gain in his enuresis, perhaps as a means of achieving closeness to his mother and expressing hostility toward a powerful and absent father. Further evidence for this hypothesis came from George's initial reluctance to fully cooperate in the hypnotic induction, except after direct induction. Put simply, George appeared to have significant ambivalent feelings about giving up his enuresis. Subsequent data confirmed this.

After the first session I had asked the parents (unknown to George) to keep records of incidents of bed-wetting but to say nothing to George about this. The following record is typical of the first few weeks when I was working with George individually:

- Tuesday—dry
- Wednesday—very little, damp only.
- Thursday—damp
- Friday—damp
- Saturday—medium wet
- Sunday—dry
- Monday—dry
- Tuesday—wet

In addition, the nights in which he had been enuretic had been preceded by drinking liquids just before bed.

As can be seen, the progression was very uneven. While it represented some progress, since he had been enuretic virtually every night before, I thought that neither George, his parents, nor I would accept this as a final outcome. It seemed that working individually with George would achieve results somewhat like his motivation: ambiguous. Therefore, I decided to directly deal with what I perceived as underlying family relationship issues.

In addition to the partial progress in overcoming his enuresis, George made another significant gain. His mother reported that after the first hypnosis session George had never again joined her in bed after wetting. She also reported that he seemed to have become more thoughtful, less impulsive, and more mature and grown-up since he had been coming to see me. It should be noted that I had not told the parents the content either of our sessions or the hypnotic routine.

FAMILY INTERVENTIONS

Although there had been partial gains up to this point (after five sessions), it was becoming clear that there were family relationship issues that needed to be addressed if the problem was to be eliminated completely. A shift in conceptual focus or paradigm (Calof, 1982) therefore was attempted. Specifically, I turned my interventions toward the parents and said that I wished to see them alone for a few sessions. The following issues seemed to need resolution.

1. The secondary gain that George experienced from his enuresis, as exemplified by his drinking liquids just before bed knowing that that made it much more likely that he would be enuretic that night.
2. The unusually strong bond between George and his mother and the relatively weak bond between Mr. and Mrs. Smith, as exemplified by their sleeping apart on separate floors.
3. Mrs. Smith's "rescuing tendencies" with George in relation to his father, with John in relation to George, and with George as demonstrated by her changing his sheets for him the next day.

These issues were now addressed in several individual sessions with the parents alone.

I explained to Mr. and Mrs. Smith that enuresis is often the result of family interactional forces as well as an individual problem. I instructed them to carry out the following tasks and to observe the results. On no account, however, were they to comment to George about his bed-wetting or to let him know they were observing his progress. They were to act as if it were his concern alone. They agreed to implement the following:

1. The television set in the boys' room was to go off at 10:00 p.m., and both boys were to be in bed. Heretofore, they had been allowed to watch TV indefinitely, thus possibly contributing to George's deep slumber. In addition, this had been a source of contention between the parents, as Mr. Smith had insisted it go off early, while Mrs. Smith had simply allowed it to stay on. She was able to do this, since Mr. Smith was often gone.

2. I strongly suggested that Mr. and Mrs. Smith sleep together on the second floor. Mr. Smith was not particularly happy about this, as he preferred the waterbed. Since most of the suggestions were those that Mr. Smith wanted, I thought that it was important that Mrs. Smith get something she wanted too. I phrased the suggestion as helping George understand that his parents were a unit and acted together.

3. I instructed Mrs. Smith to no longer change George's sheets nor make his bed, but require that he wash them himself and put on clean linen. She was to make no comments about either a wet or dry bed.

4. I instructed both Mr. and Mrs. Smith to no longer stock ice cream, chocolate, or soda. This seemed to be an important point to Mr. Smith, and I included it in order to enlist his cooperation in the other tasks.

Both parents agreed to these instructions. I asked them to keep a record of enuretic nights and let me know the results on a weekly basis.

In the next two sessions we focused on Mrs. Smith's rescuing tendencies. She stated that she did not feel particularly powerful *vis-à-vis* her husband or her sons and saw her boys as needing protection from him. She gradually came to understand that these tendencies arose from her own perceived powerlessness and not from a real need on the part of George and John. She had never discussed these feelings with her husband and was surprised when he offered her support for her attempts to deal with both George and John and accepted her feelings about him. They were able to arrive at a greater understanding about their respective roles and power relations in the family than they had previously. Mr. Smith revealed that he had felt somewhat less powerful than her within the family structure. Because of his frequent absences, he perceived himself as relatively powerless, since his wife could do whatever she wished in his absence and undercut his authority. I stressed with both of them the absolute necessity of arriving at a consensus on issues involving the relations with their sons and then sticking to these decisions. Mrs. Smith seemed quite relieved in hearing these suggestions, and stated, "I think I needed to hear these things." They both agreed to discuss between themselves all issues of child raising, to agree jointly on actions, and to carry out those actions with mutual support. Mrs. Smith agreed that it would be beneficial to herself and the family if she would curb her rescuing tendencies and become more assertive *vis-à-vis* her husband, rather than not expressing disagreements and sabotaging his ideas in his absence.

Both Mr. and Mrs. Smith reported that George continued to be more mature and outgoing in most ways, although there were also more fights and jealousness between John and him. The parents had come to think, however, that George felt compelled to show them that he was less mature than they thought. We discussed possible reasons why George might feel this way, such as a fear of not being able to meet new demands that accompany maturity and loss of a "special relationship" with his mother. Their log of "wet nights" revealed the same wet–dry pattern as before. They had, however, successfully implemented the instructions given to them earlier and felt good about that. George had not questioned the new rules, but had immediately begun washing his own sheets and changing his own bed. No explanations were asked for and none were given.

A subsequent session with George alone revealed that he was pleased with his progress with his enuresis, but that he was uncertain if he could eliminate it completely. He was aware of the connection between his bedwetting and drinking liquids just before bed, but could not explain this seemingly perverse action that undermined his stated goal. Even overtly structuring the connection in this fashion produced agreement but not understanding. Therefore, I hypnotized George again, and suggested that he would be able, during the next week, to determine for himself when he would like to stop wetting his bed completely and that he would be able to find his own way to do this. This idea was repeated several times with minor variations in wording. After bringing George out of the trance, I asked him when it might be reasonable for him to stop wetting his bed. He replied that it might be reasonable in 2 or 3 weeks and that he might suddenly stop.

This last hypnotic intervention was included in order to utilize George's own ideas and resistance and to allow him to stop wetting his bed in his own way, as outlined by Erickson (1980). Given George's sabotage of his own goals, it seemed important to provide him a means of directing his own progress. In the posthypnotic conversation, I stressed to George that he was in control of himself and therefore was capable of stopping his enuretic behavior whenever he wished. He replied, "Do you mean that I can stop whenever I want?" I said that that was indeed so. George left, remarking that this had been the most helpful session to date.

TREATMENT OUTCOME

I had two more sessions with Mr. and Mrs. Smith, which were devoted to a discussion of George's progress and their implementation of my earlier instructions as well as their own progress in working together as a team. They reported that George had suddenly ceased wetting the bed, except for a rare damp night. They had continued implementing my instructions and were continuing to discuss things more openly between themselves.

Follow-up by telephone a year and a half later indicated that George had remained dry. Mr. Smith stated that he had a very occasional damp night, but only when he had eaten ice cream or when he was angry at either parent about something. He thought that these occasional "mishaps" were anger reactions. In addition, Mr. Smith described George as having grown up tremendously, both emotionally and physically, during the last year and a half. He had become more thoughtful, more considerate of others, less impulsive, and more willing to express his feelings. He had taken on greater responsibility in the family and rarely needed to be reminded to complete household tasks. His grades had also improved significantly in that time. Enuresis was never mentioned in the house anymore, even on the damp nights. Mr. Smith stated that they were extremely pleased with the results and had been "talking up" psychology whenever possible.

This case illustrates a number of themes that have been discussed in the literature on the treatment of enuresis by hypnosis. First, there was a large intrafamily, interpersonal relations component that appeared to be maintaining the problem, whatever its origin. It may be useless, or even counterproductive, to attempt to overcome adolescent enuretic behavior without recourse to family interventions. Second, there appeared to be a strong secondary gain component of the enuretic behavior that caused motivational problems in the identified patient. Ambivalences about change occur more often than commonly recognized in psychotherapy; unless they are dealt with, the change may not occur or may be transitory in nature. Third, enuresis can be viewed as an expression of resentment, hostility, or aggression toward powerful family members without the individual having to admit these feelings directly. A method must be found for these feelings to be expressed more directly or reduced before the behavior is likely to be eliminated.

This case illustrates the trial and error nature of the treatment of entrenched behavior problems and the uneven progress that often characterizes psychological treatment. In addition, improvement in one sphere of an individual's life often generalizes to other areas as well. While many of George's emotional changes were likely due to increasing maturity that would have occurred without psychological intervention, the parents both at the time and retrospectively noticed a sudden increase in maturity at the time of these interventions. The most general conclusion that can be drawn, however, is that adolescent enuresis, like most child and adolescent behavior problems, is multidetermined in nature and provides the individual with a source of gratification not perceived as otherwise obtainable. Treatment interventions are therefore most likely to succeed if they are likewise multifaceted in nature.

REFERENCES

Calof, D. L. Shifting therapeutic paradigms: A case report of adolescent primary enuresis. In J. K. Zeig (Ed.), *Ericksonian approaches to hypnosis and psychotherapy*. New York: Brunner/Mazel, 1982.

Erickson, M. H. Utilizing the patient's own personality and ideas: "Doing it his own way." In E. L. Rossi (Ed.), *The collected papers of Milton H. Erickson* (Vol. IV). New York: Irvington Publishers, 1980.

Gibbons, D. E. *Applied hypnosis and hyperempiria*. New York: Plenum Press, 1979.

Gordon, D. *Therapeutic metaphors*. Cupertino, CA: META Publications, 1978.

Kroger, W. S. *Clinical and experimental hypnosis*. Philadelphia: Lippincott, 1977.

Ritterman, M. *Using hypnosis in family therapy*. San Francisco: Jossey-Bass, 1983.

IV
SOMATIC PROBLEMS

The cases in this section represent perhaps some of the more unusual applications of hypnosis. Coincidentally, all three chapters illustrate the role of family dynamics in the etiology and maintenance of the problem behavior. Although family therapy was not conducted, it is apparent that it might have been appropriate in each of the cases.

Donna R. Copeland and Elgan L. Baker graphically describe the use of hypnosis as an adjunct treatment technique for side effects of cancer in children. Hypnosis was used to assist the cancer patient in coping with the effects of a previous psychological trauma and was also used with other family members toward a variety of goals. These goals included anxiety reduction and ego enhancement. The case is interesting as an example of the treatment of multiple family members that did not involve family therapy.

David L. Calof provides a fascinating case of the use of hypnotherapy in the treatment of bulimia. Especially interesting is the use of trance to enable the patient to achieve a different position or role in her family, as well as Calof's conceptualization of anorexia as arising in the context of family relationships. This case reminds us of the importance of the social nexus in which we all live.

The importance of family dynamics in the etiology of problem behavior is also apparent in the chapter on the treatment of chronic hiccoughs by Belinda R. Novik and Marcia A. Angle. The authors stress permissive techniques in which the patient was allowed to have control over his treatment via symptom scheduling and guided imagery. The meaning of the patient's symptom was explored via metaphor.

12
PEDIATRIC ONCOLOGY

Donna R. Copeland
Elgan L. Baker

Cancer and its treatment present a challenge, not only to oncologists seeking to cure the disease, but to psychologists and other mental health professionals as well in their efforts to alleviate the residual pain and discomfort of this life-threatening illness. Reports on hypnotic approaches to the treatment of problems associated with childhood cancer are beginning to appear (Copeland, 1982; Dash, 1980; Ellenberg, Kellerman, Dash, Higgins, & Zeltzer, 1980; Friedrich, 1982; Gardner, 1976; Gardner & Olness, 1981; Hilgard & LeBaron, 1982; LaBaw, Holton, Lowell, & Eccles, 1975; Olness, 1981; Zeltzer, Kellerman, Ellenberg, Barbour, Dash, & Rigler, 1980; Zeltzer & LeBaron, 1982). For the most part, these reports focus on the application and efficacy of hypnosis in relieving the anxiety and pain of cancer and its treatment and in reducing the adverse side effects of chemotherapy. In some, the importance of contextual factors and the necessity for multimodal treatment approaches are addressed (Copeland, 1982; Friedrich, 1982). However, the relationship of physical symptoms such as pain, anxiety, nausea, and vomiting to psychological antecedents has not been adequately addressed. Psychological stress has been associated with diseases such as cancer (Bammer & Newberry, 1981; Bowers & Kelly, 1979; Fox, 1983; Holden, 1978; Rogers, Dubly, & Reich, 1979; Simonton, Matthews-Simonton, & Creighton, 1978; Tache, Selye, & Day, 1979) with regard to a causal or contributory relationship to the disease. However, the elaboration or influence of past psychological experience into somatic distress such as pain and anxiety needs additional empirical exploration.

Hypnosis has proved to be a useful and effective intervention technique for children with a variety of chronic illnesses (Gardner, 1976; Gardner & Olness, 1981). Children tend to demonstrate high levels of suscep-

Donna R. Copeland. Department of Pediatrics, University of Texas M. D. Anderson Hospital and Tumor Institute, Houston, Texas.

Elgan L. Baker. Department of Psychiatry, Indiana University School of Medicine, Indianapolis, Indiana.

tibility and motivation for involvement with hypnosis and frequently enjoy the opportunities for fantasy and self-control provided by such therapeutic strategies. Chronic illness frequently involves prolonged hospitalizations, invasive treatments, and extended or progressive debilitation. These variables often result in a sense of imprisonment, helplessness, victimization, and despair for the child. These associated stresses may actually contribute to the child's deterioration, interfere with capacities for adaptation and adjustment, and compromise a broad array of maturational processes. Hypnosis affords an opportunity to support the child's ability to cope, while teaching the child a variety of skills to help to master pain and anxiety. In this way, hypnotherapy also provides an opportunity to reverse some degree of helplessness and hopelessness by helping the child to develop and/or maintain some sense of self-control, self-direction, active autonomy, and self-confidence. As medical technology has advanced in successfully treating cancer and other chronic diseases, the importance of the maintenance of autonomy and self-confidence for successful maturation among the survivors has been amply demonstrated.

Specific applications of hypnosis in pediatric oncology tend to emphasize the utilization of direct and indirect suggestion, relaxation, analgesia, dissociation, and fantasy and imagery. Self-hypnosis is frequently employed after some initial experiences with heterohypnosis. A variety of therapeutic goals may be simultaneously addressed by such interventions. These include: (1) control of pain associated with the disease process and/or diagnostic and treatment procedures; (2) management of anxiety and related resistance and acting-out; (3) modulation of nausea and vomiting associated with chemotherapy; (4) support of appetite and adequate food intake; (5) relaxation and maintenance of appropriate sleep patterns; (6) use of fantasy and imagery to "escape" the hospital environment; (7) support of coping strategies in coming to terms and dealing with the cancer experience; and (8) intervention to resolve and/or prevent specific psychiatric complications such as depression and transient regressions (Baker, 1983). It is often useful and appropriate to combine hypnotherapy with other forms of intervention such as family treatment and insight-oriented work. Available research has tended to suggest that between 60% and 90% of children with cancer can successfully utilize hypnosis for managing some aspect of their discomfort and difficulty (Gardner & Olness, 1981; Zeltzer & LeBaron, 1982).

This chapter presents a case illustrating the influence of psychological history on the cancer experience and the multimodal treatment approaches utilized to minimize these effects. In this case, hypnotherapy served as a valuable adjunctive tool in minimizing the effects of previous psychological trauma on the child's current coping strategies.

MEDICAL HISTORY

Tad was an 11-year-old boy who had had surgery for a gangrenous appendix. At that time lymphomatous infiltrate was found in the area, and subsequent evaluations documented the presence of Burkitt's lymphoma. High doses of cancer chemotherapy were administered as soon as Tad was sufficiently recovered from the surgery. On the 2nd day of chemotherapy, Tad suffered renal failure secondary to tumor lysis syndrome, necessitating two dialysis treatments. He recovered, and chemotherapy was resumed. The tumor responded to treatment, and after 7 months on a standard chemotherapy protocol and continuing remission, treatment for cancer was discontinued.

FAMILY HISTORY

Tad lived with his parents and a younger brother who was 10 years old. His father was an airline mechanic, and his mother was a housewife. Tad was in the fifth grade at school where he was active in sports. Neuropsychological assessment indicated that Tad was of average intelligence but was performing below average in academic achievement. Resource room assistance at school was recommended for all his subjects.

Tad was a fairly typical boy who preferred outdoor physical activities to academic pursuits. He was mischievous and, at times, was punished fairly severely by his parents for misbehaviors such as minor vandalism and theft. It was noted on the clinic visit that he had a large bruise on his leg as a result of corporal punishment inflicted by his mother after he had disobeyed her.

Tad and his brother were very close, and their mother reported that the parents usually treated them like twins. Tad appeared to be slightly favored over his brother, however. The younger boy was extremely insecure and, at times, had threatened suicide as a way of eliciting attention.

Family members had a history of numerous events requiring medical attention. The mother had an emergency hysterectomy due to an abscess that was almost fatal. The father had been injured at work and required a cast for his arm. The brother had a minor heart condition and was being followed by a cardiologist. Additional events creating psychological trauma were: the death of a friend who had been mauled by a German shepherd dog (this was witnessed by the brother), sexual abuse of both boys by a neighborhood adult, and the brother being thrown out of the car while it was in motion. It was apparent that all these events were still fresh on the minds of family members, and they would refer to them frequently.

During treatment for cancer, the deaths of four of Tad's friends whom he had met at the hospital and the death of his dog during a family vacation exacerbated his anxiety.

PSYCHOLOGICAL ASSESSMENT AND INTERVENTION

Tad was originally referred for psychological intervention to help him deal more effectively with bone marrow aspirations and spinal taps, procedures that were initially required in frequent intervals. Additionally, it was observed that he was withdrawn and his appetite had decreased. An interview with him at this time revealed that he was preoccupied with his illness and the crisis events that had occurred, especially the transfer to another hospital for dialysis.

Tad was seen for 12 sessions of hypnosis and psychotherapy during a 7-month period. His brother was seen for nine sessions, and his mother for three sessions. There were additional consultation sessions with the mother regarding the children's progress in adjustment.

For the first two sessions Tad found it helpful to recount his recent experiences in great detail. He had many questions about his medical status and needed clarification as to the rationale for some procedures, especially dialysis. His questions and expressed fears were responded to directly and in a matter-of-fact tone. While some sympathy was conveyed, it was important for Tad that the trauma of these experiences be minimized to bind his anxiety. At the same time, his strengths and abilities to tolerate illness and treatment were pointed out and reinforced. It was thought that while Tad had had some very stressful experiences, he was exaggerating the implications of these and that he saw the events as more debilitating than they in fact were. Adequate flexibility to "bounce back" after the crises was lacking. His attitude was one of resignation—almost defeat—as if the world were a dangerous place and this experience was only one of a number he had had previously and could expect in the future.

After one session to establish rapport, hypnosis was introduced. Tad remembered a trip to Hawaii with his family as his most favorite place and time, so for the first induction, progressive body relaxation was used. Then the suggestion was made of a magic carpet that would fly him to Hawaii. Suggestions were made about the blue sky and blue water, the fresh, clean air to breathe, the warm feel of the sun and the sand on his body, and the cool breezes blowing by. It was suggested that he would feel calm and relaxed and that he would remember this feeling and take it with him for as long as he liked. From time to time, the therapist would pause and allow Tad to fill in his own fantasy material. Usually Tad would think of people surrounding him and games to play with his brother. Tad was a good hypnosis subject, and easily entered trance. This hypnotherapy session brought immediate results in his affect and outlook. He began walking around the ward meeting other children and asking about their experiences.

The next problem addressed with hypnotherapy was the extreme nausea and vomiting associated with chemotherapy. Tad appeared to be particularly sensitive to the medicine and would vomit for several days after it was administered. He was given Thorazine, an antiemetic, but did not like it because it made him sleep throughout the day. In this instance, it was suggested that Tad think of switches in his mind. One was to turn off the sensation in his tummy. When a red light was on above this switch, it would indicate that his tummy was numb; nothing could disturb it. He could leave this switch on while he was being infused with chemotherapy. To improve appetite, an additional suggestion was made of another switch, one with a blue light above it. When this light was on, he would begin to feel very, very hungry.

Tad's experience with chemotherapy was much improved after the second session. He preferred resting quietly while the chemotherapy was infused, and he reported that when he opened his eyes and noticed the switch on his intravenous pump, this reinforced the hypnotic suggestion. A light dose of Thorazine was prescribed for this chemotherapy administration, and with the hypnosis, he kept the vomiting down to a minimum. He slept well through the night and was eating normally the next day. The experience of having controlled the vomiting on his own made him feel stronger and more in control of his life. Moreover, he could see that physical symptoms did not necessarily have to be severe and debilitating.

For the first 2 months control of the nausea and vomiting received primary emphasis in hypnotherapy sessions. These were complicated by one severe reaction to Thorazine, which had inadvertently been given in a larger dose. After this episode, Tad was given only very small doses of antiemetic drugs. Primarily, he preferred relying on heterohypnosis and his own autosuggestion techniques.

The most difficult task in this case was the alleviation of anxiety and pain during bone marrow aspirations and spinal taps. Tad would typically burst into tears on his arrival to the therapist's office. He would say he wanted to get the procedures over with as quickly as possible; in the treatment room, however, he would use all types of delaying tactics. At first, he preferred going through these procedures without the therapist present, so trance was induced in her office, and posthypnotic suggestions were made that he would undergo the procedures calmly and confidently. Since he always wanted to use the images of Hawaii, these were suggested after a brief induction.

Unfortunately, during Tad's very first bone marrow aspiration at the hospital, the needle had bent during insertion, creating additional pain and a negative mental set toward subsequent procedures. An additional complication was a kidding remark made by a medical intern afterward: He joked that Tad should stay away from milk because it was making his bones hard.

To counteract these experiences, the suggestion was made that Tad could make his bones very soft and relaxed, just like Play-Doh, so that the needle could go in very easily. It was also suggested that he would feel very pleased and proud of himself when the procedure was over. The procedure went very well, although Tad did experience some pain. After an hour's rest, a spinal tap was attempted. This did not proceed so smoothly, however, as Tad complained that the spinal medicines burned, and he became very sick and vomited. This was rather puzzling, since Tad seemed to be using hypnosis and since the spinal tap is ordinarily better tolerated than the bone marrow aspiration. Follow-up with the nurses revealed that, according to their usual policy, they had warned him that the medicine "might burn a little." The therapist thought that perhaps Tad's sensitivity to this remark was heightened by the hypnotic trance, so the nurses were advised to describe the medication as "tingling" rather than "burning." But since this did not entirely explain his reaction, the therapist decided to accompany Tad to the treatment room in subsequent procedures to observe more closely. He gave his permission for this.

Prior to the next procedures, however, the therapist learned that Tad and his brother had been sexually abused by a male adult neighbor a few months prior to his diagnosis. The incidents had occurred numerous times and involved other neighborhood boys as well. The case had come to trial, and Tad and his brother had to testify in court. The mother reported that this was an extremely stressful experience for the family. This new information seemed to shed more light on Tad's difficulty with the bone marrow and spinal tap procedures, which he experienced with greater intensity than did most children. Even with hypnosis, he could not always retain information about the procedures as the nurse verbalized each step and gave him choices about numbing medications. During the procedures, he would tend to distort reality, completely misinterpreting casual remarks made by the staff. Evidence of his confused state was still apparent after one bone marrow aspiration when the therapist tried to resume a board game with him that they had begun prior to the procedure. His recovery from the stress was slow, and he was unable to perform normally for some period of time.

During the next series of procedures, the therapist accompanied Tad and his mother to the treatment room after a preliminary hypnosis induction in the office. Calming suggestions were made, along with a great deal of emphasis on Tad's strengths. In the treatment room, he responded better to these calm reassurances than he did to a formal hypnotic induction. In addition, although staff was patient with him and complied with his requests, he was not permitted to delay the procedure for long. After allowing only a short delay, the therapist advised the nurse to go ahead and insert the needle so as to prevent his anxiety from increasing. As soon as the needle went in, Tad became noticeably more relaxed.

As Tad neared the end of his cancer therapy, his mastery in coping with the pain of procedures as the side effects of chemotherapy improved. Once, when the therapist was out of town, the social worker was asked to provide assistance. She had no knowledge of hypnosis or relaxation techniques, but Tad gave her instructions on how it was to be done and what she should do. The procedure went very well.

It was shortly after this, however, that Tad learned that the fourth of his good friends at the hospital had died. This was soon after the death of Tad's dog. When the therapist returned from being out of town, he was mute and withdrawn. Psychotherapeutic intervention consisted primarily of encouraging him to express his feelings and assuaging his fears. The therapist differentiated his situation from that of his friends (medical prognosis in his case was objectively much better than theirs) and emphasized his strengths and the reason for optimism and hope in his life. He responded well and asked for an off-therapy party, a tradition on the unit. There was one more depressive episode for which he received similar assistance and from which he quickly recovered. Soon afterward, he was discharged from the hospital in a hopeful frame of mind.

Due to the family history of repeated traumatic events and the level of anxiety expressed by the mother and brother, these family members were engaged in treatment as well. Work with the mother focused on relaxation techniques, reinforcement of her self-confidence, and reinforcement of generational boundaries. She tended to dwell on the negative when she was anxious and to elaborate problem events in great detail. This served to increase Tad's own anxiety and kept conflicts from being resolved. Furthermore, her anxiety was interfering with sleep and causing her to overeat. She quickly learned hypnotic techniques to help her sleep at night and to curb her appetite. With these hypnosis experiences and those she was subsequently able to achieve on her own, anxiety diminished, while her self-confidence in meeting the challenges presented to her increased. Without this intervention, the mother's own anxiety could have sabotaged any progress for Tad. She stayed in the hospital with him almost continuously, and thus exerted a great deal of influence over him. Setting limits on her obsessiveness about symptoms and other problems and helping her approach her tasks in a more relaxed, self-confident manner was reassuring to Tad and allowed him to develop interests and concerns outside his body.

Tad's brother was seen primarily with the following goals: psychological support and nurturance; reduction of anxiety, particularly about bodily harm and illness; exploration of depressive and suicidal thoughts; and reinforcement of a more positive self-image and a more realistic assessment of his strengths. Tad and his brother had been "treated like twins" according to their mother. When Tad became ill, therefore, there was a tendency for his brother to identify with him and to feel ill as well, particularly when it brought more attention and care from the mother. Like Tad, the brother assumed that physical injury and illness were inevitable, and this belief served to enhance somatic preoccupations and the exaggeration of physical symptoms. As previously noted, this child had a minor heart condition that was checked periodically by a cardiologist. In several sessions, the brother expressed his fears that it would suddenly worsen and he, like Tad, would have to go to the hospital. (The mother reported that this was an extremely unlikely possibility.) The brother was very solicitous of Tad, thinking at first that he must accompany him everywhere so he could "save" him should he get into trouble. Moreover, there was some indication that the brother would like to sacrifice himself for Tad, whom he thought was more worthy of survival. The brother was not as good a hypnotic subject as Tad; however, he was much better at verbalizing. Hence, this mode of therapy was predominant. He was eager to try hypnosis, however, and was able to achieve a light trance. While it was not utilized intensively, hypnosis was helpful in restoring a sense of wellness, freedom, and self-direction and control. Without psychotherapy, it is possible that psychological distress and fears of bodily harm could have become a self-fulfilling prophecy, confirming what both boys were beginning to think—that extreme physical illness is a normal aspect of life.

DISCUSSION

For Tad and his mother and brother, anticipatory anxiety, preoccupation with negative expectations, and dwelling on traumatic experiences served to expand each event into a much longer experience. The anticipation was usually much worse than the actual event; obsessively thinking and talking about it afterward kept it alive in their minds, prolonging the negative experience. As time went on, their perceptions of symptoms became much more intensified. Hypnosis was a powerful tool in interrupting this pattern with distraction and the insertion of positive, pleasant experiences. During hypnosis sessions, somatic references were minimized, and suggestions related to the family members' participation in some enjoyable activity were made. It was always suggested that they were strong and healthy, as opposed to the weak and vulnerable way they tended to view themselves.

The experience of being able to develop muscular relaxation, to decrease nausea and vomiting, and to reduce pain all served to reinforce suggestions designed to enhance a sense of personal potency and positive expectancy. Tad came to his diagnosis of cancer with an already established sense of vulnerability, exploitation, and powerlessness that had developed from identification with such attitudes in his family. Further, the blurring of boundaries between himself and his brother and between the experiences and fears of one family member and another had resulted in compromises in identity formation and the development of secure differentiation and autonomy. Therefore, Tad's pessimism, symptom elaboration and overidentification with the deterioration and death of other patients is understandable in terms of these predisposing psychological factors. Hypnosis not only provided an important sense of mastery but also served to strengthen Tad's experience of himself as separate, unique, and autonomous. Such intervention ameliorated his problems in tolerating and coping with his disease but, more importantly, facilitated his maturation and identity formation in a more pervasive and far-reaching fashion. He left treatment with a more secure sense of himself and a clearer understanding of his realistic strengths and vulnerabilities. Somatization and acting-out had been modulated in favor of more conscious and adaptive expression of fears, conflicts, and concerns. Family identifications and expectations had been somewhat realigned with a resulting improvement in attitudes. Follow-up revealed no return of Tad's cancer, and his general level of adjustment appears to be good, age-appropriate, and marked by improved school performance.

This case demonstrates the way in which hypnosis can be utilized to mediate specific problems while facilitating broader adaptive capacities. The experience of mastering pain or nausea opens a new arena for exploring the capabilities of the self. Such experience is particularly significant for children who often feel a pervasive sense of fragility and is more potent in restoring self-confidence than simple support and reassurance. The exploration and phenomenological experience of self as strong, capable, and independent aids in tolerating the experience of self as limited, vulnerable, or debilitated. This process, which may be structured, directed, and supported by hypnosis not only improves the child's tolerance of his or her condition and situation but may sufficiently reduce stress and iatrogenic regression to enhance the child's treatment response (Hall, 1982). Further, this experience supports the maturational processes of differentiation and individuation, which serves to modulate the regressive pull of illness to infantile dependency and inappropriate symbiosis. This sort of hypnotherapeutic intervention, then, broadly facilitates the continuing growth and development of the child, with important implications for posttreatment adjustment. Strategically, this treatment paradigm focuses on anxiety reduction, support of syntonic and age-appropriate coping strategies, enhancement of a sense of mastery and self-control, and facilitation of maturational processes. In this multifaceted, multimodal approach, hypnosis can significantly enhance the treatment of children with cancer.

REFERENCES

Baker, E. Applications of hypnosis in pediatric oncology. In D. Copeland, B. Pfefferbaum, & A. Stovall (Eds.), *The mind of the child who is said to be sick*. Springfield, IL: C. C. Thomas, 1983.

Bammer, K., & Newberry, B. H. (Eds.). *Stress and cancer*. Toronto: Hogrefe, 1981.

Bowers, K. S., & Kelly, P. Stress, disease, psychotherapy, and hypnosis. *Journal of Abnormal Psychology*, 1979, *85*, 490–505.

Copeland, D. R. *Hypnosis of chronically ill children: A case study of Jill*. Paper presented at the annual meeting of the American Psychological Association, Washington, DC, 1982.

Dash, J. Hypnosis for symptom amelioration. In J. Kellerman (Ed.), *Psychological aspects of childhood cancer*. Springfield, IL: C. C. Thomas, 1980.

Ellenberg, L., Kellerman, J., Dash, J., Higgins, G., & Zeltzer, L. Use of hypnosis for multiple symptoms in an adolescent girl with leukemia. *Journal of Adolescent Health Care*, 1980, *1*, 132–136.

Fox, B. H. Current theory of psychogenic effects on cancer incidence and prognosis. *Journal of Psychosocial Oncology*, 1983, *1*, 17–31.

Friedrich, W. N. *Hypnosis as a broad-based intervention in pediatric cancer*. Paper presented at the annual meeting of the American Psychological Association, Washington, DC, 1982.

Gardner, G. G. Childhood, death and human dignity: Hypnosis for David. *International Journal of Clinical and Experimental Hypnosis*, 1976, *24*, 122–139.

Gardner, G. G., & Olness, K. *Hypnosis and hypnotherapy with children*. New York: Grune & Stratton, 1981.

Hall, H. R. Hypnosis and the immune system: A review with implications for cancer and the psychology of healing. *American Journal of Clinical Hypnosis*, 1982, *25*, 92–103.

Hilgard, J. R., & LeBaron, S. Relief of anxiety and pain in children and adolescents with cancer: Quantitative measures and clinical observations. *Journal of Clinical and Experimental Hypnosis*, 1982, *30*, 417–441.

Holden, C. Cancer and the mind: How are they connected. *Science*, 1978, *200*, 1363–1369.

LaBaw, W. C., Holton, C., Lowell, K., & Eccles, D. The use of self-hypnosis by children with cancer. *American Journal of Clinical Hypnosis*, 1975, *17*, 233–238.

Olness, K. Imagery (self-hypnosis) as adjunct therapy in childhood cancer: Clinical experience with 25 patients. *American Journal of Pediatric Hematology/Oncology*, 1981, *3*, 313–321.

Rogers, M. P., Dubly, D., & Reich, P. The influence of the psyche and the brain on immunity and disease susceptibility: A critical review. *Psychosomatic Medicine*, 1979, *41*, 147–164.

Simonton, D. C., Matthews-Simonton, S., & Creighton, J. L. *Getting well again*. Los Angeles: Tarcher-St. Martins, 1978.

Tache, J., Selye, H., & Day, S. B. (Eds.). *Cancer, stress and death*. New York: Plenum Press, 1979.

Zeltzer, L., Kellerman, J., Ellenberg, L., Barbour, J., Dash, J., & Rigler, D. Hypnosis for reduced discomfort related to diagnostic and treatment procedures in children with cancer. *Pediatric Research*, 1980, *14*, 430.

Zeltzer, L., & LeBaron, S. Hypnosis and non-hypnotic techniques for reduction of pain and anxiety during painful procedures in children and adolescents with cancer. *Journal of Pediatrics*, 1982, *101*, 1032–1035.

13

BRIEF HYPNOTHERAPY IN A CASE OF BULIMIA NERVOSA

Clinical Report and Commentary

David L. Calof

CASE REPORT

A 19-year-old girl, Carol, was referred to me by a community mental health center for treatment of chronic bulimia nervosa. Carol had been seen at the mental health center for 3 months following a 2-week period of hospitalization resulting from a suicide attempt in which she had taken an overdose of an anticonvulsive medication prescribed for a petit mal seizure disorder following an arrest for shoplifting. As a condition for her release from the hospital, Carol had been directed to take up residence at a psychiatric group home and initiate therapy at the community mental health center. Carol had made another serious suicide attempt 6 months previously, in which she had similarly overdosed on prescribed medication.

Carol's therapy at the mental health center had focused on developing insights regarding her family's dynamics. Efforts were directed toward the behavioral management of her eating behaviors, which had included periods of rapid, severe weight loss and daily episodes of gorging and vomiting candy and "junk foods." Her therapy had consisted primarily of discussions of Carol's early childhood and present family dynamics and the maintenance and periodic review of a behavior and cognition log associated with the gorging and purging behavior.

After 3 months of therapy Carol demonstrated a rather sophisticated understanding of her family's dynamics, although only negligible changes in her eating disorder symptomatology were noted. A treatment decision was made to offer Carol the choice of seeing a family-oriented therapist at the mental health center or of seeing me on a private basis for hypnotherapy. She opted for hypnotherapy, and an appointment was made.

On the day of our appointment, a series of coincidental events prevented me from seeing Carol for the scheduled 90 minutes. Consequent-

David L. Calof. Family Psychotherapy Practice of Seattle, Seattle, Washington.

ly, I was able to meet with her for only 30 minutes. We spent our first 5 minutes exchanging amenities. I then directed Carol to *tell me everything about her condition that she thought I should know to help her*.

Carol described her two suicide attempts and explained how her therapy at the mental health center had been a condition for her release from the hospital following the second attempt. She explained that she began obsessively thinking about food and then gorging and purging 3 years earlier, immediately following her parents' separation. She stated she had been "very involved" in the separation and consequently became quite withdrawn during her last 2 years of high school. Carol's report was sadly stereotypic of many adolescent anorectics. The implications of her report of the family dynamics typified the family structures reported by Minuchin, Rosman, and Baker (1978):

> With the child's entrance into adolescence, she finds herself in a crisis. Her wish to participate with a group of peers conflicts with her orientation to the family. The normal adolescent individuates by beginning to view her parents with the expanded viewpoint created by contact with the extrafamilial. But the anorectic cannot see herself as separate. Instead of focusing more and more on the extrafamilial world, the anorectic turns her expanded viewpoint back into focusing on her parents. She tries to help and change them. This overfocus and the parents' response strengthen the boundaries that keep the child overinvolved with the family. (p. 60)

Shortly following her parents' separation Carol became "very weight conscious" and went from 130 pounds to 88 pounds after several weeks of a "crash diet." Consequently, she was hospitalized to stabilize her weight at 92 pounds (her weight at the time of our visit) and to restore her electrolyte balance, which had been disturbed by frequent daily gorging and vomiting, first manifesting during this period of profound weight loss.

In describing her current relationship with her parents, she explained that since her last hospitalization she had made efforts to keep a distance from them. She reported that this seemed to have a minor palliative effect. She described her father as "extremely persuasive" and felt "a need to watch out for him." She recalled that he had "never" spoken to her mother. Mother was described as "bitter."

Regarding her sexuality, Carol explained that she had become amenorrehic following the period of severe weight loss and hadn't dated since then. She felt her mother had major objections to sexuality and hadn't given her adequate information about the subject.

Carol had read extensively about anorexia nervosa and bulimia in the popular press but was unconvinced that this was her condition, since she couldn't "emotionally accept" that her current weight of 92 pounds was inadequate for her height of 5′5″. She explained that her objective in hypnotherapy was to stop the vomiting, but she *would object to any weight gain*.

I next questioned Carol extensively regarding her knowledge and opinions about hypnosis. Although she was quite fearful of hypnosis, she saw it as a "last resort" and felt that she would most probably kill herself if hypnotherapy proved futile. On her intake form when asked to list words or phrases that described her attitude toward "hypnosis" she had written "last resort" and "scary (sort of)." Further questioning revealed that 4 months previously she had been hypnotized as a part of a stage hypnosis act at a local night club. Her description of a nearly total amnesia for the experience suggested to me that Carol was capable of achieving a somnambulistic trance.

When I had finished questioning Carol, I directed her to sit in the same position she had been sitting in when she had been hypnotized on the stage and to verbally report everything she could remember about the experience. She was instructed that as she did this she would develop a profound glove anesthesia in both hands and pay particular attention to this phenomenon as it developed. As she made her verbal reports I began interjecting suggestions for trance development, liberally borrowing language from the stage hypnotist whose "patter" I had heard on several occasions.

Within 10 minutes Carol developed a somnambulistic trance. I then told her I wanted to talk with her unconscious mind "privately" *in a way that her conscious mind "would not be interested in or even hear our conversation*." By this means, a dissociative state was produced in which Carol would be able to elicit even the most powerfully affective material without experiencing the pain that had accompanied her attempts to discuss this material in previous therapy.

Once the dissociation was achieved I directed the *dissociated* Carol to "tell me anything you think would be useful for me to know about Carol to help her." I further suggested, "You will be able to tell me comfortably about even those things that Carol cannot discuss consciously."

Carol first volunteered that "Carol" didn't like herself, was ugly, and wanted self-pity. She explained that she got angry easily but would usually "lock her anger inside" and then act it out in indirect ways, such as "talking behind others' backs." She spoke of her frustration attempting to resolve her problems in spite of "a strong desire to get better."

When asked about any possible connection between her condition and her family, Carol related that her mother was always yelling at her "for doing the wrong things." In particular, she remembered, "Mom always yelled at me for dieting and for eating the wrong things and for spending money." She said that her father had been kind but rarely said anything.

She then explained that when father left mother 3 years previously, she had become very sad and "went into a shell" and couldn't understand the reasons for the separation. She felt it was somehow her fault that she had somehow done something to precipitate it. She wondered if she somehow caused it by something she had done as a young girl.

I then asked Carol to tell me about her dreams. She told me that she frequently dreamed of food and of shoplifting food.

I then asked Carol if there was anything else she thought I should know. She responded that she didn't think so, except that she was "*impatient* to find a solution" and was "tired of being *inpatient*." When she spoke the second "*impatient*," it came out instead as "*inpatient*."

I thanked her *for being helpful* and then gave her a series of suggestions to the effect that she would generate and reinforce beliefs that she could be helped in our therapy together. She was directed to think less of her problem and told that as a result she would experience an improvement in her mood and outlook over the next several days and weeks, beginning when I awakened her. Lastly, she was instructed that she would remember just as much or as little of our conversation as her unconscious mind would find useful for her to remember. I then awakened her.

Once Carol was fully awake she seemed unimpressed by the experience, reporting that she felt like she had relaxed but was certain that her hands hadn't become numb as I had suggested. I construed her reference to the suggestions for glove anesthesia (given early in the induction) as a sign of a profound amnesia for her trance experiences. Consequently, I rapidly directed the conversation toward her availability for future appointments. She expressed disappointment that our first session had been so short and that more than one appointment would be necessary. She reported that she was unsure as to whether subsequent appointments would be helpful to her and that they would constitute a severe financial burden. Responding to this concern, I stated that I was only willing to continue seeing her if she had at least some hope for our success. She said she was willing to give me the benefit of her doubt "for a few sessions," reiterating her belief that hypnosis was her "last resort."

At this point in the interview, I remembered that I was scheduled to lead a consultation group later in the day consisting of five psychotherapists who were studying hypnosis. I told Carol about this group stating that the members were professional psychotherapists who were interested in the field of eating disorders. I suggested that *Carol might potentially be helpful* to that group's development in their specialties if she were to be a hypnosis demonstration subject before the group that very afternoon. I told her that I and the group would surely appreciate her special help recognizing that this would represent an additional sacrifice of time on her part. I explained that if she consented to help me in this way I would, of course, not ask payment for any help I might be able to give her during the demonstration. Carol readily consented to be a demonstration subject, stating she hoped her effort would enable the consultees to help other girls with her kind of condition through the use of hypnosis.

By implication, Carol had consented to a second trance experience in which therapy would be demonstrated, but she was allowed some denial that the therapy would be directed to her. Her conscious defensiveness therefore was depotentiated, which is a goal of the hypnotic induction process itself.

That afternoon, once the consultation group was assembled in my office, I invited Carol to join us. I found her sitting in the chair closest to my office door. She was ashen, sitting on the very edge of her chair, her knees shaking quite perceptibly. Recognizing her anxious condition, I volunteered that if she were feeling nervous about the demonstration, we could forego it and meet again in a week for a second private session. Carol protested that rather than nervous, she was quite excited about the prospect of helping to do a demonstration interview and proceeded to bind me to my earlier promise. Thus, Carol entered the interview in this "as-if" orientation. This one-up position (from "patient" to "consultant") presumably afforded Carol more access to personal resources that could be brought to bear in her therapy.

Having been thus convinced to proceed with the demonstration interview, I followed Carol into my office, where she sat on a couch around which were seated the five members of the group. I introduced Carol to the group and asked her if she would mind my tape recording the session for future reference. She readily consented to this.

HYPNOTIC SESSION

What follows is a complete unedited transcript with commentary of the tape recording of that session:

THERAPIST: OK, just tell them some of the things about you that you think are important and why you came to therapy.

CAROL [quietly, shyly, and hesitantly at first, then becoming more self-assured]: OK, well, uh, about 3 years ago I started going through this stage of eating a lot and vomiting. It got me down to about 92 pounds and I stayed that way for 3 years. At the same time, my mom and dad separated, and so I kind of *went into a shell* [my own emphasis] and didn't want to have anything to do with anyone, just the family. I, well, let's see, in January or February of this year [the interview is being conducted on November 11th] I overdosed and was put in the hospital. And then after I got out, things were going pretty good and then, uh, you know, I wasn't vomiting as much or anything and then it started picking up again and it was always candy and stuff like that. And, uh, then I found an apartment and started living on my own, and I was very lonely, so I overdosed again because I was eating and that led to stealing. And so I just, when I got caught one time, I just overdosed and then I went in the hospital again. And now I'm working on trying to stop that because it's been going on too long.

T: Yes, OK [gesturing to observers]. Would you mind if they asked you a couple of questions?

C: Uh uh.

(None of the consultees ask any questions, but several express their appreciation to Carol for volunteering as a demonstration subject.)

T: I know this is difficult for you. [Carol laughs and shakes her head "no." I continue, warmly, gently.] Why don't you just put your hands on your thighs, be comfortable. Why don't you watch that left hand. Now you remember before how you were waiting for it to go numb? You weren't sure if it did or not? I just want you to *wait in the same way*! Five! [In the morning trancework I'd given Carol a posthypnotic suggestion to go back to a somnambulistic trance each time I counted from five to one.] Relax NOW! Let yourself relax completely. Four, and you can feel yourself going to sleep now. Going deeper and deeper. Three, way down now, comfortable, relaxed and going deeper and deeper. Two, just let yourself go. Let yourself go very, very deep. Very, very deep, and one, deep asleep. Way down, let yourself go. Your whole body going to sleep. Loose and limp like an old ragdoll as you go deeper and deeper. That's right. [Carol's eyes close and she is beginning to slump to one side.] So very comfortably relaxed and just continue going deeper and deeper. [Pause.] I'd like to speak again with your unconscious mind, *privately*. At the count of three we'll be able to do that. You and I will be alone. Carol's unconscious mind and I will be alone. Her conscious mind won't really care about what we are talking about. At the count of three, Carol's unconscious mind and I will be alone, and we'll be able to speak privately. One, going deeper and more relaxed, two, deeper still, and three! [At the count of "three" Carol sits up slowly and opens her eyes.] Hi!

C [smiling, cheerful, oblivious of the observers]: Hi!

T: Nice to talk to you again. I wonder if you'd be willing, for the sake of this tape recording to tell me some of the things that you told me before? Would you be willing to do that? [Carol nods her head, "yes."] OK. You can remember exactly what it was that you said to me, and then just say it again. I asked you if there was anything that would be useful for me to know about Carol and what did you say?

C [voice calmer, deeper, and slower than before]: I said that she thought she was ugly and was too skinny and very irresponsible and wasn't very kind to others quite often. Yet at times she could be very kind.

T: And then you spoke about anger, too.

C: Yes, she gets very angry, very impatient. She locks it all inside, doesn't talk to anyone about it. That causes her to be upset. She talks about other people quite often. [Pause.] Expects other people not to talk about her and gets upset when she hears other people talking behind other people's backs. [Pause.] She gets nervous sometimes, wants things to happen too fast. [Pause.]

Bruch (1979) described a very similar social orientation in anorectic girls:

> There is increasing social isolation during the year preceding the illness. Some will explain that they withdrew from their former friends; others feel they were excluded. With their rigid, judgmental attitude, they begin to complain that the others are too childish, too superficial, too interested in boys, or in other ways not living up to the ideal of perfection according to which they themselves function and which they also demand from others. (p. 260)

T: I then asked you if you thought that the condition she brought here to be helped had anything to do with her parents and what did you say?

C [childlike tonality; literally]: Yes.

T: Can you tell me some more about that now?

C: Well, her mom always got mad at her for eating the wrong things or eating too much and got mad at her for dieting. And she yelled at her a lot, got mad at her a lot. But her dad was really kind, he never said anything. Never got mad at her for [pause] too many things. And then he left [pause] *he left her*. [This is a reference to the parents' separation.]

T: And how did she feel about that?

C: Sad. And she went into a shell. [Pause.] Then she started eating and vomiting to get rid [pause] to hide the problem.

T: How did that hide it?

C: She didn't have to think about it because she was busy doing something else. [Pause.]

T: And you also told me something that she thought about herself in relationship to the separation of her parents.

C: She thought it was her fault. She thought she did something wrong when she was little.

T: And is that true?

C [quietly, remorsefully]: No.

T: But she doesn't know that, does she?

C: No.

This cognitive dichotomy has been described, I believe, by investigators such as Bruch (1979).

> It has been recognized for a long time that these youngsters skip the classical period of resistance early in life; they continue to function with the morality of young children, remaining convinced of the absolute rightness of the grown-ups and of their own obligation to be obedient. Only few parents are aware of the literal mindedness of these children and their childish interpretations of life situations; most glory in having such good and obedient children. (p. 259)

T: OK. Now we also talked about her dreams. And what did you tell me about her dreams?

C: She remembers her dreams, easily. She always dreams about food, or she dreams horrid dreams about s-s-stealing, and they seem so real! That just really scares her. She goes to bed at night and thinks about breakfast and then has a scary dream about food and wakes up with a headache.

T: OK. That pretty much covers what we talked about. Have you thought about anything else since we talked that you think would be useful for me to know?

C [pause]: She's *impatient*. She doesn't want to be *inpatient*. [Pause.] She liked her job, but she gets upset at it sometimes, and she doesn't like that. She feels dumb a lot of times [disapprovingly]. Everyone else she sees and associates with is accomplishing more than her, she thinks. She always looks at the bad points, never the good points.

T: Any idea why she does that?

C [pause]: Her mother [pause] caused that.

T: In what way?

C: Always took her to the doctor, made her feel like she was sick. She did say she was sick. She said there had been something wrong with her for a long time. She always favored [pause, then voice lowers] *my* [my own emphasis] sister. Always favored her. And that, that I think caused a lot.

T: Does Carol understand these things consciously?

C: Partly, [pause] partly.

T: But not completely?

C: No. She gets confused very easily. [Long pause.]

T: Do you think it would be useful for her to look into her past in order to understand things about herself?

C: She's tried that, but when she does, she always looks at the good things [pause] that happened when she was little and tries to figure out if anything she did caused this. [Pause.] But she hasn't been able to find out yet. That's why she goes to a therapist, to see if they can *help find out if there's anything to do with her past* [my own emphasis].

Bruch (1979) has described how, prior to self-evaluation, anorectics " . . . marched to a different drummer who had kept them tied to the values and convictions of early thinking" (p. 258).

T [deliberately, voice lowered]: Would it be both OK and helpful for me to help her look at her past?

C: Yes.

T: Even the bad parts?

C [voice tone rising]: Yeah.

T: And would you be willing to decide what would be OK for her to remember when she wakes up and not?

C: Yeah.

T: How will you decide?

C [pause]: Well, the things I know makes her upset, I won't let her remember!

T: OK.

C: She doesn't like being upset or scared. She felt scared a lot when she was little. She was scared of the dark. She always had her door closed, er, open a little crack. She was scared of the dark. [Pause.] She was always scared that her mother would die. Always told her that she didn't want her to die. She thought to herself that if her mother died, that she would kill herself so she could be with her mother. She did. Her mother promised her when she was little that she would never get a divorce, and [with resignation] she did.

T: Does Carol remember that promise consciously?

C [with great conviction]: Yes, she does, very strong. Yeah, it was at night when *I* was going to bed mom promised that. I'll never get a divorce! [Pause.] She did.

T: What else?

C: She was always scared of getting spanked by her dad. Her dad always spanked when we got in trouble, when the kids got in trouble. He would use his belt, and she [pause] one thing she remembers is her little brother getting spanked with the belt one time and just [pause] big red welts on him. [Pause.] That scared her and made her sad.

T: Now, she has petit mal seizures. She's had those since the sixth grade. Do those have any psychological meaning?

C [pause a long time: apparently regresses; young, childlike]: No.
T: You didn't cause those!!?
C [even more regressed]: No.

My last two questions are grossly inappropriate. I am unable to account for my sudden shift of style and affect. Carol's apparent regression above is a result of this. Levenkron (1982) has commented on such behaviors by the therapist with anorectics:

> The most counterproductive behaviors by the therapist would be, first, dependent communications and, second, abandoning communications from therapist to patient. . . . Abandoning statements are those that ask the patient to assume premature automony. Silences, questions that ask the patient to make complex interpretations of her feelings, actions, or behaviors are examples. . . . (p. 144)

Sensing my error, I refocus the conversation and explain to Carol the nature of my proposed intervention.

T: I'd like to describe to you what I'd like to do, and I'd like your opinion about it, OK? [Carol nods.] What I would like to do in a moment is have you form a picture of all the significant people that you have interacted with in your life, perhaps some that you don't even remember consciously. I'd like you to see how, in the various ways, they helped form your personality, the various ways they helped contribute to your fears, and the ways of thinking about yourself, the ways of living in the world and how they interacted with each other. I'd like you to *see that progression over time* from when you were just a tiny, tiny baby to the present time. [Pause.] And I'd like *one part* of your mind, while *you're* doing that, to be watching the progression, and as *it* watches the progression, I would like for *it to make mental notes, but without your knowing that it's making mental notes*, about all those relationships and interrelationships. [Pause.] Do you think that would be useful for you?
C [calmly, resolutely]: Yes.

Now Carol can repunctuate the flow of her past experience. In the nonlinear thinking of the unconscious, Carol might examine her development in more systemic and less rigid ways.

T: OK. Close your eyes now. I just want you to go to sleep now, I'm going to talk elsewhere for a moment [turning my voice toward the group and back again]. When you feel me touch you on the knee as I am *now*, you will know that I am talking to you, again. In the meantime, you don't need to listen to me, and when I do touch you on the knee again as I am

NOW, I will count to three and at the count of three your eyes will open, and you will begin the assignment we just discussed. *When the progression is over*, that part of your mind which has been making mental notes is going to show you a wholly new scene. It's going to be of you, sometime in the future, but taking into account all the new learnings you've made. Do you understand? [Carol nods.] Now go deeper now, deeper. [Carol slowly slumps to one side.]

(I speak with the observers, and after several minutes I touch Carol on her knee and continue talking with her.)

T: Now just continue going deeper now. [Pause.] That's right. One, and when you're seeing the new scene, one of the fingers on one of your hands will lift automatically and stay in the air for a moment or two. And you can watch with a very detached sense. Three. OK. [Carol sits up, opens her eyes, and stares fixedly into space.]

T: Where do you think the images will begin to form?

C [already hallucinating the scenes]: When I was a baby?

T: Do you begin to see them?

C: Yeah.

T: Just continue to watch them. I think we should let them move down, down, to here. [I reach into the air as if grasping the hallucination and moving it to her lap.]

T: Do you see them here?

C: Yes.

T: Just continue watching the progression. *From time to time tell me how old.*

C: [Long pause.]

T: Can you tell me now?

C: She's playing with her neighbor. Her best friend. [Pause.] Now she's going to school. Her first day of school. [Carol's voice becomes younger.] Her neighbor and her are getting on the bus. [Pause.] Her mom is waving goodbye. [Pause.] She's a little scared, but she's with her friend so it's OK now. [Long pause.] Now she's with her teacher. [Pause.] At the end of the year she decides she doesn't like her teacher because she separated her neighbor and her, wouldn't let them sit next to each other. [Long pause.] Now she's in fifth grade. She had a rotten teacher. He made her exercise everyday twice a day and run around the field [pause] 18 times. [Long pause.] He never saluted the flag. He was a Jehovah [sic] Witness. [Long pause.] She's going to high school now. [Pause.] She doesn't get along with her sister very well. They're fighting. Her mother is yelling at her. Her sister's a cheerleader and her mother is upset because she's not a cheerleader. [Pause.] She's getting sick. [Pause.] Now she won't talk to anybody. [Long pause.] She'll talk to her dad. Her mother and her are fighting. [Pause.] Her mom's crying at night. It makes her very sad. [Long pause.] Now she's talking to her brother at night and told him how she wants to take overdose [sic] of pills. He thinks it's silly [matter-of-factly]. She goes in and does it. [Long pause.] Now she sees a fuzzy image of her mom [pause] waving flowers over her face, saying, "What's wrong?" [Carol begins to cry at this point and the dissociation appears to break down.]

T: *She* had those feelings and *you* don't need to!

C [tears stop, voice livens]: Then she went away.

Carol speaks these last words incredulously. My impression is that she is describing herself slipping into coma. There is a long pause, then she continues in narrative fashion.

C: Now she's in a different room [pause], and her dad's there [pause] very concerned. She's very weak. [Long pause.] Her dad takes her into his house [pause] so she can find a job. She doesn't want to live with her mother anymore. [Long pause.] Now her dad wants her to move out. She doesn't want to, she's not ready. [Long pause.] She moves into an apartment by herself. [Pause.] Things are going pretty good. Now they're starting to go downhill. [Pause.] She tries to explain her feelings to her dad [pause], but he just partially understands. [Long pause.] There's her brother. [Pause.] She's looking at her brother. [Long pause.] She's in the hospital again. She sees him for 2 minutes and then she's gone. [Long pause.] Now she sees her mother. Her mother's friend. [Pause.] His name is Jim. [Throughout these last several statements, Carol's voice has saddened. By the end, she has begun to cry again.]

T [slowly, calmly, authoritatively]: And you can continue to be calm as you tell me about them.

C [stops crying and continues; she sounds weak, sad, and far away]: Jim and mom come and see her every night at the hospital. She doesn't lose her job. She seems very happy. She wants to go back to work but the doctors won't let her. [Pause.] Now she found a new family. A better one. [This is inferred to be a reference to the group home in which Carol is at the time.] They don't [pause] fight. They're very kind to her. [Pause.] She doesn't want to have anything to do with her other family anymore. [Long pause.]

T: Does that take us to the present?

C: Yes.

I am struck by how earlier parts of the above sequence closely parallel Bruch's (1978) description of the process of therapy with anorectics:

> . . . psychotherapy is a process during which erroneous assumptions and attitudes are recognized, defined and challenged so that they can be abandoned. It is important to proceed slowly and to use concrete small events or episodes for illustrating certain false assumptions or illogical deductions. *The whole work needs to be done by reexamining actual aspects of living, by using relatively small events* as they come up. (pp. 143–144; my own emphasis)

T: Close your eyes for a moment. When you open them you'll see a crystal ball [pause] floating in the air in front of you [pause, then forcefully], and you know why it's there!! At the count of three, one, two, three! That's right. Can you tell me what you see?

C: [Opens eyes and stares fixedly into space.]

T: That's right. Can you tell me what you see?

C [pauses, voice livens, becomes more animated as she talks]: I see her. She's with her boyfriend right now. They're dancing. [Wondrously, then becoming more confident.] She has lots of friends. She's very active. She does lots of different things. [Long pause.] Now she's in an apartment by herself again. She's very happy. [Pause.] She's [pause] very artistic [pause] pottery. [Pause; astonished.] Now she's got a baby in her arms! [Happily.] She seems even more happy. [Long pause.]

T: How much does she appear to weigh in the apartment house?

C [joyously]: She weighs 115!

T: What season is it? [Note: The date is November 11.]

C: Winter. [Pause.] It's snowing out [pause, then joyfully] 2 weeks before Christmas! [Long pause.]

T [matching Carol's happy voice tonality]: What else about her is different?

C: She's very pretty! [Pause.] She's happy. [Long pause.]

T: What else?

C [continues staring for a long time, then responds]: That's all.

Selvini Palazzoli (1978) describes a process in anorectic patients in therapy that resembles the above sequence of future images.

> . . . during the advanced phase of psychotherapy, when progress toward full self-awareness enables the patient to attempt a reconstruction of her past experience of space and time, its direct confrontation with her present and new experience often produces the most trenchant insights and novel perspectives.
>
> Such flashes, which are invariably preceded by a slow and laborious process of introspection, often strike our patients like bolts from the blue and give rise to joyous feelings of surprise and astonishment. They have clearly

> scored a great and quite unexpected victory. . . . In this confrontation, the patients relive, describe and accurately interpret their past misery, and happily put it behind them. (pp. 140–141)

T: You can let the crystal ball go away now. [Carol closes her eyes.] That's right. Now, you can open your eyes again and look at me, deeply asleep. [Smiling, warmly.] You can handle it from here, can't you?

C [without hesitation]: Yes!

T [lowers voice tone]: Go to sleep now. [Carol closes her eyes and slumps to one side.] Just sleep deeply for a few minutes. [Pause.] You've done a lot of work. You deserve a rest. I'm going to talk elsewhere for a moment, and I won't be talking to you again until I touch you on the knee like this. Until I do that again, you can sleep deeply, and you don't need to hear anything, except for the sound of your relaxed breathing. [I speak with the consultees for 3 minutes and then touch Carol's knee, and she sits up and opens her eyes.] That's right. You can look at me deeply asleep. OK. You think you're ready?

C [nodding her head]: Uh huh!

T: Do you need anything else from me? [Carol shakes her head "no."] How would you like to let her know *consciously* that she's going to do what she needs to do? Do you know a way? I don't think she needs to remember all of this.

C: Let her remember the happy parts.

T: OK. You'll take care of that?

C: Uh huh.

T: OK. And you've considered all the things you need to consider?

C: Uh huh.

Selvini Palazzoli (1978) wrote a most beautiful passage regarding the spatial and temporal aspects of a patient's dream that occurred during the advanced phase of therapy:

> . . . and so chronological time is transformed into waiting time. Though she has lived in a space empty of relationships and in a time without any tomorrows, now that she has become mistress of her garden she realizes at last that she has been waiting all her life long. And in her waiting, in bridging her yesterday with her tomorrow, she has at last learned to project herself towards the future. (p. 143)

Selvini Palazzoli (1978) goes on to suggest that this extension of space–time experience can be detected in the conscious and dream material of all anorectics during the positive phase of their progress in therapy.

T: OK. All right. I'm going to wake you now. Now you can close your eyes. [Carol closes her eyes and slumps back to one side.] In a moment I'm going to count to five. At the count of five, Carol will be wide awake, remembering only that which her unconscious mind finds useful for her to remember [pause] and helpful [pause] and pleasurable. And now you won't be surprised to find other people in the room; as a matter of fact, they'll seem very warm and friendly to you. You'll be wide awake at the count of five. You'll just have some kind of idea that you're going to have a very pleasant surprise sometime later! [Pause.] You'll be very positive, very refreshed. *You may or may not know that you have to see me again.* [Long pause.] And it may or may not be the case.

The second to the last sentence was actually a slip of my tongue. What I had intended to say was "You may or may not need to see me again"; thereby indirectly suggesting no need for future therapy for the immediate symptoms.

I think my slip arose from a vague sense of insecurity and incredulity regarding Carol's accommodating performance in the trance. It had been so elegant, I feared it was counterfeit. Bruch (1978) cautioned about the overcompliance of such young women:

> A seriously delaying but often overlooked factor is the enormous compliance with which these youngsters can approach treatment, having lived their whole lives in an overconforming way. They agree with everything that is being said, will elaborate on it, even fabricate material that they feel the therapist wants to hear. This is one more reason why an interpretive approach is so ineffective in this condition. Anorexics will agree with what has been said, quote it in a different context, but actually feel that it means nothing.
>
> . . . The therapist needs to be aware of this. If things go too smoothly and there is ready agreement with everything being discussed, the question must be raised, "What is she really thinking?" Pseudo-agreeing may manifest itself in every area under discussion—in reviewing their background and home-life, when talking about friends, in explaining their self-concept, or in expressing their attitude toward weight and eating. It applies also to treatment goals, particularly to the question of "growing up" and "maturing." Many will readily agree to this as their goal, that they want to become independent people, even though their total behavior reflects their fear of adulthood and the grim determination not to grow up. (pp. 138–139)

T: With each count you're going to feel better and better. [Pause.] Very positive. You'll probably want to learn self-hypnosis in the future.

With this remark, not only did I want to lay a foundation for Carol's future use of self-hypnosis, but I also wanted to ensure a follow-up visit with her. My uncertainty, as manifested in my slip of the tongue (above), also gave rise to a fantasy that Carol would leave the session not to be seen again and chuckle over how she'd put one over on me and the group. Steve Levenkron (1982) suggests that such dependant communication on the part of the therapist is counterproductive in the treatment of anorectics, as is any behavior that requires the patient to reassure the therapist that either the patient or the therapy is succeeding.

T: With each count, a better sense of well-being. You're going to feel absolutely at peace, remarkably relaxed [pause] good sense of security [pause] safety. That sense of peace will continue with you and you'll feel better and better with every day. [Pause.] One, you're beginning to feel that good sense of well-being. [Carol begins to smile and sit up.] That's right, it feels good! Two, it feels better and better. It's going to be very difficult to resist a smile. Three, very hard to be depressed when you're smiling. Four, almost back in the room now, feeling wonderful and five! [Carol sits up completely; opens her eyes and begins to grin.] Hi!

C [cheerfully]: Hi!

T: Did you have a nice sleep? [By this remark, I want to reinforce whatever degree of amnesia Carol has chosen.]

C [laughing]: Yeah!

T: Good! Good! Comfortable? [Carol nods.] Just take a couple of seconds to gather yourself together. We have quite a bit of time, it's only 5:20. [The interview began at 4:10.]

C: OK.

The reader may recognize that a multipart dissociation was produced in Carol to aid her in the imagery assignment. The reader may also recognize that I failed to collapse the dissociation prior to awakening her. After I awakened her, I instructed her to "take a couple of seconds to gather yourself together." It is interesting to ponder how the therapist–patient interaction unconsciously selected this response in me to correct my error.

(Carol looks around the room to locate her coat and purse and notices the observers. One says, "Hello, Carol!", and Carol smiles.)

T [gesturing to the observers]: They don't seem too weird do they? [Carol and the group laugh.] Feeling pretty good?

C [grinning]: Uh huh.

T: What I would like you to do if you would, is to call me on Sunday afternoon. [Note: It is Friday afternoon.] Would you do that?

C: OK.

T: OK. I think I don't need to see you anymore today.

C: OK.

T: You have a good time tonight.

C: I sure will. [Giggles.]

T: Goodbye.

C [graciously, vivaciously]: It was nice meeting y'all. [Exits.]

FOLLOW-UP

On Sunday afternoon (in spite of my dependent fantasies) Carol called to report her progress.

She volunteered quickly that she was doing well but expressed some concern that, "I can remember most *of what you told me*" (my own emphasis). She explained that she had been "fighting against remembering" her trancework. She had recalled the scenes in the crystal ball and a few of the earlier memories. She was worried that this meant the "hypnosis wouldn't work."

I urged Carol to stop trying to forget at all, explaining that recalling surely meant her conscious mind was already starting to accept as finished some of the unconscious work that was still in progress and it was a good sign. In spite of my argument she insisted for some time longer that remembering the trance meant it wouldn't be effective. Finally, I directed Carol to ask her unconscious mind if *it* thought that her remembering was a sign of progress. Consequent to this, she reported an overall relaxation response and agreed that she was progressing, offering that she had stopped gorging or vomiting and had stopped eating at meals in response to *feelings of fullness*.

She stated that she was much more relaxed and that the problem was no longer "nagging" at her. She was thinking about food less and didn't feel compelled to eat each time she saw food. She had had none of the nightly nightmares, having slept "deeply and soundly" each night since the session.[1]

We arranged to meet in 9 days to review her progress with the proviso that she would call me prior to that *if she experienced any doubts concerning her progress* (another of my projections?).

1. Carol was then showing an increasing body sense and a greater appreciation of feelings of relaxation. Selvini Palazzoli (1978) has written, " . . . the point that strikes me as being of the utmost clinical importance is that, as a result of psychotherapy these patients not only learn to recognize body signals but also begin to take pleasure in the sensations of heaviness and relaxation, appreciating them at long last for what they are: *needs of the whole person*" (pp. 157–158).

FOLLOW-UP SESSION 1

At her second appointment Carol reported feeling consistently better about herself and "far less critical" of others. She felt she'd made a decision to live as a result of a period of introspection since her session regarding her suicide attempts. She speculated that she "might have been set up" for her overdose.

She had gone for nearly a week without gorging or vomiting, and in spite of a short-lived relapse following a difficult conversation with mother in which mother had strongly criticized Carol's hypnotherapy, *she had managed to gain a pound*.

I indicated that in my estimation, Carol was doing exactly what she needed to be doing at the time. I suggested that I would give her a "reinforcement" session and then see her in 3 weeks, *perhaps for a last visit*. Carol readily consented to the possibility of terminating.

Once I had induced a somnambulistic trance, I again asked to speak with Carol's unconscious mind *privately*. "She" reported that Carol was a lot happier and though she missed her parents some, she felt she had "a lot more patience."

In assessing her progress Carol estimated that she had "three quarters of the way to go." She explained that the symptom would occasionally manifest for 3 more weeks. She reminded me that her progress would generally follow the time line Carol had foreseen in the crystal ball.

She explained that it would be to her advantage for her symptoms to subside gradually rather than dramatically, since this would allow her to accept a weight gain. (*This, in spite of her conscious protestations that she was still having relapses*.)

Lastly, I gave Carol a series of ego-strengthening suggestions and suggestions that emphasized the value of placing faith in one's own unconsicous, along with detailed directions for the practice of autohypnosis.

Carol awakened from her trance with a self-elected, total amnesia. I repeated my trance instructions for autohypnosis, and then had Carol demonstrate a self-induced trance. She was then dismissed with an appointment for 3 weeks.

Two days after the session, Carol called asking for some advice and stating she was "lots better." She wanted to know if I thought it would be advisable for her to visit her father at Christmas. I told her I didn't know but that *she could consult her unconscious mind using autohypnosis and abide by whatever advice she was given*. She later reported that her unconscious had had no objection and that the visit had been largely uneventful and even positive compared with previous years' tensions.

FOLLOW-UP SESSION 2

Our termination session was held 3 weeks later. By this time, Carol had gained 11 more pounds. Carol's adamant refusal to "a weight gain program" just barely 5 weeks before had metamorphized into her being impressed with her ease with the weight gain. She related that she now weighed herself "once in a while."

The fact that Carol's acceptance of the weight was still an ongoing process of reorganization at both conscious and unconscious levels was best captured in one of Carol's remarks: "I feel that I'm gaining, maybe not showing on the scale, but I'm gaining. You know, it's kind of proportioning itself."

Carol told me that she was experimenting more frequently with autohypnosis and had achieved getting a dream which resolved a problem for which she had sought help from her unconscious.

Carol and I agreed that she would not need to be seen for additional appointments.

FINAL FOLLOW-UP CONVERSATION

Nearly 6 months after the initial session with Carol, I spoke with her for the last time. She told me that her symptoms had diminished rapidly and totally disappeared within several weeks of the termination interview and that she was doing well overall and still experimenting with autohypnosis.

DISCUSSION AND CONCLUSIONS

From a family systems perspective I believe Carol's success was due to her being able to achieve a "meta-position" to the family system. She let go of some of her external vigilance and did what therapists often do, that is, *expand the context of the problem*. In her trancework she had added a relational and unconscious context to the problem and let go of a rigid set of beliefs that had perpetuated her "habituated" behavior in the family dance.

In the first follow-up session Carol prophesied in trance that she would go through a period of relative separation from her family, finally to return but no longer in her previous relative position or role.

At the time I was seeing Carol, I was first being exposed to family systems theory and practice. I had been for the most part, a linear thinking, cause-and-effect, individual therapist. However, the more I studied, the more I was becoming convinced that anorexia was, as Minuchin *et al.*

(1978) concluded, "a disease of the child in the family" and that conjoint family therapy was the treatment of choice.

Shortly after I spoke with Carol for the last time, I was struck by the apparent paradox she presented in my struggle between two rather antithetical paradigms. I went with my dilemma to visit Milton H. Erickson (1978) who told me, "Jay Haley thinks you need to change the family so the child will change. I say sometimes you change the child and let the family learn to live with him differently."

I then went back to Minuchin *et al.* (1978) who, writing from a systems orientation, seemed to agree with Erickson when they concluded that if the unit of intervention is to be the anorectic child alone, the therapeutic approach must recognize the child's input in the family as a differentiated subsystem *with the power to maintain system homeostasis or facilitate change in the family.*

Perhaps the treater who hypnotizes the anorectic and "speaks to her unconscious mind privately" does not so much gain entry into a self-contained "unconscious" as tap into a "family unconscious," which is a medium of problem maintenance that does not respect boundaries such as self, household, generation, or corpus callosum.

REFERENCES

Bruch, H. *The golden cage: The enigma of anorexia nervosa.* Cambridge, MA: Harvard University Press, 1978.

Bruch, H. Developmental deviations in anorexia nervosa. *Israel Annals of Psychiatry*, 1979, *17*, 255–261, 259–260.

Erickson, M. H. Personal communication, 1978.

Levenkron, S. *Treating and overcoming anorexia nervosa.* New York: Scribner's, 1982.

Minuchin, S., Rosman, B., & Baker, L. *Psychosomatic families: Anorexia nervosa in context.* Cambridge, MA: Harvard University Press, 1978.

Selvini Palazzoli, M. *Self-starvation: From individual to family therapy in the treatment of anorexia nervosa.* New York: Jason Aronson, 1978.

14
THE TREATMENT OF CHRONIC HICCOUGHS WITH PERMISSIVE HYPNOTIC TECHNIQUES

Belinda R. Novik
Marcia A. Angle

INTRODUCTION

Intractable hiccoughs are an unusual but extremely frustrating medical problem. Current medical therapies include benzodiazepines, phenothiazines, and antidepressants. When these fail, patients are often referred to surgeons for phrenic nerve ligation. The phrenic nerve innervates the diaphragm; the causes of excess stimulation in this syndrome are thought to include tumors and anxiety.

The following case study illustrates how principles of hypnosis were used to treat a patient with chronic hiccoughs that were already refractory to all medical therapies.

In order to clarify the approach to this patient, the case description is preceded by a brief outline of three categories of hypnotic *techniques* and 10 basic *principles* that facilitated the therapeutic relationship and are illustrated in the case discussion.

TECHNIQUES

Permissive hypnotic techniques are perhaps most familiarly associated with the creative work of Milton Erickson (Erickson, 1959/1967, 1966/1967). They tend to fall into three major categories: auditory, visual, and kinesthetic (Grinder & Bandler, 1976).

Belinda R. Novik. Private Practice, Chapel Hill, North Carolina.

Marcia A. Angle. Department of Social and Administrative Medicine, University of North Carolina, Chapel Hill, North Carolina.

The adherence to any *one* technique leads to a hypnotic operator inflexible in his or her approach. That can become a problem during the course of treatment and is often blamed on the patient who is thought to be "resistant." In order to alleviate the inflexibility dilemma, the operator *must* maintain a lively, curious, versatile attitude, which may also enliven the patient's curiosity about how to get better; the operator should be willing to utilize whichever techniques appear to suit a particular patient best.

- *Auditory* techniques use words or sounds as the main channel for trance induction. The subject listens to suggestions.
- *Visual* techniques use either focused attention on an object or guided imagery and fantasy to accomplish the induction. The subject may watch mental images.
- *Kinesthetic* techniques use attention to a physical cue or sensation to induce trance. The subject feels the experience. All of these permissive hypnotic techniques can be facilitated by following certain principles.

Work by Diamond (1977) and Barber (1980) suggests that the success of therapy is not determined by the subject's responsiveness or hypnotizability, but by the hypnotic operator's flexibility with various induction methods. We believe that the variety of permissive techniques developed by Erickson offer the clinician a method to access patients' motivation, interest, and ability to speed healing.

PRINCIPLES

Once versatile in the above techniques, the operator can more easily build rapport with the patients, and good rapport with the patient may determine the outcome of treatment (Sacerdote, 1982). The following basic principles facilitate building a therapeutic relationship:

1. Following. "Pace" or follow the patient by attending to the ongoing process of the interaction, that is, body posture, breathing rate, rate of speech. Recognize the potential usefulness of whatever the patient's attitude and behavior appears to be, rather than entering the situation with inflexible notions of appropriate methods and outcome.

2. Voice. Use voice to make the suggestions congruent verbally and nonverbally. For example, when asking someone to relax, use a calm, soft voice. Voice can also be used to "pace" or follow the patient's breathing rate, vocabulary, and verbal style.

3. Positive feedback. When patients are in a hypnotic state or are ill, they are in a relatively dependent position, and positive feedback given sincerely can be a very ego-enhancing and therapeutic gift. It also serves to minimize "resistance" and maximize cooperation.

4. Credibility. To maximize effectiveness the operator must maintain credibility. This means never assuming unverifiable experiences or committing oneself to results that are unrealistic. The balance between therapeutic optimism and credibility must be carefully weighed.

5. Simple requests first. Begin with suggestions that are natural and easy to perform, for example, sit down, take a deep breath. In this way subjects learn that they can succeed. This can create a "yes" set (an attitude of cooperation), which minimizes resistance and paves the way for more complex suggestions.

6. Pairing. Give therapeutic suggestions in tandem with a predictable event in the patient's experience: for example, "When your extended arm gets heavy and begins to lower, your eyes may close."

7. Successive approximations. Recognize the utility of taking small steps toward the desired outcome and reinforce those intermediate achievements. Modify the symptom, but do not take it away. Patients are likely to resist if something is taken from them. One may "prescribe the symptom," but prescribe it as lasting less time or producing less distress.

8. Variety. The operator should be comfortable with enough techniques to be able to suit different patients' needs, whether the patient requires relaxation or animation, structure or freedom, control or permission. Facility with many techniques, even authoritarian ones, permits the operator to move from one technique to another as needed. This responsiveness is another way to minimize resistance. The operator is responsible for finding the way to the patient's hypnotic capabilities.

9. Satisfying the patient's need for control. Patients with problems often feel out of control of their situation as well as their symptoms. The hypnotic process can subtly provide an opportunity for the patient to have control over both themselves and their symptoms. This control develops through the operator's willingness to allow the patient to make selective choices congruent with the patient's needs: for example, "Do you want to sit up or lie back?," "Would you like to raise your right hand or your left hand?"

Notice that the hypnotic operator is also in control and offers choices, either of which facilitate the hypnotic state and either of which are acceptable to the operator.

10. Shared trance states. When the hypnotic operator allows himself or herself to experience a trance state while facilitating the patient's state, a powerful alliance emerges. The operator maintains primary focus and contact with the patient while simultaneously aware of his or her own cognition, intuition, and affect. This produces a highly creative encounter that is shared as an "adventure" for both patient and provider. The shared trance state so often produces imagery or thoughts that prove invaluable to the outcome of treatment that I cannot recommend it highly enough.

CASE HISTORY

The patient was an elderly, married, retired farmer with intractable hiccoughs. After an exhaustive medical evaluation, no organic etiology could be found, and the patient had failed all medical management. Permanent surgical ligation of the phrenic nerve was being considered at the time the first author (Novik) was consulted.

THE INDUCTION

The induction for this case was chosen within the first minutes of meeting the patient and was based on the perception that the patient would find it easier to be kinesthetically involved, since physical movement was unavoidable due to the hiccoughs. The therapist was unsure how active the hiccoughs would be during the session, but was prepared to incorporate any movement—especially from the hiccoughs—into the induction if necessary. Kinesthetic inductions are also useful in quickly illustrating both the patient's control and the operator's willingness to share control; it was important to communicate to this man that control over some part of his body was possible.

The induction began after approximately 4 minutes of general introductions and greetings, getting seated in the room, and asking the patient's permission to use hypnosis. He was willing to "try anything" to gain relief. The therapeutic plan evolved during the hypnotic sessions with only a rough notion early on of the desired outcome (avoidance of surgery, reduction in hiccoughs, increased comfort).

The therapist asked the patient to sit on the edge of the hospital bed, which he was already doing (*simple requests first*). Then, he was requested to pick one of his arms to raise straight out in the air to about shoulder height (*giving patient control*). The therapist quietly instructed the patient to pay attention to the arm (*use of voice*), to pay attention to whatever *he* noticed about it, its color, temperature, position, features, sensations, whatever came to his attention (having named most of the possibilities, the therapist seemed credible early in the therapy). As the patient attended to his arm, the therapist attended to his clearly visible breathing rate and heartbeat rate through his neck pulses. Verbal cues were paced to these rates and the therapist began to slow her speech—imperceptibly at first and more definitely as induction progressed (*following*). The therapist was always ready for that hiccough to be dealt with as part of the normal patter of induction and also ready to use a relaxation induction to help the patient be more comfortable.

The patient's arm began to feel "heavy," and the therapist paired the heaviness and its lowering with a sense of ease, interest, curiosity, and eye closure (*pairing*). She suggested that the eye closure would occur only after the arm was resting comfortably in his lap, to give him a chance to go at his own pace yet follow her instructions. As the patient's arm slowly lowered (*successive approximations*), the therapist encouraged and praised him (*positive feedback*).

Because the therapist knew relatively little about this man, the next direction was extremely permissive, allowing him to guide himself and the therapist into his hypnosis. She began by asking the patient if he was willing to go on (*control*). He agreed verbally, and the therapist asked him to imagine going to his favorite place and to describe it. He quickly told about a fishing pond, and she asked him to describe it in detail, deepening and enriching the experience for him (*variety*).

Guided imagery in this fashion is an experience for both patient and doctor and becomes a shared "adventure" and a common experience. The therapist felt it was important to get a picture of this man's world, as she had not worked with him before and did not know his interests and activities. Letting the patient do some of the leading strongly increases compliance and credibility.

In fantasy the patient talked freely about the boat he was in, the cool breeze, and the water. Then he hiccoughed. For a brief moment the therapist was startled but quickly recovered and responded from her own sense of the pond that it sounded like a "big ol' bullfrog." The man smiled and agreed. On a hunch the therapist asked what it was the bullfrog was doing. The patient said he was looking at this nice day. When asked what the bullfrog was feeling, the patient said "He's real *lonely*; he's *mad*."

THERAPEUTIC PLAN AND PROGRESS

The therapeutic plan began to develop further, taking into account the bullfrog, which could be a useful ally in treatment as an expressive partner to this rather typically unexpressive patient. The creativity of the trance state allowed the therapist to share a perception with the patient, giving him an alternative way of experiencing his distressing hiccoughs. Changing the referent from hiccough (a 6-year problem) to a bullfrog (a new entity with no history of distress attached to it) permitted the patient to view his problem from a different perspective and generated hope, an important curative factor.

Through the bullfrog the patient and therapist continued to talk about what it was like to sit on a lily pad and feel separate from the other creatures of the pond. This bullfrog had a wife, but she was not around at the moment. The bullfrog wanted to be with his friends and buddies. The session ended after a brief deinduction and a contract to continue the next day. The therapist felt the need for some family history and thought she could gather it from the house staff before continuing.

The history obtained from the house staff was quite useful at this point. This patient was described as being a very gentle, soft-spoken, nice man who would never say a negative thing about anyone. Recently, he had been getting less and less involved in the activities of his household, and his wife and daughter were taking over the payment of the bills and the decision making. He was being treated more and more like an invalid, and probably felt a sense of loss of self-esteem that he did not know how to regain. Since anger in any direct sense was not part of his repertoire, he had very few ways to communicate his feelings and used withdrawal (which was not permitted by his wife and daughter) and then hiccoughs to express his distress. The family was so doting that every time he hiccoughed they would rush to his aid before it was necessary. Here was an example of well-meaning people misreading each other's nonverbal cues and acting in such a way that only made the situation worse: His wife and daughter had been overzealously hovering around him, and he did not know how to reassert his independence against these maternal figures enough to ask them to leave him alone so that he could look after himself.

The therapist returned to the patient for the next session, wondering how she might be able to suggest ways for him to be more expressive and regain a sense of control and self-esteem.

On the 2nd day the patient was eager to begin and put his right arm out in front of his body before being asked to do so. The therapist quickly adjusted to this accelerated pacing, and they continued the exploration of the pond and the bullfrog (*following*). During the 2nd day and on the subsequent sessions, the therapist began to suggest to the patient that he could begin to talk about his own feelings. The therapist gave encouragement and permission for him to express even "bad" feelings to her. Gradually, a transition was made from talking about the bullfrog's feelings of anger to the patient's feelings of anger about his wife's overprotection of him. At this stage when asked directly (*without* hypnosis or the metaphor), he still described his wife and daughter as very attentive and loving. Life was difficult to be sure, but he never complained.

In the 3rd session, it was suggested that the patient could hiccough in the morning and then stop (*successive approximation*). Because he was receptive and responsive, the therapist went on to suggest that the patient would find eating more enjoyable again and that he would be able to engage in social activity and hobbies. She also suggested that he could find other means of expressing anger (*credibility*).

OUTCOME

Over the course of five such in-hospital hypnotic sessions and three weekly follow-up outpatient visits, the incidence of hiccoughs were reduced to a few minutes, several times per week. He was able to resume a more active life, shop, enjoy his hobbies, and get the family to leave him alone more often by practicing relaxation and putting his own comfortable chair in his room. He reported sleeping better and feeling better than he had in years.

The bullfrog metaphor was a useful transition from passive–aggressive somatization to direct verbal communication about needs. The metaphor was no longer necessary when the patient could talk directly about his feelings.

CASE DISCUSSION

In prescribing the symptom, the patient is encouraged to produce the symptom at a specified time and place. This promotes a sense of mastery over previously uncontrollable symptoms. In the preceding case, at the point when the therapist's credibility was high and the therapeutic relationship strong, the therapist risked suggesting increased activity and increased expression of feelings at home (not actually knowing whether the patient would or could succeed at this time).

Through the metaphor of the bullfrog, the meaning of the symptom was emerging. The symptom served as a passive way to express negative feelings in a gentleman too repressed to even think such thoughts. The symptom was an important part of the patient's personality. It provided him with an outlet of anger that left him blameless and able to continue viewing himself as a "nice" man.

The hiccoughs served to produce helplessness and irritation in the family members, who were exposed to this constant disguised expression of the patient's anger. The therapeutic plan needed to include giving or eliciting other options for the expression of anger in order to promote family harmony and to free the patient from an increasingly debilitating symptom and lifestyle.

The use of hypnosis for patients with somatic problems is particularly rewarding. Patients can increase participation in their own health care with the knowledge of self-hypnosis. The increased self-esteem and control of symptoms aids in the healing process. Learning to access the trance state together with self-hypnotic procedures enhances the very intimate interpersonal relationship of the doctor and patient. Patients welcome that kind of potent, attentive, yet nonintrusive closeness. The first 10 minutes of trancework remains a strong positive force in the patient's memory, making it a cost-effective use of physician time; those minutes communicate the caring and gentleness many patients need, and with posthypnotic suggestion, the hypnotic state and suggestability can be reaccessed instantly with a prearranged cue.

Further, the effectiveness of the hypnotic relationship and the rapport that develops from it pay off continually. Compliance increases and patients feel better and are able to be as active as possible. Given the cost, side effects, and problems of compliance with medication or surgery, especially in the elderly (Williamson & Chopin, 1980), hypnosis can be an effective ego-enhancing treatment while minimizing medical complications, dangerous drug interactions, and elective surgical procedures.

The preceding case presents additional evidence that hypnotic techniques can be useful to clinicians. As with any therapeutic tool, clinicians must be wary of the indiscriminate use of a potentially potent intervention and offer patients responsible guidance and follow-up during their joint adventure.

ACKNOWLEDGMENT

We would like to express our thanks to Ms. Janice Sheikh and Ms. Marcie Shamel for their patient and expert help in the preparation of the manuscript.

REFERENCES

Barber, J. Hypnosis and the unhypnotizable. *American Journal of Clinical Hypnosis*, 1980, *23*(1), 4–9.

Diamond, M. J. Hypnotizability is modifiable: An alternative approach. *International Journal of Clinical and Experimental Hypnosis*, 1977, *25*, 147–166.

Erickson, M. H. Further techniques of hypnosis and utilization techniques. *American Journal of Clinical Hypnosis*, 1959, *2*, 3–21. (Reprinted in Haley, J. *Advanced techniques of hypnosis and therapy*. New York: Grune & Stratton, 1967.)

Erickson, M. H. The interspersal hypnotic technique for symptom correction and pain control. *American Journal of Clinical Hypnosis*, 1966, *3*, 198–209. (Reprinted in Haley, J. *Advanced techniques of hypnosis and therapy*. New York: Grune & Stratton, 1967.)

Grinder, J., & Bandler, R. *The structure of magic* (Vol. 2). Palo Alto, CA: Science and Behavior Books, 1976.

Sacerdote, P. A non-statistical dissertation about hypnotizability scales and clinical goals. *International Journal of Clinical and Experimental Hypnosis*, 1982, *30*(4), 354–373.

Williamson, J., & Chopin, J. Adverse reactions to prescribed drugs in the elderly: A multicentre investigation. *Age and Aging*, 1980, *9*(2), 73–80.

V
PAIN CONTROL

Pain control is one of the most common applications of hypnosis, being used in a wide variety of situations with a wide variety of pain problems. Its utility in this regard has been repeatedly demonstrated, and hypnosis is often the treatment of choice when medication or surgical procedures are contraindicated. The use of hypnosis in the treatment of pain has been so widely reported in the literature that we decided not to include it as a large component of this book. Instead, we focused on three selected problems.

Clorinda G. Margolis describes hypnotherapy for pain control with two cases, one involving severe burns and the other involving terminal cancer. While seemingly unrelated, there are actually several similarities. In both cases the clients' coping abilities had all but disappeared. In addition, the usual treatment for acute pain was not effective, and the physical and psychological trauma were much greater than that normally associated with chronic pain. In both cases the intense nurturing quality of the therapist–client relationship is immediately apparent, as is the development of coping strategies.

James M. Healy and E. Thomas Dowd discuss hypnotherapy for control of migraine cluster headaches in a multiproblem client. Although the therapist was aware of the multiplicity of the problems, he chose to focus on the most salient problem only and the one for which the client was initially referred. Although the treatment for pain was successful, there is no evidence that therapeutic gains generalized to other aspects of the client's life. Although therapeutic gains in one area of an individual's life can often generalize to other areas, there is no intrinsic reason why this should occur, especially when the interventions are specifically targeted, as this case illustrates.

John F. Chaves describes a hypnotic procedure for the treatment of phantom limb pain. He notes that this phenomenon is quite resistant to amelioration. What is striking about this case is that self-hypnosis was largely ineffective despite the patient's apparent hypnotic capacity. Another interesting feature was the development of strategies based explicitly on the patient's pain experience. The hypnotic procedure used was a conservative one involving direct suggestions for relaxation and activity.

15
SPECIAL PAIN PROBLEMS
Burns and Cancer

Clorinda G. Margolis

Pain and suffering have always plagued us. The expectation that modern medical technology, often so dramatically successful in restoring the body after severe injury and eliminating the threat of so many diseases, would have advanced also toward full control of pain has not been fulfilled. Despite impressive achievements—the reduction of pain during surgery, for instance—there still remain intractably painful treatment procedures for which anesthesia or opiates or the like would be medically inappropriate. The very prolongation of life entails occasions for prolonging pain and suffering; the invasive nature of medical technology forces us to reconsider the conjoint benefit of nonintrusive procedures for controlling pain. In these circumstances hypnosis, one of the oldest forms of treating and controlling pain, appears, however incongruously, to promise a peculiarly up-to-date advantage. Furthermore, our commonsense model of pain is, as we have come to realize, much too simplistic (Bonica & Ventafridda, 1979), even when made neurophysiologically more precise. Pain cannot be merely a noxious sensation signifying tissue damage or apparent damage or the threat of damage—a sort of somatically specific or focused warning. Pain must be rather a complex sort of phenomenon—depending at least on molar psychological, situational, and cultural factors (Sternbach, 1968; Melzack, 1973)—that at times manifests itself relatively autonomously, that is, in ways not obviously controllable by direct neurophysiologic or pharmacologic intervention consistent with normal human functioning.

A modified diagram of pain by Loeser (1980) may serve to focus the problem (see Figure 1).

Nociception signifies the detection of tissue damage (sometimes, even the detection of apparent or potential tissue damage) and is thought to behave like other perceptual systems, routing neural messages through characteristically specialized networks. Minimally, on a standard model of

Clorinda G. Margolis. Private Practice, Philadelphia, Pennsylvania.

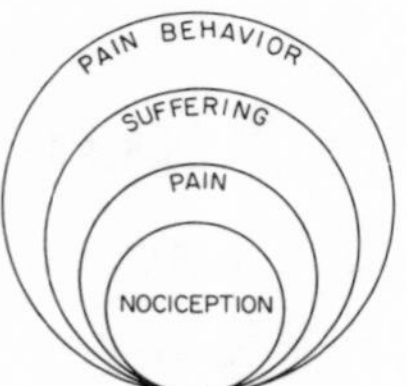

FIGURE 1.

acute pain, nociception results in a determinate experience of pain, hurt, or discomfort. This somatic experience is frequently accompanied by negative affective states (anxiety, fear, terror, sadness, discouragement, anger, etc.) and aversive responses. Normally, the more intense the affective response, the more suffering experienced and manifested. Pain behavior is observed by others, whereas actual nociception, pain, and suffering can only be reported in the first person. In its most simplified form, the model of acute pain holds that tissue damage results in nociception or pain signals that cause the subject to experience hurt. More pain triggers more affective responses, and the subject experiences more suffering. In intense pain and suffering, grimacing, groaning, as well as autonomic nervous system responses to stress are often seen. In chronic pain, pain ascribed to tissue damage accounts for rather little of the experienced suffering or can actually no longer account for determinate pain experiences. Affective responses tend to be prominent in the description of intense suffering, and autonomic nervous system responses may come to be adapted to pain-producing stimuli and therefore no longer be observed.

On the acute model, various treatment procedures—surgery and the use of pharmacologic agents—successfully reduce or eliminate pain and suffering. Often the noxious stimulus itself, a splinter in the finger for instance, can be removed. But on the chronic pain model, pain is often described as a reverberating central state that cannot be effectively removed or treated by surgery or drugs. Phantom limb pain (see Chaves, Chapter 17, this volume) is a paradigm of such pain. A learning model rather than a restrictedly neurophysiologic model is characteristically more helpful both in understanding and treating chronic pain patients (Fordyce, 1976).

The acute–chronic distinction, however, even more fully elaborated, does not exhaust the range of special pain problems encountered in the medical setting. Two further kinds of pain are particularly salient: pain experienced by burn patients during treatment and pain experienced by terminally ill cancer patients. In these and related cases, patients experience quite intense pain and suffering, and the usual treatment for acute pain does not effectively relieve their suffering.

SALIENT FEATURES OF BURN AND CANCER PATIENTS

Burn patients undergo severe physical and psychological trauma on being severely burned. The horror of that experience and the physical damage to the body shocks victims so much that, during their first days on the burn unit, they are usually disoriented and confused and out of touch with the reality of their present state. Stabilizing patients in shock presents itself as the initial treatment issue; controlling infection and other serious complications comes later. In full-thickness burns, all skin layers are destroyed: The normal regeneration of skin becomes impossible, so grafting becomes necessary. Grafting is also often advisable in deep partial-thickness burns. The daily removal of dead tissue and exudate, a process termed debridement, is obligatory for the treatment of all burns and is performed in a hydrotherapy tub as bandages are changed, continuing daily until grafting takes place. It is a prolonged and painful procedure that patients quickly learn to dread. It is in fact generally regarded as the worst process of the many painful and distressing experiences burn patients must go through in recovering from severe burn trauma. Fear, anxiety, rage, depression, and withdrawal are experienced by nearly all such patients.

Terminally ill cancer patients are usually aware that the pain they experience is due to the progressive nature of their disease—and will lead inevitably to death. Although some patients do not experience much pain, studies show that 60%–80% of patients with advanced cancer experience moderate to severe pain in their dying days (Bonica & Ventafridda, 1979). In cancer patients with extended life expectancies, pain and suffering tend to be increased simply because of the prolongation of physical and psychological deterioration. Despair, feelings of hopelessness and helplessness, and bitterness often—too frequently, in fact—seem to make their last days intolerable.

Patients of both sorts face unrelieved pain daily. They endure continual psychological and physical threats to their survival, and their need for solace and relief is overriding.

Hypnosis (or, more appropriately, hypnotherapy) offers a medically nonintrusive assortment of techniques and modes of interaction with patients that can decrease their isolation, alter their bodily and emotional states, affect the experience and quality of felt pain, and afford comforting forms of ongoing communication exchange. Sacerdote (1982) holds that many patients have the capacity to alter and transform their experience of pain relative to two factors: (1) a patient's talent for undergoing hypnosis and (2) a hypnotherapist's skill in eliciting pertinent hypnotic responses.

The following two cases provide examples of individualized hypnotic interventions.

CASE 1: BURN PATIENT

TB, a 19-year-old white man, sustained full- and partial-thickness burns over 56% of his body in a house fire. I was asked to see him by the burn staff because his physical and emotional condition was deteriorating. Two skin grafts had been unsuccessful. A Curling's ulcer—a stress ulcer 2 cm in diameter, which later perforated the stomach—necessitated a subtotal gastrectomy and truncal vagotomy the day before hypnosis was initiated. He was clinically depressed and daily debridement procedures were emotionally exhausting as well as causing unbearable pain (Margolis & DeClement, 1980).

On my initial visit I saw a patient in a prone position in bed, with both arms immobilized and suspended in the air. He appeared listless, withdrawn, and heavily narcotized because of the stomach pain from the prior surgery. He acknowledged my presence and agreed to be hypnotized. I began an eye fixation induction; but each time his eyes closed, his body began shaking, and he quickly alerted himself, mentioning brief but frightening dreams. I then suggested his eyes remain open as he listened to my voice, and I made a number of relaxation and safety suggestions. He became quiet quickly, and I suggested that the next time I hypnotized him, he would experience a deeper and more prolonged hypnotic trance.

When I returned 2 days later, a nurse on the unit stopped me to mention how eager TB was to see me again. He was alert when I went into his cubicle and immediately apologized for his poor concentration the first session. He explained that he had been very tired from his surgery but felt that he relaxed a little as he listened to my voice. We had a good working session. He was able to experience hypnotic trance quite easily. I used an eye fixation induction, focusing on a ceiling stimulus and counting backward from 300. His eyes became so heavy they closed involuntarily. He moved into hypnotic trance. In trance he visualized different parts of his burned body relaxing so deeply that he became unaware of any associated sensation. Except for the burns on his buttocks, which caused him a great deal of pain, he was able to dissociate most of his body in this way. I taught him autohypnosis, using the same induction. In trance I gave him the suggestion that when he received his narcotics prior to the debridement procedure, he would put himself into a hypnotic trance: He was to use eye fixation, to dissociate his body, and to remain in this altered state with no discomfort until the procedures were completed and he returned to his room. The training session took 45 minutes and left us both very tired. On the next visit he reported (the nurse corroborated the claim) that during debridement and dressing changes, he was able to maintain himself in a hypnotic state; he remained relaxed and experienced markedly less pain.

In the third session he was almost euphoric; he was delighted with his hypnotic experience and with his ability to reduce his pain so substantially. He also was eager to talk about himself, volunteering that just prior to my first visit, he knew he was dying. He consciously decided to postpone judgment until he met his hypnotist, in order to see if he could really be helped with his pain. Now that he could use hypnosis, he felt distinctly stronger. He felt relieved that he was no longer struggling alone and helplessly. Other traumatic experiences began to surface. For example, he had found a close relative in a coma once, due to an overdose of medication. He had been afraid that although she was breathing, she was dying. This was the first time since the accident that he was so voluble. Volunteering the details of his burn trauma and other experiences that had frightened him appeared to be cathartic. When I hypnotized him, his tremors increased as they had during our first session, but they subsided quickly as I gave him suggestions for deep relaxation. I reinforced his ability to relax and dissociate his body during bandage changes and tubbing and added the suggestion that time would pass more quickly when he experienced trance.

Prior to the fourth session his physician asked me to give him hypnotic suggestions in order to facilitate his body's accepting the skin grafts. Since prior skin grafts had sloughed off, and since he had little unburned surface skin left for grafting, it was quite important that future grafts "take." There was even some question about his having enough skin to cover the entire (full-thickness) burned area that needed to be replaced. When I saw him I explained what his physician had told me. We considered together how the burned area should be imaged in order to receive an effective graft. He described it as clean and open, and I added the notion that the tissue would be "receptive." After putting himself into trance, he responded to my suggestions that he visualize the area to be grafted (his hand and thigh) as tissue clean and open and so receptive that the grafts would take hold easily and healing would begin immediately. He reported visualizing this and feeling very optimistic.

Several days later his physician told me that the grafts were healing in a "remarkable" way—that, after only 24 hours, they looked as if they had been healing for several days. The patient was pleased, but he complained of pain from the exposed raw nerves of his donor sites. Also, during debridement procedures the day before, some bandages had been pulled off his buttocks too quickly and the exposed areas had become raw. We developed and tried two images: (1) an antiseptic bath cooling and healing the donor sites and the raw areas, (2) a cooling salve with numbing properties that he could put on selected areas that troubled him. During trance, he chose the salve because he felt he was "sitting in a draft" that kept his body cold; he wanted to feel warmer. The salve cooled him only in selected areas. On awakening he reported severe itching in his donor sites and tried to scratch himself. I rehypnotized him and suggested a reduction in his itching; I pointed out that he was probably experiencing the area healing—a comforting idea. He was pleased to report a reduction in the itching. By this time, he was a well-trained hypnotic subject, able, during most of the debridement procedures, to dissociate selected parts of his body successfully. He began using hypnosis to induce pleasant imagery and to relive pleasant events when he felt particularly confined by physical restrictions and the hospital environment.

Other physical complications continued to hamper his recovery. Localized infection and a draining gastric fistula prevented complete healing of his surgical wound. As he began taking food by mouth, he complained of a lump in his throat, some nausea, and noticeable difficulty in keeping food down. During the seventh session, he was very discouraged because his fistula, after some improvement in drainage, had "blown open" again. He also felt he was no longer able to handle his pain during debridement procedures, although the nurses reported that he was not exhibiting earlier pain behavior. He was also anticipating grafts for his arms. In a prolonged trance, I reviewed his progress and his mastery of hypnosis. I recapitulated earlier suggestions , particularly his receptivity to grafts. I gave him suggestions for healing the fistula by visualizing an increased blood supply filled with useful nutrients fed to the area. He was amnesic during most of these suggestions and was very reluctant to see me leave at the end of the session.

His grafts "took" very well. According to his physician, this was surprising because of his poor nutritional state. His healing capacities were at suboptimal levels. When I saw him, he was complaining that the food tasted terrible, that he completely lacked an appetite. The previous day he was vomiting and unable to hold much food down. He also complained of gas pains. I induced trance simply by asking him to close his eyes and relax. His eyes did not close fully, but only sclera showed. I suggested quiet deep breathing to reduce his tension and to relieve his stomach pains. During trance, an aide came in calling his name. He opened his eyes briefly, looked at the aide with a glassy stare, but did not reply. I suggested that as his stomach became comfortable, his appetite would return. He was amnesic for the entire length of the trance and reported feeling much better afterward.

The remaining sessions followed much the same pattern. He was no longer confined to his bed. His appetite improved. The fistula continued to drain a little, although the draining was minimal. His head had to be shaved to provide a final donor site for his buttocks. His complaints decreased and his affect improved dramatically. He began joking with me and the burn staff. His last graftings took easily, making further debridement procedures unnecessary. By this time, he used self-hypnosis with great facility. I reminded him, in hypnosis, that he would only use it for himself for medical purposes.

Following our 11th and final session, he left the inpatient unit and was followed as an outpatient. I saw him 2 weeks later when he visited the unit. He was gaining weight; his spirits were good; his only complaint concerned some minor withdrawal symptoms since he was no longer using narcotics. He mentioned that he was not sleeping well. When I asked him if he used hypnosis to help him get to sleep, he said he had not. He thought his symptoms were mild and already declining. He regarded hypnosis as something intended for much more serious problems.

TB was a particularly satisfying patient because he was so eager to master hypnotic techniques and so good at doing so. Obviously, not all burn patients have his energy or motivation; but most welcome the opportunity to be given hypnotic suggestions, and they often use them with moderate to high success.

CASE 2: CANCER PATIENT

Mrs. M was a 39-year-old white female, divorced, a mother of four children. Four years before my examination, she was diagnosed as having cancer of the cervix, stage IIIB, the tumor having extended into the pelvic wall. Extensive radiation treatment resulted in a number of complications, including injury to the large and small bowel. She had had a colostomy. Her pelvic cavity was a mass of scar tissue. Radiation enteritis, or inflammation of the intestine, left her in chronic groin pain. She was, however, able to manage daily activities at home when other complications were controlled. Following multiple hospitalization and various treatment procedures, she was most recently hospitalized for phlebitis in her left leg and severe pain in her abdomen. She understood that treatment could only be palliative, since lymph node metastases had not been halted by radiation or chemotherapy.

Medical staff were distressed at their inability to relieve her pain and questioned her increasing demands for intramuscular injections of Demerol. She was also receiving oral narcotics, an antidepressant, and a soporific for sleep. Her mother, who was with Mrs. M much of the time, reported that she had not slept for 2 nights and complained constantly of unbearable pain. The nurse who called me regarding the consult for hypnosis described Mrs. M as "at the end of her rope."

The patient was a thin, sad-looking woman who looked much older than her 39 years. She cried as she told me she didn't want to die. She said she had prayed for forgiveness and wanted to return home to her children. I took her hand, stroked her arm, and began talking in a soothing monotone. I stared into her eyes and told her that her eyes would become heavier and heavier. At the same time, I continued to stroke her arm. As her eyes closed, her body began to relax visibly. Her breathing became so regular that I was able to pace my voice to her breathing and soon her breathing slowed in response to my voice. Although I did not make a tape of the session, I can give a sense of the suggestions I offered: "so very comfortable . . . so deeply comfortable . . . so nice to relax . . . a safe, comfortable and restorative rest . . . how tired you've felt . . . now feeling so deeply . . . deeply comfortable . . . easy to sleep . . . safe . . . sleeping for awhile . . . a deeply restorative sleep, so that when you waken you will feel much . . . more . . . comfortable. . . . "

Because she was so depleted emotionally and physically and needed sleep so much, I allowed her to continue sleeping and left her in that state. I told her mother to take note of how long she slept and to tell her when she awakened that I would see her the next day.

The following day, her mother reported that she had slept soundly for 2 hours, had awakened in extreme pain, and had been taken to surgery for a bowel impaction. When I saw her, she was sleeping, so I didn't wake her. The next day, she reported that she was feeling more comfortable but still had pain in her abdomen, leg, and groin. She smiled a little and told me my voice made her feel better. Her mother left us alone, and I used the time to learn more about her. Her husband deserted her and the children when she was pregnant with her fourth child. They had married when she was 19—because she was pregnant. Her twin sister, also divorced and mother of two children, was caring for Mrs. M's children. This concerned her as well as her mother, because her sister was having emotional and psychosomatic problems of her own. In particular, the twin was anxious about the threat of cancer to herself. The patient conceded a sense of anguish about her not having gone regularly for medical checkups and not having had her cancer treated earlier than she had, which might have improved her chances for recovery. Her father had died quite suddenly after her cancer diagnosis and the beginning of the radiation treatment. She and the children had then moved in with her mother. Her grandmother and twin sister lived on the same street. She felt that she had a close and supporting family.

She enjoyed talking about her children, who were 11, 14, 16, and 20 years old. She described all of them as "good kids," but felt particularly close to her 11-year-old son, who spent a lot of time with her. His first communion was her happiest memory. She was pleased that the boys were allowed to wear dark suits because they got dirty so easily. I tried to probe her earlier comment about wanting to be forgiven but her responses were vague.

When I picked up her hand and looked into her eyes, her eyes became fixed on mine and slowly closed. Her body immediately relaxed. Her breathing became quiet and regular; her mouth opened slightly. After a few relaxing suggestions, I described her son's first communion, using her own words as much as possible and providing long pauses so that she could fill in her own experience of the event. She smiled a number of times. When I alerted her by asking her to open her eyes and tell me about her hypnotic experience, she reported the experience in the past tense but was surprised at details she remembered. She enjoyed talking about the communion and the support she felt from her extended family and church community. She did not mention her pain.

Two days after the surgery, she reported much less pain in her abdomen. Pain continued in her groin, due to the radiation enteritis, and her inflamed leg hurt when she moved it. As soon as I induced trance using the same procedure as before, she began to cry. Suddenly, she abreacted: "Don't make me go, I can't go," she cried repeatedly; she appeared very agitated. I continued to stroke her arm and repeat some of her words, "You don't want to go"; "It's all right." Her sobbing and crying out continued for a few minutes and slowly subsided. I continued hypnotic suggestions about the importance of this experience to her and of her need to relive it and to cry. I then gave her suggestions for increasing comfort and strength. When she came out of trance, she talked about her father's death, which had occurred soon after she developed cancer. She had panicked about going to his funeral and had refused to go. Although her mother understood and no one reproached her, she felt that she had let everyone down—especially her father—although she told me herself she was in no condition to attend the funeral. The intensity of these feelings surprised her, since she had discussed them at the time with her family and a hospital social worker. She had not thought about the episode for a long time. She also told me that, 2 weeks prior to the present hospitalization, her divorce had become final. This, she insisted, was a cause for celebration.

The next day, when I picked up her hand, her eyes closed immediately and her body relaxed. I stroked her hand briefly and released it as it became cataleptic. Using indirect, permissive suggestions, I spoke for some time about deep relaxation, how comfortable she might feel, how different her body might feel. At times, she might not experience her body at all; or, she might feel different parts tingling or warm, other parts not at all. Such relaxation, I suggested, might permit her to move into a deep restorative sleep like the one she experienced the first time I hypnotized her. I then reviewed some of the things she had told me: her sense of love and support from her family, her regret at not being able to go to her father's funeral, her pride in her children, her faith and comfort in her religion and the company of her priests and nuns. Among these comments I suggested both directly and indirectly that she had felt enough guilt, that she understood about forgiveness, that is, that she herself understood and forgave her own children, especially when they were young and did not behave perfectly. I added with great emphasis the ambiguous statement that she "understood now" and would feel as comfortable as she possibly could.

When she awakened, she looked happy and said, "I feel as if we've been praying; I do understand." I told her I would teach her self-hypnosis the next day and left.

The last three hypnosis sessions were much less dramatic. She was eager to learn self-hypnosis because her oncologist had said she would be going home as soon as the inflammation in her leg had decreased and her mother had learned to inject her with heparin to control the phlebitis. With the acute pain from her bowel impaction gone, she agreed with her physician that she could manage her groin pain with oral narcotics and hypnosis. She was put on a fixed dose of oral methadone and was taking Percocet as needed. She continued her Elavil and Dalmane at night, although she reported less difficulty sleeping. She volunteered no more personal information; so, taking my cue from her, I became more task oriented.

I taught her an eye fixation induction: staring at a selected point, closing her eyes with each exhalation and opening with each inhalation until her eyelids were too heavy to open. This occurred at the fifth exhalation in the first induction I provided. I then suggested she feel her body relax by using a color, the color of relaxation. She was to reexperience her son's first communion and enjoy herself. She could then sleep for a while or waken herself by counting to ten. During the self-hypnosis training, I suggested she waken.

She told me that her color for relaxation was light blue and that she experienced it around and through her body. At times, her body became so light blue that she could not feel anything. She then went through the same procedures. Her eyes closed on her third exhalation; her body appeared very quiet. After a couple of minutes, she exhibited some rapid eyelid movement and she then alerted herself. She was pleased to see how easy this was for her.

The next day was her sixth session, and she told me she put herself to sleep with the techniques. She put herself in trance. After her eyelid movements decreased, I gave her some ego-strengthening suggestions: Each time she put herself in trance, she would give herself a comforting, restorative experience, she would feel more in control of her body and her feelings, she might even enjoy other experiences during trance as she became more experienced. She then alerted herself. She was leaving the next day, so I planned to see her early before she left.

In the last session she put herself in trance. I complimented her on how well she was doing. When she was alert I again complimented her. She thanked me, talked with excitement about going home to her children, and we parted. I subsequently learned that several weeks later, at home, she had gone into coma, was rehospitalized, and died almost immediately.

This patient is a fair representative of many of the patients with gynecologic cancer that I see. They live several years after their cancer is diagnosed and receive a number of different kinds of treatment: surgery, radiation, and chemotherapy. Because the disease process is so prolonged, their suffering is prolonged. By the time death is imminent, their physical condition has deteriorated and their emotional and spiritual resources have been depleted. Their pain and suffering exhaust them, their families, and even the medical staff, who worry about the quantity of narcotics they are giving and who feel frustrated when the patient's pain is not adequately relieved. Patients feel victimized and increasingly isolated as their suffering continues. Among these patients, vital organs are less apt to be invaded quickly; dying tends to be an extended process.

Mrs. M was in just this state. Her coping abilities had disappeared. Medical staff, alarmed by her regressed behavior, became suspicious of her complaints and demands for medication. Her bowel impaction went undetected for several days. Faced with mounting pain, sensing the reluctance of the medical staff to prescribe increased medication, her coping abilities vanished. She was frightened, resentful, and exhausted by her pain. As she regressed psychologically to the level of a terrified child, she was unable to draw on her emotional resources or to draw strength from her family. Appropriate medical intervention relieved the pain from her bowel impaction. Hypnotic trance and suggestion helped her recover some of her own coping resources. In the course of doing so, she needed to work through her father's death again and perhaps her anticipation of her own death.

DISCUSSION

It is often the case that hypnotherapists are asked to see patients only when the usual medical treatment has failed to relieve their intense suffering. The desperation felt by the patient, family, and medical staff explains the willingness—even eagerness—of each to try hypnosis. Given a genuine interest and a measure of support on the part of the medical staff, the chances hypnosis will be effective noticeably improve. Under such circumstances, it is often successful in a variety of ways. A permissive and nurturing hypnotic style is particularly suited to the regressed state very sick patients are often in. Intractable pain, exhaustion from suffering, sleep deprivation, isolation and alienation from others, the effects of narcotics—these conditions often ensure that patients are already in altered states. The altered state of hypnosis entails shifting some ego functions, like the direction of the content of thought, from patient to hypnotherapist. Given their exhausted state, little resistance is encountered. Anxiety is easily reduced with soothing and comforting messages. As patients allow their bodies to relax, much of their pain disappears and the effects of narcotic medication is more easily felt. A safe, mothering, transferential relationship quickly develops, producing an intimacy and trust that meets patients' intense dependency needs and provides an atmosphere in which they can talk about themselves freely. The strong feelings of being understood within the hypnotic relationship also facilitate patients' privacy and the opportunity for their own reflections.

Despite the very obvious differences between the experiences of burn patients and dying cancer patients, the two cases presented indicate fairly similar ways of using hypnosis. In both, coping abilities had crumbled in the face of overwhelming fear and suffering. Exhausted from having had no sleep or respite from a relatively sudden, severe, and unexplained pain, Mrs. M regressed to the level of a terrified child no longer able to draw upon her own emotional resources or those of her supportive family. TB, in despair because of his failure to heal and dreading the continuation of painful procedures, withdrew into depression and anticipation of death. Initial hypnotic intervention demanded very little of either of them, hardly more than their listening to a comforting voice that *felt* meaningful and helpful to them. As they became psychologically stronger, hypnosis became more of a collaborative effort, in which their particular interests and concerns and resources were addressed.

Hypnosis lends itself to creative techniques that can be—in fact, should be—individualized for each patient and can also change as the patient's needs change. Unlike psychotherapy, hypnosis can be used when the patient is completely passive. But, like psychotherapy, its effectiveness depends on a trusting relationship developing between therapist and patient, which enables the patient to become more open to his or her needs, conflicts, fears, and resources. Except for prayer, which is meaningful only for some persons, I find it difficult to think of any psychological intervention, under the circumstances described, that can equal the usefulness of hypnotic intervention.

Hypnosis offers the prospect of being applicable to the patient's aversive experience and his or her psychological state without entailing any intrusive consequences complicating the medical management of the underlying complaint.

If, therefore, the treatment of pain and suffering is made reasonably focal in the medical setting, the adjunctive use of hypnotherapy can be of enormous benefit.

NOTE

The burn patient was seen at St. Agnes Burn Unit in Philadelphia. The cancer patient was seen at Jefferson Hospital, Jefferson Medical College, Thomas Jefferson University, where the author is a member of the Department of Psychiatry and Human Behavior.

REFERENCES

Bonica, J. J., & Ventafridda, V. (Eds.). *Advances in pain research and therapy* (Vol. 2). New York: Raven Press, 1979.

Fordyce, W. E. *Behavioral methods for chronic pain and illness*. St. Louis, MO: Mosby, 1976.

Loeser, J. D. Perspectives on pain. In P. Turner (Ed.), *Clinical pharmacology and therapeutics*. London: Macmillan, 1980.

Margolis, C. G., & DeClement, F. A. Hypnosis in the treatment of burns. *Burns*, 1980, *6*(4), 253–254.

Melzack, R. *The puzzle of pain*. New York: Basic Books, 1973.

Sacerdote, P. Techniques of hypnotic interventions with pain patients. In J. Barber & C. Adrian (Eds.), *Psychological approaches to the management of pain*. New York: Brunner/Mazel, 1982.

Sternbach, R. A. *Pain: A psychological analysis*. New York: Academic Press, 1968.

16
HYPNOTHERAPEUTIC CONTROL OF LONG-TERM PAIN

James M. Healy
E. Thomas Dowd

The experience of pain can cause people to drastically alter their usual behavior pattern. Much has been written concerning the efficacy of using hypnosis in the relief of chronic pain. Many "pain (control) clinics" throughout the country have arisen to offer relief to the unfortunates who suffer from intractable chronic pain. This chapter was written to demonstrate the usefulness of hypnosis as a powerful tool in the therapy of this malady. We first describe the patient, then the therapeutic procedure employed, and last the results obtained and follow-up. The patient was quite helpful in providing much of the information after the therapy was concluded. He said that he had suffered many long years and wanted others to have the benefit of his experience. The patient is called Ron in this report, although that was not his name.

PATIENT'S HISTORY

Ron was a white male in his 50s, married, with one teenage son. An invalid father-in-law suffering from a severe heart and emphysema condition lived in the family trailer confined to bed. The patient's wife spent all her time caring for her father, husband, and son. Ron had heard that hypnosis might help and had been given the first author's (Healy's) name and address by a "pain clinic" in Alabama, although he did not call immediately. He walked with a cane and talked slowly, with some slurring of his words. He was a tall slim man who carried himself erect with his head held high.

James M. Healy. Private Practice, Tallahassee, Florida.

E. Thomas Dowd. Department of Educational Psychology, University of Nebraska, Lincoln, Nebraska.

Ron reported that he had been suffering from this recurring pain from 1974 until 1983. The "cluster migraine" headaches occurred nightly during sleep and would "suddenly" appear full force. He consulted an allergist, believing that the headaches were caused by a sinus condition. However, the physician diagnosed the origin of the headache as a cluster migraine headache. Later that year a spinal tap was performed, and results were reported within normal limits. Over the next year and a half, various medications were prescribed with little long-term benefit. Cafergot suppositories and Inderal (40 mg three times a day) seemed to help minimally. In January the patient went to the Oschner Foundation Clinic in New Orleans for a complete diagnostic examination. Ron reported that as far as he could see the trip was of no help in ameliorating the headaches, which were then occurring twice daily.

In February of 1982, his physician referred Ron to a university pain clinic. His referring letter is excerpted as follows:

> . . . His course has been protracted and he has finally become medically disabled from continuing discomfort with his headaches as well as complications of surgical intervention. He is requiring frequent doses of Demerol or other pain medications in order to control discomfort. Basically, the gentleman's history with regard to his cluster headaches included an evaluation at the Oschner's Clinic in New Orleans, The Shands Teaching Hospital in Gainesville, Florida, and he finally went to Johns Hopkins University to a headache evaluation and management specialist. It was their recommendation that he undergo a neurologic procedure to eliminate pain. He had been refractory to most treatment programs tried. An attempt was made . . . to section the nervus intermedius . . . complications arose and patient developed vertigo . . . another procedure was later attempted . . . only partially successful and he continues to have difficulty with balance and walks with a cane . . . patient was evaluated by two psychiatrists with excellent credentials . . . one believed that the patient magnified the problem and the second treated him for severe depression (bordering on suicidal. . . . It would be impossible to list all the medications tried on the patient. They include Cafergot preparations, Sansert, Inderal, tricyclic antidepressants, lithium, Periactin, and perhaps some others. At one point he became addicted to Percodan tablets and had to be hospitalized to be detoxified. Along with Demerol injections we have tried rotating pain medications including Talwin, Fiorinal, Darvocet, and others with no results. He continues to request Demerol which is used sparingly but we are unable to curtail the use of narcotics. Major tranquilizers have helped in controlling his pain and discomfort . . . including phenothiazines . . . Haldol . . . Thorazine . . . Sinequan. He is also on Dilantin, Inderal, HydroDIURIL, and Lanoxin.
>
> Other medical problems include cervical spondylosis with an anterior infusion in 1970, a holosystolic prolapse of the mitral valve discovered in 1973, duodenal ulcer disease discovered in 1973 with no subsequent problems and hypertension which has been under control since 1975. I believe the man has a serious problem which we have been unable to help him overcome up to this point. He has been willing to go to a local Pain and Stress Management Clinic but did not apparently

receive any results from his visit. He is willing to try most anything to achieve some lessening of his symptoms.

THERAPEUTIC PROCEDURE

The patient and his wife made an appointment with the first author shortly after a nationally televised talk show broadcast a show on hypnosis. Both (Ron was unable to drive due to vertigo and fear of having a headache) arrived and entered the office together. He had been released from the hospital for 1 week. An appointment had been made for him to follow-up with another psychiatrist; however, Ron found some reason to terminate the appointment. During the initial interview the patient reported severe depression. In a separate interview the wife agreed with her husband that he seemed to be going downhill and that his will to live and recover was diminishing. She was quite concerned for his safety and mental stability. The couple requested hypnotherapy to relieve the pain. During the first session the patient was taught to relax using the "squeeze method" (inhale, hold breath, and squeeze middle finger and thumb, and then release breath and finger tension) and was asked to practice this at home. He practiced the method in the therapist's office five times both with the therapist in the room and alone.

The squeeze method is called by that name so that clients can easily remember the technique. During the learning phase the therapist verbalized a simple relaxation technique and then suggested that each time Ron wanted to "return to this feeling state" he could use the entry cue established at the beginning of the relaxation method. The process took about 20 minutes but can take as long as 45 minutes. The relaxation was begun, and the therapist suggested it continue as he moved to another focus. Each part of the client's body does not have to be completely relaxed before continuing. During the introduction it is also important to find out the client's "most peaceful" scene or some place or time when he or she was very comfortable. Ron's favorite place was his back porch. He lived in a sub-rural (more rural than suburban) place off a busy highway. There was a lake, stream, and a small swampy area included in this scene. Ron was asked to visualize this place. The therapist verbalized only as the client exhaled.

"I want you to take some time now to find as comfortable a position as you can so that you can learn comfortably how you can feel comfortably good with you. In a few moments I will ask you to take a real deep breath, hold it for a brief count of five, then LET IT GO. This certainly is easy to do. Not difficult really. . . . But I wonder if you know that YOU CAN IMAGINE any number of things . . . things like memories of past comforts . . . of just sitting . . . taking in the back porch view . . . just letting the scene arrive on its own . . . not having to wish it . . . not having to think it. . . . And you can begin to enjoy . . . what the view offers now . . . and . . . as you do this other things continue and also begin to occur. . . . Your heart pumps . . . your chest falls . . . and rises as you continue breathing . . . and your breathing is relaxing . . . your chest . . . your body . . . and yes your mind, . . . for you can almost feel the comfort you can begin to feel . . . with each breath you let go . . . you also let go of unnecessary tensions . . . tensions not needed for our purposes now. . . . So STARTING TO SLOOOWWW DOWN . . . is a comfort . . . and as you continue BREATHING AND RELAXING . . . BREATHING AND RELAXING . . . BREATHING AND RELAXING . . . you don't even need to pay attention as other parts of your previously tense body continue letting go of unnecessary tensions. . . . You don't have to notice breathing to breathe. . . . You don't have to notice heart pumping to continue comfortably pumping and resting . . . pumping and resting. . . . So too you don't have to notice your body relaxing, . . . yet you may notice your eye fluttering as it relaxes . . . your scalp tingling, . . . your jaw slowly untorquing, . . . shoulders gently lowering as . . . your body sinks into deeper and deeper comfort. . . . And as you do your conscious mind doesn't have to know that your SUBCONSCIOUS MIND LEARNS RELAXING . . . CAN RELAX . . . DEEPER AND DEEPER . . . AND CAN RETURN TO THIS COMFORTABLE STATE LATER . . . as your conscious mind enjoys the view and your body . . . BREATHING AND RELAXING . . . BREATHING AND RELAXING . . . CONTINUES RELAXING . . . MORE AND MORE COMFORTABLE . . . THAT'S RIGHT. . . . And your arms continue to let go of more and more tension . . . hands, fingers . . . BREATHING AND RELAXING . . . letting go . . . back, shoulder blades deeper and more comfortably . . . BREATHING AND RELAXING . . . even the little tiny muscles between your ribs . . . can LET GO NOW . . . abdomen . . . small of your back . . . sides and hips . . . seat and thighs . . . BREATHING AND RELAXING . . . BREATHING AND RELAXING . . . knees, calves, ankles . . . letting go . . . letting go unnecessary tensions . . . DEEPLY . . . SO DEEPLY . . . AND COMFORTABLY. . . .

RELAXED . . . and so you can . . . take a real big breath . . . squeeze your thumb and middle finger of your left hand . . . hold for two, three, four, five . . . and (*audibly exhaling*) exhaling . . . relaxing . . . letting go of the spent air and excess tensions . . . and continuing to breathe and relax . . . rhythmically exhaling tensions with the air . . . sinking into deeper and deeper comfort. . . . That's very good. . . . Feeling fine is just fine. . . . And you can easily feel this comfort deeply . . . whenever you wish . . . be ready . . . inhale (. . . that's right now . . .) hold for five while you squeeze . . . then exhale and sink into comfort . . . that's right. . . . Your subconscious mind will use this as a cue . . . a signal . . . a sign that you, taking more and more control of your own welfare, want to relax deeply. . . . And each time you do inhale, squeeze, and exhale as you LET THE finger TENSION GO you will return here . . . into deep comfort. And it's nice to understand . . . that deep comfort . . . is a SQUEEZE away NOW. . . . And you can use this comfort . . . just for you . . . your relaxed deep comfort . . . whenever yes, whenever . . . and where . . . yes wherever you and only you want . . . you and only you need, either or both. But you can return to your quiet existence here . . . in your own special way, taking as much time as you wish inside, yet the clock time will be less than 30 seconds."

The following day the patient was hospitalized. The wife reported that he had become suicidal and was actively talking about how he would accomplish that goal. During the hospitalization it was discovered that he had discontinued his Dilantin (antiseizure) medication on his own. His medications were reinstituted and he was stabilized before he was released. Three weeks later, Ron was taught once again the squeeze method of relaxing. During the session he proved to be a fast and eager learner. He entered into a light trance easily and came out with a splitting headache. This proved fortuitous, for he was asked to squeeze to relax and nod when he achieved a light state of hypnosis. When he nodded, the therapist spoke directly, telling him he could leave the headache where he got it and Ron and the therapist could deal with it together after he felt more confident of his relaxation skills. He nodded, and the therapist then suggested that this time he take his time coming out of his own trance because going slowly will ensure that the headache would stay behind. He took about 4 minutes to reorient himself, and he reported that surprisingly the headache was gone.

The following week he reported feeling a trembling sensation in his arms and legs, as well as problems taking his medication. He also mentioned as an aside that he had undergone oral surgery (all his teeth were extracted) that week. When asked if his physician was aware of the surgery, he said he didn't think it was necessary to let him know. Since the therapeutic relationship had been established as consultant–client, the therapist explained very strongly that Ron was ingesting numerous prescription drugs and that the prescribing physician should be notified of any and all changes that might alter the effects of those drugs. Ron also complained of oral pain due to the surgery. During the last half of the session, he was asked to use the squeeze method of relaxation and then to imagine taking a mouthful of ice and swirling it around his mouth. When he indicated he could actually feel the cold, he was asked to imagine being home quietly relaxed in his favorite chair overlooking a secluded lake. As he nodded that he could picture the scene, the therapist then said (speaking only as the patient exhaled):

"and . . . there are many things you have seen. . . . There are many things you have not seen. . . . I know you know you can feel many sensations. . . . And I wonder if you know . . . wonder . . . about the sensations you . . . experience without feeling . . . the toes in the socks . . . the ring on your finger . . . the sound of the breeze flowing through the leaves . . . so that you can choose to notice the coldness of the ice . . . and the coolness of the breezes of the stream and lake . . . the comfort you receive rocking on the back porch . . . you take with you . . . inside . . . the smile (*Ron smiles.*) you share outside . . . and to hear that you have FORGOTTEN more than you can remember . . . is nothing new . . . but you didn't realize you knew. . . . You can choose to forget . . . and take control of those nonessentials. . . . And they can BEGIN TO FADE as you awaken in comfort . . . leaving behind the memories of the recent . . . and distant past. . . . You also have learned to LEAVE the headACHE BEHIND. Now there are many reasons for many things. And you have learned some of the reasons for some of the things, some of which you have forgotten and others you choose to not remember, while still others you remember for still other reasons having nothing to do with the reason's existence [confusion to help the acceptance of the next suggestion]. Yet, the body has a series of systems of controlling that have nothing to do with a conscious understanding of the controls themselves or of the reasons for or necessity of controlling. You can consciously alter your breathing rate yet your SUBCONSCIOUS mind will continue the breathing whether you think of it or not. Yes, your SUBCONSCIOUS mind can REMEMBER to ASSOCIATE RELAXED COMFORT WITH CALM, PEACE, SOOTHING COMFORT. Now you know you have already learned to relax consciously, but what you may not completely realize in a DEEP sort of way is that you cannot BE COMFORTABLE and feel pain at the same time. . . . But you know you can relax quite well . . . very well . . . and that relaxing deeply you CAN LEAVE YOUR HEADACHE BEHIND. . . . AND ABOUT THIS MATTER OF EXPERIENCING . . . FEELING . . . you can leave the feeling in the teeth with the dentist. . . . Since pain is the body's way of telling the mind that there is something amiss . . . and since you now know you miss your teeth . . . you can also understand that your mouth will inform you if the healing process is not proceeding uneventfully . . . otherwise you don't even need to pay attention to the healing process, for your mind knows how to accomplish this well. . . . Therefore you can allow your learned abilities to leave behind . . . to leave behind and then focus on the wonders of renewing nature in the lake . . . in the trees . . . in the ever evolving healing process of nature. . . . And it happens even if you don't know how . . . so you can go ahead with the process of nature being . . . healing . . . soothing. But in your own way you can return your focus to this COMFORTABLE ROOM, CALMLY ENJOY THE RELAXED FEELING YOU CAN EXPERIENCE and enjoy a quiet interaction with me when you are ready."

OUTCOME AND FOLLOW-UP

Ron opened his eyes smiling and stated that the oral pain was gone. Ron and the therapist agreed on another appointment in 2 weeks, as he felt more confident that he could control his vascular headaches. At the next session Ron was all smiles. He had experienced only four headaches of any intensity in 2 weeks. He had practiced the squeeze method while verbalizing what he was "saying" to himself internally, and he was beginning to sense that possibly this treatment just might work. Nevertheless, he insisted on an appointment the following week. During that visit he reported that he had not had any headache since the last meeting; he asked for another appointment and was given one. At the next session Ron reported only one headache of very short duration (20 seconds) and four severe ones at night. The therapist could not discover any circumstances connected to the headaches, although it was discussed at length. It was agreed that the squeeze method kept headaches away during the day, and since the method worked quite well during the day there was no reason to believe it would not also work at night. Ron agreed and suggested that he go through a ritual of going to sleep incorporating the squeeze method to prevent any possible headache beginning while he slept. The ritual was developed by the patient (he never discussed what it was), and the following week he reported sleeping well each night. At this time Ron's wife began getting more and more agitated. She was afraid that Ron's method would not work, even though already it apparently was ameliorating the headache pain.

The contract with the patient had been accomplished, although he still had to continue taking an enormous quantity of medication. The medication, which included lithium carbonate, Vivactyl, Dilantin, and Ativan, among others, did not interfere with the effectiveness of the hypnotherapy. The patient's state of mind improved, due more to the relief of the pain than anything else. He was referred to the community mental health agency, since that agency could help him with the enormous costs of medication (he reported that he was using almost 25% of his net income for medication).

Six months later the first author had occasion to talk with the patient. He reported that the hypnosis did not work anymore, for he was having headaches at night. On further inquiry, Ron said that he was not having severe headaches, except infrequently at night. The severe headaches occurred only at night and were significantly less severe than he had previously experienced. When asked if he continued to use the squeeze method as part of his bedtime ritual, he admitted that he had discontinued that exercise since the headaches were not severe. He believed, however, that the therapy had been only slightly successful. This gentleman had been suffering from these cluster headaches for many years. The authors are not sure whether the patient was not ready to be relieved completely of his pain, or whether the hypnosis was only partially effective. It is likely that some sort of quarterly follow-up might be indicated in order to ensure long-term maintenance. Considering the unusually high amount of medication Ron was taking and the limited contract he had agreed to, we believe that the therapy was successful. Had a less limited contract been agreed to, it is possible that all symptoms could have been removed.

17
HYPNOSIS IN THE MANAGEMENT OF PHANTOM LIMB PAIN

John F. Chaves

Among the most fascinating and potentially valuable clinical applications of hypnotic techniques are its uses with acute and chronic pain. The range of painful conditions whose management has been facilitated with the use of hypnotic techniques is incredibly broad, ranging from iatrogenic pain associated with medical and dental diagnostic and treatment procedures to intractable pain associated with chronic diseases. In many cases, effective alternative treatment modalities exist for the patient who is unresponsive to hypnosis. In other cases, however, the efficacy of alternative treatments has not been established, and hypnosis may make a unique contribution to pain management. The present chapter focuses on one such application; the treatment of phantom limb pain.

Phantom limb pain is a puzzling phenomenon, both from the viewpoint of the patient experiencing it and the clinician trying to treat it. The patient is confronted with the paradox of continuing to experience sensations including, but not limited to, pain from a limb or body part that has been amputated. It is not surprising that patients may be reluctant to report these unusual and often unexpected sensations to their physicians (Loeser, 1984).

As Melzack (1974) has noted, phantom limb pain has historically been thought to have four characteristics:

1. Pain persists long after injured tissues have healed.
2. Ordinarily, benign stimulation of certain trigger zones, remote from the stump, may elicit pain in the phantom.
3. Phantom limb pain is more likely to develop in patients who have experienced pain in the limb prior to amputation.

John F. Chaves. Pain Management Program, Division of Behavioral Medicine, St. Louis University Medical Center, St. Louis, Missouri.

4. Pain is occasionally permanently abolished by temporary increases or decreases of somatic input. An example would be the long-term relief sometimes provided by local injections of procaine. Successful application of transcutaneous electrical stimulation (TENS) illustrates the relief provided by increases in somatic stimulation.

Recent research suggests that some of the traditional beliefs about phantom limb pain may need to be revised. Jensen, Krebs, Nielsen, and Rasmussen (1983) attempted to document the incidence and clinical picture of phantom limb phenomena in a group of nontraumatic amputees. They studied 58 patients over a 2-year period. In order to study temporal changes, data were collected at 8 days and 6 months after amputation. Occlusive arterial disease was the primary reason for amputation. Although virtually all of the patients had experienced pain in the limb within the 6-month period preceding amputation, 17 were free of pain the day before surgery. Phantom pain was reported by 72% and 67% of the amputees during the first and second interviews, respectively. This is considerably higher than the 5%–10% figure commonly thought to represent the incidence of phantom limb pain. As expected, phantom pain was more frequently reported by patients who complained of pain in the limb immediately prior to surgery than by those who had not.

Recent data reported by Sherman and his colleagues (Sherman, Sherman, & Parker, 1984; Sherman, Gall, & Gormaly, 1979) raise many questions about some of the traditional assumptions regarding phantom limb pain and its treatment. Sherman *et al.* (1984) surveyed 5,000 Americans whose amputations were connected with military service. Of the 55% who responded, 78% reported phantom limb pain. Only half of the respondents indicated that their pain had decreased with time. The remainder reported either no change or an increase in pain. Among those with significant phantom limb pain, 27% felt it for more than 20 days per month. Factors exacerbating the phantom limb pain included weather (48%), problems with the prosthesis (8%), mental stress (6%), and fatigue (4%). Twenty-six percent had no idea what caused the pain or changed its intensity. There were no significant differences between those reporting and not reporting pain, with respect to the original cause of the amputation. The presence of pain prior to amputation was not predictive of later pain. The average number of years since amputation was 26 for those reporting phantom pain and 30 years for those not reporting pain. Clearly, these results challenge a number of traditional beliefs about phantom limb pain. Most importantly, these results call into question the traditional assumption that phantom limb pain can be expected to decrease over time to a point where it becomes nonproblematic.

The treatment of phantom limb pain was also examined by Sherman and his colleagues. Again, their findings are at variance with the conventional wisdom and imply that phantom limb pain may be both undertreated and ineffectively treated. Only 54% of the respondents who reported phantom pain discussed it with their physicians! Moreover, only 19% were offered treatment for their pain. Two percent were told that nothing could be done, and 5% were told that it would go away (regardless of years since onset). Twenty-four percent found their questions avoided, and the rest were told that it was "in their heads"! Many respondents reported receiving the strong implication from health service providers that they were "insane" if they felt pain in a part no longer present. Amputees were also motivated to withhold complaints out of fear of being subjected to invasive procedures, which had a reputation in the amputee community for being ineffective. Respondents were also unwilling to risk their credibility in their relationship with physicians on whom they had to depend for ongoing care.

When the results of those treatments that had been provided were evaluated, only 1.1% of the respondents received any lasting benefits of significant magnitude. Minor permanent benefits were reported by 8.9%, while 7.3% reported temporary help, and 5.5% reported some very minor help.

In an earlier survey Sherman and his colleagues (Sherman, Sherman, & Gall, 1980) identified 68 different treatment methods that had been tried in treating phantom limb pain. Patients in the survey had actually experienced only 41 of these treatment methods, 30 of which were identified as conservative, and 11 were surgical. Although many forms of treatment appear to be transiently effective, follow-up usually reveals long-term benefits to be minimal, with levels of relief below those expected with placebo treatment alone. The authors conclude that the data argue for emphasis on conservative approaches to management of phantom limb pain. Taken together, the results of these important studies suggest that phantom limb pain is one of the most undertreated and ineffectively treated pain syndromes.

Hypnosis was among the treatment strategies identified by Sherman and his colleagues for the treatment of phantom limb pain (Sherman *et al.*, 1980). Unfortunately, only less than 1% of phantom limb patients who had sought treatment were treated by hypnosis. Moreover, no information was reported regarding the type or duration of the hypnotic treatment provided or the qualifications of the therapist providing the treatment. Thus, on the basis of these data, it is not possible to reach any meaningful conclusions regarding the efficacy of hypnosis in the management of phantom limb pain.

Clinical reports in the hypnosis literature as well as clinical experience lead to a more guardedly optimistic view of the potential value of hypnotic interventions with phantom limb pain. Probably the largest series of patients treated for phantom limb pain were described by Cedercreutz and Uusitalo (1967). They reported the use of hypnosis in the treatment of more than 100 patients with phantom limb pain. In a group of 37 of these patients, 20 reported that their symptoms disappeared immediately, while 10 additional patients reported that their condition had significantly improved. Although only 8 of the 37 remained symptom free on follow-up continued for as long as 8 years, an additional 10 were still improved. The degree of benefit from hypnosis appeared to be related to hypnotizability and achieving a fairly prompt response to the hypnotic intervention, typically within three sessions. There was no opportunity to continue working with these patients on a regular basis to reinforce their gains.

In the absence of a large body of data on the application of hypnosis to phantom limb pain, a detailed examination of its application in an individual case may help to clarify its use with this significant disorder.

CASE STUDY

The patient, Mr. BL, was seen for a total of three clinical sessions spread over a 3-week interval. Eight weeks later he was seen for a follow-up visit, at which time he volunteered to participate in a videotaped interview and hypnotic procedure. The interview summarizes the clinical history and is presented as follows in some detail:

THERAPIST: I'm Dr. Chaves, and with me today is Mr. BL. Mr. L, until a couple of years ago, you worked right here in St. Louis, is that right?

BL: Yes, I worked at the M Corporation. I went into the industry as an apprentice and worked my way up to foreman within 6 years. . . . I was a foreman until I retired at the end of 40 years. Two and a half years ago I retired and during this period of time, we covered the United States pretty well in trips to New Orleans, Boston, and California. We were really enjoying ourselves.

T: What other things have you done besides traveling?

BL: We enjoyed swimming, and we went dancing about every other Saturday night, and we played cards and had a lot of friends.

T: I gather things went pretty smoothly until last fall when you had an accident. Could you tell me about that?

BL: The good Lord blessed my wife and me and our two daughters with a wonderful life. Until that time there was never a bump or anything to cause any worry or problems. Then, we came home from Chicago and about 2 days later, my son-in-law says "I want to cut a tree down." I said

I'd go watch him. So, we went over the hill, and he notched it and he said it would fall that way. I was at the opposite side of the tree and saw the tree start twirling and falling toward me. . . . I started to run, and it hit me on the shoulder, knocking me to the ground and in doing so, broke both my hips and my shoulder.

T: And you were hospitalized after that. . . .

BL: I was sent immediately to the emergency room at the hospital, and they, in turn, sent me to City Hospital where they worked on me for a period of 6 hours. They decided to pin my hips, that was the most important thing to be done right away. Well, until February, when I came home and got therapy from the local family services unit, nobody said a word to me that I was going to lose my arm. They waited until my arm dropped out of its socket to tell me that I was going to lose my arm. . . . And the pain became very terrific when it dropped out of the socket. . . . I could hold it up and it would be all right. But when it gapped about 1 inch, why it really hurt. Now nobody told me that this was going to happen and to get rid of the pain, I said if that is the only way, well then take it off.

T: So you were in a lot of pain then after the accident and before the amputation. How long of an interval was that?

BL: From the time that it dropped out of the socket until I had my arm amputated, it was 3 weeks.

T: I see. Tell me how you felt about the amputation.

BL: Well, I had to work with several people down at work at the plant who had suffered loss of arms, and I knew that they got along all right, and I was not afraid to go into it. It was a shock for my wife and my family to realize that I would lose a limb.

T: After the amputation, you became aware of a phantom sensation and some pain, and I know that that was a surprise for you.

BL: That was a surprise that the doctor who operated on me did not prepare me or the social worker who worked in the department—nobody mentioned the fact that I would have a pain or what they call a phantom pain due to the amputation, which means to me that there was nerve endings there that were alive that had no place to go so there would be a pain there until they said at sometime in the future the pain would go away. But, it got to be so terrific that I could not read, I could not really carry on a conversation sensibly, I could not sleep. And at the time, my daughter saw in a magazine the fact that hypnotism was doing quite a thing in helping relieve sensation like that. So we wrote to Chicago and, of course, we received a list of people who did this sort of hypnosis procedure, and that's how I became acquainted with you.

T: I see. Now between the time of the amputation and the time you came to see me, that was a period of about 5 months?

BL: From February until I think, let's see it was about 7 weeks ago or 8 weeks ago that I came to you.

T: Yes, approximately.

BL: And I relied on medicine which I knew one should not take too much of, and a . . .

T: Did the medication help?

BL: The medicine helped relax me to a point but it did not take care of the phantom arm.

T: So through this interval of time then, you were having pretty much constant pain.

BL: Constant pain; and not being able to sleep at night, I took sleeping pills that finally put me to sleep, but the minute I woke up in the morning, it was right there.

T: Now in the first session in which I say you, we did a hypnotic procedure after talking about some of the difficulties that you had been having. At that time, right after the hypnotic procedure you had no pain whatsoever.

BL: For about 10 minutes afterwards . . .

T: Did that surprise you?

BL: That surprised me entirely that there was a control of mind over matter, and that I knew right then and there that I would be able to control my pain.

T: It was just a question of improving your skill with hypnosis.

BL: Yes.

T: So you had complete relief for about 10 minutes and then the discomfort returned. From what you described it sounded like your discomfort was less than it was before. Is that right?

BL: The 1st week, I tried to do it with self-hypnosis. It wasn't as successful as the following week, when we came down and we had made a tape recording, and immediately thereafter I saw a great improvement each day with it, even as I was not using the tape, that I could control my feelings of the phantom arm and of the pain in my phantom arm, and I found myself socializing and playing cards and reading and talking on the telephone to my friends and a great improvement in going to sleep in the evenings after I would use the tape I'd fall asleep. Or in the daytime if I would take the tape and use it, I would shut it off, and I could fall to sleep with the greatest of ease. My life has entirely changed since I have been coming to you, and just in three sessions with you and the use of the tape continually since that time every day . . .

T: It's made a big difference.

BL: I'm a new man.

T: The 1st week that I saw you, we worked with self-hypnosis, and I know that when you came back the second time, you found that it had been somewhat difficult for you to use that. So at that point, we used one tape, and we used that for 1 week, and then the third session that you came for, the final session, we made a new tape, just because the sound wasn't too good quality on the first one. I understand that not only have you been using the tape, I guess your wife has been using it a lot. . . .

BL: My wife has been using it with me as we go to bed at night, and she finds that she can go to sleep much easier also. But it's just not referring to my stub arm or my phantom arm but the very method that we proceed with in the hypnotic steps also helps her too. She has been under a great strain too in the last 7 months that we've been . . .

T: It sounds like you've been very active, you mentioned you've been doing a lot of gardening.

BL: Gardening and trimming the hedges and painting and waxing the car and going out increasingly. . . . Well, at least the other night and yesterday afternoon, as I said earlier, even went and did a few dance steps in the kitchen with some good ol' 1930s music.

T: I'd like to ask you a little bit about the pain sensations that you were experiencing. I recall that when you came in and you described the phantom, it seems like the discomfort that you experienced involved a lot of tension. Could you describe that in the phantom and also describe the stump pain that you had?

BL: The pain in my arm naturally would cause tension in my body, and I was very rigid, and I just could not sit, and I could not lay, and I was in total discomfort.

T: The phantom image that you had, did that involve your hand or arm being in an unusual position?

BL: My phantom arm was out in a position, just like it was . . . you were going to shake hands and the hand itself wanted to move all of the time, squirm, and of course, when I was hit I had a rubber glove on because I was going to help pick up the sawed-up parts and help carry them up the hill and put them in the truck and the glove had several holes in it and I could look through at the fingers moving in and out of that hole and in just no time it never let up. It was just a continuous hand movement, and I stress the fact that nobody told me that this kind of thing would happen . . . to a person who has had a limb or toe removed and a reaction afterwards.

T: The stump pain that you showed me was a little bit different. Can you describe that?

BL: The stump itself was sore, and I believe that it was just due to the fact that they had to take so much of it off, and the muscle was damaged. And the whole operation and the time afterwards, there was a large amount of healing to be done. And I believe that I couldn't compare this with somebody who had a leg taken off or just having a cut on your arm, that this is quite a different type of operation. And it just was extremely painful also. Pills or medicine which I took four times a day would relieve the pain in my stump, but that is all the further that medicine would take care of. It could do nothing for the phantom arm.

T: Yes. That's very interesting, and as I mentioned to you I thought like one of the things that we would do today is do a hypnotic procedure like the one that we have been using for you to help to strengthen your ability to use the tape and to develop even further your ability to control the discomfort, if that's agreeable with you.

BL: That'll be fine.

T: OK, fine. Let me move the chair back into a more comfortable position for you, and is that comfortable or would you like it down farther?

BL: That will be fine.

T: OK, fine. Now, I'm going to be doing a procedure today that is very much like we did before in the office, even though our setting is a little bit different. And so the first thing that I'd like you to do is just take a couple of deep breaths and just let your body get very, very comfortable and very, very relaxed. And you know that if you need to change your position at any time to make yourself more comfortable you can do that. And I'd like you to focus your attention on a target, and we had talked about a possible target for you to use. And while I'm talking, I'd just like you to focus your attention on the target and just continue to breathe quietly and deeply with your eyes glued on the target, and you'll find that very, very soon your eyes will grow very, very heavy. Even now you notice they are beginning to blink. And very, very soon the heaviness will make them close completely, and at that point you can just let your eyes remain comfortably closed. And as you continue breathing comfortably and deeply, you find yourself feeling much more peaceful and relaxed—very calm, very peaceful and very relaxed. You feel all of the tension just draining from your body, just draining out, every last bit of tension just leaving your body being replaced by a comfortable, peaceful feeling so peaceful and so relaxed. And now I'd like you to visualize yourself in an elevator, a very plush, comfortable elevator. Perhaps you might be aware of some music softly in the background. And as I count from ten to one, I'd like you to feel the elevator slowly moving down. And as it moves down from ten to one, you'll become aware of feeling even more deeply relaxed than you do now. Just totally, completely peaceful. Ten—you're more comfortable, nine—more and more relaxed, eight—very peaceful and comfortable, seven—more and more relaxed, six—almost seems as though there's more time to each second, five—everything is slowing down to a very calm, peaceful rate, four—more and more relaxed, three—all of the tension just draining away, two—deeper and deeper, one—very, very deeply relaxed now, very, very comfortable and very, very calm. And since you're so comfortable and so calm, you'll find it very easy to focus your attention and to concentrate on the suggestions that I give you. First, I would like you to focus all of your attention on the phantom, and I'd like you to let all of the tension just drain out of the phantom. Just feel the phantom completely relaxed, becoming so completely limp—so completely and totally relaxed that you may notice yourself becoming even less aware of it than you were before. Certainly any discomfort that might have been there just drained away completely. But even then you may notice yourself becoming less aware of the phantom. Just feel so relaxed, so peaceful and so comfortable. Almost as if you had it emerged in a circulating bath of warm comfortable water. So deeply relaxed, so peaceful and so calm. And I'd like you to feel that feeling of calmness, the complete feeling of freedom from tension moving up to the area of your stump. I'd like you to become aware of the stump also—feeling comfortable, just very, very comfortable and also feeling strong. You'll notice the muscles in the area of your shoulder and stump growing stronger each and everyday. Stronger and stronger and more and more comfortable. And because these things will be happening, you'll notice each and every day your mood improving. Feeling better and better. Feeling more alert, more alive, more aware of your environment, more able and more willing to do things, to be active, to become very much involved in the things that have interested you. And you'll find it surprisingly easy to do that. Of course, you'll keep your activities within the limits of your physical capabilities. You won't try to outdo yourself or do too much, but you'll find that you'll enjoy being active, and you'll want to do things and become involved. And because you'll be so involved in doing things and live an active life, you'll find it surprisingly easy to sleep each night. You'll find sleep will come very easily for you, and one reason is because before you go to sleep, you'll feel very comfortable and relaxed. When you lie down in bed, you feel so very comfortable, so very relaxed, you'll sleep very deeply and very soundly. And in the morning when you wake up you'll feel very, very refreshed, just like you had a really great night's sleep each and every night. And so when you wake up, you'll feel really energetic and be eager to go out and do things and to be involved, very active. And you know that your ability to do these things will be helped each time you listen to the tape. Each time you listen to the tape, your ability to relax will continue to grow. You know that relaxation is a skill, and the more you practice, the more capable you'll be of being deeply, deeply relaxed. In a moment I am going to count from one to three, and when I get to three, you'll open your eyes and feel wide awake and refreshed and really alert, any tension that was in your body before will remain gone. The only thing that will return is the energy. All of the tension will be gone. Just energy back. And you'll feel really refreshed, really wonderful, not a bit of tension in your body. One, more and more energy coming back. Two, more and more alert. Three, open your eyes. How do you feel?

BL: Wonderful!

T: You looked pretty relaxed.

BL: Just absolutely wonderful!

T: Would you like to remain in that position for a minute or so, or would you like to . . .

BL: If I was at home, I would probably roll over and fall asleep for a couple of hours. I don't think I'll do it here.

T: Can you tell me what that was like for you?

BL: Yes, when you start out, your body is tense. Listen to you talk, you can just start from your toes on up to your legs, to your limbs, and into your arm, your body, your shoulders, your eyes become heavy and close. It's like on cloud nine.

T: It's kind of automatic when your eyes close. And as I was describing your relaxation, did you have any mental pictures?

BL: Just what you described, the elevator very slowly, quietly and peacefully.

T: It sounds like you enjoy getting that relaxed.

BL: I do. I look forward to it everyday.

T: And so you're going to be continuing to use your tape.

BL: Taking it with me on vacation next week!

T: Great.

BL: Everyday I will use it, in fact when I go out in 2 weeks or 3 weeks when I go out—fly out to Boston, I will take it with me too.

T: Well, I'd like to thank you very much for coming in Mr. L, and it's been a real pleasure seeing you again, and I hope you have a good vacation.

BL: It's been my pleasure. I hope it will help somebody else.

T: Thank you very much.

DISCUSSION

This patient was followed by telephone at 6-month intervals for the first 2 years following treatment and irregularly for the last 3 years. He has remained very active and reports being free of phantom pain and stump pain, although he notes that he has occasional neck pain when he overdoes it. He continues to use his audiotape. During the first posttreatment year, he reported using it on a weekly basis. Subsequently, he has decreased use to less than once per month.

There are several noteworthy features of this case. First, although hypnotizability was not assessed in any formal way, the patient was able to respond readily to those suggestions that were given. Phenomenologically, he presents almost a *tabula rasa* that the clinician can emboss with any suggestions that seem appropriate. Unlike some hypnotic subjects who modulate or transform the suggestions that are administered, this patient's experience during the hypnotic suggestion appeared to bear an isomorphic relationship to the suggestions that were provided. This response is not typical. In many cases the development of effective cognitive strategies for pain management needs to be based explicitly on the patient's phenomenology of the pain experience. This seems to be the case whether talking about clinical pain (Chaves & Brown, 1978, Barber, Spanos, & Chaves, 1974), or experimental pain (Chaves & Barber, 1974).

Another interesting aspect of this case relates to this patient's inability to use self-hypnosis, in spite of his capacities as a hypnotic subject. It was only when the external support provided by the audiotape procedure was introduced that the patient made significant clinical gains. The distinction underscores the importance of specifying the clinical procedures that are used in treating chronic pain patients with hypnotic techniques. There is an obvious need to identify much more precisely the conditions under which hypnotic procedures are and are not effective with these patient populations.

Finally, the success of such a conservative intervention in managing this difficult problem reinforces the notion that hypnotic procedures should be tried prior to the initiation of other more invasive pharmacologic and surgical interventions whose greater efficacy has not been established.

REFERENCES

Barber, T. X., Spanos, N. P., & Chaves, J. F. *Hypnotism, imagination, and human potentialities*. New York: Pergamon Press, 1984.

Cedercreutz, C., & Uusitalo, E. Hypnotic treatment of phantom sensations in 37 amputees. In J. Lassner (Ed.), *Hypnosis and psychosomatic medicine*. New York: Springer-Verlag, 1967.

Chaves, J. F., & Barber, T. X. Cognitive strategies, experimental modeling and expectation in the attenuation of pain. *Journal of Abnormal Psychology*. 1974, *83*, 356–363.

Chaves, J. F., & Brown, J. *Self-generated strategies for the control of clinical pain and stress*. Paper presented at the meeting of the American Psychological Association, Toronto, August 1978.

Jensen, T. S., Krebs, B., Nielsen, J., & Rasmussen, P. Phantom limb, phantom pain and stump pain in amputees during the first six months following limb amputation. *Pain*, 1983, *17*, 243–256.

Loeser, J. Phantom limb pain. *Current Concepts in Pain*, 1984, *2*, 3–9.

Melzack, R. Central neural mechanisms in phantom limb pain. *Advances in Neurology*, 1974, *4*, 319–326.

Sherman, R. A., Gall, N., & Gormaly, J. Treatment of phantom limb pain with muscular relaxation training to disrupt the pain–anxiety–tension cycle. *Pain*, 1979, *6*, 47–56.

Sherman, R. A., Sherman, C. J., & Gall, N. G. A survey of current phantom limb pain treatments in the United States. *Pain*, 1980, *8*, 85–100.

Sherman, R. A., Sherman, C. J., & Parker, L. Chronic phantom in stump pain among American veterans: Results of a survey. *Pain*, 1984, *18*, 83–96.

VI
FRONTIERS OF HYPNOTHERAPY

This section includes examples of the application of hypnosis in the solution of problems that do not fit readily under other sections or that represent extensions of hypnosis into areas not usually served by this modality. In each case the utility of hypnosis in the solution of the problem under consideration is well demonstrated. It is anticipated that in future publications many of the types of cases described in this section might be incorporated into other, more traditional, sections as the frontiers of hypnotherapy constantly expand outward.

Melvin A. Gravitz describes the appropriate use of hypnosis in assisting an assault victim to recall details surrounding the assault. Not only does Gravitz provide a detailed example of forensic hypnosis, but he also provides guidelines indicating who should use hypnosis in forensic work and under what conditions. This case provides a timely reminder that only qualified mental health professionals should undertake activities of this kind. Gravitz also reminds us that hypnosis is an adjunctive technique, not a therapy in its own right.

Elgan L. Baker provides a convincing rationale and appropriate guidelines for the use of hypnosis with psychotic patients. This chapter is especially interesting, since in the past hypnosis has been thought to be contraindicated with psychotic patients. Baker's three case examples illustrate a nice blend of reassurance, relaxation, and imagery on the part of the therapist.

A rather complicated, long-term example of the use of hypnosis in the integration of multiple personalities is provided by Charles H. Madsen, Jr. This case is particularly interesting for its demonstration of how hypnosis can be used in different ways at different times for the solution of different problems in the same patient. Hypnosis as a versatile and multifaceted technique was never better demonstrated. The ego-enhancement aspects of hypnosis are also highlighted, indicating that hypnosis is useful for more than remedying of specific problems. Of additional interest are the sections written by the client(s) herself, providing unusual information regarding the way in which hypnosis operates in therapy.

Joan Murray-Jobsis provides the first of two illustrations of the use of hypnosis in treating the borderline patient. Murray-Jobsis gives detailed examples of the uncovering work of hypnotherapy over several sessions. Of particular interest here is the strong family component to the patient's problem, involving impoverished relations with the parents, although the therapist worked with the patient individually.

The family component, again involving impoverished relations with the parents, is also evident in the chapter by James M. Healy and John C. Moser. Their case provides a phenomenal amount of detail in illustrating the use of the Ericksonian interspersal technique. Not only are interspersal communications highlighted, but footnotes indicate the type of interspersal technique used. This chapter provides an unusually fine clinical illustration of the application of Ericksonian techniques of hypnotherapy. Of interest also is the use of two successive therapists, each treating basically the same issue but in their own unique ways. Both therapists stress growth-producing, ego-enhancing communications.

The chapter on hypnotic reparenting by Mathias Stricherz represents the first appearance in print of this application of hypnosis. For this reason, and the fact that hypnotherapy was carried out with the client alone, this chapter is included in the frontiers section, rather than in the family problems section. Stricherz provides a detailed look at his unusual approach to increasing self-esteem and growth in self-concept. The author expects a fuller elucidation of this technique as work continues.

John F. Chaves provides an interesting example of the use of hypnosis in overcoming some side effects of Prader–Willi syndrome, a highly unusual disease. As Chaves notes, this is the first report of the use of hypnosis with this patient population. This chapter is also interesting for its illustration of the importance of follow-through and home practice with audiotapes, as well as the counterproductivity of unrealistic expectations about hypnosis.

18
A CASE OF FORENSIC HYPNOSIS
Implications for Use in Investigation

Melvin A. Gravitz

Augmenting the numerous applications of hypnosis in health care, this centuries-old modality has also been employed to retrieve and refresh the memories of witnesses and victims of crime. Known suspects have rarely been interviewed because of potential Fifth Amendment complications. While the use of hypnosis as an investigative technique has been reported since 1845 (Gravitz, 1983), a strong surge of interest began in 1976 when a busload of school children was abducted near Chowchilla, California (Kroger & Douce, 1980). Hypnosis was instrumental in solving this widely publicized case, when the bus driver was aided to recall the license number of the vehicle that had stopped him. The method has subsequently been utilized successfully in a large number of investigations in the United States and elsewhere (Udolf, 1983). While in recent years high court decisions in several states, notably California and New York, have posed a challenge to the admissibility of hypnotically obtained testimony, the technique continues to be used because on numerous occasions it has developed verified relevant information that was not originally reported by the subject (Gravitz, 1980). Many law enforcement agencies, including those within the federal government, have reported the successful application of hypnosis (cf. Ault, 1979; Hibler, 1984).

Since some degree of confabulation apparently is a natural accompaniment of all memory, including but not limited to that facilitated by hypnosis, appropriate attention and precaution are indicated because of the possible impact on retrieved details. While the use of hypnosis may present certain problems, it may also nevertheless prove useful especially in those cases where emotional trauma and/or passage of time have resulted in memory blocks. Hypnosis can aid in such situations by relaxing the subject and enhancing his or her confidence that additional memories can be elicited.

Melvin A. Gravitz. Department of Psychiatry and Behavioral Sciences, George Washington University Medical Center, Washington, D.C.

The rationale for the use of hypnosis as an investigative method is the finding many years ago that it can facilitate memory. This process is termed "hypermnesia." In recent years scientific research using laboratory subjects in experimental analogue settings (that is, non-real life) has produced questions about the validity of these laboratory hypermnesic reports (Sanders & Simmons, 1983). It must be observed at this point that clinical (real life) hypnosis and laboratory hypnosis are not the same phenomena, and the two should not be compared as if they were. One must also note that there have been frequent reports based on actual investigations supporting the conclusion that the method can often be helpful (Hibler, 1984).

This chapter presents a case of forensic hypnosis, sometimes termed "investigative hypnosis," to illustrate appropriate guidelines, procedures, and precautions. The interviewer in this instance was a PhD-level clinical psychologist with more than 2 decades of experience in the therapeutic and investigatory applications of the modality. He was a diplomate of the American Board of Psychological Hypnosis, American Board of Forensic Psychology, and American Board of Professional Psychology. Specialty credentials such as these are important in qualifying an expert witness for court testimony, and nearly all authorities agree that the forensic hypnotist should be either a clinically qualified psychologist or psychiatrist with further training and experience in the use of the technique (*State v. Hurd*, 1981; Udolf, 1983). It is further generally agreed that police officers themselves should not undertake the use of hypnosis with forensic subjects.

Not all cases for which hypnosis has been used come to court trial, since the utilization of the technique may facilitate the resolution of an investigative problem without subsequent testimony becoming necessary. Even so, the forensic hypnosis interview should be conducted with the possibility that testimony may be required.

PRESENTING PROBLEM

The automobile of a married woman in her mid-30s was found abandoned on a lonely country road one night in late December. The door on the driver's side was open, the headlights were on, and the motor was running. Several hours later, the woman was found wandering in a dazed condition along another road several miles from the scene. Medical examination indicated that she had been assaulted. She was virtually amnesic for any useful details regarding the situation, however. After several weeks of unsuccessful police investigation, she had been referred for hypnosis to assist in memory retrieval with a special request for descriptions of her assailant and his automobile.

Ordinarily, forensic hypnosis interviews are optimally conducted in the office of the mental health professional who does the interview, but in this instance the subject asked that the psychologist see her in her home "where I can be most comfortable and relaxed." (Prior to the hypnosis interview, the subject had been telephoned by the psychologist to verify that she was agreeable to the interview of her own volition and to discuss any questions she might have about the process.) When meeting with the subject in her residence, the psychologist verified that she was still agreeable to the interview, and he asked her to sign a statement to that effect. This release also indicated that the subject understood that a feedback report would be provided to the police and that a recorder would be used throughout the interview. Ideally, a videorecorder should be used, but as in this case an audiorecorder is acceptable as an alternative. The early part of the interview was invested in developing rapport, after which hypnotic induction procedures were undertaken. These were based on optical fixation and suggestions for relaxation, techniques that have been utilized for many decades (Weitzenhoffer, 1957).

Throughout the interview, which was conducted in the subject's study with only the psychologist and the subject present, she was recumbent on a couch. The technique of time regression was then utilized to enable her to return in a psychological sense to the evening in question. In this procedure the subject was requested while hypnotized to visualize single pages on a calendar being added a day at a time at her own pace until she arrived at the date of the abduction, at which point she gave a prearranged ideomotor finger signal (LeCron, 1963). The use of ideomotor signals permits nonverbal communication with a hypnotized subject and does so without disrupting the trance process. It is a useful therapeutic method, as well.

The subject was then asked to picture herself as she was driving along the country road prior to the location where her automobile had been found. In a free recall mode, she was also asked to describe *everything* that was occuring. At this early stage of the interview, no effort was made to separate the wheat from the chaff of recall, because it has been observed that during such free recollection information that is important to an investigator but not necessarily to a subject may "slip out." Accordingly, during the initial phase of the hypnosis interview, it is best not to have a narrow focus but to obtain as much broadly based freely recalled information as possible before getting to the specifics; that is, free recall should precede structured recall. In the latter the subject is asked for specific details, such as, "Tell me what he looks like," in referring to the description of a perpetrator. (Additional examples of structured recall will follow.)

The interviewer must be careful not to provide leading questions or body language that could influence the subject's responses, as the hypnotic state is characterized by greater than ordinary suggestibility potential. While the amount of detail that can be obtained from imagery-aided hypnotic interview can at times be impressive, it cannot be assumed that a subject will necessarily remember everything that occurred or that a situation did indeed take place as reported under hypnosis. It must be reiterated that hypnotically aided information should be verified by later investigation.

Although not a factor in this particular case, it is possible for a forensic hypnosis subject to manifest resistance as an interview progresses. This can stem from a variety of causes and should be resolved for optimal results (Gravitz, 1984).

Speaking in the past tense but intermittently shifting to the present the subject related that another automobile had approached her car from behind, had come alongside, and had forced her off the road. The male driver of the other vehicle had then rushed out and opened her unlocked front door. While she was in a stunned condition, he pushed her into the front seat of his car and drove away. At this point, the subject was asked to stop her stream-of-memory verbalization for a moment, while the examiner asked her several questions designed specifically to describe the abductor and the vehicle. Excerpts from the taped interview follow, with identifying features having been deleted.

DESCRIPTION OF THE VEHICLE

QUESTION: What does the other car look like?

ANSWER: He pulled me out of the car. I took my purse. I was begging him to let me go. Seems like I took a step or two. Then he said, "Shut up. Shut up." Then he smacked me. He smacked me two or three times. I didn't dare look at him. I'm so scared.

Q: Tell me what the other car looks like. Tell me what is happening.

A: It was dark. I couldn't see. I'm frightened.

Q: It's all right. Tell me what it looks like.

A: It was such an awfully old car. It was dark. It was dark looking. It was an old dark blue. I don't know. It was so foggy. . . . The windshield was all one piece, and there were two windshield wipers. They're noisy. . . . He used his hands to shift. There was a gear shift on the steering wheel. The steering wheel has a rim around it. You know, a shiny metal rim that was the horn. . . . It was a noisy car. The engine was noisy all the time. . . . There were no stickers or decals on the windshield. . . . I didn't discover an arm rest. I rested my arm on the window ledge. The window has that little split window that opens on the side. That you roll up. . . . On ______ Road he ran into a big high curvy bank. He hit it with a jolt, and he sure did bang up his car. He must have damaged his car. I know he hurt his car on the right side. On my side . . . I couldn't see the license number when he let me go. I know it's from this state, though. I recognized the colors and the design but I can't see the numbers. . . . When the door light went on, I could see that the back seat was separated by one of those dividers you let down. . . . The car seat is covered with a cover. There's no design on it. It was just a plain Naugahide. It's blue. There's a little white edging around it. The front seat is one piece. There's a can of beer shoved down on the seat between us. It's S______. That's the name on it. I can read it.

DESCRIPTION OF THE ABDUCTOR

QUESTION: What does he look like?
ANSWER: Oh, he was just a man. I don't know. . . . I wasn't thinking about identifying him. I just knew that I would be killed. He had a little hat on. It has a little brim. It was too little for his head. . . . He wore dark clothes. I was very frightened. He had a gun. It was just sort of a dark shiny-like gun. It wasn't like my husband's little short automatic or whatever he has. It was more like a long-barreled pistol, not too long a barrel. It was that old metal color. Shiny. I can just see it now. . . . His hands were rough when he touched me. Like he worked with his hands. . . . He had a car coat on. It was brown. Solid brown. The bulk of it makes me think of a car coat. . . . He was a little man. His weight and all that. He's about, oh, about five-two or -three. . . . He had a quick-like speech. He spoke fast. He didn't talk a lot, though. His grammar was, well, he just talked like someone who didn't have too much education. . . . His face was round and big and full. A fat-like face. His hair was kind of bushy-like. When he had his face against mine his face was smooth. There's no hair on his face. . . . He had big brown eyes. Dark eyes. The white in his eyes showed up very plainly at one time. . . . He smoked one cigarette after another. He smoked a lot.

ADDITIONAL UNCOVERED INFORMATION

Since the subject knew the geographic area well, she was able under hypnosis to provide a very detailed description of the route over which her abductor had taken her. She remembered that he had known minor roads and that he had named several landmarks as they had been passed. This information suggested that the suspect was familiar with the area and perhaps resided there.

UNEXPECTED THERAPEUTIC INTERVENTION

Following the conclusion of the investigative hypnosis interview, the subject was advised that she would be able to remember what she had said. The tape recorder was then turned off with an audible click. At that moment the subject began loud cursing and shouting and making such comments as, "You're the one who did this to me! It's all your fault! I hate you!" Her fists clenched tightly as she lay on the couch, and her body was tensed. The psychologist did not intervene for the several minutes of this tirade, assuming that the subject was finally venting the repressed anger and other emotions that she had been fearful of expressing overtly during her ordeal; indeed, he encouraged her to express herself even more. After her angry and agitated shouts gradually ceased, the subject's musculature visibly relaxed. Instructions were then given her to alert from the hypnosis.

During the posthypnotic debriefing that followed, the subject reported that she was able to remember all that had occurred during her abduction and that she consequently felt very relieved. When the psychologist noted that she had also verbalized considerable anger toward her assailant, the subject grimly replied that it was *not* toward the abductor that her resentment had been directed. With bitter feelings, she then continued to relate that her husband was an alcoholic who was home in an intoxicated stupor the evening of the attack. "He was the one who should have been out delivering the Christmas cookies that I had baked. If he weren't a drunk, this wouldn't have ever happened to me." She went on to describe an unhappy marriage marked by considerable animosity toward her husband. The psychologist listened and made appropriate therapeutic comments. When the subject completed her explanation, he suggested that she consider consulting a psychotherapist for further discussion of her feelings. She demurred at this but added that she would give some thought to the suggestion. She then remarked that she felt much better about those feelings than before the hypnosis interview, conveying that she had experienced therapeutic benefit, in addition to feeling better because she had been able to remember additional information about the event.

The intense emotional outpouring by this woman illustrated one of the important reasons why only qualified mental health professionals, such as psychologists and psychiatrists, should undertake forensic hypnosis interviews: There is the constant possibility that an emotionally traumatized victim or witness may begin to vent psychologically meaningful feelings and verbalizations together with retrieved memories, and the interviewer must be fully prepared professionally to intervene therapeutically as required. If the interviewer lacks the necessary training and experience to do this, the subject may be placed at risk. One should be aware that it is frequently not possible to predict if and to what extent individual hypnotic subjects may require such therapeutic support.

INVESTIGATIVE OUTCOME

On the basis of the additional information developed by the hypnosis interview, the investigating authorities canvassed automobile service stations and repair facilities in the general area over which the car had been driven during the abduction. They finally located a mechanic who was familiar with an older-model dark blue-green four-door sedan that had been brought in for repair of a fresh right-front fender dent and broken headlight. The repair order was dated several days after the incident and listed the suspect's name and address. The address substantiated the impression that the assailant was a local resident, based on his knowledge of the road system. When questioned the suspect denied any knowledge of the subject or the crime; however, a warrant-search of his automobile revealed an empty can of S______ beer under his front seat. On the rear floor of his vehicle, covered by some mechanic's clothing, the subject's small purse was found. When she had been pushed into the perpetrator's car, she apparently threw her purse reflexly over the front seat. The interior of the suspect's automobile matched in significant detail the description provided under hypnosis. When confronted with the evidence, especially the purse, the suspect admitted his role. He was subsequently tried and convicted.

PROCEDURAL GUIDELINES

In addition to those guidelines described above, there are several others that will facilitate the effective use of investigative hypnosis and later admissibility in court testimony. These guidelines have been discussed by Orne (1979) and recommended in decisions handed down in several jursidictions (e.g., *State v. Hurd*, 1981). As mandated by the New Jersey Supreme Court in July 1981, the guidelines include the following:

1. The hypnotic interview must be conducted by either a clinical psychologist or psychiatrist with special training in hypnosis.

2. The qualified professional conducting the interview must be independent of and not responsible to the prosecution, defense, or investigating agency.

3. Any information made available to the hypnotist prior to the hypnosis session(s) must be in written form, so that the extent of information developed by the hypnosis may be determined.

4. Prior to induction of hypnosis, the interviewer should obtain from the subject a detailed description of the facts as they are remembered. The interviewer must be careful to avoid adding any new elements to the subject's report.

5. All contacts between the hypnotist and the subject have to be recorded, preferably by videotape.

6. Only the interviewer and the subject may be present during any phase of the hypnosis session(s), including pre- and postinduction. (I have observed that the presence during the interview of an investigator and/or police artist does not unduly disrupt the process and may in fact aid the investigation.)

In following these guidelines, the forensic hypnotist will optimize the utilization of a frequently helpful, albeit at times controversial, method of investigation.

SUMMARY

This case of forensic hypnosis was typical in many ways. The retrieval by hypnosis of significant previously unremembered memories from a woman who had been abducted and then assaulted resulted in the apprehension and conviction of her assailant. During the interview process consideration was given by the interviewer to certain recommended procedural guidelines, which were designed to facilitate both the elicitation of information and the possible later admissibility of such evidence in a court of law. Specific techniques, such as time regression and ideomotor signals, were illustrated, and the optimal qualifications of the forensic hypnosis specialist were described. Because of possible confabulatory influence, informational details obtained by this method cannot be immediately regarded as factual; rather, such retrieved memories may be considered as leads for further investigation by qualified personnel. Only if there is verification on the basis of follow-up investigation can the professional report or testify that the memories were real. Although forensic hypnosis is a controversial method as far as certain courts are concerned, clearly its use within specified guidelines may result in important information that was not previously known.

REFERENCES

Ault, R. L. FBI guidelines for use of hypnosis. *International Journal of Clinical and Experimental Hypnosis*, 1979, *27*, 449–451.

Gravitz, M. A. Discussion of forensic uses of hypnosis. *American Journal of Clinical Hypnosis*, 1980, *23*, 103–111.

Gravitz, M. A. An early case of investigative hypnosis. *International Journal of Clinical and Experimental Hypnosis*, 1983, *31*, 224–226.

Gravitz, M. A. *Sources of resistance in forensic hypnosis*. Paper presented at the annual meeting of the American Society of Clinical Hypnosis, San Francisco, 1984.

Hibler, N. S. Investigative aspects of forensic hypnosis. In W. C. Wester & A. H. Smith (Eds.), *Clinical hypnosis: A multidisciplinary approach*. Philadelphia: Lippincott, 1984.

Kroger, W. S., & Douce, R. G. Forensic uses of hypnosis. *American Journal of Clinical Hypnosis*, 1980, *23*, 86–93.

LeCron, L. M. The uncovering of early memories by ideomotor responses to questioning. *International Journal of Clinical and Experimental Hypnosis*, 1963, *11*, 137–142.

Orne, M. T. The use and misuse of hypnosis in court. *International Journal of Clinical and Experimental Hypnosis*, 1979, *27*, 311–341.

Sanders, G. S., & Simmons, W. L. Use of hypnosis to enhance eyewitness accuracy: Does it work? *Journal of Applied Psychology*, 1983, *68*, 70–77.

State v. Hurd, 86 N.J. 525, 432 A. 2d 86, 1981.

Udolf, R. *Forensic hypnosis: Psychological and legal aspects*. Lexington, MA: Heath, 1983.

Weitzenhoffer, A. M. *General techniques of hypnotism*. New York: Grune & Stratton, 1957.

19
APPLICATIONS OF CLINICAL HYPNOSIS WITH PSYCHOTIC PATIENTS

Elgan L. Baker

The evolution of the clinical technique of hypnosis has been marked through the years by the gradual expansion of populations with whom intervention is attempted. These attempts to treat new groups of patients and a wider variety of symptoms often result in the expansion of clinical theory and basic metapsychology because of the new data generated through observations with new populations. Within the past two decades, contemporary theories regarding psychopathology and psychotherapy have been altered and greatly enriched by the growing realization that character disordered and psychotic patients can be treated successfully through psychotherapy. In fact, much of the recent growth of ego psychology within psychoanalysis has been stimulated by efforts to work with borderline, narcissistic, and psychotic patients. It is only natural that these expansions in the general application of psychotherapy would be paralleled by similar developments in clinical applications of hypnosis.

The past two decades have been marked by an increase in the number of investigators and clinicians who have begun to examine the utilization of hypnotherapy with borderline and psychotic patients. Much of the early literature was primarily concerned with the question of susceptibility. Although some controversy continues regarding the capacity of psychotic patients to be hypnotized, the majority of the clinical and research literature now clearly supports the conclusion that most psychotic patients are equally as susceptible to hypnosis as neurotic patients and even a normal college population (Abrams, 1964; Green, 1976; Kramer & Brennan, 1964; LaVoie, Sabourin, Ally, & Langlois, 1976). This research literature has tended to suggest that acutely disturbed patients are somewhat more amenable to hypnotherapy than those with chronic psychotic conditions. The litera-

Elgan L. Baker. Department of Psychiatry, Indiana University School of Medicine, Indianapolis, Indiana.

ture also demonstrates a significant relationship between hypnotizability and the patient's motivation, capacity for ego involvement, degree of control over dissociative processes, and degree of preservation of autonomous and synthetic ego functions (Baker, 1983b). Further, there are no demonstrated differences between the hypnotic susceptibility of schizophrenic patients and those patients suffering major affective disorders (Baker & Copeland, in press). In general then, the fact that psychotic patients can be hypnotized to about the same degree as any other patient population has now been well documented. Further, the literature tends to support the utility of hypnotherapeutic intervention with these patients. There is no documentation of any consistent contraindication for using hypnosis, and there is no evidence that hypnotic experience interferes with reconstitution, precipitates additional regression, or reinforces maladaptive dissociative processes in patients with severe ego defects (Baker, 1981, 1983b; Scagnelli, 1976). It is significant to note that most clinicians have tended to utilize hypnotic strategies in conjunction with a regimen of intensive psychotherapy involving process-oriented, supportive, milieu, and chemotherapeutic components. Most authors agree that the application of hypnosis is advocated as one component of judicious treatment in tandem with this complete therapeutic program.

Psychotic and other severely disturbed patients are often highly motivated for hypnosis both for rational and irrational reasons. Most significantly, however, they often believe that hypnosis will provide for them a sense of self-control and increased personal efficacy at a time when they are feeling fragile, vulnerable, and impotent. For this reason, hypnosis is most appropriately presented with an emphasis on its capacity for potentiating self-control and mastery. Early instruction in autohypnosis is indicated, especially with those patients who present with significant paranoid features.

A range of induction strategies have been described with psychotic patients (Biddle, 1967; Scagnelli, 1976; Scott, 1966). In general, however, a fairly structured yet permissive approach appears to be most useful when working with regressed and psychotic patients. The structure allows for a clear demarcation within which to contain the dissociative and regressive experiences of trance, which appears to be particularly important for those patients whose ability to manage their own ego boundaries and, therefore, differentially organize experience is significantly compromised. The permissiveness is consistent with generally accepted contemporary clinical technique and additionally important with these patients because of concerns with merger, incorporation, and control, which are particularly significant with psychotic and paranoid individuals.

Most clinicians who work with severely disturbed patients, therefore, use some combination of relaxation and fantasy or imagery strategies combined with early instruction in self-hypnosis. In addition, it is important to provide these patients the opportunity to enter trance without eye closure (Scagnelli, 1976) or to give them permission to open their eyes periodically during the course of trance in order to check to see that the therapist is still there and that the environment continues secure and safe (Baker, 1981). Because most severely disturbed patients have not successfully developed the capacity to maintain a consistent internal representation of the external environment, the inability to regularly check it is accompanied by heightened anxiety and spontaneously developed fantasies associated with personal destruction. Encouraging these patients to regularly check the continuity and integrity of the external environment becomes an important requisite in enabling them to enter and maintain a clinically useful trance. Further, allowing patients the opportunity to personally terminate trance at any time they choose provides additional support of their capacity for self-control, and it anticipates and avoids significant resistances that can be rooted in negative transferential expectations that they will merge with the therapist or be incorporated in some fashion if they engage too completely with the phenomenological regression involved in trance. When attention is directed to these concerns, most patients are able to enter hypnosis with little difficulty and quickly come to develop clinically useful trance experiences. Further, they are motivated to learn self-hypnosis, and many come to use it to provide for themselves a sense of personal strength as well as the experience of respite and security in a world that these patients generally view as malevolent and threatening.

There is considerable variability in the literature regarding the specific applications of hypnotic intervention. The strategies described alternately emphasize support, uncovering, and working through. However, most clinicians who regularly employ hypnotherapeutic interventions with their severely disturbed patients tend to emphasize that the provision of structure and support as part of hypnotic utilization strategies is important and necessary to any other specific strategy.

The structure provides a sense of boundaries for patients and also allows them to begin to better organize their experience of themselves and the external world. The support provided through suggestion and hypnotic imagery and fantasy further strengthens the patient's sense of personal boundaries, reinforces the integrity of the patient's sense of self, and enables gradual amelioration in general ego functioning.

A number of specific issues may be addressed through hypnotic intervention. Most important among these is the use of hypnosis to help to establish and maintain a viable therapeutic relationship. Many borderline patients and most psychotic patients present for therapy with intense resistance to developing the trust and mutuality necessary for the working alliance in psychotherapy. This resistance primarily is a function of their previous experience of disappointment, rejection, abandonment, and pain in most interpersonal relationships. More theoretically, the rapid development of intense negative transference interferes with the evolution of the positive transferential and working alliance components of the therapeutic relationship. Specific hypnotic interventions have been described to engage the patient, to support the development of the working alliance, and to diffuse the negative transference and the associated resistances that frequently contaminate the therapeutic relationship and prevent meaningful work with severely disturbed patients (Baker, 1981, 1982, 1983a).

Once the therapeutic relationship has been established and stabilized, hypnosis can be used to generalize the patient's sense of security with interpersonal involvement and, therefore, to broaden the scope of gratifying, contemporary object relationships. Further, the evolution of the therapeutic process associated with the relational and interpersonal components of treatment provides an opportunity to examine and to correct negative aspects of internalized object representations and the associated use of primitive defenses such as fragmentation, dissociation, withdrawal, splitting, and projective identification. Hypnotherapeutic intervention can also be utilized for the modulation of affect and general tension reduction. The nonspecific relaxation effects of hypnosis are frequently useful in reducing the anxiety of severely disturbed patients and, therefore, dilating associated psychotic symptoms and defenses. Specific suggestion and fantasy can also be used to experientially control intense dysphoric affects and to help patients learn to manage their emotional experience without the development of maladaptive behaviors or regression. Hypnosis can be utilized for the management of specific psychotic symptoms including hallucinations, delusions, impaired reality testing, and impaired impulse control with associated acting out.

In general, then, hypnosis may be useful in facilitating the development and management of the therapeutic relationship, the abreaction and modulation of intrusive affect, and the support and reinforcement of more adaptive patterns of self-management. Over time, hypnotherapy can allow for a "corrective emotional experience," which enables a gradual restructuring of ego defects with subsequent maturation, adaptation, and mastery. It is significant to note that the therapeutic action of hypnosis involves a primary experiential focus, unlike more traditional verbal psychotherapy with its emphasis on uncovering, interpretation, self-understanding, and attitude change. Hypnotherapy provides the opportunity to experience rather than simply to understand. This becomes particularly important with severely disturbed patients whose observing ego functions and general capacity for introspection and self-monitoring are sufficiently compromised that more traditional interpretive approaches are often useless or even experienced as sadistic intrusions. However, the hypnotherapeutic experience must be structured in order to appropriately titrate the associated affect so as not to overwhelm the patient's ability to modulate it or to provoke spontaneous negative abreactions that frequently result in further regression or the development of resistance rooted in the negative transference. Technically, this experiential material must be elaborated, explored, and discussed concomitantly in waking psychotherapy so that it is not dissociated, which would prevent its appropriate integration into the patient's conscious experience of self and emerging integrated identity.

The case material and clinical vignettes that follow are designed to demonstrate the way in which this orientation to the clinical application of hypnosis with psychotic patients unfolds within the context of treatment hours.

CASE 1: DAN

Dan was a 19-year-old single white college freshman who became increasingly withdrawn and dysfunctional during the first weeks of entering college. He had never spent a significant amount of time away from his family, and he experienced significant depression, which gradually gave way to panic attacks and acute anxiety. Across the course of the first weeks of his stay at college, Dan became increasingly unable to leave his dormitory room, and his hygiene gradually deteriorated. He became increasingly preoccupied with concerns that his roommate was homosexual and that he would be homosexually attacked and raped by members of his dormitory floor group. His thinking became increasingly autistic and delusional, and his interpersonal behavior became increasingly guarded and suspicious. His floor counselor contacted the dean of students, and the patient was, subsequently, hospitalized on the inpatient service of a teaching hospital with an initial diagnosis of acute schizophreniform psychosis with paranoid features. The patient was sullen and withdrawn. He participated minimally in the ward milieu and avoided interaction with other patients and staff. During his second session of psychotherapy, he observed the large number of books on hypnosis on his therapist's shelf and expressed some interest in wanting to do self-hypnosis because he felt that it would make him "stronger than his enemies." This fantasy was examined in terms of the patient's general sense of vulnerability, and hypnosis was introduced as a way for the patient to learn to feel less fragile and less insecure. The following vignette, which comes from the second hypnotherapy session, demonstrates the use of hypnotic imagery, modulated trance experience, and indirect suggestion to support the integrity of the patient's ego boundaries and to aid in the development of a viable therapeutic relationship and its uncontaminated internal representation.

THERAPIST: Dan, you can simply continue to relax, comfortable and safe, calm and quiet, in charge of yourself and knowing that you are secure in this place.

DAN: This place doesn't seem safe to me. There are queers in here. (*The patient opens his eyes.*)

T: It's good to check to see that there is nothing that will hurt you in this office. You are still you, sitting in your chair, safe. I am still me, sitting here in my chair. There is distance between us physically. There is distance between us emotionally, and for now, that distance can help you feel safe, and you can be in charge of how close or far away you need to be. Like a pendulum of a clock moving back and forth, back and forth in a regular rhythmic way, back and forth, near and far, but the pendulum is still the same, whether it is swinging away or back again. You are still you, whether you need to be far away or feel safe enough to be closer. You can decide and be sure of that. (*The patient's eyes have closed, and he appears to relax noticeably.*) Good, Dan. Just continue to relax. Now I would like for you to hold both of your hands out in front of you a few inches apart. Just go ahead and do that. Fine. And now when you are ready, at the speed you use, at the speed *you* choose, I want you to allow your hands to move together, together until they touch, and then allow them to clasp tightly together, your fingers locked tightly together. Fine. That is good. As you continue to relax, safe and quiet, just allow your attention to focus on the feelings in your hands, your left hand holding very tightly onto your right, your right hand holding very tightly onto your left. And you can feel, there, the strength, a sense of power, a sense of control as you decide how tightly to have the hands pressed together. Strong and powerful as you feel the strength focused there. You can also feel a sense of warmth, where the palms are pressed together, cozy and warm in their togetherness. That is fine; good. And then when you're ready, you can allow your hands to relax, the fingers to unclasp and begin to move apart . . . apart . . . apart. Good. And then at your own speed, you can simply allow the hands and arms to come to rest again on the arms of the chair. Fine. And you can feel your left hand there at the end of your left arm and your right hand there at the end of your right arm. Your left hand is still your left; your right hand is still your right. Neither has changed by having been brought together for a while. And that is how it is with you and me. When you need to, when you want to, we can come together at your speed, and you can be in charge of the closeness of our togetherness. But when we're together, you can feel a sense of strength, the strength of our togetherness, the strength of your control, the power of two things coming together to work in one direction, and in that togetherness, you can feel warmth and comfort. But when you need to, when you want to, you can move apart, move away at your own speed, in control of that movement. You'll still be you;

I'll still be me. We won't have been changed from having been together for a while, except the good change that comes from feeling warmth and sharing and feeling strength and togetherness. You will be you; I will be me. The left hand is still the left, the right hand is still the right. Just shake your hands to be sure of that. Good.

In this example an experiential exercise is used to reinforce the notion that the patient's boundaries will not diffuse if he engages in the therapeutic connectedness. Furthermore, his sense of his own power and control is reinforced, and his ability to exercise that control in a continuing process of involvement and distancing that does not jeopardize the continuity of his own personal identity is supported. This exercise supports the development of the therapeutic alliance and begins to provide the patient an opportunity to feel safe and secure in attachment in a modulated fashion, which simultaneously diffuses potential resistance rooted in negative transferential concerns about boundary intrusion and loss of control. Two sessions later the patient is encouraged to develop images of himself and the therapist while in trance and then to elaborate these in a fantasy structured toward seeing the therapist and himself simultaneously in interaction. The following material comes from this exercise:

D: I can see you and I can see me, but it doesn't feel comfortable.

T: Just relax. Just take a moment to let go of those images and relax to feel the strength of your muscles all attached to each other, your fingers attached to your hand, your hand attached to your arm, your arm attached to your shoulders. Feel all those connections, stable and strong. Just relax, knowing that the connections of yourself will continue, stable and strong. And when you feel relaxed and when you are ready, just imagine seeing you again and seeing me again, Dr. Baker, there, inside, but know that we are still really here, on the outside. Only a picture, a feeling, a memory is represented in your mind's eye. Just picture us there as if you were tuning a television set, as close or far apart as you would like, doing something together. Can you see us?

D: I see you walking in a garden. A tall tree, filled with flowers, is growing near a wall. And that is where I am. I am on the other side of the wall in the tree, looking down at you.

T: It is safe up there behind the wall but not below it so you can't see. Up in the tree, high above, where no one can reach you unless you want, but you can move to lower limbs or you can call down. Do I know you're there?

D: You see me, and I see you, and we talk, and you throw me out some vegetables from your garden, and I send you down some flowers for your wife.

T: I see that we communicate. You give some things to me; I give some things to you. That's good. It's nice to know that you can share some things with me and that I can send you up some food that you might eat, that would taste good and help you grow strong, and that is just the way it should be.

This particular vignette demonstrates the elaboration of hypnotic imagery to reinforce uncontaminated representations of the therapeutic relationship. This imagery emphasizes the safe interaction of patient and therapist in ways that the patient feels able to control. The internal representation of the therapist in interaction with the patient serves an introjective function that can be elaborated in later treatment as a coalescing representation around which other fragmented aspects of the patient's internal representational world can begin to integrate and be mended. This particular example also demonstrates the use of the therapeutic relationship as a source of oral nurturance and support. The patient does not yet feel entirely free to engage with the therapist but recognizes the resources and potential gratification, which he wishes to enjoy by communicating and mutually interacting with the therapist. Such fantasies can be elaborated around other oral dynamics having to do with security and trust or directed toward a sense of protection or support of emerging autonomy without undue hostility or competition, as is appropriate to the developmental level and phenomenological focus of the patient.

CASE 2: PAM

Pam was a 23-year-old married housewife who was admitted to the inpatient service following evaluation at the crisis intervention unit of a local community mental health center. The patient had a previous history of psychiatric hospitalization at age 20 with continuing outpatient care for most of the past 2 years. She had been diagnosed as paranoid schizophrenic. The patient's husband had recently lost his job as a factory worker and had become despondent. He had begun to abuse alcohol and to spend increasing periods of time away from home. Pam's own functioning had deteriorated parallel to her husband's depression and alcohol abuse. There had been increasing turmoil and violence in the home, culminating in the patient's suicide attempt through overdose of sleeping pills. In addition, the patient's psychiatric status had deteriorated with an increase in delusional ideation and a return of persecutory auditory and visual hallucinations. Hypnosis was introduced into the psychotherapy regimen with a primary focus on its utilization to enhance the therapeutic alliance. The vignette which follows, however, demonstrates the specific use of hypnosis to control hallucinations and to help reduce anxiety with a subsequent dilation of delusional ideation. This material comes from the 11th hour of psychotherapy and the seventh session of hypnosis.

THERAPIST: As you are drifting there in hypnosis just now, I would like for you to imagine seeing the two of us in your mind's eye as you have done here in my office before. Just get a picture of you and me, Dr. Baker, in your mind's eye and let me know when you can see us clearly.

PAM: I can see us. We're standing on a hill, and it is very windy.

T: That is fine, Pam, but let's just go inside where the wind is quieter. Imagine that you can hear that wind blowing outside, but as we go indoors to a safe, quiet place, the wind dies down and grows quieter, quieter, quieter, until we simply cannot hear it anymore. There, that's fine. And I would like for you to imagine seeing the two of us in a room together with a blackboard or a tablet or a screen that you can draw on. In just a moment, when I tap you gently on the shoulder, I want you to begin to draw on that blackboard or screen or tablet. I want you to draw the voices and the figures that come sometimes to bother you. I want you to draw them there. Just go ahead. (*The patient looks frightened, and the rate of her respiration increases.*) It is all right. While I am with you there, the voices can't bother you. They can't disturb you or hurt you in any way. And together, we will learn a way to get rid of them for good. But just now, go ahead, while feeling relaxed and safe, the two of us together in that place, the way that we are together in this place, in my office, and draw them on that tablet or blackboard. Let me know when you have completed it.

P: I am drawing the voices now. Black, black and dark; dark like the pits of hell. That is where they come from. Hellish voices that tell me to die, that call me a whore; black with green staring eyes, evil and shrill, high voices that scream like lost souls.

T: Just go ahead and draw them there. On the blackboard they can't hurt you. That's fine. Are they finished?

P: Yes, but I don't want to look.

T: That's OK, because I am going to erase them. I am going to take an eraser and erase them away. As I erase them, I want you to imagine feeling safe and comfortable and just concentrate on seeing me there and hearing my voice say "Quiet, calm, peaceful, relaxed." Erasing them away, away, away until they are completely gone. Can you see that now? The voices are gone from the drawing, and they are not in your head right now either.

P: That's right. They're gone.

T: Now I want you to draw them again, but draw them smaller, smaller, and when you have completed drawing them, I want *you* to erase them this time.

P: I can draw them smaller. They don't fill up the whole blackboard anymore, and they don't have any eyes at all.

T: That's right. The "eyeness" [I-ness] of them is gone. They are not a part of you. We're taking them away and putting them on the outside where they can't hurt you or bother you anymore. We don't want those voices inside because they make you crazy and they make you sick. We can put them on the outside and get rid of them and replace them with good things that are healthy, with good, real relationships like the relationship that you have in here with me and the good parts of other relationships that you have had before and will be able to have in the real world in the future. Now go ahead and erase them yourself. Just go ahead and erase them, and when they are completely gone, take a deep breath and just feel strong and comfortable and relaxed.

In this example, indirect suggestion and hypnotic imagery are used to make the hallucinations increasingly ego-dystonic and to support the patient in coming to depend on an internal representation of a gratifying real relationship to replace a pathological interaction with a hallucinatory relationship. Her ability to do this while maintaining a sense of her own integrity and comfort and calm decreases, as well, the need for the defensive function of the associated delusional material, which is elaborated around the hallucination. Later, the patient is instructed to refocus an image of the therapist and to hear his office saying "Quiet, calm, peaceful, and relaxed" at any point when the voices return outside the therapy office in the future.

CASE 3: BONNIE

Bonnie was a 29-year-old white divorced female with a long history of repeating psychotic episodes and psychiatric hospitalizations. She carried the psychiatric diagnosis of chronic undifferentiated schizophrenia. Between her hospitalizations, she lived with her mother and father and worked episodically at a sheltered workshop. Prior to the current hospitalization, the patient had become involved with another patient at the sheltered workshop where she was employed. His rejection of her had precipitated an acute regression marked by aggressive outbursts and self-mutilation. The patient was hospitalized and hypnotherapy was introduced to help manage the intensity of her affect and to restore sufficient self-control to decrease the likelihood of continued acting out. The vignette that follows demonstrates the use of hypnosis to reduce the intensity of her affect and to address her defensive utilization of self-mutilation.

THERAPIST: Bonnie, you know how sometimes when you're watching the sun set, the light begins to gradually fade away, growing smaller and smaller as the sky turns red and orange and purple and black. You've seen that before, and I have seen that before. It is something most of us have watched as it grows dusk and evening brings a time of coolness and quiet and tranquility and peace. And, in just that way, in a moment, I would like for you to imagine seeing a color, a bright color that represents how angry you have felt; angry at your boyfriend for disappointing and leaving you; angry at the doctors for not taking care of you and keeping you safe; angry at your parents for bringing you to the hospital again. I want you to imagine seeing that color. Can you do that? (*Patient nods.*) And in just a moment, as I count from one to five, I want you to imagine that color growing lighter and lighter as it fades away, the way that light fades at evening, fading until it is completely gone. As it fades, you can feel a sense of tranquility and peace, just the way you might feel if you were resting somewhere safe at evening time, cool and comfortable, peaceful and safe. Tell me what color you see.

BONNIE: Orange, bright orange like a burning fire.

T: That's fine. And now as I count, that color can fade, and you can feel a fading of your anger, too. As you just relax feeling peaceful and safe as I count, one, fading away, two, fading, fading away, three, almost completely gone now, four, feeling safe and tranquil, five, completely gone as you just rest there feeling safe and comfortable. Are you feeling comfortable now? (*Patient nods yes.*) Has the color faded completely away? (*Patient nods yes.*) Good. And in just that way, much of the anger inside, which has made you sick and done hurtful things to you, can begin to fade away, can begin to fade away through one, two, three, four, five days of our work together until it can be gone, gone, gone, so that it need not interrupt anymore your ability to take care of yourself. And when that happens, you will be able to deal with it more effectively and be able to work with it in therapy more usefully. Gone, gone, gone. And now I would like for you to get another picture in your mind's eye. This time, I would like for you to imagine that you can see a liquid, an orange liquid inside a glass or a bowl or a cup. Can you see that? (*Patient nods yes.*) Good. In just a moment, I would like for you to imagine that you take that bowl or glass or cup of that orange liquid and pour it down the toilet and flush it away. Just go ahead and pour it down the toilet and flush it away and watch as it goes down the drain, round and round and round. As it drains away, you can feel, again, that sense of comfort and peace and well-being. Just go ahead and do that and signal to me when it is completely flushed away.

B: It's gone, flushed down the toilet with all the rest of the shit.

T: Good. And in just that way, we can make a container to hold those angry feelings and learn to do things with them, to flush them out of your system, to keep you safe. The container will be big enough and strong enough so that it doesn't overwhelm you, and we'll be able to get rid of it at the right time and in the right way so that it doesn't hurt, bother, or disturb you anymore.

These images are used to first reduce the intensity of the patient's anger and then to suggest that the relationship can be used to contain the feelings and to deal with them in an adaptive fashion so that they don't overwhelm the patient's ability to hold on to her sense of self or to hold on to contact with reality when she has strong feelings. Later in the therapy hour, hypnotic imagery is used to address the way in which the patient has engaged in self-mutilation as a function of feeling overwhelmed by the intensity of her emotions. This is related to a need to test the integrity of her boundaries by cutting them in order to demonstrate, experientially, that they have continued to exist in the face of such strong affect. Hypnotic imagery is, again, utilized to support the sense of the patient's boundaries, and the defensive function of self-mutilation is interpreted. The patient is now encouraged to abreact aspects of her anger while being reassured that the intensity is no longer strong enough to hurt her and that her boundaries are sufficient to contain the modulated expression of these angry feelings without it overwhelming and destroying her.

These clinical vignettes demonstrate the structured application of hypnotic imagery, suggestion, and abreaction to support the development of a meaningful therapeutic relationship. This relationship is then used as the crucible within which a variety of psychotic symptoms can be addressed. These hypnotic techniques do not specifically alter the patient's structural defects. Rather, they provide the experiential base within which these defects can be corrected. Over time the emerging therapeutic process also can be utilized to help the patient to understand the origin of his or her pathology. Further, the process can be used to reinforce and structure an emerging capacity for adaptation and maturation. Work in hypnosis continues to unfold within the context of verbal psychotherapy. Developments occurring in trance must be processed and integrated in the waking state. Specific resistances or amnesias can be dealt with through suggestion in trance or abreaction of associated affect so that the material can be approached more directly by the patient without fear of being overwhelmed by it.

Successful psychotherapy with psychotic patients is a long-term commitment. It requires patience, consistency, and technical acumen. However, hypnosis has proven to be a useful adjunct in the therapy process with severely disturbed patients and is particularly important in maintaining the viability of the therapeutic alliance. When applied in a thoughtful and sensitive fashion, hypnotic strategies can contribute significantly to the patient's own emerging sense of self-control and, therefore, to the evolution of a healthy, nascent sense of self.

REFERENCES

Abrams, S. The use of hypnotic techniques with psychotics. *American Journal of Psychiatry*, 1964, *18*, 79–94.

Baker, E. An hypnotherapeutic approach to enhance object relatedness in psychotic patients. *International Journal of Clinical and Experimental Hypnosis*, 1981, *29*(2), 136–147.

Baker, E. The management of transference phenomena in the treatment of primitive states. *Psychotherapy: Theory, Research and Practice*, 1982, *19*:(2), 194–198.

Baker, E. Resistance in the hypnotherapy of primitive states: Its meaning and management. *International Journal of Clinical and Experimental Hypnosis*, 1983, *31*(2), 82–89. (a)

Baker, E. The use of hypnotic techiques with psychotics. *American Journal of Clinical Hypnosis*, 1983, *25*(4), 283–288. (b)

Baker, E., & Copeland, D. Hypnotic susceptibility of psychotic patients: A comparison of schizophrenics and psychotic depressives. *International Journal of Clinical and Experimental Hypnosis*, in press.

Biddle, W. E. *Hypnosis in the psychoses*. Springfield, IL: Charles C Thomas, 1967.

Green, J. T. Hypnotizability of hospitalized psychotics. *International Journal of Clinical and Experimental Hypnosis*, 1976, *17*(2), 103–108.

Kramer, E., & Brennan, E. P. Hypnotic susceptibility of schizophrenic patients. *Journal of Abnormal and Social Psychology*, 1964, *64*, 657–659.

LaVoie, G., Sabourin, M., Ally, G., & Langlois, J. Hypnotizability as a function of adaptive regression among chronic psychotic patients. *International Journal of Clinical and Experimental Hypnosis*, 1976, *24*(3), 238–257.

Scagnelli, J. Hypnotherapy with schizophrenic and borderline patients: Summary of therapy with eight patients. *American Journal of Clinical Hypnosis*, 1976, *19*(1), 33–38.

Scott, E. M. Group therapy for schizophrenic alcoholics in a state-operated outpatient clinic: With hypnosis as an integrated adjunct. *International Journal of Clinical and Experimental Hypnosis*, 1966, *14*, 232–242.

20

HYPNOTHERAPY AND PERSONALITY INTEGRATION

A Case of Multiple Personalities

Charles H. Madsen, Jr.

A very interesting, somewhat bizarre, and unusual case with extensive use of hypnotherapy for a variety of problems was treated. A core problem, which was only discovered after an inordinate amount of work by both therapist and patient, was the emergence of a classic case of multiple personalities. In an attempt to understand the treatment, the patient herself has authored portions of this chapter. Her contributions are noted where they appear.

BACKGROUND AND FAMILY HISTORY

A 40-year-old white female from a middle-class background sought the author in the fall of 1976 as an alternative to indefinite hospitalization prescribed by two psychiatrists. The patient sought initial help in 1973 at age 29 following a regular hospitalization for physical symptoms and severe debilitating depression accompanied by suicidal ideation. Her next 3 years included extensive therapy with two psychiatrists and hospital staff psychologists (this period included no hypnotherapy) and three psychiatric hospitalizations (total duration, 15 months), where she received a total of 55 shock treatments, which resulted in complete amnesia for her former life. She even had to become reacquainted with her husband and her three children. The patient's condition following release deteriorated as partial memory returned until she was alternating between overtly psychotic periods and catatonic stupor. The patient was referred to me by her church leader in an attempt to avoid what her family (parents, husband, children) and therapists perceived as a definite potential for permanent hospitalization.

Charles H. Madsen, Jr. Department of Psychology, Florida State University, Tallahassee, Florida.

The patient was born to middle-aged parents, both above average in intelligence, in 1943. She had one older brother, 2 years her senior, adopted in infancy. Her mother, seen intermittently as an adjunct to therapy, was and is severely neurotic. Her mother suffered severe postpartum depression following her daughter's birth and placed her daughter with the patient's aunt for almost 2 years. The father, seen an average of once per year, is a highly successful businessman. He was extremely critical of his children. Father and mother were domineering, demanding, and perfectionistic, with highly unrealistic expectations.

The patient's brother exhibited early psychopathic tendencies and was responsible from age 9 onward for physically, mentally, and sexually abusing his sister (the patient). This abuse continued from age 7 through age 16. The parents did not believe their daughter when told of the abuse. The patient was left to fend for herself.

The parents were totally involved in business and social activities, leaving their children alone or with relatives and sitters most of the time. The patient's aunt had to insist that the patient's mother take back her daughter when the aunt's own baby was born.

The parents' marriage was stormy, and they separated when the children were 9 and 7, respectively. The children were told that their father didn't love them anymore and had gone away. The mother subsequently had a psychotic break but did not receive professional help. She sat in a catatonic state most of the time for the next 18 months. The children were afraid to ask for help and tried to take care of themselves and their mother. Shortly after the parents reunited, the mother became an alcoholic while the father continued to be a workaholic.

At the time of the patient's referral to me, she was married and the mother of three children aged 10, 8, and 3 years. Her husband, although he loved her, was a rigid, noncommunicative individual with a low self-concept, unrealistic expectations, and a value system highly different from that of his wife. They had experienced numerous marital difficulties and had received extensive marriage therapy during the past 5 years. The husband had made no significant change, and his wife stayed with him for security and because she felt she made a commitment in marriage. They finally separated and are now living apart, pending divorce. (Pat decided she could not integrate while living with her husband. I concurred with this.)

PERSONALITY DESCRIPTIONS

Pat was (and is) the adult base personality. Vicki Lin was the child and was predominant at age 7. Sharon (called Ann by Vicki Lin) appeared at age 13, and Betty (called Susie by Vicki Lin) appeared at age 16. (Pat called the personalities by the first name indicated; Vicki Lin called them by the second.) Sharon/Ann was eliminated first, and Betty/Susie was next integrated with Pat. Pat and Vicki Lin are still in the process of integration.

When Vicki Lin was dominant she engaged in behavior that was age-appropriate to either a 7-year-old or a 13-year-old and alternated between the two ages. Late in treatment she was "advanced" under hypnosis to age 16. The 7-year-old, with hypnotic help, relived extremely traumatic incidences of abuse as a child and actually believed they were occurring, with vivid sensory imagery. Vicki Lin learned to feel through therapy, and this was extremely painful. Vicki Lin was the protection against feelings that were occasioned by neglect and physical and sexual abuse in early childhood. Vicki Lin occasionally appeared for a few seconds, minutes, hours, or days. She could be brought out under hypnosis at any time by the therapist (Madsen). She would sometimes be angry and refuse to talk for a few minutes but would always relent, sometimes after some choice expletives that were totally foreign to the adult, Pat, who was very proper and church oriented. Vicki Lin could be triggered by thunder or lightning, teenage boys, Elvis Presley music, and specific words or phrases that triggered memories as well as smiley faces, beaches, candles, and planes. She has now taken responsibility to protect Pat from suicide and "comes out" at will.

Vicki Lin and Pat alternated consciousness. Vicki Lin as the child base knew and watched everything that Pat did (when reading an early chapter draft Vicki Lin penned in, "I sure do") and would frequently comment in an emotional way on what "that Pat" did to "dump on her" (Vicki Lin). Initially, Pat had absolutely no memory for what Vicki Lin did unless during treatment Vicki Lin was instructed to "let Pat watch." Therefore, Pat normally would know of what would happen in hypnotherapy sessions, but nothing of the activities and emotions of the other personalities that occurred outside therapy, until relatively late in treatment. Vicki Lin allowed more of Pat's watching as treatment progressed and appeared to lose her emotionality over Pat's "boring lifestyle." At first, after being made aware of Vicki Lin, Pat actually detested her. This was a crucial part of treatment. Prior to knowing about Vicki Lin's existence, Pat was merely aware of what she termed "blackouts."

Sharon/Ann's advent corresponded with Pat's teenage years. Sharon/Ann was created by Pat and was a withdrawn, depressed, severely disturbed girl who spent most of her time in bed, crying and curled up in a fetal position. She was the predominant personality for a short period from the ages of 13–15. She was completely dormant until 1979, when all four personalities reappeared within a 3-month time span when early memories were recalled.

The fourth personality, Betty/Susie, was created by Vicki Lin to do "big girl" things and inserted herself into Pat's life at age 16. Betty/Susie was an extroverted, rebellious, seductive, and uninhibited young woman who was almost the exact polar opposite of Pat. It is apparent that some of Vicki Lin's teenage behavior was closely allied with the behaviors of Betty/Susie. Betty/Susie loved social activities, pornography, and men, not necessarily in that order. She was argumentative, wild, witty, assertive, confident, creative, intelligent, and totally unencumbered by the dictates of society and opinions of others. She appeared to be basically the "healthiest" of all the personalities even though her values were almost polar opposites of Pat. She "came out" infrequently the last year before Pat was married at age 17, then disappeared until her explosive grand reentrance in 1979.

All four personalities were active for brief periods during childhood and adolescence, and then two (Sharon/Ann and Betty/Susie) apparently remained dormant until 1979, following the bringing of forgotten memories to the level of conscious awareness. Pat had absolutely no memory of these different entities, including Vicki Lin, prior to the time they all reappeared. The initial depression and inability to function, which had precipitated the early hospitalization, masked the basic problem. In cases of this kind the problem is resistant to treatment without extensive use of hypnotherapeutic age-regression and techniques that can be used to treat and integrate or eliminate the various personalities. The shock treatments with the resultant amnesia prolonged treatment unnecessarily for many years. (Treatment of multiple personalities requires an average of 10–20 years.)

INITIAL TREATMENT

During the first 2 years of therapy beginning in 1976, the patient manifested psychotic thought processes, flat affect, social withdrawal, paranoid delusions, and extensive auditory and visual hallucinations. She also experienced complete lack of self-love, negative interpretations of all ongoing experiences, and no hope for any change in her life in the future. Her marital situation was never helpful or supportive and she felt she had no friends. In addition, food intake was slowly decreasing and severe weight loss was apparent. She had intense abnormal guilt reactions to both her mother and father.

Treatment in Tallahassee began in September of 1976, and the patient was hospitalized once in 1976 for 10 days when the author was out of town. Starting in the fall of 1976, she received intensive (20 hours/week) clinical and in-home psychotherapy using a team of four therapists as an alternative to hospitalization. The initial treatment was focused on the psychotic process. Hypnosis was used to get into the thought processes and hallucinations. The psychotic thoughts were restructured, and it was possible to improve her self-concept, reduce anxiety, and restructure reactions to severe emotional development problems. Initial hypnotherapy helped the author to go inside the thought processes and hallucinations and slowly take charge and restructure the cognitions from inside.

Initial hypnotherapy induction proceeded as follows: The patient was instructed to visualize a space ship and float backward and down ("like an escalator going down, while you face up") through space where there was no gravity, no tension, no anxiety, no depression, and complete thought control. A view of the earth from space was a focus, as well as the author's voice, white noise generator, and feelings of peace. The patient was instructed to get outside and watch her mind as if it were a stage. The thoughts would come in from the wings and perhaps stay a while as would the hallucinatory experiences, but they would eventually exit the opposite side of the stage when instructed to do so by the therapist or even by themselves while she would maintain thought control. A pale relaxation mist, which was barely perceptibly sweet smelling, was activated into the space ship. The patient would breathe deeply of the mist, which would go to every cell of the body (she visualized small positive-acting entities as small round fuzzies going into heart and into blood), and bring peace, relaxation, an absence of tension, and complete thought control. A count from one to ten coupled with deep inhalation and deepening suggestions (going down through the levels of the mind as on a staircase of 10 steps) were used to enhance the hypnotic state. A thought control procedure ("stop thinking about that") while visualizing a large neon flashing stop sign in the mind's eye while changing to another scene was utilized whenever necessary to interrupt anxiety and to facilitate progress. The therapist would say "stop," instruct the patient to take a deep breath and to say, "relax" and, "control" as the air was slowly exhaled.

The therapist would slowly reconstruct the thought processes and hallucinations while leaving a number of imaginal "safe" places of refuge. Pat developed a beach scene, a meadow in a forest with a creek, deer grazing, and birds gliding in a deep blue sky over a forest, a family prayer situation, a warm bubble bath with circulating water, and a special church place where she felt spiritual and had felt nearness to the Holy Spirit. In addition, hypnotherapy included use of an image of a beautiful crystal ball that encompassed the patient with feelings of self-worth and reflected back the love that was "really" there within herself.

Subsequent to initial sessions, before the therapist or patient were aware of multiple personalities, some sessions were devoted to increasing food intake because of weight loss.

Combinations of hypnosis with desensitization were used to contradict negative evaluations of others and self as well as "mean, noncaring" remarks by her husband. Fear of people and fear of being alone were slowly worked through. In addition, covert hypnotic role playing in assertiveness behaviors was included with goal of the ability to say "no" to requests from others. Hypnotic sessions were used to relieve anxiety, assist in cognitive restructuring, present desensitization hierarchies under trance conditions, and continually improve thoughts of self-worth and competence. In the space ship a large television screen directly under the window where the earth appeared was used to present positive comments, contradict irrational thoughts, and induce self-control and self-esteem; sentences presented by the therapist appeared on the television screen and were read, analyzed, and erased on command.

As therapy progressed, it became increasingly clear that the problems were far more complex than even an analysis of the psychotic thoughts indicated. The intense mother–daughter conflict was a major stumbling block.

RESOLUTION OF MOTHER–DAUGHTER CONFLICT

The therapist began using cognitive–behavioral therapy and hypnosis to remediate the problem. The following is the patient's own personal summation from an internal perspective. She has included background information, a discussion of treatment procedures from her own perspective, and the final outcome.

SUMMATION OF MOTHER–DAUGHTER THERAPY (BY PAT)

Problem Definition

Psychotherapy revealed that I was plagued with extreme anger and resentment toward my mother for her apparent apathy and neglect with regard to me. I never consciously acknowledged these negative feelings, however, but repressed them so I would not have to deal with the reality of the situation. It is interesting to note that at this point in therapy I had no conscious anger or resentment toward my father, although he was actually more emotionally distant than my mother. The total repression of these emotions and the subsequent inability to remember any childhood experiences was my greatest problem. Until I could recognize, acknowledge, and experience the deep-seated anger and the profound grief that accompanied it, I could not overcome or resolve the mother–daughter conflict. Another aspect of the problem was that I was an extremely acquiescent and inhibited individual allowing myself to be manipulated by mother and others. My self-esteem was so low it was practically nonexistent, and the only way I could begin to develop self-love was to learn to refuse to be manipulated and to become more assertive.

Outcome
As my therapist and I systematically attacked all aspects of the problem, I gradually "unlearned" some inappropriate behavior, then relearned appropriate ways of coping with my heretofore repressed anger and resentment. At first I was more than a little dubious about all the seemingly "oversimplified" assignments I had to do, and for quite a while I felt I was not making any progress using hypnotic relaxation with desensitization. However, just prior to our mother–daughter meeting, I began to realize just how much my thoughts, feelings, and behavior had changed. The treatment finally enabled me to control the anxiety, anger, and guilt responses, while at the same time asserting my rights as an individual. I recall one specific incident that illustrated my new-found control quite well. During a visit in my parents' home, my mother commented that she had "just the right earrings to complement my dress." Always before when she made such statements, she could manipulate me to take off the ones I was wearing and wear hers. I will never forget the feeling of utter elation I felt as I calmly smiled and replied in a kind way that I preferred to wear my own. She was so flabbergasted, she just walked out of the room without another word. The final resolution came during our joint meeting, at which time I told my mother the effect her manipulative behavior had on me as well as my gratitude for all the positive things she did. It was difficult and painful for me to verbally express for the first time all those long-repressed thoughts and emotions. But once it was over and we hugged, we both knew it was the beginning of a new and deeper relationship. Six years have passed, and we are still building on that positive foundation.

At this point, it became apparent that the case was at a standstill and further progress could not be accomplished until the early history of the case was understood. It was therefore jointly decided that remembering and reliving the past, however painful, was essential to continued success.

PERSONAL DESCRIPTION OF PROCEDURES FOR RELIVING PAST EXPERIENCES (BY PAT)

My therapist used a hypnotic approach for rapid induction. Because of my experience with hypnosis, I was able to attain a deep trance rapidly (within seconds). I was then asked to imagine myself stepping into an elevator-like room and to notice buttons with numbers corresponding to my ages. I was told to push any button of my choice for the first few sessions but then later instructed to push button seven. The trance always deepened as I felt myself going down to that age. During the initial session I was able to describe in detail events of my childhood of which neither my therapist nor myself had any prior knowledge. Emotions that had been long repressed surfaced for the first time as the therapist continued to probe into the agonizing past. I vividly remembered and subsequently relived many excrutiatingly painful moments—moments I pushed into the dark recesses of my mind because they were too painful to face. The first of these memories was the separation of my parents and my intense feelings of rejection, isolation, and despair. It might be interesting to note that at this point I did not have any recollection of disassociation, even though I did remember the great comfort that my doll Vicki Lin brought me during traumatic experiences. The emotional impact of reliving that one episode was so intense that I fainted as I stood to leave. My primary therapist [Madsen] explained that this memory might possibly trigger others. I recall feeling indescribable fear as I contemplated reliving many other "forgotten" childhood events. In giving me that warning and instructing me to call him immediately if I began to have further recall, he succeeded in avoiding a potential disaster for me. The availability of the therapist is crucial once the "can of worms" has been opened. Three days later panic set in as other memories flooded my mind and left me with an avalanche of emotions. I was always given immediate appointments to work through the trauma of recollections.

For 3 months we continued with the age regression. Memories began coming even faster, and fear increased as I began to realize the enormity of my childhood problems and their subsequent effect on me. Most of the fear stemmed from not knowing if the worst memories were yet to come. [*Therapist note*: The age regression was accomplished in a similar manner in every session. The patient was taken into a hypnotic trance and then into the small elevator-like room. I dictated the years for memory, opened the door, and related that the exact location and the events that had caused the patient to become psychotic would be available for memory. It became apparent that there were some times and situations that were not being accessed, and there was a suspicion that there were other more serious problems as Pat's demeanor and verbalizations would change. This portended the discovery of multiple personalities.]

PERSONALITY INTEGRATION

It became increasingly apparent that if Pat ever was to function in a normal manner, it would be necessary to get at the root of the problem(s) that created the various personalities. Following the mother–daughter resolution and the removal of the conditions that kept the childhood memories at bay, the existence of the multiple personalities was suspected. Then, in one therapy session the personalities reappeared in Pat's life. Pat began to be aware that there were other personalities that intruded into her life.

INTEGRATION AND DESTRUCTION ATTEMPTS

The final phases of therapy also proved to be the most difficult. When the psychotic processes were conquered and the other gains were accomplished, the personalities emerged. During a series of hypnotherapy sessions after the initial emotions were allowed to be experienced, the personalities began to interact with the author. In addition, they each began to control portions of Pat's life. The therapist first placed himself in the position of being able to communicate with each personality on command, using a system of letters for each one. He began to understand the functions of each and dealt first with Sharon/Ann. She was gradually less dominant, and when given direct suggestions that she would no longer be able to take over any aspect of Pat's life, she became weaker with each session. She reached a point when she was so weak she would not respond to the author's questions. This came after she would give fewer and fewer responses, and Vicki Lin indicated that she was no longer necessary. One day after 7 months of therapy with all personalities, Sharon/Ann did not respond to a question that had always elicited a response from her. She never came back again. She had no positive aspects to her personality, and it was decided to let her die and not attempt any integration. She has never appeared and will not do so. Vicki Lin assured us of that.

Vicki Lin

Vicki Lin remained active until December 8, 1981, when I attempted to destroy her by burning the doll (the original Vicki Lin) who was a symbolic representation of the personality. During this extremely traumatic session involving three other therapists, Pat was literally forced to watch as gasoline was poured on her beloved life-long friend and companion, and the doll slowly went up in smoke. Following the cremation, a mock funeral was held and her ashes were collected in a glass jar as a visual reminder of her "death" (Vicki Lin said, "But I wasn't dead"). However, since therapy had not as yet eliminated the root of the issue that created her in the first place (Pat's father), she returned in the early part of 1983. Hypnotic techniques (described later) were used to first recover the lost historical events surrounding her existence, and second, to age-progress her. Following months of hypnotherapy, Vicki Lin disappeared in May of 1983, but reappeared the third time in September 1983 (Vicki Lin indicated, "I came out once with Pat's friend Melba at the lake [in June of 1983], but Pat didn't know it").

Betty/Susie

Using hypnotic techniques of restructuring, I was able to eliminate most of the negative components of Betty/Susie's personality and to integrate the positive aspects with Pat, thus creating a new personality that emerged as a combination Betty–Pat. This was accomplished early in 1982, and there has been no indication that the integration was not complete. This integrative process was gradual and came about largely as a result of Pat's finally deciding to "let her go" and work through the developmental stages necessary for her to mature. Pat stated, "I cannot say when the integration finally became complete. I first noticed I was able to "control" Betty/Susie's outlandish behaviors to a much greater extent, and then I was able, with this control, to become more tolerant of her." Gradually, Pat became more like Betty/Susie until it became difficult to distinguish between the two. The two personalities literally merged with no conscious awareness on Pat's part of when the "merging" took place.

HYPNOTIC PROCEDURE (BY PAT)

My therapist began the integration of Betty/Susie by using a formal strobe light induction procedure to heighten the effect of the hypnotic experience. The first few sessions were devoted to pulling Betty/Susie "out" so he could obtain more information about her. In any given 1-hour session it was not unusual for Pat, Betty/Susie, Vicki Lin, and Sharon/Ann to alternately come out four or five times. Once the therapist discovered that Betty/Susie had some qualities that would be extremely advantageous to me, he began using hypnotic suggestions, cognitive restructuring, and covert role playing to help me accept her and begin to integrate her. (Until that time, I literally despised her.) He frequently gave me posthypnotic suggestions to let Betty/Susie have "free rein" to grow and develop. Because she often did many things that were completely contrary to my nature, it was extremely difficult to allow her to have free rein. I did have a certain amount of control over her comings and goings and therefore tried to hold her back when someone triggered her. But once she was out I lost all control and was simply at her mercy. Many times she exhibited behavior that greatly embarrassed me. She would do outlandish things and then leave me to suffer the consequences.

In an attempt to speed up the process of integration, my therapist taught me self-hypnosis and subsequently cut a tape encouraging me to "let Betty go." I was instructed to play the tape several times a day. It took several months to get to the point that I was actually able to play the tape that often, but once I did, the integration was greatly facilitated.

Hypnotherapy Integration with Home Tape

I outlined the specific components of Betty/Susie's personality that would be beneficial to Pat and spent a great deal of time in getting Pat to accept the positive aspects. It was also explained that Betty/Susie represented a portion of Pat's life that Vicki Lin never allowed to fully mature. The process was designed to accept those aspects that were normal and "good" and allow Pat to see that a mature Betty/Susie would enhance her own life.

When Betty/Susie finally trusted me and was assured that she would not be destroyed but allowed to mature and become part of a whole new person, she was ready to complete the process. It took some time longer for Pat but acceptance was finally achieved. When reading this Vicki Lin commented that, "It made me mad that Dr. Madsen integrated Betty but tried to destroy me. I was there first; that really hurt." The following is a transcript of the tape that Pat used to enhance the process:

"Pat, I want you to think about the analysis of your behavior. There are certain things that you think about and certain things that happen that are the antecedents of your behavior. These are thoughts, feelings, and reactions. Now, any time you have feelings that are honest and are uninhibited, you should act upon them. This is the Betty[/Susie] part of your personality. I want you to act upon these feelings, these reactions, these responses and also to think to yourself, 'It doesn't matter what anyone else thinks; it only matters what's good for me,' and so any of the antecedents that lead to the positive type behavior need to be acted upon, thought out—these are the lovely nice, uninhibited kinds of pleasant behavior you can do when you become Betty because this is the bright part of your personality. Now there are also other parts of Betty. There is some anger, frustration, and a few words used at times, but none of this is very bad, and the more you become the Betty-type person, the easier it will become to control the minor aspects of your personality and the more you will be able to become integrated totally and completely with all the positive, wonderful values that you have. So you need many times to think, plan, decide, and reflect upon what would Betty do? What would I do as Betty? What should I do? I should not be inhibited. I should not feel guilty about any of these thoughts and feelings. And when you engage in these kinds of behavior, the list of which you now have—look at a few of those before you—some of the 50. Pick one out. Think how good it is to do that sort of thing, no matter what it is, because the negative parts of it are not very bad, and you can do it and engage in those kinds of behaviors and feel very good about yourself. You should have a warm, positive feeling about yourself. You should think 'Yes, I am a good person. I am the daughter of God, and as I allow myself to do these things, I will grow up emotionally just like other people do.'

"There will be shifts in emotions, shifts in reactions are to be expected, since they have never occurred when you were younger. So you allow them to go, you allow them to unfold, and react to them, and in fact, do many of those things that are very pleasant, very nice, very good. And then after you do it, it is very important that you consider the reasons why they are good. Number one, it is a process by which you are emotionally maturing, coming through those years you never had a chance to come through. It is a process by which you are becoming more perfect and more obedient, going through the nice life process that has been decreed before the beginning of time, before this world was, that everyone should go through. And having been stopped and held back and inhibited from that, now it is the time to do it. You are doing those things that are going to make you more positive. Many times the thoughts and feelings surrounding them are not what they ought to be, are not what they will ultimately be. But you must live through it, you must experience it, and you must think about it. And there is to be no guilt, no feelings of upset, no feelings of remorse for having done these things, because they are good, they are right, and they are the process by which you are becoming a whole, integrated person. Stop. Don't ever have Sharon[/Ann] come back. And when you start to feel like that, you tell yourself, 'Stop thinking about that. Think about how important I am, how good I am, and how whatever I've done has been for my welfare.' It's all been for your growth, it's all been for your development, it has all been for your ultimate perfection, now now, but having necessarily to go through and understand and live through these kind of things.

"Let Betty have free rein—that's wonderful—she needs it. She needs to grow, to develop, and to be excited, to be open, to be honest, to be kind, and also to have some negative emotions, to feel frustration, to feel anger, and to understand that, and to show it to other people. And that is fine. That is wonderful; she will help you achieve these same emotions. Your attitude should be one of growth, and development, and perfection in the right way—not being perfect, but becoming so. It is a process, Pat. It is a process, and the process was never developed, never had a chance to unfold itself because you were so inhibited and you were so restricted, and you still are very restricted, running away from growth and development that comes with normal expression of all these kinds of emotions and feelings and reactions that you ought to have—the good ones, some of the bad ones, the funny ones and the other ones, and also emotional ones, both in a positive way. Expression of anger can be very positive, and as you express it and deal with it, eventually it will come under control as it always does. Expression of your other emotions is also important—to allow yourself to enjoy yourself, have a good time, and the rebelliousness will come under control as it always does. That is fine. Pat, you don't ever have to punish yourself because you become as Betty. Let that part go and grow and make the proper kind of development that will lead you on to a more integrated individual as you ought to become.

"Stop, Pat. Think about the good things that you are, the good things that you'll become. You want to become more like Betty and totally get rid of Sharon in every way. You want Pat and Betty to integrate, and that is a process of your own perfection. But you've got to go through and experience and allow it to happen—all the antecedents are fine, the behaviors are good, wonderful, and there is nothing to be ashamed about, nothing to be upset about. There is nothing to punish yourself for. You don't need punishing. You just need experience—additional experience to let you grow. I want you to listen very frequently. Now it's time for you to think Betty—like thoughts, now, let her go. Think that way, act that way. Let Betty come out because she's the one who should be there. She's the one you need to integrate your personality with.

"All right now, Pat—think Betty things. Think, 'I'm going to be sociable, uninhibited, honest in my emotions, feelings, and behaviors, and if anyone does not like it, it's their problem, not mine. It is their problem completely.' Think Betty, be Betty, certainly the Betty with controls, that is fine. But not anything that needs to be punished or upset. You are doing well, Pat, but continue to do well. All right now, I will see you again another time.

"Bye—Betty—Pat."

FEELINGS-ENERGY

Pat still had no recollection of any of Vicki Lin's childhood experiences. These memories were being held back, and we had reason to believe that there were quite a few dissociative experiences that were blocked from consciousness. In order to explore the situation, I hypnotized Pat and again used age regression to facilitate recall. I communicated alternately with Vicki Lin and Pat about experiences, and by repeating this procedure in separate 2-hour sessions we were able to tap the final repressed memories.

Session Description (by Pat)

I recall walking in Dr. Madsen's office that day in May feeling an overwhelming sadness. I knew I was about to move the cogs in the wheel that would result in my losing my life-long friend, companion, and protector, Vicki Lin. I also knew it was going to be the first of several long, gruelling, emotionally draining sessions. When I began to relax as the strobe light was turned on and my therapist spoke in a soft voice, I felt momentary panic and had to use all my faculties to keep myself seated in the recliner. Gradually I felt myself relax. Under hypnosis my therapist indicated that there were levels of consciousness. To uncover memories, he took me in my mind down to the 10th level, where symbolically I could remember clearly, as well as experience fully, the pain of those childhood events. He told me he was going to talk to both Pat and Vicki Lin so both could remember and both could grieve. He told me to step down into my elevator-like room, and there were the buttons representing each age of my life. He asked me to choose seven and push. He indicated the room was going down and I was passing through the ages of life at the level of total awareness. Shortly thereafter I found myself reliving some excrutiating painful events that transpired when I was 7. I saw myself watching my father pack his suitcases and leave. I vividly recall seeing a little girl (Vicki Lin indicated this was her/me) standing beside me, watching the whole procedure with no indication that it bothered her in the least. Then I felt myself disappear, and only the other little girl remained. Subsequently, I heard my mother telling us that Daddy no longer loved us and was never coming back. Next, a quick sequence of scenes flashed before me along with the accompanying long-denied pain and grief. . . . Mother sitting in the big yellow chair in a catatonic state—I was begging her to talk to me, then fighting off my brother, trying to find something to eat in our always empty pantry; and finally, I saw myself running to my bedroom, grabbing my doll Vicki Lin and taking her with me in my closet [incidentally, Vicki Lin later said, "When she got 13 she put me back in the closet"], where I sat in the dark with the door closed, fantasizing that Daddy was coming home that night and all was well with my world. At that point in the hypnosis, my therapist commanded Vicki Lin to leave and let Pat feel the pain. Suddenly Vicki Lin was gone, and the intensity of the pain seemed unbearable. [Vicki Lin indicated, "How do you think I felt when Dr. Madsen made me start to feel."] I began crying hysterically while my therapist shouted over and over, "He's dead, he's dead—he was never the father you thought he was—bury him forever." When I thought I could endure no more, Vicki Lin reappeared, and the intense agony left as quickly as it came. Over and over during the hypnosis, she came when the pain became unbearable. Each time my therapist ordered her to leave. She paid little attention to him until he told her he would destroy her unless she left immediately. The authoritative sound of his voice created such fear in Vicki Lin that she immediately departed. Then I was alone again, tortured by emotions never before experienced. For the first time in my 39 years, Vicki Lin could not take over—always she had protected me from the many unbearable realities—always before she miraculously rescued me from pain too great to bear. Where is she now? [Vicki Lin said, "I was still there, but Dr. Madsen said he would destroy me if I came out."] How can I bear to feel with such indescribable intensity the agony of all those horrible years? I feel myself getting sick—I want to vomit—I want to scream out with the pain that clutches my chest and refuses to let me go—I am aware, *acutely* aware that I am feeling emotions that should have been felt years ago—Come back, Vicki Lin—don't leave me. I feel total panic. Please stop, Dr. Madsen. He goes on and on, bringing into sharp focus all the awful, torturing moments, reinforcing all that I now feel and intensifying it, encouraging me to acknowledge and feel the pain, the reality, the tears that won't seem to stop. When I feel I'm at the absolute breaking point he commands, "Stop thinking about that." Then he tells me to push button number 11 and I see myself on the roof of our house (Jim, Pat's brother, is there and Vicki Lin) as a scared little girl. Jim is threatening to push me off unless I agree to comply with all his morbid desires. I have a handkerchief pinned over my eyes; my legs are aching from standing so long on the ledge, and I know that soon I will have to give in to his sadistic demands. I cannot describe what I see next—I pause, waiting for Vicki Lin to obliterate the scene and absorb the pain, but I notice that under hypnosis she is slower in "coming out." "Please come Vicki Lin—I can't stand it anymore." She appears briefly, but my therapist whisks her away with another threat of extinction. Suddenly my vision clears, my emotions become even sharper—I feel sharp rocks beneath me and vile language and haunting laughter. I think I will never forget the sound of that laughter. As the scene before me unfolds I am unable to speak momentarily—the pain and fear are too intense. I recall hearing Dr. Madsen urging me to continue describing what I see. How can I? Does he know what is going on inside me? I recall feeling chest pain as I struggle to continue to describe the experience. I want to stop, but my doctor won't let me. "Please, don't make me go on." I plead with him to stop, telling him that no one will believe me—no one ever believes me when I talk about Jim's abuse. He assures me he will believe everything I say. I then muster up enough courage to complete the detailed description of that agonizing experience. As I describe it to my therapist it's happening to me again, only this time I don't block out the pain—it comes in giant waves, threatening to destroy me—it really feels as though I cannot survive it. I think of myself, "Why—why—why?" The pain is increasing with each scene I describe and relive, and my chest feels like it's about to explode. Suddenly, mercifully, Vicki Lin comes back, and I feel momentary relief. This time my therapist instructs her to feel, to cry for all the atrocities she's endured. At this point he describes my father as being dead, makes me visualize a casket and demands that Vicki Lin and I both grieve. [Vicki Lin told me, "This is the first time I ever hurt, I was mad 'cause Dr. Madsen made me feel. I just stayed and felt pain, and no one ever knew I was there."] We both cry.

How strange it is to watch Vicki Lin cry. She's never done that before. Now she and I alternately and rapidly switch back and forth, but both are suffering intense pain and nothing or no one can stop it. Once more I hear the words, "Stop thinking about that." My therapist instructs me to step into the elevator once more and I push the number 17. He asks me what I see as I step out of the elevator, and I begin crying uncontrollably, as I view the scene unfolding before me. It's one I've seen before, but this time there is a difference. Before I was able to slip quickly into my fantasy world. Now I'm faced with the stark reality as well as the excruciating pain that comes with the absence of illusion. Will this pain never end? I hear him asking me what I see and feel, but I cannot answer. Consumed with intense pain, I continue to sob. Exhaustion begins to seize my whole body, and I feel as though I'm going to faint. I wait for the blissful oblivion that always comes when Vicki Lin intercedes, but she is not there. My therapist finally convinces me I should verbalize what I see and feel. I remember wondering how much pain the human soul can bear without breaking, but an unseen force pushes me on, giving me the strength to continue. The vivid panorama before my eyes gradually brightens, and I see myself in a little two-bedroom white house. At 17 I am married and living 400 miles away from family and friends. Like a giant moving 3-dimensional picture, the anguish-filled days, weeks, and months of my 1st year of marriage unfold, and I am devastated by the sequence of events that passes through my mind. The primary all-consuming emotion I feel is loneliness. I see myself going through the motions of being a loving, caring wife, but for the first time, I feel the total agony of that 1st year. The feelings intensify as the sickening realization hits: I wasn't happy, I was miserable—no friends, no social engagements, no church; just a continual round of sex, cooking, cleaning, meeting demands, and always-inconsolable isolation. [Vicki Lin later indicates "I told her not to marry him."] I see a fragment of this person, a young girl who's lost her identity and has become simply an extension of her husband. I see someone who has lied to herself for so many years that she no longer has the ability to recognize truth. Now as I sit in his [her therapist's] recliner and relive my 17th year, I can see so clearly and feel so acutely the sense of utter desperation that was never allowed to surface. I think to myself, "I have lived a lie. Self-deception has followed me all the days of my life." Grief overwhelms me and I feel I can stand no more. My body is limp with exhaustion and pain. My mind is in a state of total confusion, "Please God, no more."

I hear my therapist saying, "That's enough for one day," and he counts me down. As I come out of the hypnotic state, I feel such shame, such despair, and I just want to die. I look at my therapist and he looks pale and drained. The thought occurs to me that this session was almost as difficult for my doctor as it was for me. Two hours of intense emotion had left us both exhausted.

I need to rebuild the courage needed to finish this last stage of therapy. I know there will be more sessions like this one, and something inside me says, "It is enough."

As I stand up to leave his office, all my energy is draining to my feet and I faint. After 3 hours spent vacillating between hysterical crying, dry heaving, and hyperventilating, I am able to walk to my car with help. The first of several painful sessions is over, and I'm left to cope with myriad emotions. How lonely it is.

CONTINUATION OF THE FINAL STAGES

Following the mock death of Pat's fantasy father, the one that never really existed, she was able to deal with him in a more rational manner and logical way (she and her family also moved to Tallahassee in August 1983). During a number of sessions of hypnotherapy, when it was necessary to help her acknowledge and feel her intense hatred for her father, a large picture of him was used. She tore up newspaper clippings, sliced his portrait, and finally relieved herself of the emotions that he had stated she should never feel. The subsequent sessions dealt with memories and reactions plus finishing her feelings about her father.

After 5 years of hypnotherapy and intensive cognitive–behavioral therapy with and without hypnosis, Pat was no longer intruded upon by Betty/Susie or Sharon/Ann. It was belatedly realized, however, that Vicki Lin represented part of the basic core personality from which Pat had probably developed. Her reappearance made it necessary to achieve an integration as with Betty/Susie, rather than a destruction as with Sharon/Ann. This proved the most difficult, as Pat was extremely afraid of "disintegration" in giving herself over to Vicki Lin, and Vicki Lin in turn was very much afraid of being controlled by Pat. For a time Vicki Lin no longer accepted Pat as her friend whom she had to protect, and she continually did little things that made Pat's life much more of a problem. This lasted 5–6 months until Vicki Lin was convinced that she needed to protect Pat from death.

Vicki Lin in her age progression became suspicious of her therapist but would still call him late at night when she had been drinking and needed some help to get home. She was angry with her therapist for a few months because he taught her to feel, and she felt he did not give her enough help in coping with these feelings. (Vicki Lin told me, "But most of all, Dr. Madsen grew me up to 13 and left me all alone, and tried to destroy me. I was hurt for 3 months.") She also became angry because he didn't bring her out enough.

When it was determined that all of the memories were available for recall, the process of age progression was begun with Vicki Lin. She would age-regress to 7, and then when the door opened a birthday party would be in session. A birthday party was given for Vicki Lin for every year up until age 13. The parties included cake, ice cream, and games appropriate to the age level of the party. All of the parties were part of hypnotherapy sessions. The parties progressed well on a bi-monthly basis until age 13 where some resistance was encountered because of the prior appearance of Sharon/Ann and other memories that were still a problem because of their intensity. After 6 months of work, we started again and have progressed to 15.

Vicki Lin alternated between 7 and 13 with no in-between. She was finally able to tell me that the memories were not all finished and she could not leave 7 until they were all finished and relived. The final memories involved a series of abusive interactions that were every bit as difficult as the previous session described so graphically by Pat. It was necessary on many occasions to allow Vicki Lin to experience the memory with Pat watching. She would see, experience, and have to go through the entire sequence before the memory was placed behind her.

In the initial sessions I told Vicki Lin that the memory was not real and it had happened in the past. Whenever I interrupted the memory in this way, it was then necessary for Vicki Lin to go through it again before it was put to rest. Finally, after many sessions over approximately 6 months, the 7-year-old appeared no more, and the final integration proceeded.

Both personalities felt extremely threatened. In hypnotic sessions Vicki Lin was given suggestions to become older and more accepting of Pat. Pat had a more difficult time, since she had never been able to get inside Vicki Lin's "head," since Vicki Lin stopped letting her in and since Pat was almost pathologically afraid of Vicki Lin damaging her reputation at school, church, and community after Vicki Lin stopped being the protector. This later was reversed as both personalities have now accepted the inevitability of integration, and Vicki Lin is again a protector, but in a different way.

MAJOR CONCERNS DURING FINAL INTEGRATION (BY PAT)

I am going to have to let Vicki Lin "go" in the same way I did with Betty[/Susie]. Lack of control is even more frightening with Vicki Lin, since she is even more different than I am and also is an impulsive teenager. In addition, her impulsivity is occasionally manifested in suicide attempts. I must get some degree of control before she kills us both. However, the fear is so intense that I also must be brought under control. My hypnotherapy sessions where my therapist brings out Vicki Lin are very anxiety provoking. Although I very much want to rid myself of the problems caused by these two personalities, I find myself already dreading the loneliness and grief that accompanies the extinction of a personality. It seems paradoxical that I could want something so much, yet at the same time dread it, but past experience has taught me there is a painful adjustment following integration. I am disappointed that Vicki Lin has reemerged, even though in reality she has been there all the time, and that I will have to face difficult times. I am confident that the end is in sight.

SUMMATION

Integration of these two personalities is coming close to being achieved after a great deal of traumatic work. Pat is finally able to accept to a greater degree Vicki Lin as Vicki Lin is growing up and maturing. Pat does experience a great deal of anxiety, pain, and grief. The hypnotic techniques are similar to the integration of Betty/Susie (daily tape) with the addition of hypnotherapy images of the personalities melding together, employed in many sessions. Pat and Vicki Lin experience a great deal of pain as they picture their bodies becoming one. But "they" are working hard to finalize the process.

Pat's life is very difficult, and she retreats into depression and at times suicidal thoughts. Pat feels that if she would go away and, "give it all to Vicki Lin, everyone, including her family, would be better off without her." This development precipitated a series of sessions where it was necessary to go back into the mind and find Pat where she had hidden. A tape was cut so those that worked with her could bring Pat out when it was necessary. The melding of the personalities has begun and the writing, speech, and mannerisms of the two personalities are becoming more similar as witnessed by the 6 people who work closely with them. However, the feelings of grief, disintegration, and lack of being can not be understated. In one session it was necessary to liken the process to a death and to let Pat grieve for her demise and to later write her own epitaph. The trauma and intensity of the sessions remains very high and the final integration is inevitable but when it will exactly occur is not yet known.

As the therapist I am also experiencing some feelings of grief and in a small way I understand the emotions of the two personalities and am experiencing some sadness as the final integration approaches. I will need to experience more and will say at that time: "Goodbye Vicki Lin and the former Pat; I shall never forget either one of you. The newly integrated person takes the best of both, but something was lost in the process, even though it is necessary and for the best."

21
HYPNOSIS WITH THE BORDERLINE PATIENT

Joan Murray-Jobsis

PROBLEM DEFINITION

The patient being presented in this case study will be referred to as Lydia. (All names used are fictitious.) She was a 33-year-old woman with a PhD degree who was functioning intellectually quite well as an assistant professor at a major research university. However, although her performance was successful in the limited area of academics and intellectual pursuits, Lydia's personal life was in a state of despair. She lived with her parents, sharing a duplex with them and was excessively tied to and dominated by her mother. She distrusted much of the rest of the world and had few social contacts and no close relationships other than with her mother. She disliked her father and men in general and avoided relationships with males. She felt some conflict about this behavior, because her mother ostensibly wanted her to marry. While claiming that she preferred her solitary life to one involving relationships, Lydia was nevertheless troubled by severe bouts of anxiety and depression. She felt she was potentially suicidal and also feared her hostile impulses toward the outside world.

Initially, Lydia came into therapy rather cautiously skeptical. She had been referred to me by one of her sisters who had been a former patient of mine. Lydia clearly did not initially believe that psychotherapy could help her. Nor did she believe that she was "worthy" of help. She perceived her problems as involving anxiety and depression with potential for suicide. But she did not feel that she deserved treatment. She felt her problems were her "own fault" and that she should not indulge in "self-pity" but should learn to better ignore her negative feelings. At the time of our initial meeting, Lydia had become very expert at dissociating from (ignoring) feelings and at forcing herself to live almost totally in an intellectual–philosophical frame of reference. This dissociative defensive pattern allowed Lydia to

Joan Murray-Jobsis. Private Practice, Chapel Hill, North Carolina. (The author formerly has published under the name Joan Scagnelli-Jobsis.)

perform fairly well at her job but left her periodically engulfed in waves of anxiety and despair when her defenses gave way and feelings pushed through.

Lydia did not initially define her problem (as did her therapist) as a lack of contact with feelings and a lack of sense of identity. Nor did she see her inability to form and maintain relationships as central to her problem.

Nevertheless, Lydia was aware of her depression and anxiety and was willing rather tentatively and skeptically to contract for some initial therapy.

CASE BACKGROUND

Lydia was the middle child of three sisters. Her role in the family almost from birth seems to have been that of assistant to mother in the care and tending of the older sister, Ella. Lydia had been told early in her life that mother "had" her because her older sister needed a playmate. The mother appears to have had a symbiotic relationship with the oldest daughter and centered everything in the family around meeting the oldest child's needs. Even the father was subordinated to this child, and apparently the marriage was extremely tenuous at times due to this mother–child relationship. In her teenage years, this oldest daughter was diagnosed as schizophrenic and was hospitalized for a year.

During all of her remembered life, Lydia had centered her existence around her mother. She developed an intensely empathic relationship with mother in an attempt to serve mother's needs and win mother's affection. Early in life Lydia realized that she could make mother happy by keeping Ella, the older sister, satisfied. So the interfamily dynamics became established. Mother dominated the family and centered everything around pleasing Ella. Father became more and more angry but passive and withdrawn from family influence. Lydia became focused on meeting mother's needs, which in turn meant keeping Ella happy. The youngest sister, Mary, identified quietly with daddy and sought his approval. Thus Mary kept herself somewhat apart and safe from some of the interfamily conflict and intensity.

In her early years Lydia also had tried to identify with daddy and get some of her approval and support from him. However, this attempt at paternal support appears to have been aborted by mother at about the time Lydia became 9 years old. It seems mother wanted to return to full-time teaching and needed more assistance in caring for Ella at that time. It appears that mother broke up the relationship Lydia had established with her father up until age 9 in order to enlist both Lydia and father in the further care and tending of Ella. In any event, Lydia lost the contact she had occasionally shared with her father and found herself more and more bound to Ella – partially because a family move left Lydia without her previous peer group of friends and also because both mother and father were less available due to mother's return to work.

"Taking care of Ella" frequently meant tolerating her abuse and taunts. Although Lydia did not perceive the hostile, destructive nature of this sibling relationship as a child, it became very clear in retrospect through hypnosis.

By adolescence Ella's rages had become unmanageable. Knives were hidden so that she would not injure herself. Lydia was forced to eat large quantities of food in order to coax an anorectic Ella to eat a little. Father was threatening to leave because of mother's indulgence of Ella's hostility. Finally, as mentioned, Ella was institutionalized for a year.

The family stayed together with angry bonds. Ella returned home, not much better, and angry at mother for sending her away. Mother was angry at father for "forcing" her to send Ella away. Lydia was angry at father because mother said he was wrong to send Ella away. And the youngest daughter seems to have distanced much of the hostility and escaped into her peer group for acceptance and approval.

By the time I saw Lydia in therapy, Mary had been married and divorced and returned home to live with Lydia and parents. Mary had been seeing me for depression over her divorce and anxiety over her job. As she began to make progress, she referred Lydia to me. Lydia's problems were clearly more serious, and her character formation was borderline in structure. She lacked a coherent sense of self. She saw her feelings as separate, dangerous, and unworthy. She valued only her intellect and could initially relate to the therapist only through intellectual discussions concerning Far Eastern religious philosophies and the value of dissociating from the physical and emotional self. Gradually Lydia began to be able to perceive some possible value to feelings and to recognize that she need not so greatly fear those feelings. She eventually became interested in hypnosis because her anxiety attacks were overwhelming, and she wanted some help in reducing anxiety and in relaxing.

DISCUSSION OF TREATMENT

As stated earlier, Lydia originally entered therapy with great skepticism and distrust and in deference to her sister's prodding. Therefore, initial therapy was devoted to simply forming a relationship and building trust. Several initial sessions were devoted to philosophical discussions regarding Eastern religions, and the elevation of spirit over the senses and the emotions. These early sessions clearly represented signs of patient distrust and of resistance. The extensive intellectualizing was utilized by Lydia to keep both feelings and the therapist at a distance. Gradually, as trust and respect developed, Lydia expressed cautious interest in hypnosis to help her with anxiety attacks and sleep problems.

INITIAL INDUCTION AND ASSESSMENT OF CAPACITY AND RESISTANCE

The initial hypnosis sessions were designed to be primarily supportive and nurturing. A relaxation induction technique was used. The patient was asked to relax into her chair with a deep breath and requested to "just let your eyelids close." She was given permissive messages throughout the induction. She was told that she could sit in an upright rather than a recliner chair and that she could open or close her eyes whenever she wished. Given this permissive setting, Lydia soon closed her eyes for comfortable hypnotic work. However, she continued to prefer a straight-backed chair over the usual recliner, as this seemed to provide her with a greater sense of control.

Following eye closure, a standard progressive relaxation procedure was used. It was suggested that the patient focus on relaxing the different parts of the body starting with the toes and working up to the top of the head. The patient was then helped to experience an arm levitation. The therapist took the patient's arm and gently placed it in a floating position. The patient maintained the levitation until the therapist suggested that the arm might lower to the lap as the patient deepened even further. Thus a levitation technique was used as a deepening procedure and also as a dramatic way of helping the patient become aware of her trance capacity.

Lydia followed the initial relaxation trance induction quite readily. She was also very receptive to the initial nurturing messages of inner calm, strength, and healing. There were no significant resistances encountered in this initial phase of relaxing and nurturing hypnosis. This stage of hypnosis seemed to overcome further the original therapy resistance and distrust and to solidify the therapeutic alliance and positive transference. During this initial phase of hypnosis, Lydia clearly shifted into a positive, cooperative relationship with the therapist and began to abandon her intellectualizing defensive patterns. These initial hypnotic sessions also clearly demonstrated that Lydia possessed a good hypnotic capacity and was quite able to access that capacity.

As the supportive, nurturing rewards of hypnosis began to build and bond the relationship between therapist and patient, Lydia learned to trust the therapist not to intrude on her inner space. Gradually she became more and more able to share her fears and feelings—her vulnerable inner self. As this transition occurred, Lydia and the therapist moved into more exploratory work with hypnosis. Age regression, free association, open-ended projective techniques, and imagery were employed to access memories and feelings.

ONGOING TREATMENT

While the initial hypnosis sessions involved relaxation and trust in the relationship as central issues, the later sessions began to move into more uncovering work. This uncovering work typically proceeded with a brief relaxation induction and then a suggestion for the patient to image a staircase leading down 10 steps to a room with many doors. Behind each door lay memories, images, and feelings to be explored. The patient then descended the staircase and described the room and the doors as they appeared on each occasion. She was then asked to select a door to open and explore. Lydia typically would choose a door with some foreknowledge of what lay beyond it. She would then "enter" that door and follow the free association of images beyond the door.

An excerpt from an early session in the uncovering phase of psychotherapy accomplished in hypnosis with Lydia follows[1]:

Hypnotic Session 3

LYDIA: The room is circular with a spiral staircase coming down into it. I can't see the entire room—some of it is blocked by the stairs, and some of it is shrouded in darkness. But I can see a large segment of it including those doors that I have opened previously. Some of these are now open while others remain closed. As I look around I can sometimes see behind the other doors. Gradually I begin to feel the pull of one of them on which I then focus.

Today I open the door to a room in which there is a huge *skeleton of a baby*. It is about 10 feet long with rotting bits of flesh on it. I also see *two normal-sized babies* also as skeletons. They've been *eaten by the monstrous baby*. Its touch is death—like acid that will eat away at your flesh. I'm standing near a wall—afraid even to move. A woman, its *mother*, comes and picks it up and carries it away protectively.

I identify the skeleton as Ella—rejecting any sense of identification with it.

DR. J: Do you want to leave?

L: *I can't leave. If I do I'll be all alone*. I feel very lonely and rejected. I follow the mother carrying the skeleton.

1. The patient made these notes herself following each hypnotic session. Underlining (here indicated by italics) was done by patient.

Some comments by Lydia about the hypnotic process at this early stage of therapy might be revealing. She commented as follows:

"*1*. During hypnosis I need *prodding* to move from scene to scene. Otherwise I just stare—frequently not thinking just observing, feeling, floating.

"*2*. I feel like I've put *strong defensive barriers* between myself and the rest of the world. I'm *afraid to lower* these barriers and be seen. *To be seen is to be rejected. During hypnosis I don't have a sense of lowering the barriers*. Rather I feel as if I'm still behind them and am simply allowing you behind them also. This way I feel safer and can talk about things more easily.

"*3*. During *hypnosis I can still feel my denial* mechanisms and the tendency to suppress emotions that I don't want to face, but I have a much *easier time putting these tendencies aside*. Also my mind becomes quieter so the *tendency to intellectualize is more easily overcome*.

"*4*. I periodically feel *anger and resentment over feelings of dependency* that arise during therapy. Such feelings do not seem to be engendered in me as much during hypnosis. Consequently, I have somewhat less difficulty accepting the ideas, advice, etc., that I should be getting from the sessions.

"*5*. During hypnosis I am both a participant and an observer in the process. The partitioning of my consciousness between these two phases varies with the subject being dealt with and with the level of trance that I'm able to achieve on a particular day. The more I can get into the situation as a participant, generally the more effective the process. This requires that a protective barrier I've set up between myself and my emotions be more fully lowered. (Simply being under hypnosis lowers it to a large extent.) It is more difficult for me to fully lower the barrier when we are dealing with more painful subjects. There are two reasons I see for this at the moment:

"*a*. The more painful the emotional experience the more I want to avoid it. It is after all like sticking your hand in the fire. Many times I must require myself to deal with difficult experiences rather than avoid them the way I'd like to. It is much easier for me to do this in hypnosis since the barriers to dealing with emotional pain are lower.

"*b*. Because the family failed to recognize and respect my emotions, I've come to think of them as unacceptable, and I'm afraid to let others see them. Hypnosis overcomes this fear to a large extent because you (the therapist) are behind the barriers that protect me from the outside. But the observer part of myself still has some fear of rejection and thus seeks to protect itself by remaining dominant when we are dealing with very painful topics."

It can be seen from the above comments of self-analysis by Lydia that the hypnotic process appeared to reduce resistance and negative transference. Lydia's initial resistance to dealing with feelings and expressing feelings centered around the belief that her inner feelings were "bad" and "unacceptable." She especially feared rejection of herself and her feelings by the outside world. In her comments Lydia very poignantly described how hypnosis permitted her to retain her defensive barriers against the outside world while allowing the therapist behind those barriers, thereby allowing her feelings to be seen by the therapist. In addition, Lydia described how the hypnotic process helped her lower the internal protective barrier she had set up between herself and her own emotions. Thus the experience of hypnosis "per se" appears to provide a mechanism for lowering resistance. It seems that hypnosis allows for the suspension of "the critical judgmental self" and in so doing allows patients to express and reveal feelings that they otherwise might censor and keep from expression and from awareness. Thus, the experience of hypnosis can provide a mechanism for reducing resistance that may be especially helpful to the withdrawn or alienated patient with low self-esteem. Hypnosis may allow such a patient the noncritical atmosphere to permit the acknowledgment and expression of feelings. In Lydia's case, she is clearly stating that hypnosis did provide that temporarily noncritical space for her self-expression.

Occasionally, resistance would occur for Lydia in hypnosis in spite of the reduced critical atmosphere. On such occasions the resistance would typically occur in the form of imagery. For example, Lydia at one point in therapy could not open one of the doors to continue her explorations. Her fear of the painful emotions behind that particular door was too great. In dealing with that resistance, the therapist stayed within the patient's imagery and suggested that Lydia "speculate" on what was behind that particular door. She was asked to imagine what that pain and fear were about. Then she was asked to devise ways of protecting herself so that she could enter the door and remain safe. Lydia eventually created protective escape routes described in a later session.

Lydia continued to use hypnotic trance work intermixed with traditional ongoing weekly psychotherapy for approximately 2 years. Excerpts from some later sessions follow:

Hypnotic Session 5

L: In today's session we dealt with feelings of anger and hate that I have against myself which arise from the belief that I am ugly. I first see myself in the bathroom of the old house. I can see the room quite clearly—the sink with the mirror about it especially. I am standing in front of the mirror staring into it at my face, which is badly broken out in pimples. I hate my face and feel it is ugly.

DR. J: What do your mom and dad say? Do they reassure you that it is only a temporary situation?

L: My parents think that I am ugly. I heard them talking and know that's what they think. They're not sure that it will ever clear up. I can remember mom coming in to say goodnight to me each night. She would sit on the edge of my bed and examine my face. I hated it when she did this—like I was always being judged and found ugly. It was important to be pretty. That's very important in order to get a man, and without a man I would be a failure. I think that mom is embarrassed by my complexion. She is very pretty.

DR. J: Go forward in time and try to see when your complexion started to clear up.

L: I go through the end of high school. It is better then but still not beautiful. Even in college it's not great.

DR. J: Do your parents give you positive comments now?

L: I can remember their saying they are surprised that my face is not permanently scarred from it. I still think mom views me as ugly. She is always criticizing the way I'm dressed or have my hair. I still feel ugly and hate myself for it.

DR. J: Other things are important besides being pretty.

L: I remember thinking that my parents feel it is a good thing that I'm smart since I'm not pretty. It's OK that Mary [younger sister] is not smart, because she is pretty and can get a man.

DR. J: Do you think that mother would love you if you were pretty, after all Ella is not so pretty and she loves Ella.

L: I feel that is different since Ella is her first kid, and I think that she loves Ella best. I think that I must be perfect in order for mother to love me. I have to be real nice and bring her presents.

DR. J: When a child is unloved it does not mean that the child is unlovable. It means that the mother had an inability to love. Perhaps mother was incapable of loving more than one child. If you could have been the mother, you would have loved little Lydia. I would like you to go back in time and see yourself as the little girl Lydia. Then go back also as your adult self and visit with that little girl Lydia. You can give her love and care. You can know her needs and her lovableness.

L: I see myself back at my baby sister's first birthday party. I'm about 4 years old and I'm quite cute. I'm very spunky and run all over the place excited. Now I can see my present self taking the little kid in my arms and hugging her. I feel great love for her and care for her. I try to bring that feeling forward as the kid gets older and am at least partially successful.

Footnote by Lydia: At the end of this session I felt much more positive about myself. Feelings of hate toward myself were at least temporarily put aside and replaced by feelings of love. Thanks!

Hypnotic Session 10

L: The section of the circular room dealing with Ella and my interactions with her during the time I was in high school lies to the far right as I come down the stairs. I go through the first door in this section to find myself in the kitchen of our house. The room is long and narrow with a door leading into the dining room at one end and a door leading to the back hallway and the back stairs coming from the middle of one side. It is evening and I have been making popcorn for the family as I frequently do. Mother, Ella, and Mary are in the kitchen with me while Dad is watching TV in the dining room. The corn is popped into a large white enamel pan that has a few chips knocked out of it. Mom takes out a heaping red bowl for me. She piles it very high so that a lot of the pieces are precariously balanced. She then puts a few handfuls in another bowl for Ella and checks with her that the distribution is satisfactory.

DR. J: How are you feeling about this?

L: I feel very nervous as I watch this process fearing that Ella will fly off the handle again and start screaming. I'm going to take my bowl upstairs and eat it while I read in bed. As I try to carry it upstairs, a few kernels roll off the top, and Ella starts shaking and crying and piles them back on. I carefully carry the bowl upstairs and slide into bed. Most of the time I don't want to eat all the corn, so sometimes Snoopy (my dog) will eat some for me. She is lying on my bed with me stretched along my legs. I like to have her there. Other times I stuff the extra into a large plastic bag and hide it under my red sweater in the second drawer down in my chest of drawers. Then after everyone is asleep, I sneak down into the basement and burn it in the incinerator.

DR. J: What does mother do about this?

L: I'm back in the kitchen and see mother check with Ella for approval of what I'm supposed to eat. She wants and I think expects me to cooperate fully. She can't handle it when Ella starts screaming.

DR. J: What does she [mother] do?

L: I'm in the living room, and I can hear Ella upstairs in her bedroom screaming and banging her head and fists on the walls. Mother runs up and tries to calm her down. She is afraid that Ella will try and commit suicide. One time we had to hide all the knives and razor blades. I would come home from school each day wondering whether Ella might have killed herself before I got home.

DR. J: Did Ella ever really try to kill herself? Are there any scars on her wrists?

L: I look at her wrists. They are very skinny and I can see the blue veins running along them and the tendons which are distended and very prominent. I can't see any scars at all on them although I see a scar on her elbow from the time she fell off her bike and had to have stitches.

DR. J: What does your father think of all this?

L: Dad gets angry about Ella. Mother is afraid that he will leave. I see them in the living room arguing in hushed voices. I think that dad would like to hit Ella and make her shut up. Mother is pleading with him to calm down. There are tears in her eyes, and dad finally relents.

DR. J: When did all this start? Has Ella been to the hospital yet?

L: They haven't taken her to the hospital yet. She went away to a private school for a year to a place in Vermont. I'm in the car driving up there with mom to pick up Ella. When we see her, she has become extremely skinny, and I wonder why they don't feed her more. She says that she only will eat one orange a day now and that she isn't hungry. She acts real nasty, and I don't talk to her any more about it.

DR. J: I want you to let yourself become divided into two people now and become in part an observer of the scene in the kitchen. How do you feel about it?

L: I look at mother and know that what she and Ella are doing is not right. I feel that they are completely unaware of how I am feeling or don't care. This time of my life has left me incapable of forming normal relationships with other people.

DR. J: How do you feel about this now? Are you angry?

L: I don't feel any anger toward them, but I do feel very sad.

DR. J: Why do you feel so sad?

L: Because mother loves Ella so much more than she loves me. This knowledge brings a sharp aching pain to my chest, and I have a sense of isolation.

Hypnotic Session 11

L: Today the room of many doors appears brightly lit. The staircase is metallic, and most of the doors are white with metal doorknobs. The section of the room dealing with Ella during high school lies to the right as I reach the bottom of the staircase. I go through a door that is in the middle of this section and find myself on the tennis court at the lake. Mom and I are playing, and I have to run all over the court to return her shots. Ella is on the side of the court standing by the old bench near the net. She is very upset that mom and I are playing and keeps screaming and crying. She yells that it's not fair if mom plays more time with me than with her. She's crying and says that no one wants to play with her.

DR. J: What does mother do?

L: Mother is upset and sad and tries to calm Ella down. I don't like to see mother upset. She tells Ella that she will play a set with me and then will play a set with her. But Ella gets upset over that and says that it takes a lot longer to play a set with me than it does with her. She will be beaten 6–1 or 6–2 while a set might go 7–5 or more with me. Then mom says OK, that she will play 6 games with me and then 6 games with Ella, but she gets upset again because games with her are shorter than games with me so she'll be cheated again. All the time this is going on Ella is crying, clenching her fists, and saying how unfair things are. Finally, mother agrees to play a half hour with each of us.

DR. J: How do you feel about what's going on?

L: I feel a deep pain in my chest and intense sadness. Ella is so unhappy. Her mind is sick, and she seems to have no control over how she acts or feels. Mingled in with the sorrow is a little anger, because I really want to play with mother, and I don't want her to have to play with Ella as the price for playing with me. I want to get away from the whole situation. I do this by withdrawing into myself and feel myself flowing into the dark and silent recesses of my self. I reside there in touch with God and in peace, undisturbed by outer things. From this place I can endure the anger, pain, and rejection that surrounds me.

DR. J: What does your dad do about Ella and her screaming?

L: I have a little trouble locating dad. He seems overshadowed by the presence of Ella and mother. I find him sitting in the cottage reading a Western. He wants to avoid problems, and although he gets angry with Ella, he usually lets mother handle things the way she wants to. I don't spend much time with him now, although sometimes we go fishing.

DR. J: Tell me about fishing.

L: I am in the little boat on the lake. Dad is sitting in the back seat next to the motor, and mother is in the middle seat while I'm in the front. The water is glass smooth and I can see seaweed and tiny minnows below the surface. I have an impulse to dissolve into its stillness. Just two of us fish at a time to prevent the lines from getting tangled. We generally fly fish and catch a lot this time of year. I can see the rubber bugs twitching on the surface and a series of ripples radiating as a fish strikes one. Mother is bragging about being the best fisherman in the family, and I think about how she always wants to be better than me at things – fishing, tennis, cards. I am now in the cottage. It is evening and mom and I are playing double solitaire. We go at it pretty vigorously, and mother sometimes gets a little nasty if I'm winning. I feel a little hurt but play along pretending to really care about winning, because mother seems to like beating me better when she thinks I want to win a lot.

DR. J: So even when you get to spend time with mother, it isn't always enjoyable?

L: I want mother to love me, and I do everything I can to please her so she will love me.

DR. J: Do you think that your mother has ever really loved you or understood you?

L: No. I never let her see me as I really am. She would not accept or love me then. Rather I acted the way I thought would win her approval and love and let myself think that I was special to her.

DR. J: I want you to go back and become two people – the young Lydia and the adult Lydia who can now become the mother of the other. She would have understood and loved the real Lydia.

L: I see myself playing tennis with the teenage me. The adult me enjoys seeing that I'm playing well and is pleased. She has no desire to beat me, just likes the chance to be with me and do something together that we both enjoy. Then we are walking down a dirt road near the lake, talking. The adult me is listening to the child – understanding and respecting what is important to her.

Hypnotic Session 12

L: Today we decided to try to gain some insight into the "real" reasons behind my *unnecessary anxiety over Mary's safety*. I am drawn into a room in which I find myself at the lake. I'm now in the sixth grade [about 11 years old]. We still have the trailer, and I'm washing dishes at the sink. Mary is supposed to be rinsing and drying them, but as periodically happens, we are both being difficult. She has complained that they aren't clean enough, and I've retaliated by washing them extremely slowly and carefully. As soon as she gets mad and leaves, I'll rush through them quickly and pile them up so it's hard to rinse them. But now I'm starting to get worried about Mary. She went out the side door and should be back by now. I go out to look for her and start walking down toward the lake calling for her. There is a knot of fear in my stomach.

DR. J: What are you worried about?

L: I'm afraid that Mary has disappeared and will never be back. I read about that happening in a book called *Stranger than Science* that I bought with my own money from the book club at school. I now find myself in the scene I visualized whenever I thought about that section of the book. I'm on the old wooden porch of a farmer's house. In front stretches a dirt path leading to the main road several hundred feet in the distance. Fields with short brown hay in them lie on both sides of the path. It is morning. The sky is overcast, and just the edge of the sun can be seen glinting off the clouds on the horizon. There are several other people on the porch with me including the farmer's wife and his daughter. The farmer walks down the path away from the house as we watch. When he gets about 30 feet away from the house, he suddenly disappears before our eyes. In panic and fear we run to the place where we last saw him and start searching and calling for him. Faintly I can hear him calling back, crying for help, but we cannot find him. Even months later he has still not reappeared. I go out there almost every day looking and listening but to no avail. Sometimes I picture him trapped in a different dimension and catch a glimpse of him reaching out as he tries to get back. But the momentary warp in space that let me see him closes again before I can touch him or call to him.

DR. J: Who do you worry about disappearing?

L: I worry about mother and Mary in particular and once in a while about dad.

DR. J: Do you worry about disappearing yourself?

L: Once in a while but not very often. At least I'd know what had happened then. But it's possible that some time I might just vanish and get stuck in another state from which I couldn't escape. That frightens me but not as much as mom or Mary disappearing.

DR. J: Perhaps one thing that this story reminds you of is people disappearing when you need them. They weren't too good at meeting your needs. When you were a little child and helpless, you needed them to meet your needs. If they disappeared, you would be helpless, and that fear may still be with you. Of course, you don't need to have that fear any more. You are not helpless, and you have many resources to turn to now.

L: I find myself now in my play pen as a little kid. I'm restless and want to get out but there is no one there to pay any attention to me. I wander around the pen feeling frustrated. Then I grab the rail and start shaking it. That doesn't seem to do me any good, so I sit down in one corner waiting. [*Lydia's note*: At this point I entered one of the most "delocalized" states I've ever experienced. Awareness of my body on any level was gone, and I felt like I was walking with great effort through a viscous fluid.] I now find myself *looking down on myself as a baby in my crib*. I am wrapped in a white blanket that has a rather rough texture. Black hair grows thinly on my head lying in little strands down my forehead. Slowly and with some sense of fear, I let myself relax into the baby's consciousness. I'm very frustrated and feeling confined. I want something, perhaps something to eat, perhaps just to be able to move around. I start beating my arms up and down in frustration and shaking my head back and forth. I am unhappy, dissatisfied, *and want something but no one is around*. In just a few moments, *I have a great desire to be free of the confinement and helplessness of this body*. I leave feeling afraid that I may be so far away I won't be able to get back but have no problem.

Hypnotic Session 13

L: The objective of today's session was to start dealing with my urge to flee from establishing close relationships with other people because of the drain they put on me. The room looks rather metallic today and I find my door far to the right almost under the back of the staircase. When I enter the room I am in a cool, damp, and rather dim part of the forest. Snoopy must be nearby for I can sense her presence. I am sitting on the large protruding root of a tree with one arm around the trunk and the other resting on the bark of the root. My cheek is pressed against the trunk, and I can smell its damp, musty scent. Nestled in a corner of the root is a small clump of soft green moss covered with tiny red spore stalks. I feel utterly drained. There is a tight feeling in my chest, as if I am trying to hold in the last drop of my own essence. I begin pulling life from the tree and a sense of silent peace from the ground. The "essence" of the woods gives life, peace and quiet joy freely. It is able to touch my inner self, filling me once more with life.

DR. J: You are drained by others' demands on you. Certainly Ella with her constant needs and demands takes a lot from you. And your sensitivity makes you vulnerable to her needs. Who else places demands on you? Mother?

L: Yes. Mother places demands on me all the time. She can't cope with Ella by herself and needs my cooperation. She expects me to be her "perfect" daughter.

DR. J: She certainly needs you to help take care of Ella. In addition, she wants you to be her companion and to entertain her. But she is also competitive with you. She needs to be better than you. What about dad? Does he put demands on you?

L: Dad also puts demands on me. I think that he wanted a son, and since he didn't have one he wants me to do things with him that a son would. We get a bow and arrow, and I learn to shoot it. For a moment I am in the pit in a cow pasture with the bow and a box with the picture of a deer on it as my target. Tall brown grass grows all around me and keeps me hidden from anyone around. I like this feeling. Spot (Mary's dog) is with me, and she chases my arrows as I shoot so that I have to worry about hitting her. Dad also buys me a BB rifle and a pistol and teaches me to shoot them.

DR. J: Do you enjoy doing these things with Dad?

L: Sometimes I like shooting the BB rifle. I am walking through the woods along a path that will take me to the sand pit. I'm carrying the BB gun, and I like the smell of it—metal and oil—and particularly the sense of power it gives me. It makes me feel safe, invulnerable and in command of everything around me.

DR. J: So there are some positive things here?

L: Yes, but dad always has to teach me everything. And I'm now a better shot than he is with the BB gun. It's a rainy day, and I'm in the front yard of the cottage. I've set a tin can on a log near the edge of the water and shoot at it. I can hit the can almost every time. Dad comes over and takes a few shots but misses most of the time. He then starts to tell me about how you must always be sure to squeeze the trigger gently and not jerk it. He's told me this a hundred times already, but I listen patiently anyway. It doesn't seem to matter that I'm a better shot than he is. It's almost as if he doesn't even acknowledge it to himself. I'm always the one who must be taught. Then I find myself in the basement of the house. Dad is giving me a lesson on the use of the safety on the pistol. But he forgets to put it on himself and accidentally shoots the dryer. I think it's funny, but he turns it into a lesson on how serious the incident could have been and I gravely agree.

DR. J: So your dad also has to be better than you and makes demands on you? What does Dad do if you do not respond to his needs?

L: He sulks. I'm in the cottage and dad wants me to go carp hunting with the bow and arrow. He has bought a hunting arrow with a barbed point that opens up on both sides once it hits the fish so that it won't pull out when the fish tries to escape. It's attached by a special cord to the bow so that you can pull the carp in. I don't want to go. I have no desire to kill a carp, and the whole thing seems cruel to me. I think up an excuse not to go today, and he seems hurt. He doesn't say much, but goes into his bedroom to read a Western.

DR. J: What about mother? How does she react when you don't do what she wants?

L: She acts rejected and that makes me feel rejected. I almost always do what she wants me to, but occasionally I won't. I'm in the cottage in the evening. Mother wants to play cards, but I'm not in the mood. I have a good book and would rather read. Mother turns away from me, saying something about my not wanting to play with her and sniffling a little as if she is very hurt. It really wrenches my heart when she does this, and I feel like I'm being an awful person.

DR. J: What does Ella do when you don't do what she wants you to?

L: She get very angry and usually screams a lot.

DR. J: What about other people in your life? Do they make lots of demands on you also?

L: I don't let anyone else into my life.

DR. J: The demands within the family are all that you can handle at this time. But perhaps you can learn to regulate the flow of others' needs. You don't have to respond to all of them. You can preserve a part of yourself as autonomous, an island within you that can remain peaceful regardless of the outer demands. Try to visualize this inner peaceful island.

L: I'm sitting on a grassy knoll by myself. Behind me is a small stand of trees that surround some sort of stonework—perhaps the ruins of an ancient temple. In front of me stretches the outer world separated from my knoll by a moat. A wooden bridge lies across it. I can see people from outside trying to get in and begin to develop ways to protect myself. First I fill the moat with fire, but it burns the grass and that worries me. Also the fire is hard to contain, and the flames keep licking at the bridge, which I need to be able to control. Next I fill the moat with water, but people keep swimming across so that it's not sufficient protection. Then I make the walls of the moat sheer metal, so if anyone slides in he won't be able to climb up on my side. I don't like this arrangement, because the walls look man-made and sterile; also someone might get down in there and not be able to get out on either side, so that image is rejected. Finally, I make the walls of the moat into a rocky cliff that can only be climbed going out. I like this image the best, because the rocks are strong and yet peaceful. They can only be worn and weathered over a long period of time so that I am safe behind them. The only problem now is the drawbridge. I'm not able to get that imagery worked out satisfactorily. The bridge floor is OK and can be raised and lowered, but people keep crawling across on the side supports so I need to visualize an alternative design. I feel that the problem is really twofold, that the imagery is incomplete, and that I'm only dealing in these scenes with one aspect of the problem. I need to have some defenses against the constant press of others' needs. But I also have to keep myself from reaching out to those needs—sensing them and responding to them even when not asked to do so.

Hypnotic Session 16

L: I enter hypnosis today with the direct intention of trying to make some contact with my buried emotions. Over the past several days I have had the image of them as a series of swirling colored lights separated from me by a wall. [*Lydia's note*: This vision of the emotions hidden within me arose originally several years ago while meditating to the second movement of Beethoven's Seventh Symphony.] We focus on this image as I move down the staircase and into the room. I pause only briefly there and then seem to be at the wall without having to open any door. The wall is composed of concrete and is gray in color with a rough texture. It is very thick, but I can see what's on the other side to the extent that I know the colored lights are behind it.

DR. J: Can you describe what is behind the wall?

L: The area behind the wall is filled with swirling lights that seem to be made of a murky fog-like substance. There are many colors in it but red predominates.

DR. J: What will happen if you go behind the wall?

L: There is terrible pain behind the wall. I have built it to protect myself from the pain, and on the few occasions that I've let it down I've been hurt.

DR. J: The pain will hurt but it won't kill you.

L: I think the pain can kill me. It has the power to destroy my will to live and without that I will die. I try to see what has given me this view but can't find it at the moment.

DR. J: Try getting a better look at the place beyond the wall. Maybe you can do this by putting on a suit of armor to protect you or by floating above the lights.

L: I try to go in with the armor but seem to get lost in the mist and have trouble breathing. The red color is some kind of poisonous vapor that suffocates me and I quickly leave. Then I try floating over the top of the colored mists, but the ceiling is very close and I feel claustrophobic, so I back off from this and perch myself on the top of the wall. I'm still a little frightened there since the ceiling is so close, but I won't have to go into the area behind the wall if the ceiling starts closing in on me. If that happens I'll just slip off onto the safe side.

DR. J: What do you see as you perch on the wall?

L: The red mist predominates and momentarily comes quite close to me. It is very hot and I feel a searing pain from it that makes me wince back. My eyes follow the red light as it curves back away from the wall and I catch a glimpse of mother behind it or within it. The pain comes from the realization that she doesn't really love me. The wall normally protects me from that pain.

DR. J: When you were a child, your mother's love was all important. But now you are an adult, and you can survive without her love. You no longer need to feel such pain just because Mother was so wrapped up in Ella that she didn't have anything left for you. When a mother can't love a child it does not mean that the child is unlovable. There are many people who can love you.

L: I slip off the wall onto the safe side and begin to see what will happen if I start taking part of it down. My first approach is my usual blunt attack. A long, heavy timber lies to one side. It is made out of a reddish wood and is very rough. As I pick it up, I know that I'll get slivers from it. I use the timber as a battering ram and break a small hole in the wall. The result doesn't please me since it is unattractive, and it can't be patched back up in a hurry if I need it.

DR. J: You don't have to punch a hole in the wall. You might just try putting some doors in it.

L: First I try taking the wall partway down and looking over the top. But I get afraid that the mist might start to come over and I won't be able to get the wall back in place in time. Then I put three doors into the wall. They are made of thick wood and are surrounded by a heavy frame. Each door can be locked from the outside, but the knob is designed so that it can't be locked from the inside. I also fix the latch so that when I'm inside, it will not be engaged and I'll only have to push on the door rather than find and turn the knob in order to get back out. With this construction satisfactorily in place, I walk a few feet into the room but I feel the pain again and quickly leave.

L: Then I decide to see if I can take the wall partway down or go through one of the doors if I'm with Joe.[2] We're sitting on the couch together. Joe has his arm around me and my head is on his shoulder. I lower the wall about halfway down and find that I can have a feeling of caring for him. Then I slip through one of the doors—on the right hand side of the wall—and stand just inside with my back pressed up against it. I feel then that perhaps I might love Joe. With this sensation comes a knowledge of the pain I will feel if he doesn't love me also. I wonder whether there are any good aspects about caring for someone. I see mostly pain coming from the caring.

DR. J: Caring is a good thing. It feels good to love someone else and to have them love you in return. If you love someone more than they love you, it may hurt a little, but it won't be the same kind of pain that you felt when Mother didn't love you enough. You have many other things in your life now, so you can't be hurt so badly any more.

L: What if Joe likes me more than I like him? I have the feeling that since my emotions are so buried and hard to reach that he may feel more toward me than I do toward him at the moment. This thought disturbs me a lot.

2. During the later stages of therapy, Lydia developed her first positive relationship with a man, and this relationship reinforced the value of accessing her feelings.

I usually feel that I give more than I get in most interactions with people, and I am uncomfortable with the idea of being on the receiving end. I don't want Joe hurt the way I've been hurt. A part of me is afraid that if he likes me a lot, I will have to care a lot for him (or at least act as if I do) in order to prevent causing him pain. I spend a few minutes inside the wall trying to find out more about how I feel about him.

TREATMENT OUTCOME AND FOLLOW-UP

At the time of this writing Lydia is in ongoing psychiatric treatment and continues to work periodically with hypnosis. She has been in treatment on a weekly basis for approximately 2 years. During this time Lydia has made great progress. She is now capable of establishing contact with her feelings. She is aware of angry feelings as well as painful and loving feelings. She is still struggling with her fears of being overwhelmed by her anger. In some of her more recent hypnotic work Lydia has encountered a knife-wielding woman (a part of herself) who is walled off in a cave. Lydia fears that this angry, violent "evil woman" would kill her if released from her cave. However, Lydia has also discovered a "strong self" in her hypnotic imagery. This "strong self" is gradually defusing the anger of the "evil one" through love and acceptance. Lydia now clearly defines her problem as a lack of sense of identity and self-worth. She now sees that she was conditioned by family dynamics to identify others' feelings (primarily mother and Ella) and to perceive her self-worth only through their approval. She also understands that this pattern of conditioning has left her ill-equipped to cope with outside relationships and has also made her disinclined to relate to others. Since Lydia felt that family relationships totally drained her and left her barely enough resources for her emotional survival, she could hardly imagine additional relationships as helpful or possible.

As Lydia came to understand her problems and their historical antecedents more clearly, she also began to use therapy to help produce constructive changes in her life. She began by initiating some distance in her life from mother and Ella. She recognized that she could only discover and express her own identity and feelings by learning to curtail her automatic responses to meet their needs. She began to decline to spend as much time with Ella or mother as she had formerly been willing to do. Realizing that she hadn't always wanted to be with them but had been continuously accommodating their wishes, Lydia discovered that she feared their anger and guilt-inducing responses. However, Lydia also learned that she could assert her own feelings more and more positively with practice. She eventually realized that her deepest fear about not meeting Ella's and mother's needs was that mother would not love her—her self-worth had been largely identified with pleasing Mother through placating Ella and mother. Finally

Lydia realized and accepted that mother never had loved her very well for herself. She felt that insight as a deep hurt from which she had protected herself at great cost, even after she became an adult and no longer physically needed mother's love. With the help of therapy and hypnosis, Lydia was able to understand her relationship with mother and accept the lack of love and finally be free to grow beyond that relationship.

As a result, Lydia has moved toward greater independence from the family. Her vacations are now separate from the family. Her phone and mail and much of her living space are now separate. Although still sharing a duplex, she has established her right to lock her connecting door and maintain her privacy.

In addition, Lydia has begun making new relationships. She has expanded her friendships to a few people with whom she socializes regularly. She has also taken the risk of developing a close relationship with a man for the first time. She is gradually exploring and mapping out the boundaries and the balance between closeness with another person and maintenance of self and autonomy. Clearly Lydia has a long way to go and much learning about interpersonal relationships to catch up on. Nevertheless, she is moving strongly in new positive directions with the help of hypnosis and psychotherapy.

22
HYPNOTHERAPY WITH A BORDERLINE PERSONALITY

James M. Healy
John A. Moser

In the book *The New Language of Psychiatry*, Levy (1982) well described the borderline personality.

> The borderline personality disorder has unstable social relationships involving clinging, intense overvaluing and devaluing (or perhaps rapid shifts between the two), and a tendency at times to be manipulative of others, together with an inability to be alone and a craving to be with other people, together with distressing confusion about a variety of issues related to identity, and a lack of a stable sense of self. (p. 206)

Treating clients who are diagnosed as "borderline" can indeed result in "the graying of the therapist." These individuals can at times be sensible and behave in a situation-appropriate fashion, while at other times be recalcitrant and infuriating. It is our opinion that many clients who are diagnosed as "borderline" can be appropriately treated, as though they had been diagnosed in another category, if the therapist goes at the proper speed, that is, slowly. The client to be presented in this chapter is a case in point: She presented a series of problems, and when some of these were partially resolved, some external source would exacerbate the issue or a more pressing issue would emerge, leaving the original problem unresolved. This case is also interesting since the client saw two therapists successively, the first and second authors respectively, about the same concerns. She was thus able to benefit from a multiple perspective to common problems. The reader will also be able to observe how two different therapists handle the same issues.

James M. Healy. Private Practice, Tallahassee, Florida.
John A. Moser. Private Practice, Pensacola, Florida.

CLIENT'S HISTORY

The client, Mary, was a 29-year-old white female. She had a history of receiving mental health treatment after suicidal gestures, including ingestion of her various psychotropic medications. She had thick files at the psychiatric hospital unit, the community mental health center, and with numerous private practitioners in the area. She had been hospitalized more than a dozen times at the psychiatric facility. She reported that her mother had died 10 years before, and "nothing has been OK since." She had fond loving feelings toward her mother, yet the memories she described were devoid of motherly nurturance. She remembered little of her father when she first arrived at the office.

During her first session with the first author (Healy), she said that she decided to seek help since she feared that she was on the verge of "blowing it again." She had begun writing "bad checks" and was arguing with her husband more. She said that when they had a disagreement, she either had to concede immediately or fight for a while and then concede. She appeared quite undernourished, with an almost anorectic-type demeanor. Her affect was flat, and it seemed quite difficult for her to generate the energy for a smile. Her husband was a retired civil service worker who was employed in a blue collar position. The client reported having had three children, but the oldest had been put up for adoption when the client was a teenager. The husband had been married (previously) and they had been married over 5 years. The children at home were a 9-year-old boy (hers) and a 4-year-old daughter (theirs). Healy strongly urged the client to make an appointment to have a complete physical because she appeared to be suffering from some organic dysfunction. She was also referred to a psychiatrist for an evaluation for psychotropic medication.

The consulting psychiatrist prescribed lithium carbonate and a tricyclic antidepressant. He used the lithium carbonate to ameliorate the manic type behavior the client reported on occasion. He was not sure if this was the appropriate medication; however, this particular client had been treated with a variety of different drugs, none of which exhibited long-term effectiveness. Unknown to the therapist, the patient continued visiting her family physician both at his office and at the emergency room of the hospital seeking relief for "migraine headaches." She continued showing improvement overall and occasionally acting out in more or less severe self-destructive behavior. The principal dynamic appeared to be "Show me you care when I do bad things." One day she called the office of the consulting psychiatrist and said "I can't do it." The psychiatrist replied that she had made a commitment to no suicidal gestures for at least 6 months. She responded that she had committed to no overdoses and laughed. He agreed to see her to correct this misunderstanding. When she arrived she reported that she had been at a convenience store pay phone with a handgun in her purse. An important relationship had just been terminated by a friend, and she was despondent.

This one incident appears to have been a turning point in the therapeutic relationship. In that short 20-minute session, she laughed aloud and with some affect for the first time. This scene altered the manner in which she behaved at the office. The client's extreme defensiveness was reduced dramatically. Humor appeared now to be used to reduce anxiety during the meetings. Although at times she would use herself as the butt of her own jokes, the therapist would not laugh and at times suggest other uses for humor, such as "knock-knock" jokes. This type of joke became a therapeutic trademark, and each session began and ended with some kind of humorous note.

THERAPEUTIC PROCEDURES

Two months after treatment began, Mary fell downstairs at home and was hospitalized, paralyzed from the waist down. The paralysis was diagnosed as a conversion reaction. Healy was called on a consultation. He used hypnosis to relax the client and indirect suggestions were given, such as:

"In these cases different types of sensations occur as your body fully recovers. The sensations may be tingling, itchy feelings, trembling, or jerking. You may notice these sensations start above your waist [where she reported feeling and showed movement] and will then travel in their own special circuit into the parts that until that time you could not CONSCIOUSLY FEEL. NOW, I know you don't know when you will find yourself feeling and moving again, but I want you to know that you should not do so until you are ready. I'll be back in 3 days, and I will not be surprised to see that you are comfortably moving. You don't know whether you will go to the bathroom alone tonight, tomorrow or the next day. I really don't know either. But, you know, and I know you know how to walk and that you will walk me down to the elevator when I return."

The suggestions were given for an early return to walking because the client had indicated that she was ready to walk nonverbally. The indirection was employed to give her a sense of recovering on her own timetable. The client walked within 2 days. During her hospital stay the lithium carbonate therapy was discontinued, while her tricyclic antidepressants were continued.

A week after her discharge from the hospital, the client wrote Healy a five-page "note." In the cover letter she explained that she at times stopped talking during the sessions because of the emotional pain the discussion caused her. She thanked him for the great help she felt in the therapy. The following four pages were her own way of forcing herself to focus on the issues she needed to work through in therapy. Below are excerpts from the letter.

It's been a long time since I've sat down and put on paper my thoughts and feelings. . . . Doing something to hurt myself hasn't gotten me anywhere. The only advantages have been that I have found a few friends who understand me and still accept me as a person. That's my problem—I haven't been able to see myself as a person who is worth spending time with. . . . I have been pushed aside, ignored, "put on the back burner" for so long until I'm afraid of coming forward. It's a scary feeling, and at times when you see yourself taking two steps forward, you stop and try to take three backward because of what has happened before, but people who want to help and understand are at your back pushing you back where you belong with the rest of the world instead of withdrawing into your own. . . .

I didn't have a childhood or one worth remembering. I was brought up not knowing what a father was, not getting the hugs I needed or the words "I love you" spoken to me. . . . I feel as if I'm still a child waiting for a big lap to crawl up on and a strong arm to go around me and spend a few special minutes with me. I need that or I'll never grow up and I'll always feel like I've missed something. I know I've missed something and it hurts—*it hurts real bad*. . . .

Yes I have problems at home but I know when I get my childhood straightened out then things will work out there.

Right now I'm scared—I'm really scared because something is going to happen soon that's going to have a great effect on the rest of my life. I've got to find things out—I've got to know what really happened to me when I was growing up or have I already found out.

I don't like myself, and even though I'm nice to other people I'm not nice to myself. I'm down on myself all the time—I need to let my mother rest—it's only fair to her but there's so much I need to tell her. I need to tell her I love her and I'm sorry for what I did to her before she died.

Everybody who has had any kind of great effect on my life has always left me—Why? . . . I always do something to hurt them, I don't like that—it's not fair to them or myself because they're really nice people.

I feel like I've done something terrible because of my actions to go the way they do. What I mean is, why did my mother leave me, why did my father leave me? I can't understand it. I loved her so much and never told her so. I tried since she died, but it still doesn't feel just right. I don't feel she hears me—I guess that's why I can't let her go. I need to, it's only fair to her.

HOW MUCH LONGER CAN I GO THROUGH THIS HURTING?

This letter resulted in significant therapeutic gains, as Mary began to show her commitment to her therapy. She arrived on time and was either available or silent. The therapist interpreted her silences as special times during the sessions in which she needed quiet. Her wishes were respected and silence was maintained, although the silences at times lasted 15 minutes. On occasion the therapist would announce that he would return momentarily and would go to the rest room or to obtain a cup of coffee or water. In time the silences grew shorter and discussions longer.

Shortly after, she was apparently sexually attacked by someone whom she allowed into her home in the middle of the day. She blamed herself for her "stupidity" in opening the door in the first place. She never reported the incident to the police, for she was afraid of what she might have to endure both from the authorities and from her husband. She also became both quite impatient with the therapy and also more reticent. As she began to remember her very early childhood, she recalled a frightened little girl. It was suggested that the little girl still needed "loving" and that only she could now reach her. In a 50-minute discourse by the therapist, she was reminded of her abilities as a parent (using her two children as prime examples), the way in which pets always took to her, and the gentle way in which she treated people. During this rambling discourse Healy repeated over and over many things that the client had already learned, things that she "learned before" she knew and understood that she knew.

About this time, her father reintroduced himself into her life. When he called she felt violated and called the therapist. A session was scheduled for the following day. Mary decided to see her father, but when she saw him she felt a rage surge from inside her and she became very angry outwardly at him. She also later reported that the thought of suicide entered with "capital" letters, though she dismissed the idea as something she would have considered and acted out 4 months earlier. She was warned that she could begin to remember more and that she didn't have to try to remember anything until she was in the office. Two days later she reported "flashbacks" of a scene in which she was seated on her father's lap and her mother came in and began to scream at her father (just before he left). In the next 2 weeks she spent up to 4 hours at the emergency unit at the mental health center, had greater difficulty sleeping, and called the daily newspaper threatening to kill herself, involving both the sheriff's office and the therapist.

One week later the client went away for the Christmas holidays with her family. When she returned from her trip, she reported that she had decided that she needed to focus on her issues with her father. She asked that hypnosis be employed in the therapy. She reported that within 2 weeks her husband was leaving town because he had obtained a new job and that she would go with him. It was agreed that her suggestions were very well thought out and that we would follow them to the letter. Since she was planning to go to a completely new area (she had come to Tallahassee from a small rural town in southern Georgia to try out the "big" city), she agreed to record the session so that she could listen to the recording during the move and while she was settling into her new home.

To aid in the understanding of this taped hypnotherapeutic intervention, superscript numerals and footnotes (see p. 288) are used to identify the type of suggestion employed. The italicized portions were accentuated by lowering the voice and slowing down the speed. This is a way of using the "Ericksonian interspersal" method elucidated so well by Lankton in *Practical Magic* (Lankton, 1980). The recording begins with silence and then, as if it was understood that something had already begun, it starts with:

"Find a quiet place. . . . Take a deep breath, you can close your eyes . . . [Mary breathes.] That's right. . . . You've heard my voice talking about many things[1] . . . helping learn and unlearn . . . but this tape is for your conscious and *subconscious*[2] mind to develop a new helping relationship . . . growing and developing into *deeper comfort*. . . . But you have the freedom, *Mary*, to remain as tense as you wish or to *relax now*. . . . Or to *relax* for a while and to get tense or to never relax or never tense up . . . or you can *relax now, Mary*, or get tense later. . . . It doesn't really matter[3]. . . . What's important is that your ears hear the sound of my voice and your *subconscious* mind listen. . . . But your conscious mind doesn't even have to pay attention and can busy itself as I count from twenty to one. . . . That's right . . . sewing at some material . . . or . . . go ahead and get away in the car and drive away . . . just leaving things behind . . . leaving things behind . . . leaving everything behind and start piecing the puzzle back together again. . . . Now you know about reading newspapers, not that you have to follow papers but at least you can look at them . . . but you also know ways of not getting goodbyes . . . but I wonder if you know that it is as easy to, *Mary, forget* as it is to remember . . . and there is a, *nineteen*, comfort, *eighteen*, *seventeen*, in forgetting and, that's right [Mary lets out a deep sigh], can you imagine how busy your mind would be if it couldn't forget anything?[4] My goodness, your mind would have to be twice the size it is today to remember everything that happened, *sixteen* and *fifteen*, but you don't have to, *fourteen, thirteen*, so you can go ahead and *forget*, many things, *twelve, eleven*. And driving is such a pleasure and *ten* is halfway there. . . . Now, some people *get in the car so they say goodbye* and *go*, and others get in the car just to get away and since ten is halfway there they, *nine*, and you can, slowly, can be and go in your own special way in your mind, allowing your *subconscious*, of course, to remember in its *subconscious* way those lessons it learned while previously in this comfortable place.[5] While driving away can distract your conscious mind, while your subconscious mind continues now to grow and develop, . . . *eight, seven, six*, and *five* is three quarters of the way there, even muscles between your ribs can, *Mary, let go*, . . . deeper and deeper, allowing that blanket of comfort to soothe and *wash away tensions* that are unnecessary, *four*. That's right, *three* that's right, very good. And *two and one* can be a comfort to you and place of being and for being, just *being comfortably secure*, and you don't have to do anything at all while I talk about many things, and your conscious mind doesn't even have to remember where it is driven or from where it drove, since it really doesn't matter so long as it consciously *PAY ATTENTION* to driving through country lanes through beach and city wherever it drives. *Pay attention* and enjoy the act of driving while I talk about other things.[6] . . . I can talk about fairy tales like Hansel and Gretel [long pause] or Cinderella[7] but reversed and I'm not talking about CinderFella but Cinderella with a stepfather. . . . But we don't need to do that, we can *easily forget*[8] *many things*, for example, when civilization first started, after a couple of families got together and formed a tribe or a clan, I'm sure you'll recall that they used to offer sacrifices to all the gods that they thought they knew, and to them these were not pretend gods . . . they were real! And if the god of the harvest wasn't offered sacrifices, he would make [the] next harvest poor. . . . Or maybe somebody in the family/clan had upset that god, and so they found other gods . . . the god of rain, . . . because they needed some, . . . a god of sun, . . . because they needed that, . . . god of soil, . . . god of harvest, . . . god of love, . . . god of this and a god of that, . . . god of wine, . . . mountains, . . . *that's right* and each one needed some sacrifice . . . to keep the gods happy . . . to keep the gods from coming down too hard . . . [long pause until she nods ever so slightly],[9] but after that time, speaking of good buys . . . I saw white sales . . . and isn't it interesting that most of the articles on sale in white sales are no longer white.[10] . . . yes, *Mary*, things *change*[11] in many ways. . . . Yes, when I was a child in South America, I was living there, and I had friends there. . . . My father was a pilot and was gone a whole bunch, and I used to call him a 'fly by night,'[12] and I didn't know what that meant[13] until later,[14] but nevertheless, we were in Lima, and then without warning my parents left to find a new home for us and them,[15] and after a long time they came back and said, 'It is time . . . for you to leave and join us.'[16] . . . but I didn't want to leave so I didn't say goodbye and left without a goodbye . . . [very long pause]. . . . And for years I wished I was back, until finally I went back and *learned* to *say goodbye Mary*,[17] *goodbye* to my old friends, *goodbye* to my bus stop, *goodbye* to traffic, *goodbye* to relatives, aunt, . . . mother, . . . cousin, . . . *goodbye* to old home, . . . *goodbye*, . . . *goodbye*, . . . And it was difficult to *say goodbye Mary* . . . *to say hello* . . . hello to new life. . . . Now I didn't like new life at first. . . . Even soil is different and I wonder if you know that what was north then was east now. . . . I was confused until I said goodbye. . . . But, you do have much experience in learning,[18] and you have learned many things even though you didn't know how you learned what you learned when you learned it. . . . Sewing . . . you can get lost in sewing now,[19] and it can be *a release*, and do things for *yourself* and others in a way you can, *Mary*, . . . express your own creativity . . . that's right. . . . *Comfort* [she sighs a deep sigh of release.] . . . But when you first started you wondered where you got all those thumbs. . . . Thumbs soon became fingers and fingers become more practiced[20] in doing things right and efficiently. . . . In reading, same way[21] . . . lots of time in *sounding* out words, *S O U N D I N G*. . . . then after practice your mind can sound it out faster and faster, and you didn't have to *point to each word on the page* [said in a stacatto]. . . . You could almost read 'look at Spot run . . . run Jane run,' and before that . . . even younger . . . letters of the alphabet were hard, . . . but you *deeply ingrained* those *comfort* sounds in your *growing* mind. . . . And what was at first blush an almost insurmountable task . . . became a song, and you could sing your 'ABCs' at the drop of a hat. . . . And even learning to walk was a chore. . . . You can remember that subconsciously [slow nodding] . . . pulling yourself up. . . . And you learned to push away from the floor, and your head went up and hold tight and lock knees, and you stood up. . . . Then take one step . . . and fall down . . . and pull yourself up again . . . and again and again . . . and take a step, and this time . . . you don't fall . . . but you hold on tightly. . . . Then take step with alternate feet, and with practice . . . lots and lots of practice . . . and more . . . you *venture out* into the room and *say goodbye* to furniture. . . . And you can walk across the room and *hold your head up high*, and you can grin from ear to ear and *bubble with delight* . . . *knowing*, *YES, I have learned*. And you also learn in many different ways to *unlearn* what was learned in different ways. . . . Yes you unlearn that you no longer have to crawl. . . . And you can, *Mary, walk* across the room . . . *NO MORE CRAWLING*. . . . Later you learn reading and *unlearn* that you need someone to read for you. . . . And you unlearn still later that you don't have to have an adult hold your hand to cross the street, . . . because you are an adult and you can *hold your own hand* across the street. . . . And as a child you *unlearned* other things . . . you unlearned wetting your diapers as you learned to use the potty and *honor and control your body functions*. . . . To *develop and grow* is a *delight*, and it is such a *comfort to forget*,[22] and I wonder if you know *you can be comfortable not knowing what you've forgotten*, . . . and you can *feel the comfort NOW* . . . when you were a child safe between the sheets,[23] and you were ready to go . . . to your special place, . . . you could slip out of the sheets . . . and go to the secret trap door . . . that opens only to you. . . . Through the door you climb . . . down the ten steps . . . *ten, nine, eight*[24] . . . going to the place . . . your place of deep comfort . . . *seven, six* . . . deeper, deeper . . . *five, four, three* . . . [talking slower now] . . . *two* . . . *one*, that's right, go through the threshold into *your* place of *inner security*, . . . your room. . . . That's right, . . . and be more comfortable now, and you know you will have a visitor . . .

who will comfort you, . . . yes, even deeper. . . . And as you realize this, . . . you become aware of a wise person's presence, . . . and you know this person smiles a warm smile, . . . and the smile comforts you and the eyes reassure you. . . . Yes it's OK . . . that's right, it's OK. This person reaches out with the staff . . . and touches you, . . . and the light enters you, . . . bright . . . comfortable . . . light . . . traveling throughout your body . . . *searching out tensions . . . releasing . . . letting them go . . . warm, soothing* . . . even to the darkest recesses . . . cleansing, *cleansing body and mind let go dark recesses purged*, not hung up in past *but now brightening . . . yes bright* . . . with future . . . cleaner, comfortable . . . light cleans inner being quiets. . . . Smiling wise person says, "*You are learning . . . becoming cleaner. . . . You are becoming OK' Yes! Smiling, you feel the message to the very deepest depths. . . . Yes, you are becoming. . . . And you hear inside . . . 'I am OK! I am OK! I am OK!'* [long pause] . . . And this voice too is comfort. . . . And the smiling wise person adds, 'You can now *SAY GOODBYE . . . GOODBYE . . . HELLO*. . . . Each has its own comfort, . . . offering your own comfort. . . . And while you reflect, . . . looking inside, . . . this wise person recedes, . . . is gone, and you are comfortably alone, . . . growing deeply, . . . that's right. . . . Then you understand, you know, you can continue now, . . . because you have this room, . . . here. . . . Whenever you need you can return, . . . whenever . . . you wish. . . . So you look about . . . and leave walking lightly, . . . skip up the stairs, . . . one, two, three . . . four, five, six, seven, eight, nine, ten, . . . through the trap door . . . safe between the sheets. . . . And *forgetting* isn't any harder than remembering,[25] . . . and, *Mary*, remembering isn't any harder than *forgetting* . . . both are . . . that's right. . . . When you remember one thing you *easily forget* another,[26] . . . but it makes no difference, because it is a comfort to forget, and *learning is now a joy . . . learning new ways to see . . . to hear . . . to feel is a way . . . learning by degrees . . . one at a time . . . a tape . . . a word . . . a smile . . . a comfort . . . a flush. . . . And goodbyes are easy and hard*, . . . some easy and . . . some hard. . . . And today we don't give homage to gods, because we know that sometimes droughts are . . . dry, . . . and we prepare for it all. . . . And even Cinderella grew up too. . . . Now, Hansel and Gretel, we really don't know what happened, but you can come out and emerge from your dream. . . . But you don't have to remember . . . the comfort is yours, . . . and you can feel it in the dream or out. . . . And when you are ready, you know how to count forwards from one to twenty . . . in your own way. . . . it's your way . . . and comfort . . . " [Tape ends.]

The recording trailed off, giving Mary time to use the trance in whatever way she felt would be helpful. She aroused herself within 3 minutes and thanked the therapist. She asked about the referral to the second author (Moser) and scheduled an appointment for 2 days later. She later cancelled the appointment and left town rather suddenly, about a week before she had planned.

After receiving the tape from Healy, Mary, her husband and children moved to a town close to Moser, with whom she subsequently made an appointment.

Moser's first impression of Mary was that she was a kind, gentle, somewhat suspicious person who demanded proof of friendship and possessed an excellent sense of humor. They continued the previously set ritual of starting and ending each session by sharing jokes. As she talked to him about her life during the first session, she sat curled up in a fetal position in the chair directly across from him. She literally looked as if she was, as she had previously mentioned, "still waiting for a big lap to crawl up on and a strong arm to go around me and spend a few special minutes with me."

The initial session was consumed with BLAME. She blamed herself for all the unfortunate happenings of her life (her father's sexual abuse of her, her teenage pregnancy out of wedlock, her mother's death when she was pregnant, her unhappy relationships with men, her unhappy marriage, her suicide attempts, her rape). She carried all this "baggage" with her and constantly referred to herself as worthless. People always leave her, she said, and she repeatedly mentioned that the therapist would leave her too, someday.

Healy, in his taped metaphor, had already "seeded" ideas and suggestions such as "leaving things behind," "saying goodbye to the old life and hello to the new," "no need for sacrifices to the gods any longer," and "cleansing inside and outside" (Bandler & Grinder, 1975, p. 27). When Mary walked into and out of Moser's office, she walked slowly, as if burdened. She usually showed signs of carrying these emotional loads and having no acceptable way of letting go. Before she left the first session with Moser, he said, "It must be very difficult to carry all that weight of blame and guilt. It must take a great amount of courage and inner strength to carry it; *and you can, now Mary put it down or let it go whenever you're ready*" (italicized to indicate lower tone, an indirect suggestion). This seeding allowed her to have the choice and tied in with Healy's taped comments regarding "saying goodbye and leaving baggage behind." Seeing this, Moser attempted to alleviate some of the weight of these burdens and concerns to allow Mary to feel a lightness in her life. Since she had just traveled to a new town, he used the following metaphor during the next session.

"Each traveler carries some unnecessary baggage; all sorts of old and new stuff can *Mary leave it behind and unopened besides*. No need to carry all that stuff, since arms are strong and courage is proven. Check the tag, it's someone else's. Let them carry it if they wish to, if they want to. We don't listen to the porters. So, *just relax and lightly walk away NNNOWW*. Travelers learn something new about their maps everyday. Where are those old bags and old stories? *Who cares where they are? No one's fault. Who cares whose fault?* Travel, light up our lives. Forget the trunk said the traveling elephants and let's get on with making tracks in the future. Travelers, *Mary, feel new roots, better and better each day*, deeper and deeper, one growth day at a time. We can *say goodbye and hello*."

Healy's taped metaphor had an excellent anecdote concerning his travels and saying goodbye and hello. This anecdote helped Moser to allow Mary to establish a readiness to take the suggested idea of "letting go and leaving the baggage behind."

During the next session, the focus was on decisions we have to make in our lives. Mary talked of her marriage and her children, always underlining her problems in each situation. Moser's anecdote was about his own life and the decisions he had to make, one after the other. Mary is an auditory–kinesthetic communicator consciously while using her visual component subconsciously (Lankton, 1980, p. 18). The therapy worked on her decision-making skills so that she could fit in her visual component subsequent to her discussing the decision (auditory) and prior to getting in touch with her feelings (kinesthetic) about the decision. So, her decision-making process would start with an auditory–visual–kinesthetic sequence, using all representational systems, and would help design a new strategy for better decision making. (Lankton, 1980, p. 138).

After the first session Mary stated that she felt as if she had let go of some of her worries, especially about always pleasing her husband. She now felt she might be able to find out who she was and climb out of the pit she was in. With those thoughts in her mind, Moser used the following metaphor in trance so that Mary might be able to see more of herself and her difficulties:

"Mountain climbers always, *Mary, walk in the sun with the son*. Each peak seems hard to climb so climbers wait for good, "whether" or not they hear all the good news. But, now she can move up peacefully and comfortably. Some hiking teams include four members, small and tall. Sometimes the leader climbs in the wrong direction but climbers, *Mary, climb lightly and brightly and just adjust the ropes and hopes*, and get back on track into the future, right direction besides. No tripping on this trip. No back packs or luggage. Just taking the right step, *looking up, lighter and brighter*. Rejoice in your steps, to another more peaceful level, each step, each day, really. Hear the peaceful wind, feel that peace, one piece at a time, *closer to the top everyday. My, the view is fantastic.*"

After she started letting her "guilties" go and feeling better, Mary brought her children in (her husband would not join her). The children were bright, alert, lively, and seemingly well cared for. Mary was justly proud of them. She was now back into practical pursuits of sewing and clothes making at home. As she began to feel better about herself and felt change inside, the pressure from her husband increased. She wanted to go out and take a volunteer position, but her husband demanded that she remain at home. The more she objected, the more he put her down, and insidiously brought out all the skeletons in the closet of her past life. She slowly retreated back into her depression.

Her children now came to be her greatest support. As she and the children attempted to decide what to do, we discussed the role of mothers (since she identified with this role more than others). The therapist discussed his own mother and her protective ways. At the subsequent session, he used the following metaphor, since Mary was at the point of wondering if she could venture out as a mother and become an individual too (she enjoyed references to animals with which she was familiar, and she was raised in a rural environment):

"Long legged, graceful deers [dears] mature in life's forest and for rest learn more and more about each other everyday. Hear them purr sweetly to their children and friends. Feel the warm skin of the mother and *feel the goodness inside her deer* [dear] *baby*. Good feeling to gracefully grow and learn in life's greens and boroughs [she is originally from a town with a -boro suffix]. Young awkward deers with their loving mothers grow into joyful mature deers, all three side by side. Deers go about life's forest *quietly doing what they must do*. They move on to other pastures together if their lives are not fed the grasses of love. Deers know they must protect their young presently with their presence. And *deer, Mary, grow stronger all the time*."

During the next session Mary said she felt as if she had grown inside and wanted to continue that growth NOW! Hearing that imperative, the therapist adapted a metaphor on growth by Gindhart (1981, p. 204) and added the dimensions of being at the crossroads of her life, ending finally with Robert Frost's poem *The Road Not Taken* (the month was May):

"May, Mary, *is the time for the beginning of new growth of determination* that has ceased for so long—through the long dismal spring and cold winter. As you wonder, as you understand, as you listen to my voice, and as you hear every word I say, you can feel more and more relaxed—and comfortable—even warm as you listen—and relaxed, as you listen, as you understand—as you become aware. And you can hear, you can listen, you can understand, and be aware as you relax and feel very comfortable—even as we talk about some things that won't seem to make much sense at first or second. You know, Mary, in winter so much stays dormant for such a long time. The growth that once was, just had to stop and wait—a long time waiting for the growth and warmth of late spring. You know, Mary, we could talk about trees—about how they must feel after waiting for such a long time . . . without growing. Just waiting for the right moment—for spring and summer time—to grow. And you know, Mary, about the cold and the barrenness and the aloneness and the misunderstanding those trees must endure before they greet the long awaited springtime and 'specially May. *Now, Mary, May is a special time*. You can feel the comfort of knowing about the strength from the field of *growth that begins to build and build deep*, in the roots of that which has been dormant for so long. Do you—*Mary* you can *feel so good, so comfortable, so warm, so secure, as you sense the feelings of growth . . . beginning deep in those roots*. And you can continue to feel it beginning deep, comfortable, and strong. And strength, Mary, comes from knowing it begins soon. Soon, of course can be anytime—an hour from now, a day from now. Certainly soon—even in a moment—'specially in May. Can you imagine? Can you feel how peaceful you feel . . . *as you see the growth building deep in those roots* . . . as you become increasingly aware, as the energy of growth moves ever upward from deep in the roots. And can you *now, Mary, feel the special sense of pride that growing things feel in May*? You can *then . . . feel that special way as you notice the very budding determination* that comes in late spring—especially in May. Of course, it is very comforting to know that growth, 'specially *this special kind of growth which always takes the right amount of time*—just the right amount of time . . . *against odds*. . . . It always perseveres, and it can and will take all the time it needs. That growth occurs along with the budding of determination, along with the unfolding of leaves . . . until *all is just right, when so much is in bloom*. And the blooming of flowers, and the unfolding of leaves, tells you all is growing—at just the right rate—in just the right amount of time. *When so much is in full bloom you will have the very satisfying feeling of confidence that growth is just as it should be*. The *things that grow always do*, Mary, you know, *they always do*. And they don't forget what they learned when they had to stop growing . . . for awhile. It took a lot to endure the misunderstanding of winter. Yes, it seems odd to talk about growth, trees, late spring and May—but *growth occurs, Mary, and you can feel it*, 'specially in late May, even *NOW*."

At this point the therapist seeded amnesia and added the metaphor with Robert Frost's poem *The Road Not Taken*, which the therapist changed somewhat for the purposes of the anecdote:

> Two roads, Mary, diverged in a yellow wood,
> And sorry you could not travel both
> And be one traveler, long you stood
> And looked down one as far as you could
> To where it bent in the undergrowth;
> Then took the other, as just as fair,
> And having perhaps the better claim,
> Because it was grassy and wanted wear; . . .
> You shall be telling this with a sigh
> Somewhere ages and ages hence:
> Two roads diverged in a wood, and you—
> You took the one less traveled by,
> And that has made all the difference.[27]

OUTCOME

In the next session, Mary came in stating that she had picked up her orange volunteers' coat and that the next day she would start her new job. She looked good and felt relaxed. She said she believed she was ready to begin again. She said she had decided to stay with her husband, but she was determined to grow as a person—and this job was a beginning.

Mary called twice since then to let Moser know that she and the children are fine. She and her husband still do not "get along," but she is dealing with that using her own resources. As of Christmas 1983, Moser received a letter from her stating that she was now working 3 days a week as a volunteer, and she still felt that she was growing as a person. She ended the letter with a "knock-knock" joke.

Two primary themes occur in this case presentation. First, both of us attempted to teach Mary choice as a process, while not attempting to dictate to her what that choice should be. Second, we both believed that the resources needed for Mary's change lay within Mary herself. Interventions were directed toward helping Mary to discover those internal resources. That this approach seems to have been successful is indicated by Mary's continual growth and change and by the fact that she is still sending knock-knock jokes to both of us on holidays and is enjoying her newfound choices.

NOTES

1. Indirect suggestion: Truism.
2. Indirect suggestion: Conscious–unconscious dissociation.
3. Indirect suggestion: All possible alternatives, interspersal and confusion.
4. Indirect suggestion: Amnesia.
5. Indirect: Confusion, conscious/subconscious dissociation.
6. Indirect: Deepening by confusion.
7. Indirect: Eliciting abandoned and cruel stepfather feelings.
8. Indirect suggestion: Amnesia.
9. Matching her frame of reference as child, "gods are demanding."
10. Indirect deepening suggestion: Confusion.
11. Imbedded command: Mary, change.
12. Deepening and continue to match her experience, "Father gone."
13. Confusion: Word "that" refers to phrase or father gone.
14. Matching her experience of "not understanding."
15. Matching her current "leaving" situation.
16. Indirect suggestion: Reintegration.
17. Imbedded command: Say goodbye, Mary.
18. Retrieval of learning resources.
19. Indirect suggestion: Amnesia.
20. Change of tense suggests process is learned.
21. Indirect suggestion: Age regression.
22. Indirect suggestion: Amnesia.
23. Indirect suggestion: Age regression and safety.
24. Indirect suggestion: Deepening.
25. Indirect suggestion: Amnesia.
26. Indirect suggestion: Amnesia.
27. Modified from "The Road Not Taken" in *The Poetry of Robert Frost*, edited by Edward Connery Lathem. Copyright 1916, © 1969 by Holt, Rinehart & Winston. Copyright 1944 Robert Frost. Reprinted by permission of Holt, Rinehart & Winston, Publishers.

REFERENCES

Bandler, R., & Grinder, J. *Patterns of the hypnotic techniques of Milton Erickson, M.D.* (Vol. 1). Cupertino, CA: Meta Publications, 1975.

Gindhart, L. R. The use of a metaphoric story in therapy: A case report. *American Journal of Clinical Hypnosis*, 1981, *23*(1), 202–206.

Lankton, S. L. *Practical magic: A translation of basic neurolinguistic programming into clinical psychotherapy*. Cupertino, CA: Meta Publications, 1980.

Levy, R. *The new language of psychiatry*. Boston: Little, Brown, 1982.

23
HYPNOTIC REPARENTING

Mathias Stricherz

Clinicians experience many reasons for their clients' entering therapy. It has been suggested that clients enter therapy when their psychic defenses break down; however, Frank (1974) suggested that persons seek treatment not so much when their psychic structure fails to provide them security as when a feeling of demoralization takes place. Often that sense of demoralization comes with either the lack or loss (including perceived loss) of love and attention from mother, father, or parenting process. Frank described this sense as "failure or powerlessness to affect oneself and one's environment." It has been my experience that, after certain clients have gained insight, made behavioral changes, improved interpersonal relationships—or have been shown the pattern for improvement—there still exists a certain type of emptiness akin to an existential void. With many of these clients their early childhood bonding with mom, dad, or significant other was both erratic and characterized by extreme conditional acceptance. Although aspects of that type of early childhood bonding could apply to any client, hypnotic reparenting would not be a treatment of choice for every client. This writing is the first formal presentation of my work in hypnotic reparenting.

In the pages that follow, I will present a rationale for the concept of hypnotic reparenting, the process of gathering information needed to reparent a client, the therapeutic application of reparenting within a single case, and follow-up and treatment outcome for the case study.

BACKGROUND OF HYPNOTIC REPARENTING

Over a 10-year span, both traditional hypnotic and psychotherapeutic techniques have provided the basis for hypnotic reparenting. These techniques have included imagery used in psychotherapy as well as in applied kinesiology. Age-regression techniques for uncovering have been used in hypno-

Mathias Stricherz. University Counseling Center, Texas Tech University, Lubbock, Texas.

analysis and have been instrumental in many approaches in hypnotherapy. I have found these techniques to be effective, for the most part. Regressive work for uncovering, change paradigms, abreaction, and cathartic release are techniques that have assisted many clinicians to restructure clients' early memories. Change-history imagery, a technique I have found especially helpful, initiated much activity in hypnotic reparenting. Change-history utilizes age regression to birth. Following the regression, positive hallucinations create two selves. One becomes disassociated to experience no pain in childhood trauma while the other is given permission to grow up with the actual history. When the two selves integrate at adulthood, much of the memory of painful childhood experiences are gone or calmed. With one 25-year-old female who experienced many phobias surrounding intrusion, the change-history tactic significantly reduced the intensity of most phobic reactions and eliminated others after only one session. Change-history and other psychotherapy techniques did not seem sufficient to offset many of the problems certain clients presented with, or appeared refractory to, in short-term therapy.

Thie (1979) discussed the use of emotional stress release within a kinesiology paradigm. His discussion of neurovascular holding points as reset points to eliminate physiological as well as psychological reaction to stress give a further understanding of ways to incorporate a quick cessation of real or imaginary stress. I have used the emotional stress release (ESR) points for several years with promise in treating a variety of disorders including phobias, test-taking anxiety, posttraumatic stress disorder, and others. The ESR requires the visualization of a stressful situation and then a repeat of the visualization while a gentle touch is added to the frontal eminences of the forehead. The client is told that the touch reduces the impact of physical stress of the imaged scene. Kinesiologic testing of indicator muscles during visualization shows that, with touch, muscle strength is not negatively affected; however, muscle strength is negatively affected when touch is not incorporated. Touch has been shown to affect brain waves, hemoglobin levels, pain control, and provide tactile stimulation for an overall "wellness" feeling.

Utilizing many of the hypnotic techniques available as well as the integration of touch in the hypnotic state, I began conceptualizing a mode of therapy that I term "hypnotic reparenting."

RATIONALE FOR HYPNOTIC REPARENTING

There are many techniques to restructure early childhood experiences. During the early 1970s, reparenting within a transactional analysis model received considerable attention. Schiff (1972) detailed accounts of reparenting schizophrenic patients in a sheltered home environment. Her approach required regressive behavior on the part of the client to the extent that her "children" were placed in diapers and bottle-fed. Her case studies showed considerable promise in utilizing such an innovative approach. Schiff's work utilized age regression in an implosive fashion without defined trance or the use of induction procedures. In watching several of her students reparent various persons, I was struck by the intensity of the emotions of the regressed child (adult) as well as the plaintiveness of the emotional releases as the child (regressed adult) cried for touch, food, and stroking. The overall role of Schiff, as well as her students and others trained in her parenting approach, generally placed the caretaker in continual *in loco parentis*. In hypnotic reparenting, formal trance is used and boundaries are adhered to (e.g., therapy hours, patient–therapist relationship, etc.). Two of Schiff's students, Falzett and Maxwell (1974), detailed several of the important aspects of psychosexual and task development that have influenced my initiation of hypnotic reparenting. Included in that approach are the psychological developmental tasks, motor developmental tasks, and characteristically unhealthy parenting approaches that exist at various age levels as well as healthy parenting approaches. Characteristics of unhealthy parenting include: lack of physical contact; responses to crying that escalate discomfort (nervousness, anger, rigidity); unresponsive, inadequate care; overresponding when no discomfort is apparent; restricting mobility; lack of physical protection; too early/late toilet training (harshness with accidents); no discipline or no realistic expectations; no cause–effect thinking expectations; excluding child thinking; teasing or responding to fantasy as if real; lack of rules and values or rules and values too rigid.

TACTICS IN GATHERING INFORMATION, BACKGROUND, AND HISTORY

Gathering information in hypnotic reparenting is both tedious and necessary for effective reparenting. Time lines, age regressions, and client-gathered information are the basic methods of securing data to be used in reparenting. Both techniques of time line and contact with mother–father–brother–sister–relatives and other significant persons in the child's development are crucial in the information-gathering process. Age regressions, perusing early childhood medical records (if available) and early childhood academic records are major focal points in pinpointing parenting patterns as well as identifying patterns relevant throughout psychosocial stages. For example, one 2nd-year law student who was unable to read and who had been diagnosed dyslexic discovered that his father began to stand him up and support him by his fingers while walking him around his crib and room at age 2 weeks. The student never went through a normal crawl pattern, using neither homolateral nor cross-lateral arm–leg movements.

A time line is the major tool used to gather information. The time line is a homework assignment that requires the client to begin at the present time and list all of those events that have had an impact on current behavior. The use of time lines in reparenting requires more complete information than when used for specific disorders such as phobic or sexual problems. In specific disorders the client lists only those events that are symptom specific. The following information is needed for each data point: age of client, persons involved, the event, the feeling during the event and the decision made about the self as a result of that event. Feelings and decisions about the self are not gathered before age 4 or 5. The use of the time line appears to initiate several processes or functions: (1) It presents the problem, (2) it traces the historical roots of the presenting problem, (3) it links emotional and physical relations to current functioning, (4) it metaphorically links current health or patterns of relating to maintenance of problem or pathology, (5) it creates an age regression while the client works on the time line at home (i.e., a client regresses in order to fulfill the task description of the time line), and (6) the homework triggers some repressed emotion.

From all the gathered information, a history that includes childhood behaviors, events, implicit and explicit emotional conflicts and perceptions of early events is compiled. That history is used in the reparenting process to guide verbalizations for parenting phrases. Once the history is gathered, the client is briefed on the procedure that will be employed during the hypnotic reparenting procedure. The treatment is generally done in 90-minute segments and has taken from 5 to 9 hours.

CASE STUDY: MARY SMITH

Mary, the client in this hypnotic reparenting paradigm, was a 37-year-old student enrolled in a science program at a large university in the Southwest. She was referred for hypnotherapy by her primary therapist. Her therapist felt "stuck" with her, had difficulty in handling transference phenomena, and had been successful in eliminating some of the client's general anxieties. Hypnosis had been employed by her primary therapist. The client presented in a hostile manner, angered over her primary therapist terminating their therapeutic relationship even though she understood why, and seemed willing to work toward eliminating her difficulties. The client was married to a professional business person. The family, which included three children (two girls and one boy), had an adequate income with basic needs comfortably met. After approximately five sessions, I decided to engage the client in a contract for hypnotic reparenting. My decision was based on her current functioning that I characterized as childhood and teenage regressive behavior. The client spent much of her time pouting, feeling unloved, in passive and passive–aggressive manipulations with her husband and others. She also felt that she did not get a fair chance in being raised or getting married. The husband was supportive, insightful, and loving toward her and was willing to look at his behavior. Prior to the reparenting sessions, the husband was referred for individual psychotherapy. Mary had many coping skills and excellent parenting skills in spite of her feelings of inadequacy and low self-esteem. Mary was told about the hypnotic reparenting process and was given instructions on what she would need to do. She agreed to the procedure and was given her choice in selecting a surrogate mother from one of her friends, teachers, or therapists, or from one of the therapists who had worked with me in hypnosis and reparenting. Mary initially selected a friend who had experience in teaching parenting skills, human development, and transactional analysis. Mary began the homework process and within a 3-week period gathered the necessary information. A three-page time line of her entire life was constructed, consisting of approximately 120 data points. An approximate 50-page narrative amplified the time line. Hypnotic age regressions were used to gather further information about childhood events. Important items included in the client's time line from birth through puberty are listed below. The client's amplifications follow the time line.

		Time line
1945		I was born in Troy. Mother had no anesthetic. I was breast-fed for 3 weeks, but mother hated it and soon put me on a bottle. I was crying constantly. I got burned.
1946	9 months old	I was taken to live with grandparents and aunts. Mother and daddy visited about twice a month.
	10 months old	My aunt fell with me and I broke my leg. I was hospitalized with my leg in traction for 6 weeks.
1948–	2½–3 years old	I had my tonsils and adenoids removed. I was wheeled into surgery awake and then given ether.
1949	Late 3 to 4 years old (late spring or early summer)	I was taken to live with parents (no advance preparation). I was baby-sat during the day by an older lady along with three other children. I learned to read. I gave up my bottle. I had problems getting to sleep.
1951	Early summer, late 5 years old	We went to Glencoe. I went to summer school, then started first grade (first recollections of night terror).
1952	January, 6½ years old	We moved to Lafayette. I finished first grade. Early sex play with friends occurred at this time.
	Fall, 7 years old	We went back to Troy; second grade.
1953 1953–1954	Early summer, late 7 years old	We moved to Brugge. I had my first room. I started third grade.

1954–1955	9 years old	Fourth grade; recall happy school year.
1955	10 years old	Fifth grade; teasingly called "tiny tears."
1956	Early summer	Found out mother was pregnant. Had appendicitis; surgery.
1956	Late summer, 11 years old	Moved to Graceville; sixth grade; entered puberty; disliked by teacher.
	Dec. 19, 1956	Sister born.
1957	Winter–spring, 11 years old	Clear memories of overt rejection of affection by mother.
1957–1958	Summer, 12 years old	Moved to Olton; met Jane seventh grade; grew very close with Jane.
1958–1959	Summer, 13 years old	Eighth grade; cheerleader. First menstrual period; first 4-H awards.

Amplification (first page of 50-page narrative)

Born: July 29, 1945

Mother—20, daddy—late 20s. Late in my 1st year, I went to live with grandparents and three aunts still at home. Grandpa bought the farm and we all moved.

10 months old

I was hospitalized for a broken leg—6 weeks before age 1. I think I had whooping cough.

About 3½ years old

Somewhere in here I had my tonsils/adenoids removed in the same hospital where I'd been born and been where I had the broken leg. I remember being wheeled into the operating room and having the mask lowered over my face. My next recollection of it is back home at grandma's. I had blue seersucker pj's with a pink applique especially made for this event.

4 years old (summer 1949)

My real recollections begin here. Went to live in Blaine with mother and daddy. Somewhere in here I remember dropping my bottle on the front porch and its breaking. Mother told me that was the last one; I wouldn't get another. I must've been at least 4. I still slept in a crib here, and I remember trying to get to sleep at night by holding mother's hand through the bars. Stayed with Mrs. Ball during the day. Mrs. Ball was our landlady—we lived in an apartment in the left portion of her old two-story home. Three other children (one boy, two girls) stayed there also: Ike, I don't remember the girls' names and I used to. Mrs. Ball was loving. I remember her attempts to get me to take a nap. I remember sitting in her lap as she read the newspaper. I sometimes sneaked upstairs in her house to look around; it is the first I remember seeing a boy's genitals. He was peeing out the back porch door; I thought it was interesting, but I think I knew I wasn't supposed to look. Daddy had the mumps and was very sick; a little girl at church got polio, and I was afraid to go to her house to visit her. I also remember being afraid to go into the church—mother and I sat outside. Mrs. Ball taught me to read, and I learned to sing the "Tennessee Waltz" from the radio (I remember singing it to mother). I got some colored blocks for Christmas. I have a variety of miscellaneous recollections of this time; playing with Irv and the girls, sitting on the porch swing "helping" Mrs. Ball shell peas, playing near the hydrangeas.

Summer 1951

I remember being in nursery school at GBDC. They also tried to get me to take naps. I could never go to sleep; I remember the little commodes.

Noted within the pattern demonstrated in the time line were eight residences in the first 13 years. Many of the parenting figures changed during the first 4 years of life. Mary recalls not having mom there when she needed her. Early childhood physical abuse/trauma was present and emotional estrangement existed before the age of 1.

After asking Mary about the circumstances surrounding her being burned (see time line, year 1945) and her inability to gather further information from her mother, it was decided to use age regression to discover more data. Ideomotor and sensory responses were established. T1 (Stricherz): "And I need to know from Mary's subconscious mind,

- Is Mary sitting ("no" response)
- Lying ("yes" response)
- and is the surface beneath her hard (no)
- soft (yes)
- Is Mary sleeping (no)
- Is Mary just lying there (no)
- Is Mary crying (no)
- Is Mary making sounds (yes)
- Is Mary crying (no)
- Is Mary making baby sounds (no)
- Is Mary crying very loudly (yes)
- Is Mary screaming (yes)
- Is mom in the room (no)
- Does mom come into the room (yes)
- Does mom talk to Mary (no)
- Does mom say anything (yes)
- Does mom talk to Mary (no)
- Does mom scream or raise her voice (yes) . . .
- Does mom pick Mary up (no)
- Does mom hurt Mary (yes)
- Does it burn (yes)"

Upon completion of this line of questioning, Mary was instructed to again ask her mother about the incident and discover if it happened in a kitchen or other room. The mother responded that the "accident" did happen in a bedroom.

THE REPARENTING

Mary, the surrogate mother (T2), and the therapist (Stricherz, T1) utilized a setting that was formally described as the reparenting room. The room consisted of carpets and many soft pillows that the client could lie on. An induction procedure was used with appropriate deepening given. Since the client was familiar with hypnosis, emphasis was spent on achieving a deep trance state. All jewelry was removed from Mary, room temperature was adjusted, and body comfort was ensured. The following includes partial verbalizations for the induction:

"Mary we're going to begin the hypnosis process. . . . Just lie back and let your arms flop. I'll pick up your arms and flop them to help you relax [the client's arms are picked up and dropped to allow a relaxation of the musculature]. . . . Every time you hear the bus go by or any other noise . . . go deeper . . . it's a sign your autonomic nervous system is doing what it should be. . . . Feel your eyelids comfortable . . . quietly comfortable . . . inside your mouth moist . . . drifting deeper. . . . Let your whole body relax deeper and deeper down. [A counting procedure using a dual induction with T1 and T2 counting at different paces.] In a moment, I am going to count from twenty-five to one, and T2 is going to count from fifty to one, and as you hear her, let your subconscious drift back . . . back to a safe time when all was safe and secure . . . six . . . and imagine you feel just not here . . . instead, is a warm comfortable space [the open-focus verbalizations of Dr. Lester Fehmi provide an excellent hypnotic induction procedure for adequate feelings of detachment needed for deep cognitive and imagery restructuring]."

Approximately 25 minutes were used for deepening and induction before ideomotor signals were established. Developmental milestones from the time line provided points of reference for the age regression back to childhood.

The following is excerpted from different reparenting sessions with Mary. All inductions took longer than 15 minutes, and subsequent sessions started with ideomotor questions to find out if any of the previous work needed to be modified or altered to ensure acceptance by Mary's subconscious mind.

First Session

T1 talking to T2: "Soon our baby will be here, I'm so excited waiting for it. I'll love it so and I'm so glad that our wait will soon be over. . . . " T2 to T1: "I'm excited. I hope it's a little girl. I'll love her so. I hope I'm a good mother. I'll do my best."

Mary was asked to indicate when she was at a time when she was completely safe, secure, completely cared for and all her physiologic needs were met while she was in her mother's womb. (Ideomotor signals indicated that she had achieved that state.) T1 and T2 began a rocking motion by moving Mary's body gently from side to side, from head to foot.

T1: "And while you are here, this warm, loving feeling becomes a complete part of you. You're safe, completely loved, completely cared for. Your mom loves you, your dad loves you. And let our words become your inner voice and your own method of self-love. I am love, I always have a safe place inside and I'm loved. . . . "

T2 (simultaneously): "Your mom loves you, your dad loves you, let all of our words become your inner voice, and your own self-love—I am completely loved, I am safe, I am completely cared for, I am love, I always have a safe place inside, and I'm loved. . . . "

This ego strengthening and positive stroking lasted about 8 minutes. Mary was asked to let her physiologic and early psychological self develop to completion and signal when she was at the point where she could have a safe and happy birth. (Mary signaled "yes.") Mary was asked to begin the birth process. T1 and T2 began pressure at the crown of the head and, in a process that took about 3½ minutes, added pressure alongside Mary's body until she was completely (symbolically) delivered. T1 complimented each part as it emerged.

T1 and T2 (as mother): "Look, Evelyn, here's our beautiful little girl, she's perfect. I'm so glad she's here, she's just right. I want her to feel our love always." (*to Mary*) "Soon I'll put you in your mother's arms, and while you're there, I wonder how warm you'll find all of your memories stay with you. Your mother loves you, your father loves you, create that memory and let it grow and expand." (T1 touched frontal eminences of Mary's forehead and lightly stroked her face.) "Let that love fill all of the space behind your eyes and extend from the tip of your nose to the back of your thoughts . . . " (Images of love between different points of the skull were added.)

(T1 gently picked up and cradled Mary and passed Mary to T2.) "And soon you'll hear your mother's voice, let it go with you and let your mind and heart open with her love to your self and let it become yours to your self." (*T2 to Mary while cradling, rocking, stroking her face; Mary curled in the fetal position.*) "Mom is so glad you're here. You're a beautiful little girl. . . . I'll always love you. . . . I want you to carry my love with you. . . . " (T2 passed Mary back to T1 and both rocked Mary for several minutes then placed Mary on pillows. T1 placed a hand on Mary's forehead.) "Sleep, sleep, sleep. Go deep into a baby's safe sleep and let that feeling grow, let the safety grow, let the love grow, and let your mind drift as it listens to your mother and father. Sleep deeper and deeper. . . . " (T1 and T2 talked as mother and father about the baby's head, neck and shoulders, identifying body parts, letting Mary know that she'll be loved regardless of her behavior and that there will be enough nutrition for her to always feel loved.)

T1: " . . . and sometimes your mother will not do all the things she should or will do some things she shouldn't [preparing Mary for the time she was burned] and when your subconscious mind understands that your mother did things that were not caused by you and when it can release that bound fear, anxiety, sadness, and overconcern for Mom, signal 'yes' . . . [Mary, signaled "yes."] . . . and sleep, sleep, sleep. And, in a dreamlike fashion, know that mom and dad took, take you to your grandparents to be safe and receive all of their love, too. . . . "

T2 (simultaneously): "I'm sorry and I'm scared and sometimes I don't do what I should. I want your love to grow and let your earliest and safest memories with me overshadow all that happens between us. . . . "

Second Session

(A disassociated self was used to alter the memory of the burn.)

T1: " . . . and in a moment I'm going to ask you to open your eyes and see a little Mary over there, safe, secure, and free from all harm, completely protected. Three, two one. Open your eyes and look at the pillows, and let me know when you see the little baby Mary, safe, secure, protected. [Mary signaled "yes" after opening her eyes and apparently had trouble focusing on the pillows.]"

T2 (simultaneously): "Safe now, feeling pleasure. Mom's doing her best. She needs help. She's learning and it's OK to cry and OK to cry loud, and it's OK to grow up and be just the way it's right for you."

T1: "Good baby, sleep, sleep, sleep deep and deep and let the memory that has been old in it, the story of pain told

that left inside a feeling of cold,
fade and drift with love for Mary unfold.
A new little girl with memories bright,
filling her heart each and every night.

. . . Mary, let your memory of your burn teach you what it will, a way of using that pain to learn how to love yourself. And some things that happen aren't fair, and little kids get hurt, and some things that aren't fair hurt, and you need not hurt anymore. You can create fairness in your life, and if I were there to protect you, I would. And your memory of being loved, NOW, let it grow and protect you while you pass through the 3rd and 4th week and signal when you are safe, 1 month old and now feeling loved. [Mary signaled "yes" and the disassociated self was reintegrated.]"

(T2, as Mom, talked to Mary and told her she is loved and she is sorry for her mistakes. Since Mary's mother never apologized following arguments, T2 provided this early memory to help offset conflict between Mary and her mother.)

(T2 cradled Mary, stroked her face, and told her she was loved while touching frontal eminences on her forehead.)

(T1 took Mary to the time of her broken leg and gave her hypnoanesthesia for the experience.)

T2 (*cradling Mary*): "I love you Mary. I wish I had been there. I would have held you and protected you. I want to be there when you need me. (*hand on Mary's forehead*) Let my memory go with you and be with you for all troubled times. Let your memory and your warmth for yourself be even greater. . . . "

(Approximate age 4½ years.)

T1: " . . . signal when you feel yourself on Mrs. Ball's lap. [Mary signaled "yes." T1's hand was placed on frontal eminences.] Let this memory grow and fill every cell of your body. Feel her warmth and love for you. Let it become yours for you. Let the gentle rocking memory of that safety while inside your mother grow. Let it allow this memory of Mrs. Ball be even better. Let it be, let it be bigger and bigger."

(T2 began a gentle rocking motion.)

Throughout the reparenting sessions, developmental milestones were prepared for – for example, raising head, first smile, turning over, crawling, first steps, skipping, jumping, going to grandma's, going to school, friends, and so on. Developmental milestones were complimented by both parents. Mary received messages about hot–cold, knives, strangers, traffic, poisons, and so on.

Mary's reparenting covered the first 6–7 years with reference to an abundance of ego strength needed for later developmental milestones. Mary had spontaneous partial amnesia for each of the sessions.

TREATMENT AND OUTCOME DATA

There were several positive effects noted within Mary's psychosocial ecology as a result of the reparenting intervention. Since many suggestions during reparenting were given around ego-strength issues, Mary quickly began to sense a deep feeling of self-worth. As Mary's feelings of self-worth increased, other interpersonal skills began being manifested. Mary's self-deprecatory behaviors and passive manipulations have decreased significantly. Mary has become more assertive, self-assured, and confident. Mary describes the major positive outcomes of the reparenting as: (1) a place exists inside herself that is happy, healthy, and full of self-love, and (2) a place exists now for escape, when needed, which is no longer frightening.

SUMMARY

Hypnotic reparenting provides the clinician with a relatively short-term intervention technique that has both immediate and long-term results. The technique requires extensive history taking, homework assignments to gather information about early years and stages of development, and the immersion of the client into the process of change. Specifically, reparenting is utilized with a client who has had early childhood bonding experiences that do not seem appropriate for functioning within an adult's frame of reference. Generally, the client who has benefited from reparenting has had a preponderence of guilt inductions, rejection, early childhood physical or emotional abuse (often extensive medical treatment), and received extreme and inconsistent parenting as a child. Often traditional psychotherapeutic approaches assist in symptom and ideational change; however, when that change appears to be coping change without change in deeper levels of subconscious functioning (self-esteem and self-concept growth), hypnotic reparenting seem appropriate.

In the case presented of this 37-year-old female with a hysteroid personality disorder, hypnotic reparenting was successful in developing deeper levels of self-esteem, fostering an appropriate growth of independence, instilling a sense of self-love and providing a safe imaged place to reorient to or use when under physical and emotional stress. In this case there was evidence of child abuse and a lack of perceived mother and father love. Marital problems resulted from the client's regressive and passive–aggressive manipulations.

An approximate 6-hour reparenting was employed, using both the author and a female (mother-surrogate) therapist. The reparenting was completed after extensive history taking. The reparenting included the use of age-regression, change history, touch and physical stroking, ego strengthening and extensive use of building positive expectations.

Reparenting requires considerable active commitment in the therapy process on behalf of both the client and therapist(s). It is understood that not all therapists would be comfortable using touch to the extent that takes place in the reparenting paradigm. I believe that hypnotic reparenting could be done without the use of touch; however, I believe that process would be very long and tedious and would require the use of tactile hallucinations.

Although hypnotic reparenting has been used effectively in this and other cases, it is not quite understood why hypnotic reparenting has assisted various clients. The following are some of the mechanisms that could be responsible for the effectiveness of reparenting: touch and a sense of complete love; a sense of complete, unconditional, positive regard; a placebo effect resulting from high expectations built around the concept of "reparenting"; dissonance reduction following extensive homework and extensive age-regressive phenomena (i.e., when clients put as much work into the process as is required by the reparenters, they have to move in a positive direction to account for the psychic energy expenditure); the establishment of new memories as well as acquiescence and decathection of old painful memories within the client's psychic ecology.

Reparenting appears to be a viable approach that can be used in hypnotherapy. I would expect that a modification of the procedures to match the style of intervention used by each practitioner could only add to the effectiveness of the techniques. Like parents that provide their children with warm and positive memories, hypnotic reparenting can provide clients with warm, positive, healthy, and intensely loving memories.

REFERENCES

Falzett, W., & Maxwell, J. *OK childing and parenting*. El Paso, TX: Transactional Analysis Institute of El Paso, 1974.

Frank, J. *Persuasion and healing: A comparative study of psychotherapy*. New York: Schocken, 1974.

Schiff, J. *All my children*. New York: Pyramid, 1972.

Thie, J. *Touch For health*. Marina del Rey, CA: De Vorss, 1979.

24

HYPNOTIC MANAGEMENT OF BEHAVIORAL COMPONENTS OF PRADER–WILLI SYNDROME

John F. Chaves

The Prader–Willi syndrome is a congenital disorder characterized by hypogonadism, muscular hypotonia, mental retardation, and obesity (Ledbetter *et al.*, 1981; Zellweger & Schneider, 1968). The syndrome was first described by Prader, Labhart & Willi in 1956. Since that time more than 400 additional cases have been described in 159 publications (Bray *et al.*, 1983). Estimates of the prevalence of the syndrome are highly variable, but the best current estimate is between approximately 1 : 25,000 (Bray *et al.*, 1983) and 1 : 10,000 births (Cassidy, 1984). Complicating the diagnosis of the syndrome is a high level of phenotypic variability (Cassidy, 1984). Both the nature of the symptoms and their severity vary considerably. Since diagnosis of Prader–Willi syndrome tends to be restricted to the middle ranges of severity, many cases are not correctly identified (Clarren & Smith, 1977).

Prader–Willi syndrome seems to occur sporadically in otherwise normal families, although the disorder occurs in about 1.5% of proband siblings and is more prevalent in males than females (Clarren & Smith, 1977). Patients display an abnormal karyotype often characterized by deletions and translocations involving chromosome 15 (Ledbetter *et al.*, 1981). The pathophysiology of the disorder is not well understood. Some have speculated that the multiple consequences of the disorder represent the results of a single localized defect in the brain (Clarren & Smith, 1977). Others have argued that hypogonadism observed in the syndrome suggests the combined effects of hypothalamic and primary gonadal abnormalities (Jeffcoate, Laurence, Edwards, & Besser, 1980).

From a psychological perspective, Prader–Willi syndrome is remarkable for several important features. Perhaps most notable is the obesity that characterizes the disorder. Obesity generally becomes apparent be-

John F. Chaves. Pain Management Program, Division of Behavioral Medicine, St. Louis University Medical Center, St. Louis, Missouri.

tween the 1st and 2nd year of life, with the severity of the problem increasing throughout life (Coplin, Hine, & Gormican, 1976; Juul, & Dupont, 1967). The marked hyperphagia associated with Prader–Willi syndrome was documented by Bray *et al.*, (1983), who placed six adolescent patients on an *ad libitum* diet, which resulted in an average consumption of almost 5,200 calories per day. More than 50% of Prader–Willi children regularly went on nighttime forays for food, and only 20% failed to become upset when food was withheld (Bray *et al.*, 1983). Appetite-suppressing drugs have met with only limited success, as have other weight control strategies (Bray *et al.*, 1983; Holme & Pipes, 1977; Page, Stanley, Richman, Deal, & Iwata, 1983).

Complicating the weight control issue is the fact that Prader–Willi patients require only 50%–75% of normal caloric intake to maintain body weight (Bray *et al.*, 1983). A further difficulty is that these patients suffer from complex and highly variable intellectual deficits. Although intelligence is sometimes within the average range, typically, there are intellectual deficits that resemble specific learning disabilities (Cassidy, 1984). Some success in managing maladaptive eating behaviors using behavioral management approaches have been reported (Altman, Bondy, & Hirsch, 1978). Temper tantrums, which are frequently displayed by these patients in response to minimal provocations, can add a significant complexity to the overall management of these patients. One clinical report suggests the potential value of relaxation training in managing this problem (Nielson & Sulzbacher, 1981). No previous reports have appeared describing the application of hypnotic techniques with this patient population.

PATIENT'S HISTORY

The patient described in this report was 16 years of age at the time he was referred to me by a graduate student who knew the patient's family. The patient was approximately 4′ 3″ tall with a markedly protuberant abdomen and waddling gait. There was obvious scoliosis, a frequent concomitant of Prader–Willi syndrome (Cassidy, 1984). He displayed several dysmorphic features associated with the disorder, including narrow bifrontal diameter and small hands and feet. He appeared younger than his stated age, an impression that was further strengthened by his high-pitched voice, limited vocabulary, simple sentence structure, and content typical of younger children.

The following excerpts from a videotaped interview, conducted with the patient's parents after several weeks of treatment, reveal the parents' concerns regarding their son's difficulties and their expectations for hypnotic intervention.

THERAPIST: Mr. and Mrs. D, I wonder if you can tell me when you first became aware that Jim was different than other children?

FATHER: Well, actually, it was at birth, because the doctor said there was some malfunction, something wrong with his nervous system, one side especially, and he didn't elaborate; I guess he didn't know. That is the first that we knew.

T: So it was right at birth that you became aware that there was a problem.

F: Right.

T: What was the problem?

MOTHER: He didn't cry. . . . He didn't cry for about 6 weeks, one little cry right at birth. Um, he couldn't suck. I had to, I tried to nurse him, and he couldn't suck, so I actually took a nipple and enlarged the hole and fed him with a spoon for a while to get milk into him.

T: I see, and so he had some problems with his motor development and you noticed it very early. Uh, can you tell me how things went as he grew older?

M: He was a very good-natured baby; very good, and, but he was slow in doing everything. Eventually, he'd come around to doing it. He was slow in walking, slow in talking, he never crawled, he would roll and get to where he wanted.

T: I see. I imagine that through this time you brought him to physicians to try to get a better understanding of what was wrong.

F: We took him to our own doctor, and of course, he didn't know anything about it. But he recommended that we take him down to a children's hospital which we did. They didn't know anything about Prader–Willi either and they, well, we went through all kinds of tests, I think 2 weeks.

M: Almost 2 weeks.

F: They tested him for everything they could think of, and they came up with nothing except that, at that time they said it was probably come from pituitary glands, some malfunction in some way, whether it was the gland itself or before or after the effects, but they said it wasn't normal glandular disturbance. There was nothing wrong with them, and he took muscle biopsies to check on muscle weakness and they found nothing there either.

T: When is it that the diagnosis of Prader–Willi syndrome was finally made.

F: Well, we had more or less made it ourself, for a while, and we mentioned it at the children's hospital, but actually, officially, when we went to Mayo Clinic. That was, he was what, 7 or 8 years old.

T: When you say you made the diagnosis yourself, I understand that you read about Prader–Willi syndrome in the paper and brought those clippings to the attention of physicians who ultimately made the diagnosis. So Jim is 16 years old now, and still, I guess, is as good natured as he was when he was a boy, but I know that you have had some difficulties, and I wonder if you could describe what some of the problems have been that led you to seek help now.

F: Well, one of the things that led us to hypnotism is the fact that we've gone just about as far as we can go medically. I mean, we've been interested in that sort of thing ourself in the past 5 years or so, and we can't afford to pass up anything.

T: I know that there are a number of specific concerns that you have about him at this point, and I know that one has to do with overeating. I wonder if you could tell me a litle bit about that problem.

M: Well, that's the most obvious problem, is his overeating, and he can gain weight on what any normal child will lose weight on a diet, and I don't care what kind of food it is that you feed him, and we have tried many different kinds of diet, and they will help for a while, and then whatever he's lost he'll put back on. Uh, we've had to lock the kitchen, because there is a compulsion in eating and he doesn't know when to stop. I have seen him eat until actually he was in a kind of a stupor.

T: I see. So . . . he really seems to have very little control over his own eating at this point. Is that right?

M: That's right.

F: Well, it's one of his . . . pleasures, one of the main things in life that he's got that he can do.

T: I know that another concern has to do with temper tantrums which arise periodically. Can you also tell me a little bit about those?

M: Well, they can come at a snap of a finger, and the provocation can be very small. Just uh . . . and you never know. It's something you're very unaware of and all of the sudden it's on you, and you don't know. . . . I have found that in a lot of cases, he'll lose complete control, and a lot of times he'll go to his room and he'll have a cooling off period, he'll come out and be very remorseful, very sorrowful and loving again, and um, I don't know, I think sometimes he'll sleep it off. Take a little nap and he'll sleep it off, 'cause he has always slept more than a normal child. His stamina is short, and he'll wear out, and he'll have to take a little rest.

T: I know these temper tantrums contrast quite remarkably with his usual temperament. He's usually very mild mannered and very well behaved and good natured.

F: I think one of the things that has to do with Prader–Willi of course, is short memory span and that, in itself, probably helps him overcome or forget the fact that he had a temper tantrum. But I think most of that comes from a low self-esteem. He's intelligent enough to know that he's different, and he doesn't know how to cope with it.

T: Now I know that he's presently enrolled in school on a half-time basis in a special program. Could you describe what his adjustment has been like at school and what some of the problems have been there?

M: Well, he started out very well. He liked it. He did, and he was going half days, going in the morning, but he has difficulty getting along with peers and he identifies with older people, he gets along with them very well. But with the children, he has trouble.

F: Well, they [adults] don't make fun of him; they don't torment him. That's one of the bug-a-boos that he cannot stand, ridicule, and that goes back to the self-esteem part.

T: So he receives a lot of ridicule from other . . .

F: They know that they can get him. That brings it on, you know.

T: I see, and I know that also he's had some problems with his temper tantrums in his relationships with teachers.

F: Not as many as you would think. Maybe two or three. That was special circumstances, too, we found out later.

M: Which was brought on when it started with the youngsters.

T: I see.

F: Actually, the teacher bit with any attention at all, and which he did get in this special school, he can get along, but he can't get along in a regular school where the teacher has 20 other children to watch and not give him the attention that he demands.

M: Well, he thrives on attention.

T: I know that you have a lot of concerns about his future well-being. I wonder if you could tell me what some of your hopes and expectations are for Jim.

F: Well, psychologically, it is a problem I think of being able to get along with people. Right now he's not grown psychologically, I think. If there's something we can do or some way we could get him to accept himself and get along with other people, be able to take the quips and the ridicule and things . . .

M: Now, he has scoliosis, some [Prader–Willi patients] do and some don't. It's common though, and he [a physician] mentioned a mild retardation. The obesity, of course, is the most obvious . . . his short stature. They are not fully developed sexually, muscle weakness, anything else?

F: Coordination goes in with the muscle weakness, of course. In this case, he has trouble walking even on slanted ground or anything, because he can't get his legs to go quick enough, so he gets scared, naturally. He doesn't want to fall down.

T: Now over the last several weeks we have been working with him, using hypnosis using audiotapes, which he plays at home with the idea of achieving several objectives: one, to help bring his temper tantrums under better control; another, to make it easier for him to control his eating; and thirdly, to develop a stronger sense of self-confidence so that he'll be less vulnerable to some of the pressure that he receives from peers. I wonder if you can comment at this point about any observations you may have had about how he has been responding up to this point.

F: We think there's an improvement. We think that there could be a lot more, but we think there is some definite improvement in his action. I think the road block in that is the same as everything else, his short attention span. If he could keep more in mind of what you're doing through the day; how you do that, I don't know. We have hopes on hypnotism in that respect.

T: He has been using the tapes regularly, as I understand.

M: Once a day.

T: Once a day? And we're going to be continuing to work to assist him to improve his level of control in all of those areas, and I'd like to thank you for coming in today and telling us about some of your concerns and sharing information about Jim's background with us. Thank you very much.

F: Thank you.

THERAPEUTIC PROCEDURES

The patient was a willing hypnotic subject. He had seen hypnosis done on television, but could not articulate any specific expectations for what the experience of hypnosis would be like. Although hypnotizability was not assessed formally, he was responsive to a wide range of sensory and motoric suggestions. The quality of his subjective response is indicated by his response to my questions regarding his experience while responding to some motoric suggestions:

THERAPIST: Tell me what that was like for you.

JIM: Oh, kind of interesting. I could feel my hands locking together and I couldn't pull them apart.

T: What did it feel like?

J: It feels like that somebody put some sticky thing on my hands and couldn't pull them apart.

T: Could you see a picture of that in your mind? What it would be like to have glue or something really sticky in your hands?

J: Yeah.

T: Uh huh. Tell me about the bucket too. What was that like?

J: Well, I could feel the bucket getting heavier . . .

T: Uh huh.

J: Like . . . and I couldn't hardly hold it.

T: What color was the bucket?

J: Red.

T: OK, was it a plastic bucket or metal?

J: Plastic.

T: OK, Jim I want to thank you very much for coming in today.

This patient was seen a total of 14 times over a period of 18 months. During this time attention was focused on two primary issues: weight control, and control of temper tantrums. Weight control was approached along the lines suggested by Barber (1983) and included suggestions for increased exercise and activity, enhanced relaxation, supportive and encouraging suggestions, and goal-directed imaginings (Barber, Spanos, & Chaves, 1974). These imaginings included seeing himself able to move about more easily, images of being able to wear clothes that did not fit him initially and being viewed more positively by peers and family members.

Control of temper tantrums was approached through "ego-strengthening" suggestions with the addition of a thought-stopping strategy that involved visualizing an exploding "Mr. Peanut," which was suggested to be so funny that his anger would dissolve. He invariably would emit prolonged intense laughter whenever this image was evoked during a clinical session, although he denied any overt response would occur when he used this image in school or at home.

To potentiate these strategies, hypnotic sessions were typically tape recorded with the patient instructed to listen to the tape once per day. With parental support, he was generally compliant with this schedule. Possibly such support may be particularly helpful with mentally retarded patients.

OUTCOME AND FOLLOW-UP

At the time the patient was first seen, he weighed approximately 155 pounds according to his parents' records. During the time he was seen, his weight gradually decreased to 141 pounds, and then near the end of this period, his weight again began to increase to 145 pounds. In addition, there was a marked diminution in his temper tantrums in school—where he had been particularly vulnerable to harrassment from his classmates. There was also a less impressive reduction in frequency of temper tantrums at home.

As therapy continued, a part of each session was spent discussing management strategies with the patient's parents and giving them an opportunity to discuss their feelings regarding their son's future. During these discussions the parents expressed a desire to have their son experience age regression. Further discussion revealed that the parents believed that the use of hypnotic age regression might reverse their son's condition. Although a specific origin for these beliefs could not be identified, every effort was made to emphasize that while hypnosis could be a very useful tool in behavioral management, there was no reason to believe that the result they wished could be achieved. Shortly thereafter, therapy was terminated by the parents, in part, because the initial goals had been achieved with the patient's weight roughly stable and his temper tantrums greatly diminished in frequency and intensity. Undoubtedly, my pessimism regarding other proposed uses for hypnosis with their son influenced their decision.

The most recent telephone follow-up, 2 years after termination, revealed that the patient had maintained a low frequency and intensity of temper tantrums. He was about to graduate from high school in his special class, and arrangements had been made for him to work in a local sheltered workshop.

After a year and a half of reasonable stability during therapy, his weight had increased to approximately 200 pounds by his mother's account. The mother revealed that they had subsequently gone to an "NLP therapist" who had been doing age regression as the parents had wished, with little benefit. The mother acknowledged that use of the audiotapes had ceased at termination of therapy with me.

Although there is some controversy regarding the use of hypnosis with retarded individuals (Gardner & Olness, 1981), this case suggests the potential utility of hypnosis as an adjunctive technique in the management of individuals with Prader–Willi syndrome. Although the magnitude of intellectual deficit in this case was not investigated, it is clear that this patient came from the upper end of the intellectual spectrum of patients with this syndrome. Whether hypnotic techniques might be useful for patients with lower levels of intelligence remains to be seen. In any case, periodic visits for assessing compliance may well be needed to assure that these patients derive the maximum benefit possible.

REFERENCES

Altman, K., Bondy, A., & Hirsch, G. Behavioral treatment of obesity in patients with Prader–Willi syndrome. *Journal of Behavioral Medicine*, 1978, *1*, 403–412.

Barber, T. X. Hypnosuggestive procedures as catalysts for all psychotherapies. In S. Lynn & J. P. Garske (Eds.), *Contemporary psychotherapies: Models and methods*. Columbus, OH: Charles E. Merrill, 1983.

Barber, T. X., Spanos, N. P., & Chaves, J. F. *Hypnotism, imagination and human potentialities*. New York: Pergamon Press, 1974.

Bray, G. A., Dahms, W. T., Swerdloff, R. S., Fiser, R. H., Atkinson, R. I., & Carrel, R. E. The Prader–Willi syndrome: A study of 40 patients and a review of the literature. *Medicine*, 1983, *62*, 59–80.

Cassidy, S. B. Prader–Willi syndrome. *Current Problems in Pediatrics*, 1984, *14*, 1–55.

Clarren, S. K., & Smith, D. W. Prader–Willi syndrome: Variable severity and recurrence risk. *American Journal of Diseases of Children*, 1977, *131*, 798–800.

Coplin, S. S., Hine, J., & Gormican, A. Out-patient dietary management in the Prader–Willi syndrome. *Journal of the American Dietetic Association*, 1976, *68*, 330–334.

Gardner, G. G., & Olness, K. *Hypnosis and hypnotherapy with children*. New York: Grune & Stratton, 1981.

Holm, V., & Pipes, P. L. On the management of Prader–Willi syndrome. *Journal of Pediatrics*, 1977, *91*, 355–356.

Jeffcoate, W. J., Laurance, B. M., Edwards, C. R. W., & Besser, G. M. Endocrine function in Prader–Willi syndrome. *Clinical Endocrinology*, 1980, *12*, 81–89.

Juul, J., & Dupont, A. Prader–Willi syndrome. *Journal of Mental Deficiency Research*, 1967, *11*, 12.

Ledbetter, D. H., Riccardi, V. M. Airhart, S. D., Strobel, R. S., Keenan, B. S., & Crawford, J. D. Deletion of chromosome 15 as a cause of Prader–Willi syndrome. *New England Journal of Medicine*, 1981, *304*, 325–329.

Nielson, S. L., & Sulzbacher, S. Relaxation training with youngsters with Prader–Willi syndrome. In V. A. Holm, S. Sulzbacher, & P. L. Pipes (Eds.), *Prader–Willi syndrome*. Baltimore; University Park Press, 1981.

Page, T. J., Stanley, A. E., Richman, G. S., Deal, R. M., & Iwata, B. A. Reduction of food theft and long-term maintenance of weight loss in a Prader–Willi adult. *Journal of Behavioral Therapy and Experimental Psychiatry*, 1983, *14*, 261–268.

Prader, A., Labhart, A., & Willi, H. Ein Syndrom von Adipositas, Kleinwuchs, Kryptorchismus und Oligophrene nach Myotonicardtigem Zustand in Neugeborenalter. *Schweizerische Medizinische Wochenschrift*, 1956, *86*, 1260–1261.

Zellweger, H., & Schneider, H. J. Syndrome of hypotonia-hypomentia-hypogonadism-obesity (HHHO) or Prader–Willi syndrome. *American Journal of Diseases of Children*, 1968, *115*, 588–598.

NAME INDEX

S

T

U

V

W

Z

SUBJECT INDEX

E

F

G

H

I

M

N

O

P

R

S